A Commonwealth of Hope

THE AMERICAN MOMENT

Stanley I. Kutler, *Series Editor*

A Commonwealth of Hope

The New Deal Response to Crisis

ALAN LAWSON

The Johns Hopkins University Press
Baltimore

© 2006 The Johns Hopkins University Press
All rights reserved. Published 2006
Printed in the United States of America on acid-free paper
2 4 6 8 9 7 5 3 1

The Johns Hopkins University Press
2715 North Charles Street
Baltimore, Maryland 21218-4363
www.press.jhu.edu

Library of Congress Cataloging-in-Publication Data

Lawson, R. Alan, 1934–
A commonwealth of hope : the New Deal response to crisis /
Alan Lawson.
p.   cm. — (The American moment)
Includes bibliographical references and index.
ISBN 0-8018-8406-3 (hardcover : alk. paper) — ISBN 0-8018-8407-1
(pbk. : alk. paper)
1. New Deal, 1933–1939. 2. United States—Economic policy—
1933–1945. 3. United States—Economic conditions—1918–1945.
4. United States—Social conditions—1933–1945. I. Title. II. Series.
E806.L365 2006
973.917—dc22   2005029020

A catalog record for this book is available from the British Library.

For Mary Beth
Who gives life to hope

Contents

Series Editor's Foreword

Today's memories of Franklin Roosevelt and the New Deal belong to a dwindling remnant of Americans. Their children and descendants, indirect heirs of the governmental efforts at the time, now, amid unprecedented material comfort, view the past through a prism of mixed images and ambivalence.

The very term *welfare state* is charged language, reflecting concern about higher taxes, cheats, irresponsibility, illegal immigrants, and troublesome minorities. Those under thirty or forty, confident of their immortality, seem readily amenable to proposals to drastically alter present-day guarantees of the Social Security system. But those same cynics certainly insist that banks belong to the Federal Deposit Insurance Corporation, and they would be dismayed at the sizeable monetary losses their ancestors suffered resulting from bankers' culpability. Ambivalence indeed.

As the Great Depression hardened and deepened by the time of FDR's inaugural in 1933, one of every three American workers was unemployed; manufacturing and foreign trade had plummeted; personal debt soared while savings were lost in the multitude of bank failures. Only Abraham Lincoln assumed powers under such dire conditions.

Roosevelt offered a clarion call to action—a "New Deal"—and the American people responded. They heartily welcomed an activist government, one that would eventually be an employer of last resort. This was no moment for blind religious faith; this was not the time for diversionary "cultural" issues; it was the idea and role of government, *not fear,* that inspired people and forged another historical link in the American character.

Alan Lawson's *A Commonwealth of Hope* thoughtfully provides a broad, extended historical context for the new political, social, and economic developments of the 1930s. The crisis of the American capitalistic system was no momentary event—stock market crash, unemployment, and depression—but rather reflected deep-seated, longstanding malfunctions of the economic order.

Further, Lawson demonstrates that the Franklin D. Roosevelt administration's response to the crisis was not mere improvisation but had roots in earlier notions of a progressive, cooperative commonwealth—ones that provided a wide array of reform measures to better peoples' lives and ameliorate the ravages and excesses of industrialization. The vision included reform and regulation of large, vital, and unbridled national business practices. All this served as a foundation for government's activist, interventionist, and compassionate role that emerged in the 1930s, dovetailing with the nation's keen desire for economic recovery and security.

Seventy years later, President George W. Bush, unlike his Republican predecessors who followed the New Deal, has systematically sought its virtual repeal, favoring an unbridled, unregulated "free market" economy and the reinstitution of trickle-down economic policies. Following his re-election, Bush dedicated his "political capital" to the transformation of the Social Security system. But the burden of the Iraq war eroded much of his capital and prevented the fulfillment of his fondest hopes. Ironically, that would have been his contribution to "revolutionary" policies to advance "liberty"—in other words, his "New Deal" in new garb.

The New Deal doubtless established a fresh framework and vastly more important role for government. Can anyone doubt that if the United States again found itself so devastated by comparable economic disaster, the government would assume enormous responsibility for providing relief and mitigating its effects? And once again, the American people would resume their familiar historical role of distrusting government, yet when convenient demanding vigorous governmental efforts to mitigate such a disaster.

Stanley I. Kutler
Madison, Wisconsin
University of Wisconsin

Preface

This book takes its title from the tremendous ferment that took place during the last years of the nineteenth and the first years of the twentieth centuries—the time when the leaders of the New Deal were forming their ideas and forging their careers. "Commonwealth" was the official designation of several colonies from their beginning, including the most important crucibles of American republican polity, Massachusetts Bay and Virginia. In the late nineteenth century it became a favored term to describe the ideal American society by those with a hopeful vision of America's governing prospects. These "men of good hope," as Daniel Aaron's portrait of the leading reformers of the late nineteenth century called them, took that view because they saw great possibility in the way the nation's activities and institutions were consolidating into ever larger interdependent units. Industries, agriculture, the professions, social organizations, and, in a more laggard way, politics gained power and wealth as they expanded within webs of interconnection. Utopians witnessing the transformation dreamed of a perfected society of shared abundance and harmony, while the more moderately sanguine praised cooperation as the way to replace poverty with shared abundance, if not to perfect human nature itself.

Against that hopeful vision of commonwealth an array of strivers took the tradition of American individualism as a warrant to seek their own fortunes with little regard for others except as competitors. From the scramble for advantage amid America's growth into the world's most productive industrial and agricultural nation emerged a cluster of transcendently rich entrepreneurs, trailed by a new class of large landowners and industrialists who formed an American aristocracy of wealth. Although they shaped vast interdependent enterprises that expressed the consolidating tendency of the time, these plutocratic leaders fostered a myth of self-reliance to cover their uneasiness over the necessity of relying on an increasingly complex network of brains, muscle, professional expertise, and government support. For them the prospect of a commonwealth of shared abundance was far from reassuring—indeed, it was decidedly ominous, a threat to their power and possessions.

And, so, the lines were drawn—*Wealth against Commonwealth,* as the title of Henry Demarest Lloyd's key reform tract put it in 1894. Fifteen years earlier, Lloyd's predecessor, Henry George, also spoke to the unhappy polarity in American life in the title of his influential call for the redistribution of wealth and opportunity, *Progress and Poverty* (1879).

The phrase that best captured the optimistic ideal was coined by the Danish immigrant and Marxist Laurence Gronlund in his utopian novel, *The Cooperative Commonwealth* (1884). His utopia would rely on the new technological advances that were dazzling so many observers at the time. Within that clocklike society, individuals would be utterly subordinated to the overall design. America's most famous labor leader, Eugene Debs, adopted Gronlund's cooperative commonwealth theme as the key to building an American Socialist party, but Gronlund's regimented version of a cooperative commonwealth had limited appeal to most of his reformist contemporaries. Edward Bellamy's utopian novel, *Looking Backward* (1889)—which Gronlund graciously acknowledged was the superior and vastly more popular book—also touted technology as the key to generating wealth and improving surroundings, but the novel stressed the personal freedom it would provide rather than the interdependency underpinning that freedom. In turn, America's leading philosopher, John Dewey, who admired Bellamy's shrewd analysis of how a system of wealth for the few and misery for the rest could be converted into a communal order of shared prosperity, took the lead in arguing the necessity of social interaction to guide that evolution intelligently and shape the individuals within it .

These critiques developed within the drama of large-scale confrontations. Seeking a fair return on their labors, farmers pressed the cooperative commonwealth principle forward in the form of alliances that eventually produced the Populist Party in 1892. Although Populist fervor failed to gain much political power, the party's 1892 presidential campaign platform, which declared that "the conditions which surround us best justify our co-operation," set a standard for future reform by advocating a commonwealth that would promote the welfare of farmers and workers through federal ownership of the railroads, establishment of a uniform national currency, enforcement of an eight-hour workday, and reservation of public land for homestead settlers.

Neither Populists nor utopians were able to overcome the resistance of business and financial forces to create a new cooperative order. Nor could they remove the barriers between workers and farmers, between ethnic groups, between social classes, and between races. Yet the logic of a consolidating society pressed an irresistible case for interdependency of some sort. The leaders of the American Federation of Labor, for example, kept its membership independent of government and focused on immediate workplace issues. Yet the AFL also became a shining example of the cooperative ethos of the time in creating the largest and most successful union by drawing independent craft unions into alliance. So, too, did the burgeoning social welfare organizations adopt the ethos. Middle-class idealists who flocked to settlement houses in slum areas at the turn of the century accepted a duty to share their lives directly with the poor and disadvantaged. Study centers such as the National Bureau of Economic Research, the Municipal League, and the Brookings Institution were formed in the belief that experts could accomplish more within a group setting than on their own. The Civil Service Reform League sought a similarly ramified influence by drawing reformers together within a cooperative structure dedicated to virtuous and rational governance. Even fiercely competitive corporate leaders saw merit in forming trusts and pools that tried to convert individual advantage into mutual advantage.

In light of the consolidating trend, a wave of conceptual thinkers, often within the rapidly growing universities and professional associations that were key indicators of the trend, explored ways of making society more rationally cooperative. Sometimes these heralds of a newly enlightened age rhapsodized about the project's prospects. Charles Horton Cooley, a leader in the new field of sociology, in *Social Organization and Human Nature and the Social Order* (1902) envisioned that "our democracy might be a work of art, joyous whole, rich in form and color, free but chastened, tumultuously harmonious, unfolding strange beauty year by year." Other progressive thinkers agreed, if less ecstatically, that there were strong grounds for optimism. Simon Nelson Patten at the University of Pennsylvania insisted that the new technical prowess and modes of production meant that the economists' dismal idea that scarcity was the general rule could be overcome through intelligent planning by universal abundance. In search of evidence to prove this providential case, a coalition of civic leaders and university professors created the National Bureau of Economic Research. Under the leadership of statistician Wesley Clair Mitchell, the Bureau compiled economic data relating to business and government on the conviction that they would prove useful for progressive reform. The principle of cooperation between university experts and government was most fully advanced at the University of Wisconsin, which was just down the street from the state capitol building. Charles Van Hise, president of the university, made an influential appeal in his major work *Concentration and Control* (1912) to replace much of the competitive distance between business corporations with cooperation, which would be regulated by government commissions in order to protect the public from unfair monopoly practices. Within Van Hise's university, fellow economist John Commons commanded an army of university researchers in the project of supplying state government with precisely the pertinent information needed for such control, aimed especially at creating social insurance that would protect workers against disability and unemployment and provide them with decent pensions when their work was done.

On the edge of professorial thought, Thorstein Veblen—university trained but estranged from the establishment because of his scandalous disregard for polite conventions—made the most sensational impression. The entire business-centered society, Veblen insisted in mockingly incisive terms, was a fraud, its opulence and pretensions of virtue merely a wasteful cover for the barbarian aggression that really undergirded the competitive capitalist system. Veblen was a cynic; yet he also shared the cooperative ideal and so argued for a transformed society in which the engineers who devise modes of production and the workers who carry them out would determine policy for a society of shared abundance.

Widespread advocacy of a cooperative commonwealth ideal inspired a range of specific reform initiatives, centering on the hardships inflicted by industrialization. Decent working conditions, abolition of child labor, unemployment and disability insurance, food and drug standards, access to public schooling, and regulation of public utilities were in the forefront. The term, *progressive,* first used to describe the cooperative reformers of 1890s London, came to be the most common label that such advocates of cooperation in the United States applied to themselves. When Herbert Croly, the leading apostle of progressive reform on a national scale, wrote his influential book *The Promise of American Life* (1909), the promise he had in mind was of a nation shaped into a true commonwealth by cooperative design.

It was within this atmosphere of hopeful thought and action that most New Dealers came of age. When it was their turn to run the country in the 1930s, they repeatedly drew upon the concepts of interdependency to devise remedies for the woes of average Americans. Rather than simply react to the crisis of the Depression by inventing strategies on the spot, New Dealers mobilized the progressive ideas they had imbibed in their youth and had hailed in World War I for their value in preparing the nation—only to see them selfishly and irresponsibly cast aside during the 1920s. In the depth of the Depression of the 1930s, these latter-day progressives allowed themselves to hope that the crisis would give them the chance to revive cooperative commonwealth formulations in order to realize the promise of American life. The laws and policies that resulted—and the various storms weathered along the way—is the story told here.

My intellectual and personal debts are greater than my ability to acknowledge them all. From the outset several of my students found illuminating items that helped steer me in the right direction. These researchers and shrewd interpreters include Joe Cugini, Michael Dungar, Marc Ferrara, George Harding, Jeff Malanson, Judy Maas, Joe Mitchell, Carol Obertubessing, Jennifer Pish, Bill Scaring, Peter Spellman, and Brad Thompson. Several generous colleagues have subsequently read drafts and offered critical suggestions that frequently saved me from myself, while lending encouragement to continue. I am glad for this chance to express gratitude to Alexander Bloom, John P. Diggins, Lancelot Farrar, John Heineman, James Kloppenberg, Krister Knapp, and John Saltmarsh. I wish to express my deep gratitude to the readers for the Johns Hopkins University Press, Patrick Reagan and Robert Zieger, for their crucially insightful commentaries.

My admiring thanks go also to the Boston College librarians, especially Michelle Baildon, Adeane Bregman, and Robert Bruns for their expert guidance in using the many data collections that have been brought together in the library system.

Similarly invaluable assistance and good will have been forthcoming from the staffs at the Columbia University Oral History Collection, the Library of Congress Manuscript Collection, and the Franklin D. Roosevelt Library.

At the Johns Hopkins University Press, Henry Tom and Stanley Kutler have shown admirable forbearance through my various detours and uncertainties; toward the end Claire McCabe, Martin Schneider, and Carol Zimmerman steered the work across the finish line surehandedly.

My family did the rest, maintaining a balance of support, healthy diversions, and accomplishments that set just the right examples. Thanks beyond measure, then, are due to Mary Beth, Nell, and Richard. I hope they find this book some small recompense.

A Commonwealth of Hope

Introduction

The New Deal stands as the most comprehensive moment of national reform in American history, the culmination of the American progressive tradition. For its inspiration the New Deal looked back to the struggle at the outset of the republic against attempts to establish a moneyed aristocracy, to the antislavery crusade, to the extension of civil rights during the Reconstruction period that followed the Civil War, and finally to campaigns of Progressives and Populists championing the welfare of farmers, workers, and other victims of the Industrial Revolution at the turn of the twentieth century, when most New Dealers were coming into social awareness. Hence, in creating the New Deal mystique President Franklin Roosevelt was able to identify with progressive heroes of both major parties—Republicans Abraham Lincoln and Theodore Roosevelt and Democrats Thomas Jefferson, Andrew Jackson, and Woodrow Wilson.

Yet, despite the practical and symbolic lessons the New Deal drew from the history of prior reform, it was fated to be distinctive. Because it took shape within a unique moment of crisis, it tested in new ways the basic proposition that America could somehow reconcile individual liberty with communal order—that free enterprise and welfare state could coexist, that local traditions could be respected while federal limits on discriminatory practices were imposed, and that free expression could be left unhindered by state-sponsored cultural and artistic programs.

What mainly determined the uniqueness of the moment was the unusual tenacity of the economic crisis of the 1930s. The baffling and catastrophic new reality made Americans more receptive to change. Since 1819 America had suffered boom and bust cycles approximately every twenty years. In each instance national institutions held the line against rising discontent and clamor for drastic changes in the system. After a brief period of pain, prosperity returned under the auspices of conservative "business as usual" policies. By spending less as revenues declined to keep the budget balanced, Presidents Monroe, Van Buren, Buchanan, Grant, Cleveland, and Taft all helped establish the principle that austerity was called for while the private economy readjusted itself to create a new prosperity. Progressive reforms were left to flush times, when the nation could afford to ameliorate social ills and lift up the poor and afflicted without deficits or high taxes.

In the wake of the Crash of 1929, the pattern broke down. Even with Herbert Hoover, the "Great Engineer" and a proven genius at organizing disaster relief, in the White House and his fellow Republicans firmly in control of Congress, the economy did not rally. Angry and disillusioned, the public in the election of 1932 for the first time responded to economic crisis by choosing a liberal reformer to be president. The New Deal to come truly had to be new. Since the captains of industry and titans of finance had failed to rescue the government by the usual means and public patience with them had worn exceedingly thin, the government for once had to do more than merely preach austerity. And that meant breaking traditional barriers against government intervention into the economy. For those long-frustrated advocates of social planning and reform, the situation seemed to provide an unprecedented opportunity. If they could settle on the right agenda, they might just be able to integrate the two traditionally competing American ideals of civic responsibility and individual liberty.

In that spirit, the New Deal Brains Trust that coordinated Roosevelt's presidential campaign turned to national planning concepts that had been brewing throughout the era of progressive reform. Plans to relieve farmers of their surpluses, to end unemployment, to revive business profitability, to provide social insurance, to govern labor union formation—merely the most prominent examples—quickly surfaced. It was from the sum of these plans that a new deal would emerge.

The will of the New Deal to take action against the Depression depended greatly upon the optimistic character of its leader, Franklin Roosevelt, and his ability to inspire support from a hard-pressed electorate. Roosevelt's confidence stemmed from a remarkably simple and persistent set of core beliefs that provided a framework within which the diverse policies and maneuvers of the New Deal could be contained. From his privileged and morally serious upbringing, Roosevelt absorbed the lesson that he would be a leader in the service of Christian charity and democratic ideals. When Roosevelt achieved the pinnacle of that expectation as president of the United States, it was easy for him to explain his philosophy to newsmen: "I am a Christian and a democrat; that's all." As far as he could see, those values accommodated all benevolent aims and needed no ideology or dogma. To critics who complained of inconsistency in that broad embrace, Roosevelt, had he thought of it, might have echoed the poet of democracy, Walt Whitman: "Do I contradict myself? Very well, then, I contradict myself. I contain multitudes."

Sure that he could fit all American experience to his ideals, Roosevelt set himself to champion both the individual and big government—the latter to serve the former. Unlike those who have seen America as a fundamentally divided society—by class, race, ethnicity, gender, or some other alienating measure—Roosevelt assumed common ground. The human condition, he believed, favored cooperation and an empathetic government intent on careful planning to protect the right of each to share with all. Accordingly, Roosevelt could also assume that protection of individuals and local communities sometimes required the active intervention of the federal government.

Roosevelt's optimistic vision of a cooperative commonwealth drew support from those hurt by the depression, even as it was hindered by uncertainty about the causes and lessons of the crisis. How could the historic American faith in progress have been so confounded? Had the glittering prosperity of the 1920s been only a momentary extravagance? Or had some sinister forces—whether within or without—sabotaged the nation's soundly based progress? Whichever explanation puzzled Americans chose, they had a difficult time deciding how to respond to the crisis. Was this the moment to write off the old American individualist dream as a mirage and seek to build anew along more radical, collectivist lines—as in, say, Russia after its revolution of 1917 or Italy after Mussolini's triumphal march on Rome in 1922? Or was the opposite conclusion closer to the mark—that the economy had collapsed because too many Americans went on a binge in the Roaring Twenties, meaning that stricter individual discipline was needed to bring the nation back to the old straight and narrow? For those inclined toward the former view, it was time to build a new consciousness leading to a planned and cooperative society. For proponents of the rueful latter view, salvation seemed to depend on rediscovering the basic values that had gotten lost in the careless Twenties.

Disagreement over the lesson of the Depression was reflected in the division of opinion about economic remedies. New Dealers and their reformist allies took up a concept called "underconsumptionism," which concluded that the widening gap between rich and poor had caused the economy to collapse once too few people were able to buy what the wealthy produced or occupy the buildings they financed. In that view, taxing and regulatory powers seemed necessary for a redistribution of wealth that would strike a just balance between supply and demand and ensure a decent standard of living for all citizens. Conservatives, opposed to interference with the free market on principle, argued that unwise governmental policy was responsible for the economic slump. Had foreign state banks and the Federal Reserve System made enough money and credit available, the private economy would have righted itself.

As for the millions of ordinary victims of the Depression, they wavered between support of bold action and a yearning for security. The ordeal left on them what Caroline Bird calls "an invisible scar," making them forever anxious about new signs of trouble. Rejecting a drastic overhaul of the system, each segment of society clung to the hard-won New Deal benefits that affected it directly, such as the right to organize unions under federal auspices, farm subsidies, and the old age and dependency benefits of the Social Security system.

The modest aspirations of the common man were praised by New Dealers but disappointed more radical reformers. One of them, critic John Chamberlain, fashioned his shrewd "limited racket" theory of government as a kind of surrender of his socialist hopes to the New Deal reality. Thoroughgoing reform went against the American grain, Chamberlain argued in his bestseller *Farewell to Reform* (1932). What the public wanted was just enough security to feel free to carry on private undertakings. Thus, as soon as the fearsome aspects of any major problem confronting society—war, depression, or other—are alleviated, reform enthusiasm gives way to business as usual. No permanent, full-fledged welfare state could possibly emerge from such a national mindset. Only partial cures for social ills could be expected within the American political system, which operates as a "broker state" where special interests make deals and trade favors with politicians and bureaucrats.

Soon after the New Deal ended and Chamberlain himself had grown conservative, the concepts of self-limiting reform and a broker state came to seem prophetic. After being buffeted by new trials of hot and cold war against totalitarian powers, in 1946 Americans voted Republican and shrank from any extension of big government while different segments of society sought public support for their own special concerns. The legacy of the New Deal froze within an ambiguous frame of reference. Relief and gratitude that the Depression was finally overcome, together with determination that the nation would not be vulnerable to another crash, maintained the New Deal's hold on public sympathy and installed

Roosevelt as the president most admired, after Lincoln. At the same time reaction grew against the New Deal as a form of socialism creeping along the road to serfdom. When Republicans regained control of Congress in 1947, they hastened to pass a constitutional amendment limiting presidents to two terms, so that no future Roosevelt could establish such a charismatic hold over the electorate. It was a sign of the unheroic times that the majority, who had after all been rescued by the New Deal, accepted this repudiation of their own experience without complaint.

Revulsion against further expansion of the scope and power of the New Deal regime reflected concern that America had become an administrative state with an imperial president. But could there have been a New Deal otherwise? By the late 1960s, accelerating discontent with the postwar system as a devil's bargain whereby the majority secured soulless affluence by oppressing the minority at home and carrying out imperialist raids abroad led critics to look upon the New Deal as a missed opportunity to enact a welfare state comprehensive and systematic enough to create a good society. From that perspective Roosevelt was put down not as an imperial president but as a patrician with limited vision. His New Deal was lamented as a brand of cautious opportunism that failed to realize the full seriousness of race and class issues or to appreciate the potential of either Keynesian or Marxist economics to achieve prosperity and social justice.

Doubt about the lasting impact of the New Deal has also been cast in terms of ethics and morals. When critics speak of the fall of the New Deal order, they include defects in will and character that have tended to thwart reformist intent. They gloomily point out that regressive taxes and excessive entitlements have undermined Social Security; that biased legal maneuvering and the stacking of the National Labor Relations Board with opponents of organized labor have led to the decline of union bargaining rights; that lavish subsidies have enabled agricultural barons to bankrupt the family farms the subsidies were intended to help; that the civil rights gains have roused conservatives to desert the Democratic Party and create Republican majorities in the South hostile to the project of remedying past racial injustices; and that regulatory agencies have become training grounds for experts in the pay of private business to promote deregulation. Capping the case for decline and fall is the public disillusionment described in E. J. Dionne's *Why Americans Hate Politics* and that backlash described in Kevin Phillips's history of the American rich, *Wealth and Democracy,* as an elite of wealth in the 1980s and beyond acted to reinstate the yawning gulf between rich and poor that had characterized the glittering 1920s. Feeling themselves excluded and exploited by a privileged political establishment beholden to special-interest money, the very common people the New Deal was pledged to redeem have increasingly withdrawn from the process except to protect local and personal interests and, occasionally, to egg on maverick candidates who talk of shaking up the national system and "sending a message" to Washington that never seems to arrive.

And yet, the New Deal has remained at the vital center. All national administrations since the New Deal have, as William Leuchtenburg put it, operated in the shadow of FDR. They have at least paid lip service to the ideal of protecting the common man, and their policies have been framed in the light of judicially endorsed federal authority over the economy and the recognition of civil liberties as preferred freedoms. Social Security, regulation of the stock market, federal guarantees of labor's right to bargain collectively, farm subsidies, public housing, regional power development, conservation, and policies to advance racial equality have remained the prime legacies of New Deal reform.

This book approaches the centrality of the New Deal by focusing on where the impetus and the plans for the New Deal originated, how Roosevelt and those closest to him sought to fashion a cooperative commonwealth, and what happened when the impulse for collective unity was thwarted. First I describe the impact of the Great Depression on the prevailing system and trace the fortunes of the major social sectors and elements of the New Deal as the drive to create a cohesive plan for reconstruction unfolded and then was blocked. In later chapters, I continue the story of those main sectors during the last half of the 1930s and into World War II, as new and more partisan approaches to reform were tried. The New Deal, this sequence indicates, did not move from innovation to plan, as one might expect from an experimental approach, but from plan to innovation, as circumstances demanded.

The question raised at the start of the New Deal has remained at the center of efforts to evaluate it: Did the New Deal represent the true American way or was it an aberration—a stopgap to meet an unusual crisis that would last only until the old order was able to reassert itself? Historians have always been divided on this question. For every one who describes the New Deal as mere anomaly or holding action, another has hailed the New Deal as a genuine expression of the nation's original democratic ideals.

This account argues the latter case of the New Deal as a special opportunity for reformers who sought to build in the American grain and who were therefore prophetic in warning of the turmoil and loss of faith that would result if New Deal aspirations were not met. Elements of the New Deal welfare state and the powerful presidency have remained in force, and Roosevelt's reputation as a great president seems secure. Yet in recent years the struggle over whether to advance or reverse the New Deal has tilted toward those who want to limit government in the interests of a corporate and financial elite of the sort Roosevelt called "economic royalists." Considering all the uncertainty and backtracking of their ideological heirs, New Dealers could do no better than echo the plaint of Frank and Jesse James's mother that "I done the best I could with what I had." Which, in the case of New Deal, was considerable. For better or worse, the New Deal's mobilization of the progressive legacy made it the political colossus that looms over every national effort to guide social policy and conscience.

CHAPTER ONE

Prelude

The Fall of the American System

The collapse of the stock market in 1929 and the economic paralysis that followed confronted Americans with an unprecedented reversal of their expectations of endless progress. As the Great Depression deepened, astonishment that an era of high prosperity (with the assurance of more to come) could suddenly vanish gave way to fear and anger. Grim, bewildered faces stare out from the photographic record of the time; veterans of the Depression ever afterward brooded about the stifled air of foreboding that smothered the nation. A deadly quiet settled on the city streets, so different from the previous decade, when a jazzy clamor announced America's ascendancy to an affluence never before approached. The shutdown of factories, which left U.S. Steel operating at about 19 percent capacity and its fulltime employees pared from 224,980 in 1929 to exactly none in 1933, was one of the main contributors to the quiet. It was further extended by the demise of most of the companies that had created the great automobile boom of the 1920s—including the most elegant among them, like Cord and Duesenberg. The rail industry faded also. After having produced an average of 600 locomotives a year during the 1920s, the American Locomotive Company turned out only one in 1932. "Once I built a railroad," lamented one of the popular songs of the year, "Now it's done. Brother, can you spare a dime." The phonograph industry that spun such laments was out of dimes itself, dropping from a fifty million dollar volume in 1929 to only $250,000 in 1932, thus adding to the stillness.

As national income declined from $87.4 billion in 1929 to a scant $41.7 billion in 1932, displaced persons appeared in the quiet streets, wandering over the countryside in search of work, standing in long breadlines before somber churches, or huddled disconsolately in doorways—human "junk," as one bitter writer put it. Less visible were the scavengers who haunted alleys behind restaurants or picked over garbage dumps in search of edible scraps. One observer who witnessed such scenes of desolation was especially struck by the elderly woman, formerly of means, who always took off her glasses so that she wouldn't see the maggots crawling over what she was eating.

The specter of starvation was never far. In New York City four hospitals reported ninety-five deaths from hunger in 1931. But mostly the problem was chronic, enervating malnutrition. The Children's Bureau determined that one of five schoolchildren was not getting enough to eat. A poignant vignette summed up the situation for one investigator, who remembered a little boy proudly displaying his pet rabbit at school, while his older sister whispered out of earshot: "He thinks we're not going to eat it; but we are."

The worst hardships naturally befell the jobless and their families, estimated by *Fortune* magazine to include thirty-four million persons. But those still at work felt a severe pinch, too. The average weekly wage in 1932 was only $16.21; below that, some paychecks dwindled to the vanishing point. A Chicago investigation revealed that the majority of working women in the city received less than 25¢ an hour. That was a sharp comedown; but elsewhere things were worse. In the lumber industry hourly rates fell to 10¢, in general contracting to 7½¢ and in the sawmills all the way down to a nickel. In all, wage payments dwindled from $50 billion in 1929 to only $30 billion in 1932. A sure sign of the loss of confidence in American prospects was a drop in the birth rate for the first time in American history. The attitude of those who had come from other nations to seek opportunity in America showed a similarly dismal reversal. Between 1931 and 1936, 240,000 more aliens left the United States than were admitted.

To address this catastrophe, the nation was equipped with the worst welfare system in the western world, a patchwork of voluntary institutions and pinchpenny state and local agencies. For a family of four without any income, the best the city of Philadelphia could do was provide $5.50 per week. And that was comparatively munificent. New York City, where the greatest number of welfare cases gathered, could give only $2.39 per week to such a family. In Mississippi the figure was $1.50; Detroit, devastated when the bottom fell out of the auto industry, allotted 60¢ and went bankrupt anyway. As the indigent tide thus mounted, hospitals began limiting admission to those who had prepaid, while state agencies required utter destitution before granting aid and even then were forced to limit help to families with children. In a desperate act of fear, ten states withdrew suffrage from those on relief rolls, alarmed at the prospect of whom the down-trodden might elect. The grim realities knocked playwright and storyteller William Saroyan from his famous high trapeze of optimism long enough for him to state plausibly that "hardly anybody is interested in anything much. Hardly anybody *is* at all."

The term *Depression,* coined to avert the hysteria that might ensue if the customary word to characterize economic collapse—*panic*—were used, neatly captured the trauma of the era. Undoubtedly the shock was deepened by a 180-degree disjunction between the hard times and what the nation had thought was in store for it. President Calvin Coolidge, who with saturnine smugness had presided over the prosperity of the mid-1920s, closed out his last full year in office with this message to his legislative colleagues: "No Congress of the United States ever assembled, on surveying the state of the Union, has met with a more pleasing prospect that that which appears at the present time. . . . The great wealth created by our enterprise and industry, and saved by our economy, has had the widest distribution among our own people, and has gone out in a steady stream to serve the charity and the business of the world. The requirements of existence have passed beyond the standard of necessity into the region of luxury. . . . The country can regard the present with satisfaction and anticipate the future with optimism."

In a time when people were impressed with advancements in the science of measurement, many objective measurements seemed to buttress the Coolidge view. After a brief dip in the economy as the nation converted to peacetime production following World War I, prosperity surged forward. The gross national product rose from $74 billion in 1921 to $104.4 billion in 1929. An exhilarating factor in that burst was the 30 percent rise in productivity per worker. The marvelous technological virtuosity and human vitality on display led the nation at its high point to the production of 25 percent of the world's goods and 40 percent of its manufactured items. Wartime national debt gave way to a surplus in the federal budget, which Andrew Mellon, secretary of the treasury and one of the world's richest men, cited as justification for his policy of stimulating the economy by reducing taxes. Mellon's pet theory was that most of the relief should be directed to the upper income brackets, so that there would be more money in the private sector available for investment in America's wondrous industrial machine. The profits accruing to men of great wealth like himself, Mellon insisted in a phrase that has shown great durability, would "trickle down" to the humblest level and thus justify his president's confidence that the nation's affluence had "the widest distribution" and managed to "serve the charity . . . of the world." Indeed, so carried away with his doctrine did Mellon become that he ordered the Internal Revenue Service to provide an expert to help him find ways of eliminating his own taxes altogether. By the end of the decade the Mellon policy helped 60,000 families at the head of the economic procession to gather assets equal to those of the twenty-five million persons who brought up the rear. Especially striking was the way income from dividends had risen by 65 percent, an indication that the wealth rescued from taxes was not trickling down but was rather being swept up into the stock market and the bank vaults.

The combination of Mellon's policy of steering surplus federal revenues to private investors and excitement over economic prospects brought avid attention to the stock market. Leaders of both parties pressed the theme that the poor would rise to affluence within a speculative paradise. When he accepted the nomination for the presidency in 1928, Herbert Hoover announced: "We shall soon with the help of God be in sight of the day when poverty will be banished from this nation." And the following summer John Jacob Raskob, chairman of the Democratic Party and head of General Motors, went even further in an article entitled "Everybody Ought to Be Rich." Published in the *Ladies Home Journal*— despite the fact that women were barred from the floor of the Stock Exchange— the article exuberantly sketched a stock investment plan that could not help but bring lavish gain. The advice illuminated the strength of two perennial lures: The something-for-nothing formula and the individualist belief that, with luck and pluck, the common man—or lady—could break out of the mob and find room at the top.

The stock market craze was remarkable as much for the illusions spun about Wall Street as for its actual destination. Like the youths who in an earlier era had read Horatio Alger tales of success and dreamed idle dreams of matching them in real life, most Americans during the 1920s merely beheld the stock market from a distance. Post mortems after the great binge ended in 1929 showed that only about two to three million persons traded on the Exchange; only about half that number, roughly one for every hundred of the 120 million Americans at the time, bought on margin. Yet, speculative excitement reached everywhere. The Associated Press devoted five to ten thousand words to the market every day; the *New York Times* filled about a third of its columns with news about finance. Tip sheets made their first appearance, and myths abounded about the inside dopesters, of the sort immortalized in the stories of Damon Runyon and Ring Lardner; they could be found in shoe shine parlors, washrooms, Chinese laundries—everywhere. Between 1925 and 1929 the number of people employed in the field of finance went up by 400,000, establishing a speculation empire that left America permanently saddled with a far higher proportion of corporation lawyers, accountants, and stockbrokers than other countries in the modern world. The prices of common stocks between 1923 and 1929 increased by 176 percent, as the number of traded shares climbed from 236 million to one and a quarter billion. Between 1925 and 1929 alone, the market value of stocks rose 250 percent, from 27 billion dollars to 67½ billion.

The accompanying business boosterism ascended all the way to heaven. "The man who builds a factory builds a temple," intoned Calvin Coolidge in a rare moment of spirituality. "The man who works there worships there." To Bruce Barton, senior partner of a leading advertising firm, Jesus was "The Man Nobody Knows"—the greatest of business executives and admen, who took twelve motley fishermen and stragglers and welded them into a dynamic corporation that spread the Good News of the Kingdom around the world. Did the Savior not explain that He had appeared on earth in order to be "about my Father's business," Barton asked ingenuously? Accordingly, people flocked to the stock exchange temple, and little branch shrines where they could trade even began to appear on ocean liners. The general ardor for speculation finally induced businesses to reverse the traditional practice of seeking loans through stock and bond issues so as to finance productive enterprises. Instead businesses began to make investment loans themselves from the surplus profits that Mellon's policy had helped them accumulate. In 1929 alone the Cities Service oil company, riding the crest of the automobile boom, loaned more than $285 million to speculators, including $42 million in a single day.

Among those swept up in the exuberance was one Franklin D. Roosevelt, recently returned to his New York City law practice after his service as the wartime assistant secretary of the Navy and an unsuccessful run for the vice presidency in 1920. Roosevelt's speculative forays involved him in freight dirigibles, frozen lobsters, wildcat oil, and other long shots but yielded little return except a rebuke by the Society for Promoting Financial Knowledge for lending the prestigious Roosevelt name to doubtful undertakings. A certain offhandedness, even playfulness, about the way he approached the Exchange marked Roosevelt as definitely not an exemplar of the earnest, money-making, nation-building patriot ideal favored by the presiding Republican establishment.

President Hoover, on the other hand, seemed a bit too earnest. Alarmed that stock prices were rising beyond any reasonable relation to the true value of the companies issuing them, Hoover sent an emissary to Wall Street to ask the Exchange to curb speculation. But the euphoria rolled over the dour president as well, and the gap between investor assets and the face value of stocks purchased continued to widen until it reached twenty-five to one. And so the maxim that "Everybody Ought to Be Rich" drove the nation onward, past old-fashioned caution.

Ultimately, what went up had to come down, as had happened to similar speculative crazes in the past. A slight loss of altitude in stock prices in mid-October of 1929 indicated that there might not be enough hot air left to keep the speculative contraption aloft. Then on October 21 the collapse began with a vengeance. On Thursday, October 24, almost thirteen million shares were traded on the New York Stock Exchange, climaxing a week in which billions were lost as shaky margin accounts were called in and inflated stocks tumbled toward their true value. Some enraged Chicago gangsters, not used to losing money on anything marginal, dynamited their stockbroker's home and threw stink bombs into the brokerage offices. Herbert Hoover issued assurances of essentially firm business foundations to allay the dangers about which he had futilely warned the plungers. A worried nation then greeted the weekend respite in hopes of a return to normalcy. It was not to be. The next Tuesday witnessed the greatest volume of trading the Exchange had ever seen—not to be exceeded until 1968—and an average decline in stock prices of 24 points. On Wednesday *Variety,* the theatrical arts trade journal, summed it all up in a banner headline: "Wall Street Lays an Egg." From there the market kept dropping until it finally bottomed out on November 13, with losses of $74 billion, some three times the total cost of fighting World War I. The rest of the devastated economy was sucked downward in its trail, toward the grim electoral conditions of 1932.

Puzzlement over the Crash has continued since the initial inability to understand their fate first paralyzed worried citizens. Of course, the inflated stocks, inside pools for sharing information not available to the public, holding companies that kept the best of new stock issues for themselves, and comparable swindles—all of these had much to do with the crisis. But the stock market was only the lightning rod for a wide range of economic weakness. For example, while the Coolidge-Hoover business sector was riding high, agriculture remained in a depressed state, persistently below its pre–World War I level. In the year of the Great Crash, the average income for those on the farms was $223, while for those elsewhere it was $870, despite the labors of many on the land from "can see" to "can't see." Beyond that comparison was a more comprehensive fact of income distribution. Low average incomes, including six million families eking out less than $1000 a year, contrasted sharply with the precipitous rise of corporate profits. In the all-important steel industry, for example, there was no wage increase between 1924 and 1929, a reflection of the industry's success in quashing the strike of 1919. But during those years Republic Iron and Steel racked up profits of 208 percent, while other industry leaders were not far behind. Where, under such circumstances, was the great industrial juggernaut to find enough customers to buy all the things it was producing? The slowdown of new construction after 1927 and the inventory backlog on the eve of the Great Crash indicated that America was, in the new term of the day, suffering from "underconsumption."

Complicating the issue was the imbalance of trade in a period that saw the United States move from debtor nation to creditor. The destructiveness of World War I, combined with postwar reparations from the vanquished and loans due the United States from its allies, left European nations at a competitive disadvantage. For a time, America enjoyed selling far more goods abroad than it was buying; by the end of the decade the ability of foreign nations to come up with money, aside from American loans, to pay for the stream of goods had seriously diminished.

Yet another shaky base was the banking system. Unlike every other advanced nation, the United States had no central bank. The scattered array of independent banks, many of them with small, vulnerable holdings and poorly trained management, was a weak bulwark against the sort of enormous pressure for support funds generated by large waves of speculation.

The remedies proposed as the Depression worsened were a sign of palpable fear and uncertainty. One retired Army major suggested mercy killings for those too old and weak to support themselves. Rather more humane was the proposal of health faddist and journalist Bernarr McFadden to develop some way to put the unemployed in cold storage, to be thawed at the return of prosperity. Roger Babson, a highly successful financial analyst esteemed especially for his accurate prediction of a market crisis, urged people to turn to religious revivals to gain the strength for recovery. Others rallied around Texas Congressman Martin Dies, who would later make his mark as a hunter of subversives on the House Un-American Activities Committee, when he urged that all aliens be deported and their jobs turned over to "real Americans." Henry Ford, the patron saint of the production line, turned back to his rural roots by insisting that his employees grow what unfriendly critics called "shotgun gardens." In a comparable appeal to national morale, J. P. Morgan, the living symbol of America's financial community, defended the importance of maintaining an economic elite. "If you destroy the leisure class," he informed a congressional committee investigating ways of redistributing wealth, "you destroy civilization." When pressed about how to define the leisure class, Morgan said it would include all those who could afford a maid—about twenty-five to thirty million people, he supposed, until informed that there were only about two million servants in the whole country. Morgan's obliviousness was typical of many from his class who were called forward to testify. Under scrutiny, those who had presided over the debacle and now sought to lead the nation back into the same old promised land showed how little they had troubled themselves to learn about the society that had made them rich.

Herbert Hoover, the nation's president during the disastrous reversal of fortune, was the most formidable public figure of the time. Self-made millionaire, heroic leader of relief for civilian victims of World War I, and a fount of ideas for economic growth who made the Department of Commerce the most dynamic agency of government during the 1920s, Hoover bears careful examination as the personification of a principled "American System" that purported to represent individualism at its best. Through his unique combination of business and political success, Hoover managed to establish a monumental presence that won him an admiring audience for his ideal of a society bound together by voluntary cooperation. As early as 1909, in his influential text *Principles of Mining,* he expressed the concept of shared achievement in business, which he felt was borne out in his career as the world's wealthiest engineer. The key, Hoover declared, was finding a common bond among freely motivated strivers. On the labor side, unions for workers to pool their strengths were "normal and proper antidotes for unlimited capitalistic organization." As for management, he believed that "the time when the employer could ride roughshod over his labor is disappearing with the doctrine of 'laissez faire' on which it was founded." To be in tune with modern forces, the virtuous engineer or employer must understand how "inspiration to increase exertion is created . . . by recognition of individual effort, in larger pay, and by extending justifiable hope of promotion."

At odds, thus, with laissez-faire orthodoxy on the right and the varieties of state socialism and welfare state capitalism then rising on the left, Hoover instead took to the White House the nineteenth-century Whig view that a combination of natural abundance and democratic freedom had provided America with a unique opportunity. Like Benjamin Franklin and Abraham Lincoln and the boosters of pluck and ingenuity who followed them, Hoover believed that the human disposition toward cooperation would, if allowed to develop without institutional interference, form a wise and just community, prepared to make good use of the resources at its command. That faith, contrasting American democracy and prospects with the inequality and restricted opportunity he saw elsewhere in the world, conditioned Hoover to stand aloof from other nations and to champion the booming business expansion of the 1920s against those who equated free enterprise with sheer self-interest. Designs that would curb private initiative and responsibility by imposing state controls Hoover considered the authoritarian offspring of wicked European ideas.

The intense way Hoover embodied classic nineteenth-century Whig attitudes mirrored the rags-to-riches heroics of his own life. The child of strict Quakers in Iowa farm country, Hoover was orphaned in 1884 at the age of nine and shunted off to live with an uncle in Oregon. In struggling to adjust to drastic loss and change, young Hoover created an identity that both strengthened and consoled him, though it never fully rid him of anxiety. Hoover biographer David Burner shrewdly links him to the title character of F. Scott Fitzgerald's signal novel of the Jazz Age, *The Great Gatsby* (1925) on the grounds that both were skilled at willing things into existence, even against the force of circumstances. As Burner put it, "much of his career would be occupied with getting power and control for himself, and with creating order and stability around him." Self and other would thus be balanced, with ample distance set between them. To complete the analogy and suggest what is apt to happen when self-created reality eclipses experience, Burner might have added that both his and Fitzgerald's heroes were eventually overcome by realities they were not able to will away.

Sometimes Hoover paused to think of himself in more forlorn terms, as a latterday David Copperfield, the bereft orphan left to the harsh ways of his stepfather. That was the wounded side of Hoover, which made him wary of close relationships and resistant to criticism. In later years he liked to attribute his success to being forced at an early age to learn how to handle difficult relations stoically. Able to trust only himself fully, Hoover kept going by inner determination, not warmth for others. A friend from boyhood recalled that he had never heard Hoover laugh, let alone cry; at the most Hoover would only open up with his wife and close friends to the shared joys of intimacy, well out of the line of duty.

Hoover's choice of a career as a mining engineer perfectly suited his temperament and life strategy. He loved the rough outdoor work, the solitary freedom, and the chance to wrest value from raw nature. His nineteenth-century individualism took him beyond the closed frontier of America to the remaining frontiers of Australia and China, where the chances were greatest to dominate his surroundings. Before he was done making his fortune and reputation, he had fought roughnecks and adventurers for control of the mines, been shelled during the Boxer Rebellion in China, and prevailed in clashes with native rivals, whom, in typical imperialist fashion, he mostly regarded as menial inferiors. Fulfilled and proven, Hoover moved to London in 1910, where he became a type his fellow expatriate Henry James liked to write about—the upright American businessman in vigorous early middle age searching out new experience and refinement among the upper classes of the Old World, yet feeling lonely and displaced. Hoover gained entry as a wise man with an exotic past. He offered advice to the English financial elite, set up his family in a large house, and entertained almost nightly in high Edwardian style, thus exemplifying his maxim that a man who is not a millionaire by the age of 40 is not worth much. It was during this time, safely away from the anxieties of his upbringing, that Hoover cultivated his public persona as one whose peerless competence entitled him to take the lead in public affairs, even though his own identity and achievements were rooted in distant places. He thus stood above the crowd as a superior being who could appear on his own terms to solve crises. In Asia and England he served as the heroic entrepreneur from the West; in America he later became known as the savior of Europe's starving millions during World War I and the Great Engineer from remote frontiers. Never fully integrated in, or subordinated to, his surroundings, Hoover's world view was thus, like his own character, self-contained and to a considerable extent self-created—even invented, mythical. The result was a neatly rounded consistency but also an innate resistance to events and policies that called his own judgments into question.

Hoover outlined the faith that sustained him in *American Individualism* (1922), a slender book he wrote as secretary of commerce under President Warren Harding. Couched in vigorous terms, little softened by Hoover's Quaker legacy of mild benevolence, *American Individualism* was emphatically self-assured—yet ambiguous. It never succeeded in drawing the crucial dividing line between individual freedom and responsibility to the community and was vulnerable to vital questions: How could government actively encourage individual enterprise without encroaching on private initiative? Could a government dedicated to individual choice ever shape a coherent national purpose? Could such a state, however activist, legitimately get beyond the suggestion and encouragement of means to be itself responsible for the attainment of inspiring ends? Hoover was able to leave these questions hanging until the needs of the Depression forced the issue. Then his grudging willingness to use state power only as a last resort left him anxious, exhausted, and alienated from the public and his ebullient successor, Franklin Roosevelt, who sought action less fettered by old principles.

Hoover's strong record of public service, then, was progressive, but in nineteenth-century Whig terms of encouraging free enterprise autonomy that were uneasily out of step with the twentieth-century movement of progressive thought toward reliance on government to advance the common good. Accordingly, though Hoover's actions in the public realm on many occasions earned him heartfelt admiration, they are best understood as the product of a sense of duty fighting a rearguard action to keep public policy and private lives as separate as possible. That embattled disposition was notable in his most famous mission of mercy. Stranded in London at the outbreak of World War I, well before America's entry, Hoover accepted the daunting task of arranging for food and other forms of aid to reach war-torn Belgium. So brilliantly successful was the effort that Hoover became one of the most celebrated men to emerge from the war. The word *Hooverize* even entered the common language as a term for making a little bit go a long way. And yet, true to his beliefs and temperament, Hoover did not seek compassionate ties with the people he had rescued; they were clients with lives of their own to lead, was the way he seemed to approach them. Warm-hearted Secretary of the Navy Josephus Daniels was repelled by Hoover's aloofness. "He told of the big work in Belgium," Daniels reported, "as coldly as if he were giving statistics of production. . . . From his words and his manner he seemed to regard human beings as so many numbers. Not once did he show the slightest feeling or convey to me a picture of the tragedies that went on." The head of the effort to enlist public support for American war aims, George Creel, extended that response to a judgment about the whole man. To Creel Hoover's aloofness made him seem nothing "but a stretch of blank wall . . . a citadel where every drawbridge is up and every portcullis down."

But Daniels and Creel missed the hurt child in Hoover that was to surface later, in the face of his fight with Roosevelt. What they construed to be indifference may, indeed, have masked the fears and disappointment of one who cared very much about what people did and what they said about him, even as he felt obliged to separate his official actions from the private lives of the people he served. Hoover's strict moral sense also came into play. He felt displaced in Europe, averse to the way caste distinctions separated people and denied opportunity for those at the bottom. The sordid, selfish ways European politicians undermined Wilson's peace hopes further dismayed him and left him feeling that his relief work had been dishonored. Afterward he always looked resentfully upon Europe—from a carefully calculated distance—as inferior to America in ideals and as the source of many of America's problems.

Hoover's aversion to Europe reinforced his preference for virtuous American individualism over the mass movements he associated with European backwardness. That aversion to the "mob," along with his innate shyness, made addressing large gatherings, even the adoring ones most politicians crave, an ordeal. Hoover revealed himself as one who was intimidated by the masses, not merely disdainful of them. "I have never liked the clamor of crowds," he recalled privately. "I intensely dislike superficial social contacts. . . . I was terrorized at the opening of every speech."

For most of the decade after Hoover's wartime success his anxieties were in abeyance. The prosperous 1920s seemed a perfect time for implementing Hoover's vision. Widespread national pride in victory naturally fed a desire to return to the deferred quest for material progress. Americans, Warren Harding realized as he campaigned toward his landslide presidential victory in 1920, wanted "not nostrums but normalcy." They remained loyal to the American faith in progress but not to the reform zeal of earlier progressive campaigns, which seemed to have led to revolutionary upheaval and a war that failed to make the world safe for democracy. Agitation of the sort that had produced legislation regulating the abuses of business and providing safer workplaces now seemed disruptive and un-American. When a series of strikes erupted in the basic mining, shipping, and manufacturing industries during the postwar depression of 1920–21, public opinion supported harsh measures. Even Franklin Roosevelt in his 1920 vice presidential campaign applauded authorities' use of lethal force against strikers when they resisted the American Legion vigilantes besieging their headquarters. Soon afterward the law barring child labor, whose passage in 1916 had culminated a long, arduous campaign for child welfare, was struck down by the Supreme Court as an unconstitutional infringement on individual rights.

In this atmosphere, the two great progressive triumphs at war's end, women's suffrage and the prohibition of alcohol, almost immediately began to disappoint their adherents. The first election in which women could vote, 1920, saw the lowest turnout of eligible voters in the nation's history. And the sweep of conservative Republicans to control of Congress and the presidency mocked the hopes that newly enfranchised women would advance reform and social welfare causes. As for Prohibition, defiance by the general public made bootlegging the era's most lucrative criminal activity. Reformers thus faced an uncomfortable choice. Either they could come to terms with the dominant forces of business practicality and so hope to have a benevolent influence on the new consumer public, or they could continue the old crusades and be branded radical or naive.

The situation was made to order for Hoover to become the most admired figure in public service. He exemplified rags-to-riches enterprise and described himself as a progressive in the sense that he wanted improvements in productive efficiency and an enlightened partnership between leaders of free enterprise and government. This was top-down progressivism, managed by those who had proven themselves through business and professional success. It was a progressivism which assumed that a well-run economy would provide individuals with what they needed most—opportunity and the confidence to seize it. Progressive reformers could try to ensure that efforts to substitute privately run "corporate welfare" for state regulation would truly benefit ordinary workers. As for those who would not or could not gain a favored place within the new system—the "American System," Hoover called it—the pity of private charity could cushion their weakness.

Harding's appointment of Hoover as secretary of commerce provided him with an ideal staging area. His first task was to solve the depression that ensued when wartime mobilization ended. Finding new jobs and markets for food no longer needed for the armed forces was the crux of the matter, and Hoover responded by trying to adapt the lessons of industrial efficiency that had been devised during the twentieth century and demonstrated in the highly centralized war effort. Voluntary associations of producers, Hoover believed, could best achieve a rational balance between supply and demand and an allied harmony with the state at all levels. A network of state and local committees sprang up to solidify his corporatist faith by persuading employers to create jobs and government officials to provide community support. Throughout the rest of the decade hundreds of conferences and committees studied problems of organization, efficiency, and welfare and were greeted with a steady rise in prosperity, which led to the assumption that the high-energy efforts at what came to be called "associationalism" proved Hoover's case. On most economic fronts the impressive results supported the booster spirit that characterized the period. Corporate profits went up about 50 percent from 1923 to 1929, while corporate dividend payments doubled from $4.6 billion to $9.2 billion.

Workers also had a taste of progress. After a desperate postwar decline in which unemployment went from 560,000 at war's end to over five million in 1921, recovery swiftly took hold and left only some 1,550,000, or 3.2 percent, out of work in 1929. At the same time, by 1929 wages had ascended to 136 percent of what they had been in 1913, enough to keep ahead of the cost of living, which was almost 60 percent higher than in 1913 but remained level during the 1920s. For those outside the productive economy, funds for welfare and education increased markedly, if not nearly as fast as corporate and financial profits. The $4.3 billion allocated to these concerns in 1929 on the federal, state, and local levels was four times the amount spent in the high-water Progressive year of 1913.

Thus, if the United States was often decried culturally as the "Babbitt Warren," materially it seemed peerless. Indeed, it was precisely because prosperity was so commanding that many American artists and writers fled to Europe in despair over their perceived inability to make a dent in their countrymen's materialistic values. On those foreign shores the exiles found the same dreadful awe: "The whole world is now fascinated by the United States," wrote the eminent Spanish critic, Salvador de Madariaga in 1929. "So, American life becomes the model which, consciously or unconsciously, all life is now imitating." This praise, another critic declared in an essay describing the United States as "a first draft of the United States of Europe," reflected "the belief that there, by the agency of a reasoning intelligence, had been achieved the miracle of permanent prosperity which no crisis could destroy."

The vision of permanent prosperity was a triumph of American salesmanship. Dazzled by the confident show of goods and money, observers tended not to notice the trouble lurking beneath the surface. Of central importance was the growing maldistribution of income. Between 1923 and 1929, the top 1 percent of Americans increased their income share almost by a fifth, to about 15 percent of the total. At the pinnacle, the upper 1 percent had as much money as the bottom 42 percent and fully a third of the nation's wealth was held by the richest 5 percent. This concentration of affluence, which bankrolled the displays and escapades that wrapped the decade in myths of golden romance, rested on fundamental changes below. Under the goad of technological advance, more efficient mass production, and long hours, industrial workers' productivity rose by more than 40 percent. Their income, however, increased by less than 10 percent; the remaining fruits of their labor went into increased profits, which rose overall by almost two thirds during the decade. Largely unreported after the wave of postwar strikes fizzled out and labor union membership declined from about 5,110,800 in 1920 to 3,444,000 in 1929 were living conditions that belied the prevailing image of prosperity. Even before the Great Crash, almost 8 percent of workers in the industrial sector were unemployed, a consequence of technological advances and higher worker productivity that the euphoria of progress overshadowed. Not until the disenchanted year of 1934 did a study by the Brookings Institution, *America's Capacity to Consume*, finally reveal that over 70 million persons in more than 60 percent of America's families during the 1920s subsisted at less than the $2000 per year needed to acquire basic necessities. A mere 25 percent of the 21.6 million nonfarm families could afford an adequate diet. Especially ominous for the economy was the unheeded downslide that most people experienced even before the Great Crash; between 1928 and 1929, the meager overall rise in income since World War I reversed into a 4 percent decline for 93 percent of the nonfarm population.

The farm sector, comparably beset, became the crucible of economic discontent. While industrial labor was neglected because of weakened unions, lack of prestige in an era of business and celebrity, and minimal political representation, farmers retained their yeoman status and fervent support from southern and midwestern congressmen and senators. For farmers the roaring of the 1920s sounded only from a distance. Their postwar depression did not end until 1925, and even then farm income remained below the level of 1914 for the rest of the decade. Although farmers could eat better than urban workers, they were at more of a disadvantage in the consumer cash economy. The average annual income of the 5.8 million farm families at mid-decade was only $240, and, although modern technology and increased money at the top for land speculation had produced an elite of large growers, 54 percent of all farmers earned less than $1000 per year. Steadily, farm mortgage debt rose while commodity prices and land value declined even though the cost of manufactured goods increased and nonfarm land values almost doubled. At the center of the trouble was the galling way that farm productivity kept rising, in accord with the American ethic of progress, beyond the limits of available markets. A sure sign of imbalance in the economy had appeared, but only the beleaguered farmers seemed concerned—or even to notice it.

The farm bloc reaction to the crisis was to press for legislative authority to dump the surplus abroad. In 1924, Senator Charles McNary of Oregon and Representative Gilbert Haugen of Iowa presented a bill that would be hotly debated for the rest of the decade. Their plan called on Congress to establish a fair return to farmers for what they grew, based on a comparison of what farmers received in 1914, and then arrange to buy for export whatever farmers could not sell at home. The difference between the established fair, or "parity," price and what the government could recover by "dumping" the surplus would be made up to the government by an "equalization fee" levied on dealers and processors.

This "equalization fee" became the nub of controversy over the McNary-Haugen Farm Relief Bill. Both Coolidge and Hoover opposed it on the grounds that the fee amounted to price-fixing and unconstitutionally levied taxes for purposes other than raising revenue. Furthermore, opponents charged that a device to raise prices while a surplus existed violated the "natural laws" of the marketplace. In Congress the bill failed when first introduced mainly because southern farm interests—primarily cotton—stuck with their region's traditional opposition to tariffs, correctly seeing McNary-Haugenism as a means of extending what amounted to tariff protection to agriculture. But when cotton markets shrank after 1925, and profits with them, Southern agrarians changed their tune and were ready to join midwestern farmers in the dumping program. This time the lines were clearly drawn: the farmers vs. President Coolidge, the Republican establishment, and the bulk of professional economists who, as usual, were nervous about changing the status quo.

Out of the contention emerged a new McNary-Haugen bill in 1927—only to be vetoed by Coolidge in sharp language. No one supported the veto more emphatically than Hoover, whose devotion to the free market was joined by his conviction that means for improving commerce, such as the marketing provisions in McNary-Haugen, should properly be left to his own Department of Commerce. Farmers would make their greatest contribution, indicated the Republican leaders, by providing surplus-bogged food cheaply enough to sustain workers who, in turn, could then allow American goods to be priced competitively abroad. So serenely confident was the Coolidge administration's conviction that "the business of America is business" and that farmers should expect to serve that truism that Treasury Secretary Andrew Mellon, one of the wealthiest men in America, was moved to chide Representative Haugen in a show of lordly disregard for the farmers' plight. McNary-Haugen's farm export assistance, Mellon charged, would amount to "the unusual spectacle of the American consuming public paying a bonus to the producers of five major agricultural commodities, with a resulting decrease in the purchasing power of wages, and at the same time contributing a subsidy to the foreign consumers, who under the proposed plan will secure American commodities at prices below the American level." The obvious inconsistency between this dismissal of agriculture and the administration's support of high tariffs to protect industry and the hard-sell delegation from Hoover's Commerce Department to drum up markets for manufactured (not agricultural) goods abroad was not lost on the farm insurgents.

To counter McNary-Haugenism, Republican farm policy offered the Cooperative Marketing Act of 1926 and the Federal Farm Board, set up in 1929, when Hoover was president. The objective was to foster voluntary association among farmers to govern crop yield and provide each other with assistance, along with governmental advice and loans, to stave off hard times. Hoover showed his affinity to the business point of view and earned plaudits from the Business Man's Conference on Agriculture in 1927 when he declared that farming was like any other industry and, when "sick," should be treated with more efficiently organized marketing arrangements and the doses of higher tariffs that had been standard Republican medicine since the late nineteenth century.

And, yet, Hoover remained largely stymied by the farm situation. He had once announced to an Iowa banker his belief that "if we could get 25 sensible men in a room together without the pressure of either publicity or politics I believe the agricultural industry of the United States could be put on a basis more stable than any other industry." But no such room or men materialized to make the unspecified insider policy possible. Rather, at the triumphal moment when the Cooperative Marketing Act was passed, he confided to a friend: "I confess I do not know how to go about it at the moment." The ever mounting resistance of farm interests to his associationalist panacea was worrisome; Hoover may well have wondered whether such widely dispersed enterprises as wheat farming and cattle raising could ever be brought into the tight cooperative arrangements he had admired in the California fruit fields of his youth. When the time came for his nomination to the Presidency in 1928, many farmers adamantly opposed him.

The impasse over agriculture was the major symptom of difficulty in Hoover's approach, but it wasn't the only one. His careful avoidance of declaring national ends—whether out of deference to the rights of individuals to determine their own purposes, or from shyness, or because he possessed no such ultimate spiritual visions—left an aching void. When it came time for Hoover to try for the presidency, after Coolidge's cryptic "I do not choose to run" statement in 1927, the drawbacks of Hoover's stolid and mechanical approach became evident—even as his stature and Republican prosperity guaranteed a landslide. In the primaries he lost in the home states of all the favorite son candidates. Even staunchly Republican *Time* magazine argued that "the central fact militating against candidate Hoover is that many people cannot understand what he stands for. He is no forthright protagonist of an ideal or program. . . . Material well-being, comfort, order, efficiency in government and economy—these he stands for, but they are conditions, not ends. A technologist, he does not discuss ultimate purposes."

One of the dampening factors was the lack of enthusiasm the laconic Coolidge had shown for the busy organizing schemes of his secretary of commerce and heir apparent. Silent Cal became especially exercised when Hoover, through the sort of inconvenient facts and figures that always annoyed Coolidge, warned that irresponsible speculation in the stock market was undermining the economy. Rebuked for such crepe-hanging, Hoover backed away from his criticism, consoled by the confidence that, when retribution for the orgy of speculation came, the fundamental soundness of the system would absorb it without serious damage. Yet Coolidge remained a wet blanket, blunting the point of Hoover's onward thrust. In the spring of 1928, the retiring president summed up the problem of Hoover from the status quo conservative standpoint with his usual bluntness: "That man has offered me unsolicited advice for six years, all of it bad!"

Coolidge's exasperation reflected a state of mind whose power Hoover did not fully appreciate. Hoover, the rational engineer, believed that careful assessment of the evidence would make the case that personal and community interests were mutually supportive, when voluntarily acted upon. However, that progressive logic did not move Coolidge and his moneyed supporters. They thought in more divisive, even feudal, terms and so would insulate the wealthy and powerful from the collective pressures of government, unions, and public interest lobbies. Hoover could thus rouse applause at the 1922 convention of the National Association of Manufacturers when he declared that to make sure the Commerce Department "shall be of the greatest service to commerce and industry, it should be maintained on a non-regulatory basis, that its whole relationship should be one of cooperation with our business public." But Hoover's view that cooperation should include elements outside the business community, among them organized labor, was not applauded. Julius Barnes, believing that as president of the United States Chamber of Commerce he spoke for the nation, insisted that "America conceives that the prime obligation of government is to preserve to the individual the reward of superior effort or superior ability." And that, as Vice President of the National Association of Manufacturers Charles Fay explained, meant that the federal government did not have the positive role of fostering cooperation but the negative one of blocking invasions of personal space and property. What private citizens alone could create it was the duty of the federal government to defend, with diplomatic and armed forces "to protect all citizens against foreigners; and the law, justice and police establishments, to protect them against their fellow-citizens." Secondary functions like education and other public services could be left to state and local discretion. Underneath this formula, championed by the most important business associations in the nation, lay the bedrock of belief in the primacy of competition. The dominant true believers still accepted the obiter dicta of the communal spirit's most caustic critic, sociologist William Graham Sumner. In his classic *What Social Classes Owe to Each Other* (1883), Sumner did not mince words. What the social classes owed each other was nothing. Christian charity for the weak had its place, but the strong deserved what they could get, and it was from them that society derived its progress and glory. Against such a creed, Hoover's hope for cooperation between businessmen for the benefit of society at large, even if it could avoid running afoul of antitrust laws, was not likely to succeed.

Hoover had only a few months to promote the vision he had mapped out before crisis engulfed him. The situation unfolded like a Greek tragedy. Hailed to preside over permanent progress, Hoover spoke at his inaugural of a nation "filled with millions of happy homes; blessed with comfort and opportunity. In no nation are the fruits of accomplishment more secure." Instead, Hoover was swept toward the great stock market crash and a shattered economy precipitated by policies he had warned about and energetically sought to prevent. Once over the edge, in part because the business and financial sectors would not cooperate, Hoover relied on beliefs and devices that were fatally flawed. Like poor War-ren Harding in the midst of scandal, Hoover might have lamented that his great handicap was not his enemies but his "goddamned friends."

And, he might have added, his inflexible, naive hope that business leadership would abandon its ideological commitment to competitive self-interest in favor of the cooperative associationalism he preached. For Hoover's way was, no matter what, to remain stoically loyal to his own conceptions. At a conference for "continued indus-trial progress" in December 1929, Hoover told the assemblage of industrial and labor leaders that the economic crisis involved far more than just Wall Street. It proceeded from complex national and international forces which only an ear-nestly coordinated effort by the citizenry could control. With an understanding that historians have often failed to credit, Hoover spoke of the need for industry to help ensure that consumers would have money to buy what manufacturers produced. Hoover echoed his long held dictum that "the essence of great produc-tion is high wages and low prices." At the same time, Hoover urged a no-strike pledge on labor to assure the nation that its businesses would bravely carry on.

Government would do its part by trying the same techniques that had proved so successful in 1921. Expert study and legislation would remedy flaws in the operation of utilities, railroads, and other defective industries. A public works program would provide jobs for the unemployed. Lowered income taxes would return money to businessmen for investment. And frugal paring of governmen-tal services would keep the budget in balance and public confidence correspond-ingly high. At the local level, government agencies would help private charity dis-tribute voluntary contributions to those clearly unable to fend for themselves.

As usual, Hoover's hopes for a surge of voluntary, self-sacrificing altruism were unrealized, and the results from his plan proved far too limited in scope to halt the decline. Hoover then placed greater stress on causes outside the Ameri-can System. He might have focused his wrath on the way businessmen were violating his high-wage, low-cost formula by resorting to their old habit in hard times of cutting wages while keeping prices up in order to maintain high rev-enues. He might have been more alert to the drastic inadequacy of private char-ity. And he might have been quicker to see that cooperative self-reliance could not keep the farm sector afloat. Instead Hoover looked abroad, influenced by his jaundiced attitude toward Europe as deceiver and troublemaker.

Default on the war debts owed to the United States seemed especially criti-cal. Now in arrears, the Allies blamed the Germans, who by 1931 owed almost $5 billion and showed little inclination to pay. Pressure by French creditors in the form of withdrawing funds from German and Austrian banks only weakened those nations' banking systems until May 1931, when Austria's largest bank, the Credit-Anstalt, went under. In the ensuing panic it became apparent that some extraordinary measures needed to be taken. Hoover's response was to declare a one-year moratorium on all international debts so that there would be time for the troubled economies to right themselves.

But they did not right themselves. The moratorium became permanent despite Hoover's opposition on grounds that obligations should be met fairly. With that permanence, the concept froze in Hoover's mind that default on the debt in 1931 was equivalent to a collapse of the entire European economy; by withholding both the trade and the borrowed cash that America needed, Europe was responsible for dragging the American economy down with it. That conviction of European culpability was hardened when Britain went off the gold standard in 1931 in order to supplement its dwindling gold supply with other assets as backing for the nation's currency. Hoover always subscribed to what his banker ally, Thomas Lamont, called the "old-fashioned religion" of the gold standard as an indispensable safeguard against monetary chaos. A corollary of that orthodoxy was belief in a balanced budget, which enabled the government to support its expenditures with gold-backed revenues. Thus Hoover was reluctant to stimulate the domestic economy through deficit spending and opposed the expedient resort of gold-strapped nations to paper currency, barter, or other unconventional means of trade.

Within that tight ideological framework, about the only means available to Hoover for balancing the domestic economy against world conditions was the tariff. He turned for guidance to the fact-finding commission created in 1916 to come up with a "scientific" way for the federal government to arrange equal opportunity (somewhat more than equal for Americans, that is) in international markets. Mainly that meant preventing cheap foreign agricultural and manufactured goods from undermining the American standard of living while still giving imports a chance to compete at a "fair price" with domestic goods. But the efforts to revise tariff schedules at the end of the decade made it evident to many economists and other experts that the pressures of special interests to establish barriers *against* competition were prevailing over Hoover's enthusiasm for scientifically determined fair competition. As they feared, when the Hawley-Smoot tariff, featuring greatly increased rates on many items, appeared on the president's desk in the spring of 1930, Hoover ignored the pleading of over a thousand economists and the threats of retaliation from twenty-four foreign governments and signed the bill into law. In less than a year's time, twenty-five nations raised tariffs, and the gap between American exports and the (now decreased) volume of imports widened. But Hoover ever afterward denied that the

Hawley-Smoot tariff upset the scientific balance. He continued to view the tariff as a hedge against depression and averted his attention from the ominous way the import-export imbalance was draining foreign funds and so diminishing the ability of foreign economies to absorb American goods or pay the debts Hoover so staunchly insisted must be honored.

Hoover's concentration on foreign problems also supported his aversion to direct federal intervention into the economy. Locating the cause of Depression abroad enabled him to suggest that domestic remedies were secondary and, in the last analysis, at the mercy of foreign devils anyway. He also harbored bitterness over the way the world crisis pressured Americans toward statist measures that would undermine the true laws of progress he had described in *American Individualism*. In that aggrieved mood, Hoover sought to make his voluntary concepts work at home. He created an Emergency Committee for Employment in the fall of 1929 whose mission was to elicit cooperation from businessmen to create jobs and make recommendations for governmental aid. At the same time the president busily fended off congressional attempts to pass public works bills that violated his precept that the government could only finance projects such as river and harbor improvements and public housing, which would pay for themselves and furnish employment in the private sector. Other projects, like roads and public buildings, that did not provide continuing employment Hoover decried as "raids upon the Public Treasury."

That rigid approach was no match for the pressures that were throwing people out of work, and soon the Emergency Committee's hapless chairman, Walter S. Gifford, also president of the American Telegraph and Telephone Company, was reduced to desperate claims that through volunteer action "America will feel the thrill of a great spiritual experience" and "the fear of cold hunger will be banished from the hearts of thousands!" At last, on July 21, 1932, dire conditions forced Hoover to sign an Emergency and Relief Construction Act providing $2 billion for public works and $300 million for relief in direct loans to the states. Hoover's rationale that the new bill would support local options and only provide for productive jobs, rather than relief, was a fragile expression of the old commitment to self-reliance that the crisis would soon blow away altogether. Hoover's own faith in personal initiative was indestructible, however. During the prosperous 1950s he looked back on the ragged peddlers who had come to symbolize the Depression and noted in his autobiography that "many persons left their jobs for the more profitable one of selling apples."

To combat depression in the farmlands, Hoover used the Federal Farm Board to administer $500 million for loans to farm cooperatives and purchase of surplus. Although the surplus-buying proviso, especially with the tacit corollary that the commodities bought would eventually have to be "dumped" somewhere, smacked of McNary-Haugenism, Hoover reluctantly agreed to the measure because it promised to stimulate the marketplace. Where he stood firm was in his opposition to those who pointed out that the farm problem could only be ended by requiring farmers to grow less. Hoover was willing to urge farmers to reduce their crops and so eliminate the fundamental problem of low prices because of too much supply, but he declared himself "unalterably opposed" to a government role in buying and selling commodities. Duty, not policy, was at stake. "Certain vital principles," Hoover lectured a special session on agricultural problems in 1929, "must be adhered to in order that we may not undermine the freedom of our farmers and of our people as a whole by bureaucratic and governmental domination and interference." What followed was a debacle. In times of low prices, as experience had repeatedly shown, farmers are inclined to grow more, not less, so that they can recoup lost income through a high volume of sales. The result in the desperate Depression years was unsaleable surplus and plummeting prices. Into the breach the Farm Board stepped with the creation of stabilizing agencies, most notably in cotton and wheat. But, despite energetic efforts, surpluses kept mounting. After depleting most of its $500 million, the Farm Board decided that it had to liquidate its attempt to hold the line. The surplus cotton and wheat was sold for a fraction of what it had cost, much of it, in effect, "dumped" on foreign markets. But despite the graphic demonstration that overgrowing was the villain, Hoover remained adamantly opposed to crop controls, and farmers drowned in their own fruitfulness.

A large rural segment was also cursed by an opposite plague: Beginning in 1930 vast areas of the southwest suffered drought. That circumstance led to the crowning irony of agricultural impasse. At the same time that Hoover was opposing intervention to ease overproduction on prosperous farmlands, he was also opposing intervention to aid drought victims, who were unable to grow, by giving them food from the surplus the government was stockpiling at great expense. And yet, to compound the irony, the formula allowed feed to be provided to livestock, presumably because they were freed from the human obligation to show self-reliant initiative. Disgust over this rugged individualist doctrine run amok was captured in the Biblical parody of Hoover's words by Senator George Norris of Nebraska, one of many Progressive Republicans who opposed the administration on moral and efficiency grounds for its unwillingness to deal directly with suffering: "Blessed be those who starve while the asses and mules are fed."

Disasters mounted beyond all precedent. Farm prices in 1932 dipped to 48.2 percent of what they had been in 1926, a time when reformers were already making a case that the standard of living on the farms was too low. By 1932 nearly a million farms had fallen into the hands of mortgage holders, and total income had declined from $12 billion just before the Great Crash to $5.3 billion, giving the average farm family only a little over $200 for that grim election year. By the end of Hoover's unhappy term, farmers were sliding so far down the social scale that one acute observer noted the resemblance between many of them and the masses he had observed in the Mongolian hinterland. Apropos of this rural misery, the famous English economist, John Maynard Keynes, when asked if there had been anything like the Depression before, recalled another peasant age: "Yes, it was called the Dark Ages, and it lasted four hundred years."

The group most fully benefited by Hoover's policies was the financial sector. That was because, for all his praise of the way democracy develops through open opportunity from the bottom up, Hoover's support for free enterprise really aided the Coolidge "trickle-down" approach. The great concentration of business assets meant that investment money went to relatively few sources and that whatever prosperity watered the grass roots had to filter down from wealth in full bloom at the top. Thus, in trying to meet the growing banking crisis, Hoover was enveloped by the leading financiers: they were the ultimate beneficiaries of government aid to smaller operators, whose debts were to the big banks. The system made it especially difficult for Hoover to maintain his distinctions between direct and indirect aid and between private enterprise and government intervention.

In October 1931, Hoover persuaded an important segment of the banking and insurance community to join in the creation of a National Credit Corporation, which would use $500 million of entrepreneurial funds to underwrite the shaky bank paper. The reluctant efforts of the private bankers did little to stem bank defaults, but they did stimulate hope that some large undertaking by the government might succeed. Hoover was reluctant to accept the obvious analogy pointed out by Eugene Meyer, governor of the Federal Reserve Board, between the need of the moment for financial expansion and the similar need during World War I, which was managed successfully by the creation of the War Finance Corporation. Such intervention into the private realm worried Hoover, but since it involved loans rather than direct investment and built on the close relationship between government and private banking in existence since the creation of the Federal Reserve Board in 1913, Hoover endorsed the legislation creating the Reconstruction Finance Corporation in January of 1932.

As Hoover's biographer Joan Hoff Wilson so aptly emphasizes, the creation of the RFC meant, ironically, that "the ill-fated Hoover administration became the first in American history to use the power of the federal government to intervene directly in the economy in time of peace." However, the collectivist implications of that innovation were emphasized as little as possible. Hoover made the RFC his prime weapon against the Depression with an uneasy, evasive determination not to be lured into the swamps of statism. At the signing of the law he was careful to reiterate a bootstrap faith in American individualism by stating that the RFC was not intended for big banks and industries. Those enterprises, Hoover insisted in his best confidence-inducing manner, could take care of themselves. Then the RFC set out under a cloak of secrecy, which Hoover defended as a way of maintaining the confidence of recipients, to disperse $1.5 billion of its $2 billion during the remainder of the year. Although over 90 percent of the total number of loans went to institutions in small cities and towns, the lion's share of the money went to the giant banks. Two-thirds of the first $61 million went to three banks, and a fourth bank received $90 million soon afterward. Furthermore, much of the money granted to small banks found its way up the line because large banks held the liens that forced the smaller banks to request RFC help in the first place. After the Democrats in Congress passed an amendment opening RFC operations to audit, the imbalance of the assistance became clear.

By doing little to revive business at the grassroots level, the RFC could not head off disaster. It did, however, buttress the deluded concept, held by Hoover and the business community alike, that prosperity stemmed from stability at the top. Let leading businesses and their investment banker partners flourish, and in their train workers will have jobs and farmers will find markets. That article of faith undergirded Hoover's conviction that the American System was on the way to recovery. He was not as foolishly optimistic as Vice President Charles Curtis, whose remark that "prosperity is just around the corner" has often been mistakenly attributed to Hoover, but he was convinced. The key, as always, was fortitude. Decrying Communist Russia's five-year plans for their misguided haste, Hoover avowed that the right twenty-year plan could ensure America's future. On that note, eyes raised to the horizon beyond the troubles all around him, Hoover embarked on his campaign for reelection.

CHAPTER TWO

The Shaping of Franklin Roosevelt

The emergence of Franklin Roosevelt as the one to lead the Democratic Party against Hoover in 1932 disappointed many. The myth spread by journalistic pundits and some party regulars was that Roosevelt was a lightweight opportunist who had gotten ahead mainly on his family name and his urbane manner. Even the famously astute journalist Walter Lippmann wrote him off just before the 1932 nominating convention as "an amiable man with many philanthropic impulses, but . . . too eager to please." Four years of Roosevelt might be a welcome relief from Herbert Hoover's cheerless regime, but there seemed little chance he could generate any thorough blueprint for recovery.

The critics were right about Roosevelt's ability to please. From the beginning he impressed people with his Grecian profile, his energy, and his engaging manner. One old politico recalled first seeing Roosevelt as a new state senator in 1910 and feeling keenly "when he strode down the aisle to take the oath" that "there's a bird who will have to be watched." From then on Roosevelt was in demand as a representative of the Democratic Party who could be counted on to make a good impression.

In the face of so much charm, however, what tended to be missed was the alertness and shrewdness behind it. Roosevelt was a remarkable calculator of the possibilities residing in each situation. He struck a balance between affability and cunning reticence that buffered him against the competing pressures and enigmatically reflected the operating principles of his life.

Roosevelt's complex nature derived from circumstances that were just enough at variance with typical upper-class life to make a significant difference. In the

1880s, when Roosevelt was born, wealth and prestige were concentrated in the entrepreneurial elite that were in the process of driving America toward becoming the world's leading industrial power. Energy and ambition were the dominant characteristics of the era—and the class. But Roosevelt's father James was by then in his fifties whose energies were diminished by heart disease and his ambitions checked by disapproval of the ruthlessness he had encountered in the business world. James had turned his back on the competitive inferno of New York City in favor of a more genteel existence as a country squire on his handsome estate overlooking the Hudson River. He had wealth enough to be comfortable and sought to use his wealth to experience the moral satisfactions of being a preeminent benefactor in local civic and church affairs.

Thus young Franklin grew up in an atmosphere as close as an American could get to the British aristocracy. His was a cherished, privileged, yet lonely existence as an only child with access to few companions, especially of his own class. He turned to his benevolent father for guiding principles and learned to evade his class-conscious and domineering mother Sara by developing his talent of seeming to agree with others while carefully leaving room for pursuing his own ends. Except for tutors and governesses, the boy made do largely with his own company—reading, collecting stamps and toy soldiers, roaming the estate, and sailing on the Hudson or in the ocean off of Long Island. Roosevelt's children, Anna and James, declared that their father had "learned loneliness" as a child and then developed it into his famous inscrutability. His ingrained trait of keeping others away from his innermost being served him well as a shield—but it also isolated him, leaving even his wife Eleanor to describe him to a friend as a "stranger." As Roosevelt's public life unfolded, the irony grew apace that this most gregarious of public figures could seem almost a personal friend to the troubled Americans who depended on him and hung on his reassuring words yet remained an enigma to family, friends, and political associates—and to his biographers as well.

At age fourteen Roosevelt was sent to the Groton School, one of several boarding schools started in the late nineteenth century to prepare upper-class boys for leadership. By then he was firmly rooted in a set of essentially simple characteristics: an undogmatic Christian faith, belief in the superiority of the countryside over the city, a sense of civic obligation toward neighbors, love of the sea and outdoor sports, and a yearning to become part of a loyal community in which he could excel and thus attain leadership, as his father had over his small domain. Groton provided a fair field for Roosevelt to nurture these traits and ambition. Ardently, he gave himself over to the leadership of the school's overbearing headmaster, Endicott Peabody, an Episcopal minister who drew his inspiration to establish a school from the "Muscular Christianity" he had encountered in British schools, blended with his upbringing in the social reform atmosphere of Brahmin Boston. Peabody imposed a spartan regimen that combined ascetic living quarters, cold showers, and rugged sports with a curriculum similarly devoted to mental exercises rather than to creative imagination. Roosevelt responded with a zest for action, a corresponding indifference to theory, and confidence in Peabody's idea that the experience ideally equipped the privileged to rise to the challenge of serving the nation and ministering to the needs of the less fortunate.

What crucially distinguished Roosevelt from most of his fellow Grotonians was that he retained his devotion to the official ideals of the school throughout his later encounters with the world. Peabody's Groton and the characteristics Roosevelt's life at Hyde Park had instilled in him were perfectly suited. In contrast, the majority of boys, sent to Groton from families caught up in the urban mainstream of business, finance, and the professions, veered from Peabody's earnest moralism when it showed itself out of accord with the world of practical affairs. If they chose to retain the altruism they had learned at Groton, they had to compartmentalize it away from the competitive self-interest of the marketplace. Roosevelt underwent no such discontinuity. From the time as a Groton boy that he accepted the headmaster's plea to do mission work at a nearby chapel that ministered to the poor, he stayed with the Peabody credo as an extension of his own father's uprightness in another special enclave deliberately removed from the corruptions of modern life. Indeed, so strong was Roosevelt's fealty to Peabody that he ever afterward turned to him to preside over crucial events. He was married by Peabody; his children were baptized by the headmaster and later welcomed to Groton. Had Peabody lived a little longer, according to the president's will, he would have conducted Roosevelt's funeral. Roosevelt only differed from his mentor by applying the family allegiance to the Democratic Party, thus avoiding the stress Peabody encountered in remaining loyal to the party of Lincoln when it strayed into the disastrous materialism of the 1920s and then in trying to quell the shrill opposition of the Groton community to his devoted former student when Roosevelt became president.

Peabody responded to the division between Roosevelt and the conservative Republican Grotonians by seeking to be loyal to them all. He voted for Hoover in 1932 as standard-bearer of the party of respectability but thereafter supported Roosevelt, while lecturing other graduates, mostly in vain, about loyalty to one of their own and respect for how the New Deal sought to enact Grotonian ideals of charity and public service.

Roosevelt, however, had long before accepted the gap between himself and most others of his class as unbridgeable. For a time at Harvard and during his subsequent young manhood, Roosevelt tried to belong to the social elite, which misled Joseph Alsop, the journalist who also grew up in that gilded setting, into claiming that Roosevelt only became a "maverick" reform Democrat, as his cousin Theodore Roosevelt Jr., angrily called him, when he realized that his conservative Republican peers would always find him wanting in sophistication and athletic prowess. But, although Roosevelt suffered somewhat from this lack of full acceptance, he understood that his destiny had been determined elsewhere. Reflecting his father's example, he preferred the country to the city and was disdainful of what, in a speech for New York Governor Al Smith, he called the "crass materialism" of commerce. Nor was he suited for the professions, given his mediocre student record and lack of focused intellectual interests. Yet his restive ambition and high energy would not allow him a life of dignified retreat as a country squire either. Instead, although he was moderately interested in the economics he studied in college and later gained admission to the New York bar without bothering to finish law school, Roosevelt found that politics alone energized his special gifts of empathy, communication, and strategic judgment.

Out of the distinctive pattern of his own experience and temperament Roosevelt created an outlook that set him apart from politics as usual. Franklin did not share his father's attachment to the conservative Democratic Party coalition of rural hierarchies, characteristic of Hyde Park as well as the "Solid South." He also tended to disapprove of the ethnic machines of the cities, with their patronage favoritism and casual approach to the law; yet Roosevelt also criticized civil service reformers and advocates of efficiency for their desire to curb mass democracy with elite standards for office-holding and public policy. Instead, Roosevelt blended his father's concept of local community and the activist temper of his presidential cousin Theodore into a vision of progressive reform. Roosevelt's clear sense of self and destiny led to early musings on how to advance a career in politics that would achieve his goal to become the center of his world, as his parents taught him was his due. Soon after Roosevelt's death, Grenville Clark, a fellow clerk in the law firm where Roosevelt worked briefly after his admission to the bar, reminisced in the Harvard yearbook on how amused the other clerks were to hear one of their lowly number describe how he would follow the example set by "Uncle Ted": a post in the Navy Department, then the governorship of New York and on to the White House. In Clark's telling, amusement had turned to awe over how everything had worked out as predicted.

Roosevelt's success owed a great deal more to his good fortune in marriage than to his skill in foretelling the future. At the time of his engagement to his distant cousin Eleanor, one of her rejected suitors, who soon afterward committed suicide, advised Franklin of his excellent luck. Yet, not even one wholly smitten with Eleanor could have imagined the remarkable outcome of their complementary characters. Eleanor was tall, awkward, not at all the belle that her beautiful mother had been. An orphan who had survived her mother's disappointment and the harrowing demise of her alcoholic and morphine-addicted father, she did not fit the expected mold of an innocent, carefree New York debutante. Franklin vaguely sensed the qualities she brought instead, qualities needed for his own fulfillment. She had a serious, intellectually curious outlook on life that stirred Franklin's earnest side and helped him reflect sensibly on the frivolous self-indulgence and narrowness of experience that went with upper-class privilege. From the start Eleanor encouraged Franklin to develop his abilities and interest in public service, rather than follow his mother's desire that he succeed his father as squire of Hyde Park or slip into the sort of conventional business and professional life marked out for his classmates and friends.

The creative tension between Franklin and Eleanor that helped each of them grow also stemmed from their educations. At Groton, Franklin's preparation for life came more through character training than scholarship. Eleanor, however, had been influenced in a very different direction. For two years she attended Allenswood School in England—"the happiest years of my life"—where she came under the spell of the remarkable headmistress, Marie Souvestre. Mademoiselle Souvestre infused the school with a Gallic love of beauty and art, a feminist consciousness of the need to open society up to women's creative gifts, and a corresponding affinity with daring aesthetic experiments and political reform. Where Peabody consorted with clergy and business leaders, Souvestre and her staff found their allies within the most creative circle of England's Bloomsbury artists and Fabian socialists. In that atmosphere Eleanor developed a passion for learning that was open to all sorts of new ideas and experiences. Fluent in several languages, steeped in a wide range of literature, and trained as a writer, Eleanor offered a balancing breadth of cultural awareness to Franklin's more prosaic, practical inclinations.

So, too, in their temperaments did Eleanor and Franklin form a balanced whole. Where Franklin was ebullient, self-centered, and confident in the simple beliefs inculcated in him, Eleanor had a subtler appreciation for nuance and uncertainty. She, who had never had a stable home and in her early life often felt like an outcast, was more inclined to accept a broad diversity of persons and ways of being. In 1903 she joined other idealistic young women from the Junior League to do volunteer work at the collegiate settlement house on Rivington Street in the lower East Side tenement district. Soon afterward she joined the National Consumers' League to further Progressive efforts to ensure fair business practices and safe products. At her urging, Franklin visited Rivington Street and saw for himself that both Progressivism and Eleanor spoke from a basis of fact.

For Franklin, finding his place within the Progressive movement meant having a political career within the Democratic Party of his father. Eleanor urged him on and provided an ever-expanding scope through her experience in social service organizations. As his father and Peabody had taught him, Franklin concentrated on character issues. Aligned with a group of "insurgents," he focused his successful campaign for the state senate in 1910 on corruption within the Tammany Hall machine that ran New York City. The strategy was shrewd as well as moralistic; by running as an upstate reform Democrat against urban and ethnically different Democrats, Franklin was able to convince Republicans, as well as Democrats in his rural district, to vote for him. Eleanor cautioned him, however, not to lose sight, in his maneuvering and righteousness, of grassroots issues having to do with working conditions, housing, public health, and education. Gradually, she made Franklin understand that the Tammany machine he sought to purify was also the only agency available to help the most needy and despised people of the city. For material as well as moral progress, the task was to incorporate the ability of city machines to reach the lower depths within a more efficient and honest system of welfare and regulation. The central challenge of progressivism, Eleanor pressed upon Franklin, was to devise means of improvement that would cut across class lines to create a single mutually concerned and beneficial community. That meant going beyond the noblesse oblige that enlightened persons in their privileged station tended to favor. Creating what the most committed Progressives termed a "cooperative commonwealth," in which all had a share and a voice, was the ideal to which Eleanor, and increasingly Franklin, subscribed.

Roosevelt's timetable for his political rise received a crucial boost the same year he won his state senate seat when fellow Democrat Woodrow Wilson was elected governor of the neighboring state of New Jersey. A similar sort of progressive moralist, Wilson compiled such a rich record of legislative reform in his first year that Roosevelt was moved to make a pilgrimage to Trenton with an offer to do whatever he could to gain New York delegates for Wilson's try at the presidency in 1912.

Roosevelt's association with Wilson in the successful campaign that followed altered his tendency to prefer the country and Jeffersonian self-sufficiency over city life in ways that reinforced his wife's advice. Since Wilson was running with Tammany and other urban support, Roosevelt had to consider both city and country, both local and national issues. Gradually, as Theodore Roosevelt and Wilson carried on their campaigns against each other, a new synthesis began to form. Wilson's "New Freedom," a restatement of the traditional Democratic preference for small units of government and business, drew from Theodore Roosevelt an acknowledgment that the efficient coordination of large enterprise had to be balanced by checks against monopoly and to allow for labor union organization. Wilson, in turn, conceded that the dictum, attributed to Jefferson, that the government is best which governs least no longer held. Government had to keep technological advances and great private wealth in check if individual initiative were to survive. Wilson followed the reasoning of the reform-minded lawyer Louis Brandeis that the true Jeffersonian must now favor an active federal government that through regulation would strive to prevent dangerous concentrations of power. Not Jefferson the self-sufficient yeoman but Jefferson the statesman, guiding the nation to become an "empire of liberty," became the model for the Progressivism Wilson took with him to the White House.

Franklin Roosevelt was astute enough to anticipate the balance between the New Freedom and the New Nationalism at the very beginning of the campaign year. In March 1912, he concluded a speech in Troy, New York, with the declaration that the pressing issue of the time was a "struggle for the liberty of the community rather than liberty of the individual." The nation needed a leader who understood that cooperation for the general good should always take precedence over individual ambition. Competition, he declared, "has been shown to be useful up to a certain point and no further. Cooperation must begin where competition leaves off and cooperation is as good a word for the new theory as any other."

Subtle questions of where to strike a balance between personal initiative and communal loyalty and between local and national interests would engage Franklin Roosevelt for the rest of his career, as he strove to crystallize his version of the perennial American yearning for a cooperative commonwealth. One criterion he always favored was that of the strategic necessity of convincing people that political activism did not mean governmental tyranny. In that regard, the general belief that cooperation was in the American grain, from Puritan town democracy to the frontier, could be used to advantage. "If we call the method [for progress] regulation," he once told supporters, "people will hold up their hands in horror and cry 'un-American' or 'dangerous.' But if we call the same identical process cooperation, these same old fogeys will cry out 'well done.'" Cooperation had sustained the pioneers on the frontier; lack of cooperation had led to an "every man for himself" devastation of natural resources. Without cooperation, Americans in cities and farms had falsely concluded that their interests were antagonistic; so too had labor and capital, by competing rather than cooperating, stunted progress. Roosevelt insisted early in his career that "there is no such thing as a [necessary] struggle between labor and capital."

The cooperative principle of progress could also serve in times of crisis as the basis for a unified defense. With a simple analogy, used many times over, Roosevelt sought to show how foolish divisiveness is when collective welfare is at stake. What would people think, he asked in support of American preparedness for World War I, "if they saw the members of the volunteer fire department stop in their headlong rush toward the conflagration and indulge in a slanging match as to who was responsible for the rotten hose or lack of water at a fire a week ago?" In 1932 on the presidential campaign trail he added further definition to his cooperative commonwealth ideal in order to reassure those who were devastated by the way the Depression had swept away faith in self-reliance. Roosevelt's adroit manner of drawing strength from weakness shone through the argument in his pamphlet, "How I Will Conduct My Responsibilities," that the key to progressive recovery was "*inter*dependency—our mutual dependence one upon the other—of individuals, of businesses, of industries, of towns, of villages, of cities, of states, of nations."

By steadfastly resisting dogma and ideology in favor of lessons drawn from experience, Roosevelt avoided the dilemma that so often bedevils the principled person of having to choose between abstract beliefs and concrete results. Without self-conscious resort to philosophical reasoning, Roosevelt's beliefs and moral principles were pragmatic in that he judged action as right or wrong according to consequences. As for motives, Roosevelt's adherence to a generalized Christian faith and the gentlemanly code of his youth led him to disapprove of cruelty and dishonesty in others while armoring himself against any doubt about his own virtue. This self-assured mix of faith, moral standards, and practicality guided Roosevelt along a progressive track. At the same time, his unsystematic approach enabled others who had developed theories and social designs that fitted with Roosevelt's concept of a cooperative commonwealth to gain a sympathetic hearing and, in many cases, an opportunity to experiment with government policy.

Thus Roosevelt came to enjoy the best of political balances: he remained himself the exemplar of American improvisation, unfettered by the rigidities of systems, while having around him in empathetic orbit a galaxy of persons devoted to the sort of detailed, coherent, even abstract, conceptualization and collective planning that he himself eschewed. Many critics, following the lead of Roosevelt's biographer and political scientist, James MacGregor Burns, have seen the situation in terms of divided character—Roosevelt as alternately the lion and the fox of Machiavelli's cynical anatomy of practical politics. But the situation was not a matter of inner dualism but of flexible symbiosis between Roosevelt and those around him who supplied each other with what was needed for an operationally effective, if sometimes disjointed and inconsistent, whole.

Roosevelt's reward for championing Wilson's cause was an invitation to become assistant secretary of the Navy under Wilson's kindly old friend, Josephus Daniels. Four peacetime years to take the measure of his duties—and of Washington politics—equipped Roosevelt well to take on the arduous task of mobilization when war struck in 1917. The experience stimulated both his admiration for detailed efficiency and a certain Grotonian flair for heroism. Though dissuaded by Daniels and Wilson from enlisting in the fighting ranks, Roosevelt was at least able to spend time at the front, where he gloried in the dangers. With a sort of frenzied relish, Roosevelt toured the war zone until, beset by illness and fatigue, he was taken home on a stretcher. Although only a grand gesture, the battlefield tour climaxed an intense wartime period that thereafter left Roosevelt inclined to approach public problems as foes against which to mobilize the warrior spirit.

Roosevelt's first period in Washington reached its pinnacle when he was named to run for the vice presidency in 1920. James M. Cox, the presidential candidate, was an unexciting, moderate former governor of Ohio. While enough of a regular to gain the support of Tammany Hall, Cox had shown a capacity to support the old, largely small-town and rural virtues of the party and so, it was hoped, might head off a reaction against the self-righteousness of Wilson and his attempt to lead America into entangling alliances through the League of Nations. Roosevelt offered a fresh face to the eastern wing that had marched behind Wilson and crucial help in carrying New York. The young man had shown dash and a capacity for hard work—but no well-defined political philosophy to trouble a nation weary of causes and eager to get on with prosperity.

Exuberantly, Roosevelt set off on a hectic cross-country campaign. He proclaimed the Democratic platform—support for the League of Nations and a vague pledge to advance progressive measures—with the enthusiasm of a game loser. After the Republican landslide he spoke jauntily of "a most interesting experience" that had given him a prime opportunity to get to know the country.

Then began a period of trial and reflection. The Republicans, with their talk of "normalcy," sidetracked progressive reform and League of Nations internationalism in order to concentrate on building a "business civilization." Barriers arose against immigration, while many artists and writers fled to Europe to escape the dull materialism at home. The prevailing mood favored a kind of crassness that grated against Roosevelt's ideals of service. But his discouragement was tempered by the chance to return to New York and bolster the Democratic reform spirit that lingered there. He always liked to recall how persuasively Lord Bryce, a family friend and author of the great critique of American life, *The American Commonwealth* (1888), had argued that the genius of the American federal system was that states could serve as laboratories for reform. New York could be such a laboratory and also enable Roosevelt to complete his early design of stepping someday from the governorship to the White House.

Roosevelt's conviction that a long season of Republican reaction lay ahead helped him accept his new private status gracefully. He practiced some law with a downtown New York City firm and in 1922 became president of the American Construction Council at the request of his wartime friend Herbert Hoover, who was then secretary of commerce. On the side he corresponded with Democratic Party leaders far and wide to see what he could do to knit the organization together. Demonstrating his adaptability to the need for building a new consensus, Roosevelt filed down all the sharp edges of his public positions: He no longer spoke out against the Tammany bosses and abandoned his fervor for the League of Nations. The cause of progressive social legislation he allowed to lapse without much protest.

But fate had in store something grimmer than a carefully programmed rise to the top. In August 1921, Roosevelt went sailing with friends at his summer camp on Campobello Island off the coast of Maine. Characteristically, Roosevelt's idea for "rest" was a hectic round of activities. After a hot day of sailing, jogging, and fighting a brush fire, punctuated by icy plunges in the Labrador Current waters, Roosevelt experienced a strange chill and then sank into the fever of polio, which left his legs permanently paralyzed.

Roosevelt might then have given way to the urgings of his strong-willed mother, Sara, that he retreat to the life of Hyde Park squire, as his beloved father had. Instead, the force of his passion to overcome crisis and continue his political plan pressed him back into the world of affairs. Heeding the lesson of the favorite poem of his youth, Alfred Lord Tennyson's "Invictus," that one be the master of his own fate, Roosevelt pushed himself through excruciating exercise in a hopeless effort, which he never abandoned, to get back on his feet. He had time, also, to read and to develop his powers of concentration. From being one who had always moved restlessly about while doing any sort of work, he learned to endure immobility. Adaptable as always, Roosevelt developed a laughing unconcern about his handicap that kept his spirits up and disarmed others who might have felt pity or embarrassment.

Around this struggle has grown a legend of Roosevelt's transformation—a "twice-born man," as his uncle, Frederic Delano, termed him. Frances Perkins, secretary of labor in the New Deal, described the ordeal as having changed a rather unfeeling, supercilious young man into a champion of the underdog. But Roosevelt's son James and his close adviser Rexford Tugwell disagreed. No traits were changed, they argued, only intensified. Roosevelt raised his stoic resistance to pain and fatigue to a fine art, and he made his always sheltered inner feelings even more hidden. The optimistic resolve that kept him a believer in simple moral precepts had always been there. Like his feelings, it simply became more invulnerable to challenge.

Roosevelt emerged a more convincing champion of the common man after the advent of his crippling disease. He must also have learned something about loyalty; his wife and his other most important aide, Louis Howe—the self-styled "medieval gnome" who had guided his political campaigns from the start—showed depths of intelligent encouragement without which Roosevelt's strength might have failed him.

While Howe remained devoted to his task of grooming Roosevelt for his eventual election to the presidency, Eleanor prepared herself for the path-breaking role she would then play as First Lady by becoming an accomplished journalist and a political force in her own right. Relieved of the need to defer to her husband's career, Eleanor took on ever-increasing responsibility in the effort to enlarge women's participation in public affairs. She served as director of the New York State League of Women's Voters, the organization spawned by the passage of the Nineteenth Amendment, and joined other activists in founding and editing the journal *Women's Democratic News*. In close alliance with the Women's Trade Union League she undertook intense but inconclusive legislative battles for the 44-hour work week and an amendment to ban child labor. Her work as finance chair of women's activities for the New York Democratic State Committee led to national prominence in 1928 when she became director of the Bureau of Women's Activities of the Democratic National Committee, the most powerful party position a woman had ever held up to that time. Soon afterward, she became a member of the campaign staff guiding the bid of New York reform governor Alfred E. Smith for the presidency and from that vantage helped argue Smith's case that Franklin should run to succeed him as governor.

Smith hoped that the Roosevelt charisma would rub off on his national campaign and attract voters. But Roosevelt was more fortunate as inheritor of Smith's reform innovations. Along with his pioneer work in shaping welfare and regulatory legislation, Smith's outlook, shaped within the poor immigrant life of

New York City, well suited the accelerating shift of the Democratic Party center from the rural South to the urban North. Smith put together a reform coalition of ethnic groups that balanced Roosevelt's ties to the decentralized legacies of Jefferson and Wilson and helped pave the way for the ethnic coalitions that would characterize the New Deal. As well, Smith's organizational talent rebuilt the state administrative machinery so that it could enact reforms and still pare the budget—$17 million from the 1924 budget alone. When he left the governorship in 1928, Smith bequeathed to Roosevelt a state with a model employment merit system, streamlined finances, a strong start in conservation (especially by keeping hydroelectric power out of the hands of private developers), and high standards of enforced public health, industrial safety, and maximum hours of work for women and children.

In return, Roosevelt used all his persuasiveness and contacts to help the "Happy Warrior," as he had dubbed Smith at the 1924 national Democratic convention. But the balance of city and country that gained election for Roosevelt as governor did not work nationally for Smith, whose Catholic, urban ways alienated both southern Democrats and voters in the North who credited prosperity to Republican business leadership. Smith was further upset when he discovered that his protégé was determined to govern the state on his own terms—terms that would allow him to overcome the party weaknesses that had sunk Smith and fashion a larger vision that would carry him to the presidency.

From a starting point that combined Smith's legacy of efficiency and urban reform with a new rural emphasis, Roosevelt groped toward realization of the progressive unity he had sketched at Troy in 1912 and again in his 1920 national campaign. He decried the prevailing economic ethos of laissez-faire self-interest—indeed, he was always skeptical of the "laws" touted by economists—and posed instead a communal ideal in which economics would be regarded as tool, not immutable law; a servant, not a master. The ideal was never precisely formulated, but it was real and central in Roosevelt's mind. He used it steadfastly throughout his public career as a counter to selfishness and dogmatism. Often bewildering others in the way he incorporated the most unlikely bedfellows within his blueprint, Roosevelt seemed generally confident that all social elements could serve his spacious aims. That outlook did not rise to the level of true pragmatism, as devised by moral philosophers like William James and John Dewey, because it did not show careful concern to have its means and ends logically and ethically consistent. But if it was opportunism, it was of a special moralist sort; for Roosevelt acted not as one who believed that the ends justified the means but with trust that the right ends would subsume many means and make good of them. Thus, Roosevelt could with cheerful optimism parley with shady city bosses like Tom Pendergast of Kansas City and Frank Hague of Jersey City and with reactionary, racist southerners like Senator "Cotton Ed" Smith of South Carolina. And he felt few pangs about departing from conventional policy to try new, even hastily improvised, ways of meeting needs, radiating benevolent confidence that it would all work out in the end so long as people acted on humane motives.

Roosevelt's plans for building a record of prosperity and reform were displaced by the Depression. The realization that economic crisis had replaced thoughts of the steady march of progress raised demands for emergency action. As the chill of winter in 1930 deepened and the savings of the growing army of unemployed vanished, the chipper promises of business leaders that an upswing was imminent lost their power to keep the business index and the stock market from plummeting. Private charity, though gaining a temporary boost through the public-spiritedness of wealthy donors and volunteers, also lacked sustaining power. Roosevelt had no systematic relief concept in mind—indeed, he had not yet strayed from the orthodox belief that charity was a last resort that sapped initiative. But the flood of letters to him from desperate people calling for help roused his compassion. In March 1930 he initiated a state committee on stabilization to explore remedies, even as his own energies were being mobilized to bring the dispossessed into the cooperative commonwealth vision.

As always, Roosevelt's first overtures were to the private sector, and, as usual, he was disappointed by the reluctance of that group to enter into any firm partnership with government. The insurance industry balked at a plan for unemployment insurance, even though it would rest heavily on worker contributions and use private insurance companies. Labor unions opposed a plan to place unemployed workers in unused plants to turn out goods they could barter among themselves—too much danger that the government would become a competitor of private business, the AFL insisted. Farmers registered comparable objections to Roosevelt's Jeffersonian enthusiasm about helping unemployed city dwellers take up the healthier, self-supporting rural homestead life. Putting more land into production that way, farm spokesmen complained, would only worsen the agricultural glut and lower farm prices even further.

Turning of necessity to the state sector, Roosevelt in 1930 convened a conference of governors of eastern states, where nearly half of the nation's wage earners lived. The conference proved highly informative for leaders in a nation whose welfare system was far less developed than those of other industrial nations and spurred Roosevelt's departure from orthodoxy. The following summer he told the national governors' conference in French Lick, Indiana, that New York would point the way for state initiative against the Depression. Soon afterward Roosevelt's plan for a Temporary Emergency Relief Administration became law in New York.

Fortunately, TERA came under the direction of veteran social worker, Harry Hopkins. A sickly yet tough and energetic administrator with the breezy manners of the racetracks he frequented, Hopkins set down rules that eventually guided New Deal relief policy. The unemployed who could establish that they were destitute gained work on tasks deemed socially useful, yet of a sort not profitably undertaken by private industry. Within those strict guidelines Hopkins oversaw a state agency that aided well over 100,000 persons per month by the end of Roosevelt's governorship, at a total cost of about $25 million.

Even that effort was not enough to check the spread of unemployment or, with its meager monthly outlay of $23 per relief recipient, restore a reasonable measure of prosperity. Roosevelt became so impressed by the need for a massive rescue effort that he abandoned another orthodox tenet, the balanced budget, by approving a $30 million bond issue for relief in the cold early days of 1932.

By then Depression had eclipsed Roosevelt's original intention to create a cooperative commonwealth of mutually supportive farm and business interests in New York and then extend it nationally through election to the presidency in 1936. With the nation in heavy weather—needful of revised conceptions, more compassion, and above all immediate repair and rescue action—Roosevelt became convinced that the time had come for him to displace Hoover. The American System had discredited itself, and its architect was evidently vulnerable to challenge. With a mingling of personal ambition and a sense of national urgency, Roosevelt began to gird up for the campaign of his life.

CHAPTER THREE

Landslide

A combination of dire conditions and shifting loyalties drove the greatest reversal of electoral fortunes in American history—from a landslide victory in 1928 for Hoover and his American System to a landslide defeat of Hoover by Roosevelt and his New Deal in 1932. The collapse of the economy, for which Hoover was bitterly assailed, may have been enough reason for the reversal of fortunes. But changes in the demographic landscape had begun a realignment toward the Democratic Party even before the Depression struck. All during the 1920s cities increased their numerical advantage over the countryside. Within them children of the 13 million immigrants who poured into the United States between 1900 and 1914 were coming to voting age. When Alfred E. Smith, a Catholic son of immigrants and a leader of efforts to improve industrial working conditions, ran for president in 1928, the urban masses and progressive reformers found their hero. But their time had not yet come. The old ethnic and religious prejudices, combined with the power that Republicans had forged in the Civil War and as captains of industry, swept Hoover into office. Yet the solidification of ethnic urban discontent in the hands of a majority of these new, mostly lower-class voters, including many women, gave the Democrats unprecedented victories in five of the nation's twelve largest cities. The makings of a winning coalition of the urban working class, the Solid South, and reformers soon to be activated by the Depression loomed as a way to unseat Hoover.

Franklin Roosevelt's legal counsel, Samuel Rosenman, set the course for a crucially altered approach to campaigning when he wisely persuaded the candidate to enlist new advisers with specialist credentials and a broad national perspective. This was no time, Rosenman recognized, for politics as usual; nor did he and Roosevelt's other advisers in Albany have the experience needed to grasp the profound troubles that were shaking the country.

To organize the group, Roosevelt and Rosenman settled on Raymond Moley, a professor of government at Columbia who had impressed Louis Howe when they worked together on the New York State Commission on the Administration of Justice. The very model of a sharp blackboard strategist in his rumpled, pipe-smoking, slightly caustic way, Moley prided himself on his practical savvy. He came from the small town of Berea, Ohio, and had long balanced a career of scholarship and political involvement. As a youth he admired the idea in Henry George's classic polemic *Progress and Poverty* (1879) of a single tax on land that would prevent speculators from cornering productive resources and thus blocking the initiative of others. Some years later Moley tempered his single tax enthusiasm with the argument by Charles Van Hise in *Concentration and Control: A Solution of the Trust Problem in the United States* (1912) that large industrial concentrations are both inevitable and efficient in modern technological society. Codes of fair business procedure with regulation by government commissions along the lines pioneered by Van Hise's home state of Wisconsin, the book insisted, were the way to create a cooperative commonwealth under modern conditions.

At the same time that he was absorbing Van Hise's formula, Moley approvingly observed the way that Woodrow Wilson moved from scholarly life into the White House. Accordingly, Moley used his study in law and political science for a career that fluctuated between teaching politics at Western Reserve and public service—including, even, a term as mayor of tiny Olmsted Falls, to which he frequently referred later with amusement as his sole executive experience.

Moley's first choice to join him in what the *New York Times* correspondent, John Kieran, would dub the "Brains Trust" was his Columbia colleague, economist Rexford Tugwell. Tugwell added a handsome, dashing presence—like a "cocktail," Moley observed, "his conversation picked you up and made your brain race along." Tugwell's ebullience reflected the way he had been influenced at the University of Pennsylvania by Simon Nelson Patten. With evangelical fervor, Patten in his teaching and writing, especially in *The New Basis of Civilization* (1907), advanced the hopeful concept that the United States had passed into an era of abundance. Americans should cease honoring the old values of frugality and the belief that business had to be a competitive war for resources too scarce to satisfy everyone's needs. The economic problem now, Patten and Tugwell insisted, was to distribute abundance fairly and efficiently and then perfect the sensibilities that abundance would free. This would be a job for carefully constructed social institutions that would guide cooperative action, not for competing individuals at the mercy of obsolete "laws" of the free enterprise jungle.

In thus arguing that society could choose abundance, rather than the scarcity that classical economics insisted was mankind's lot, Tugwell stood alongside Hoover as well as Patten. But he diverged critically from Hoover's insistence that heroic individual strivers, coordinating their efforts only on their own volition, would make good on the promise of abundance. Tugwell inclined rather toward Roosevelt because they shared a belief in the need for the state to be an active partner in creating a cooperative commonwealth through persuasion of the general public that the shared use of resources, with some degree of self-sacrifice for the common good, was not only more humane than individual free enterprise but also necessary if America was not to burn itself out. The great issue in approaching the task of building such cooperation—which Tugwell termed a "concert of interests"—was determining how far conventional capitalist arrangements should be changed or eliminated.

Tugwell was more precisely aware than Roosevelt of the spectrum of views that had developed about how to deal with that problem. Early in 1931, as the crisis was deepening, Tugwell outlined to a fellow economist the choice of models that were most prominently available. In assessing the school of "institutional economics," so named because it focused on the actual workings of sociopolitical institutions, rather than theory, Tugwell noted that most institutional economists merely "state conditions, . . . [and] describe the materials with which we must deal." He reserved his praise for the more reform-minded few who believed that an increase of precise knowledge entailed understanding what should be done to make things better. To them, such understanding, like science, had general applicability and pointed toward collective social action.

Into that progressive category fit the labor organization analysis by John Commons, the charting of economic cycles by Wesley Mitchell, and the detailed reports on various segments of the economy by such early examples of think tanks as the Brookings Institution and the National Bureau of Economic Research. At the far end of the institutional spectrum were the writings of Thorstein Veblen, the maverick economist of the late nineteenth and early twentieth centuries who treated capitalism with disdain as a duplicitous means of transferring wealth from those who created it to absentee landowners, bankers, and other manipulators of honorific titles and paper transactions.

Tugwell followed Patten's lead in trying to find practical solutions to pressing problems through the use of creative imagination that could inspire readers— even economists—to reach beyond the usual in order to transform the capitalist

system rather than overthrow it. Deploying what he called "experimental economics," Tugwell projected a vision of change that was, indeed, like an intoxicating cocktail. He confessed to "repressed hopes, a certain yearning for re-creation." He wished
to "clear away the rubbish" of the dismal science of economics and "substitute for
these a growingly realistic analysis of men's tragic and beautiful experiences with
the material of economic life." During the 1920s Tugwell became a leader of insurgent economists whose manifesto, *The Trend of Economics* (1924), he edited.
These rebels against the conventional view that economics was an abstract science
insisted that economic and political leaders had to take account of the full spectrum of human experience—art, literature, philosophy, and psychology included—
before they could hope to govern society effectively. Properly understood, then,
economics was an agent of transformation of the whole society, not a fixed set of
precepts or a technical tool to advance business and financial interests.

In approaching economics as an inclusive and evolutionary public pursuit,
subject to the ethic of democratic fairness, Tugwell accepted the Van Hise case.
He recognized the inevitability in modern life of large concentrations of economic power and added his own cautionary words about technology. Tugwell
believed in expert guidance of modern technology: with it, prosperity and jobs
would abound; without it, technology could run amok, like the sorcerer's ap-
prentice, eliminating jobs and producing more goods than people could buy. In
his search for principles of efficiency, Tugwell praised Frederick Winslow Taylor,
inventor of time-and-motion studies, as having led the way to the phenomenal
growth of productivity per man-hour. But for ways of efficiently making abundance serve the general welfare, Tugwell could not rely on Taylor, servant of the
steel industry's profit-takers. He had to look elsewhere. Eventually, in 1928, the
quest took him to the Soviet Union. Like so many other observers at that time,
Tugwell concluded that the Soviet experiment was a key economic breakthrough,
despite its rigid political control. Through planning and education, the Soviets
had begun to lift a poor nation out of chronic poverty and toward the sort of social
integration that was the object of Tugwell's "repressed hopes."

The ensuing crash intensified Tugwell's belief in the need for planning to cure
a disastrous spiral in which technology displaced workers, resulting in lessened
purchasing power, which in turn led to lowered production and more layoffs,
and so on to the bottom of a trough where deprivation existed alongside idle productive resources. When he was selected for the Brains Trust, Tugwell had just
published *The Industrial Discipline and the Governmental Arts,* in which he spoke
for an economic council to plan cooperation between industry and government.
The major aim was to "discipline" industry so that there would be an abundant

balance between production and consumption. This would be no merely technical accomplishment. At the heart of Tugwell's analysis was the yearning of a romantic idealist. Reflecting Patten's influence, Tugwell spoke for the kind of modern economy that would free Americans from purposeless striving in blighted
and autocratic work settings. Tugwell lamented, "Industry is rolling forward of
its own weight. . . . But there [are] no values which a free people would have
recognized." For the radical task of building a democratic, humane setting, labor unions had proven too submissive—asking for "nothing but larger bribes
for greater degradation." Only representative government had the power and
breadth to educate workers as to their own best interests and to mobilize expertise so that technological advances would serve those interests, rather than
crushing them. Tugwell disavowed the current talk of revolution. What would
be the point of an uprising? It was perfectly plain that "we possess every needful
material for Utopia, and nearly everyone knows it." There was no good reason,
let alone the general desire or power, to exchange the prevailing system for any
socialist or fascist alternative. One should rely instead on the "quite simple conclusion in most minds that control ought to be taken out of the hands of people
who cannot produce [Utopia] from the excellent materials at their disposal."

For all his grappling with industrial questions, Tugwell entered the Roosevelt
campaign mainly on the strength of his special experience with agriculture. He
had grown up in Sinclairsville, New York, not very far from Hyde Park, where
his father had a cannery and some farm holdings. That gave him a feel for farm
problems and an immediate rapport with Roosevelt. Beyond that, Tugwell, like
Roosevelt, believed that the crux of the Depression lay in the hard times that
had afflicted agriculture after World War I. Tugwell emphasized that farming
was subject to surpluses, which would continue to be unmanageable until some
means were found to persuade farmers to grow less. How that was to be done,
in the face of farmers' insistence that a bountiful harvest was the surest sign of
virtuous endeavor, became Tugwell's special assignment.

The second key member of the Brains Trust recruited by Moley was Adolf
Berle, a member of the Columbia faculty who specialized in the relationship
between law and corporations. Only 37, his youth accentuated by his small size,
Berle was something of an enfant terrible. At twenty-one the youngest person
ever to earn a degree at Harvard Law School, he could be austere and superior in
tone. Yet he shared the commitment to social work common to many who were
attracted to Roosevelt. Berle had lived for a time at the Henry Street settlement
house. His father was a social gospel minister, an immigrant's son who placed

great store in learning and rejoiced upon graduating from Harvard that he could be a model of uplift for the poor, rather than merely serving among them as an equal. The extraordinarily quick Berle took in the whole drama. He noted the frozen bodies huddled in doorways when he walked to school from his father's mission in Chicago, and he responded superlatively well to the pressure that he rise through Harvard to model stature. At the time he was contacted by Moley, Berle and the statistician, Gardiner Means, were on the verge of publishing *The Modern Corporation and Private Property* (1932), a work that made them famous and has remained a classic to this day. The study showed in detail that majority control of the nation's industries lay in the hands of about two hundred corporations. Moreover, control over those giants had become divorced from ownership. A class of managers now ran the industries, a change that Berle and Means considered an economic revolution.

The timeliness of *The Modern Corporation*, as well as its incisive brilliance, accounted for critical acclaim few other books of the century had enjoyed. The historian Charles Beard, who had long struggled to understand the relationship between politics and economics, noted that it might well be "the most important work bearing on American statecraft" since the Federalist Papers. Legal scholar Jerome Frank added that the book "will perhaps rank with Adam Smith's *Wealth of Nations* as the first detailed description in admirably clear terms of the existence of a new economic epoch," while *Time* magazine noted shrewdly that it was "the economic Bible of the Roosevelt administration." Berle himself had large ambitions for the work. His wife recalled him confiding to her that "his real ambition in life is to be the American Karl Marx—a social prophet," with *The Modern Corporation* presumably being his *Das Kapital*.

Though the anxiety to find answers to the Depression accounted for some of the fervent response to *The Modern Corporation*, Berle and Means did, indeed, have a vital cooperative lesson to draw from their study of financial and industrial concentration. Armed with statistics on those few who dominated the economy, the authors concluded, "It remains only for the claims of the community to be put forward with clarity and force. . . . When a convincing system of community obligations is worked out and is generally accepted, in that moment the passive property right of today must yield before the larger interest of society." Thus, "if the corporate system is to survive . . . the 'control' of the great corporations should develop into a purely neutral technocracy, balancing a variety of claims by various groups in the community and assigning to each a portion of the income stream on the basis of public policy rather than private cupidity."

Berle sometimes convinced critics that he was a pessimist by warning that the American System might turn into a kind of corporate, even fascist, dictatorship. But he more characteristically chose to look on the bright side in a way that showed his social gospel conditioning. Now that the tycoons, like Carnegie and Rockefeller, who had both owned and managed the giant firms, were giving way to professional managers, Berle believed that the classical emphasis on *homo economicus* was due to decline. As personal ownership became more and more limited to consumer items, people could detach themselves from the old Horatio Alger aspiration of becoming plutocrats. The new heroes need not be captains of industry but servants of the public who would help distribute wealth on behalf of the general welfare. Indeed, as corporations moved toward becoming mere "passive" providers—neither owned by their managers nor managed by their owners—business was apt to pale. "Not impossibly," Berle argued, "the teacher, the artist, the poet and the philosopher will set the pace for the next era." For the first time American individualism faced alienation from economic production; consequently, the way was open for a humane appreciation of how redistribution of wealth would improve the general quality of life, even as it gave new stability to industry by insuring broad consumer purchasing power.

The visions of a humanely integrated social life entertained by Tugwell and Berle partook of a longstanding insistence by progressive reformers that the drive for money and power that characterized the late nineteenth century needed to be tempered by attention to the arts and improved in moral character. Society could not count on fanciful "natural laws" of the marketplace or of the survival of the fittest to create a good community. There must instead thrive a willingness to experiment with explicit plans in the spirit of the new science and technology, based on careful study of actual conditions and the way to achieve spiritual satisfaction. The salient faith was reliance not on natural law but on the resolve of the public to do the right and intelligent thing when the true nature of social organization was shown to them.

This progressive view generated widespread interest in planning as a way out of the Depression. As the period after World War I unfolded, revolutionary fascism and communism also caused Americans to look abroad for examples of social planning in action. Mussolini's apparent efficiency commanded tentative respect. But the Soviet Union made the greatest appeal with its sweeping promise, in a land of immemorial suffering, for raising common humanity to shared abundance and an ideal of brotherhood through the exercise of modern technology and organization. Stuart Chase, a popular writer on economics and technology, summed up the ebullience of American planners after returning from his trip to Russia with Rexford Tugwell: "Why should the Russians have all the fun?"

Evidently, the reading public wanted to pursue Chase's question. After carrying only a few articles on factory management during the Coolidge years, the popular journals during the Depression-wracked Hoover regime were filled with arguments outlining the pros and cons of planning. "To Plan or Not to Plan?" asked a journalistic Hamlet in the *Literary Digest* of 1931. The next year the mostly orthodox *American Economic Review* published Tugwell's pro-planning article on the "Principle of Planning and the Institution of Laissez-Faire," while the friend of the weary businessman, *The Saturday Evening Post,* denounced "The Craze for Planning." In a pair of timely summary gestures, the *Annals of the American Academy of Political and Social Science* devoted its July 1932 issue entirely to planning, just in time for Roosevelt's nomination, and the following March, when Roosevelt was inaugurated, published another special issue on planning as it applied to the problems of workers.

This reading fare was complemented by a wave of conferences. Wesley Mitchell, the most notable statistical economist of the day, warned a 1930 gathering of mechanical engineers of the dangerous inconsistency between technological efficiency and planless competition. H. S. Person, the president of efficiency engineering's most eminent body, the Taylor Society, offered similar advice. Social workers echoed the concern of engineers and economists over careful management of the marketplace. In 1931 a broad array of social justice groups at a Conference on Permanent Preventives of Unemployment cheered George Soule—a key spokesman for welfare economists—when he told of the urgent need for the forces of social work and planning to close ranks. Hoover's overdependence on providence and individual initiative, Soule and his audience agreed, had left the old free enterprise faith a "dry well."

Roosevelt's broad communal vision and experience as a progressive politician made him receptive to planning long before the Depression. In remarks given at the Subsistence Homes Exposition on April 24, 1934, he recalled how the presidential run with Cox had made a believer out of him:

> During three months in the year 1920 . . . I went to forty-two states . . . and got to know the country as only a candidate for office or travelling salesman can get to know it. In that trip, the one great impression I got of our country was that it had grown like Topsy, without any particular planning. . . . And because the country was so vast, during nearly all of those three hundred years nobody seemed to suffer very much, because there were plenty of new opportunities.

But as I went over the country I became impressed with the fact that in those
latter days we had come, to a certain extent, to the end of that limitless opportunity.
. . . I realized that the time was ripe, even overripe, for the beginning of planning.

Roosevelt sought to drive the argument home by specifying each dimension of
the national need. There must be, he asserted, "planning to prevent in the future
the errors of the past, and planning to meet in the future the errors of the past,
and planning to meet in the future certain perfectly obvious economic and social
needs of the nation."

Throughout his term as governor, Roosevelt followed through with several
planning initiatives; he began a system of state roads and, over Al Smith's laissez-
faire objections, instituted systematic resource conservation, reforestation, and
park development. In an enveloping statement he declared that "family, church,
community, state, and all industry are subject to [planning's] influence. . . . Study
and investigation of technological advances and their social implications consti-
tute one of our most important American planning problems."

While Roosevelt's approach was forming, attention to planning increased in
Congress. The Senate Committee on Manufactures served as a focal point for
several of the leading conceptions of planning when its chairman, Robert La Follette Jr., Republican Senator from Wisconsin, announced hearings for February
1931, on a bill to establish a National Economic Council. The legislation would
incorporate the Hoover approach of carefully researched cooperation with the
Progressive penchant for regulatory agencies. Thus, a council would monitor
business conditions, formulate proposals for solutions to problems in an annual
report to the president, and initiate trade associations to define the rules for the
nation's businesses. Two other proposals were important for defining the main
alternatives facing those who would conquer the Depression. Representing the
status quo, the Chamber of Commerce suggested that industry, rather than government, appoint a council of economists, statisticians, market analysts, and the
like. By coordinating the individualistic genius of business—hitherto anarchic—
the council could surely defeat any problems that might arise, the Chamber argued. To the other side of La Follette was the plan by Stuart Chase. A young man
looking for bearings during World War I, Chase was much impressed, as Roosevelt had been in similar circumstances, with the patriotic efficiency of the War
Industries Board. From the vantage of 1931, after a national binge of profit had
ended in collapse, Chase looked back hopefully on what carefully harnessed national purpose had been able to do. Accordingly, he proposed a Peace Industries
Board with extensive power over production, distribution, waste, and the needs

of public health and sanitation. The board would tie its expertise in with agencies like the Federal Reserve Board, the Interstate Commerce Commission, the Federal Power Commission, and the Federal Trade Commission. At the same time the board would stay in close touch with private bodies like the Chamber of Commerce and the unions, thus completing a giant circle of national cooperation.

In the midst of intense national debate over reform plans, the Brains Trusters maintained harmony, despite their differences on specific points, largely because they deferred to ultimate arbitration by the candidate himself. Roosevelt listened intently and contributed zestfully from the experience and facts stored in what Tugwell called his "fly-paper mind." Steadily there developed arguments on behalf of a cooperative commonwealth in response to Hoover's *American Individualism.* Tugwell's bitter pamphlet "Mr. Hoover's Economic Policy" (1932) spearheaded the argument for state leadership. Hoover had always presented himself as a man of facts, Tugwell noted, when the president was really captive to the abstract idea that an active government was taboo and selected his "facts" accordingly. An objective look at reality, Tugwell argued, would reveal that a high degree of economic concentration and technological interdependence made the old nineteenth-century individualism obsolete. Tugwell countered that his "concert of interests" approach would recognize the need for "discipline" to subordinate the hitherto unaccountable activities of private enterprise to the general welfare. Otherwise, the wealth accumulating at the top would not "trickle down" but stagnate in savings and possessions, leaving the consumer economy in the doldrums. The crying need, then, was to redistribute wealth, especially through steeper income taxes and levies on excess profits and corporate dividends. A corollary to tax reform would be public spending to get people back to work while adding to the nation's stock of buildings, roads, and other assets.

The farm crisis called for other measures to combat powerful taboos. Rather than a problem of getting idle hands and factories together, farm woes stemmed from too much productivity. This much was clear to all, but disagreement persisted among the major farm organizations, Hoover, and the Brains Trust on how to fix it. Farmers wanted to dump the surplus; Hoover favored voluntary crop reductions; the Brains Trusters, recognizing the disparity between farmers' inclinations and what Hoover would have them undertake voluntarily, urged mandatory crop controls.

When Tugwell traveled to Chicago to do advance work on the farm plank for the Democratic nominating convention, he found a plan to suit his inclinations for collectivist direction that would not mortally offend farmers' sense of free will. M. L. Wilson, a professor at Montana State College, convinced Tugwell of the merits of his Voluntary Domestic Allotment Plan, a formulation that would combine government supervision of crop reduction with voluntary action by paying farmers who agreed to withdraw land from production, the money deriving from fees on processors. Farmers would sign up because they would enjoy good prices for what they grew and compensation for land left fallow, pegged at "parity" with the prices received during the golden years of 1909–14. Tugwell enthusiastically explained that under Wilson's plan consumers would pay a fair price, farmers would prosper, and due respect would be accorded the traditional precepts of a free marketplace.

A number of other less precisely defined remedies were called for to round out the new "discipline" Tugwell urged to generate a "concert of interests." The Brains Trusters, for example, favored tighter regulation of the stock market and the banking institutions—with Tugwell unsuccessfully arguing for a nationalization of the banking system such as existed in other western nations. There was also agreement that a relief program massive enough to re-employ much of the almost 24 percent of the labor force out of work would entail an unbalanced budget. That need only be temporary, the Brains Trusters argued, because the revived economy would make up the funds expended at the low point. Tariffs, all agreed, should be lowered and modified in the direction of a system that would include reciprocal trade agreements.

A prime focus for greater public leadership was the power industry. As governor Roosevelt had sought control over the great hydroelectric capacity of the St. Lawrence River. The Brains Trusters joined Roosevelt's advocacy of public power with a resolve to conserve natural resources. Rising demand and the closing of the frontier meant that resources should no longer be considered limitless and freely subject to private exploitation.

All these positions, which awaited the campaign for testing on public opinion, challenged approaches that both the Democratic and Republican Parties had developed during the 1920s. The primary question was how far the old decentralist small-enterprise party of Jefferson and Wilson could accommodate such collectivist leanings. Roosevelt was determined to bring the Brains Trust innovations to fruition within a new progressive synthesis, Tugwell reported, in a discussion that had made an "indelible impression." The patient work of reshaping, Roosevelt assured his most impatient adviser, would be done in the foreseeable future. "I'll be in the White House for eight years," Roosevelt remarked. "When those years are over, there'll be a Progressive party. It may not be Democratic, but it will be Progressive." The candidate couched his determination in a sense of urgency. To a friend who ruminated that, if Roosevelt succeeded, he would stand as the greatest president, and if he failed, be remembered as the worst, Roosevelt responded rather melodramatically: "If I fail I shall be the *last* President!"

Both the Brains Trust positions and the gravity of the situation found expression in Roosevelt's opening pre-nomination salvo. Drafted largely by Moley, the speech cited the need for planning, restoration of purchasing power to workers and farmers, massive unemployment relief, and tariff revision. Zeroing in on the "trickle-down" approach, Roosevelt warned that "these unhappy times call for the building of plans that rest upon the forgotten, the unorganized but indispensable units of economic power . . . that build from the bottom up and not from the top down." That "forgotten man" speech of April 7, 1932, also made a case for planning by recalling the hugely successful effort to mobilize for World War I.

Roosevelt fended off conservative complaints about socialism and class warfare, including Al Smith's florid declaration that he was ready to take off his coat and "fight to the end any candidate who persists in any demagogic appeal to the masses of the working people of the country to destroy themselves." At the annual Jefferson Day dinner on April 18, Roosevelt elaborated on the "concert of interests" theme, defying the risk that he would be branded socialistic and making it plain that he would not bow to pressure from the conservative wing of the Democratic Party. Then he retired to his polio rehabilitation spa in Warm Springs, Georgia, to get ready for the final drive to nomination.

During Roosevelt's hiatus in the South, two other noteworthy events climaxed the first phase of the campaign. On May 19, Moley sent the candidate a memo outlining much of the program that Roosevelt's administration later tried to carry out. Moley offered a progressive blueprint of public works on a grand scale, taxation of undistributed surplus corporate income, social insurance, banking and investment regulation, and a foreign policy including more reciprocal trade agreements and recognition of the Soviet Union. These aims, Moley emphasized, would be coordinated by an economic council of planners. In taking that stand for planning, Moley fixed on the crucial difference between Hoover and Roosevelt: "It is all very well for those who speak for the present administration to speak of economic laws. But men starve while economic laws work out. And it is a fair question as to whether economic laws exist which cannot be controlled by the laws of men." What people yearn for most of all, the memo concluded, is work and security—the twin concerns that would always be the core of Roosevelt's New Deal.

The second event was a speech by Roosevelt at Oglethorpe College in Georgia, which set out the items of the May 19 memo in a way notable mostly for its devotion to experimental planning. Roosevelt insisted that: "The country demands bold, persistent experimentation. It is common sense to take a method and try it: If it fails, admit it frankly and try another. But above all, try something. The millions who are in want will not stand by silently forever while the things to satisfy their needs are within easy reach."

A day later the cause of the forgotten man was vividly dramatized by the arrival in Washington of several thousand ragged, desperate World War I veterans in search of advance payment of the service bonuses due them in 1945. For a month this Bonus Expeditionary Force, as it called itself, bivouacked on the marshy flats of the Anacostia River while Congress debated a measure to grant them the bonus. After the bill died in the Senate, the BEF hung on through the hot summer, waiting for a word of comfort from the White House that never came. The pathos was acute, for these forgotten men were the tattered remnant of the very mobilizing effort Roosevelt insisted that the nation must duplicate in order to win the current war against economic distress. In July Hoover played his role as Scrooge by ordering General Douglas MacArthur to herd the BEF demonstrators back to their camp. MacArthur, in fine dress regalia, did more than his duty—by leading a charge against the camp itself! The rout of the BEF by tank, bayonet, and tear gas, with the aristocratic general talking nonsense about quelling revolution all the while, sealed Hoover's reputation as the heartless enemy of the "forgotten man"—by then on his way to becoming a national symbol of the Depression. Humorist Will Rogers put the matter succinctly: "You can get a road anywhere you want to out of Washington, but you can't get a sandwich."

Although Roosevelt gained the nomination while such disasters were mounting ever higher on Hoover's cold doorstep, the Democratic nominee backed away from continuing his strong expression of Brains Trust positions. Instead he chose to construct the broadest possible coalition so that his mandate would be large enough for him to take action as president, unfettered by the old guard. Thus, his campaign tacked and veered between bold experimentation and reassurance that the old sureties of balanced budget and free enterprise would be respected—an ambivalent performance that reflected the argument between Roosevelt's orthodox political strategists, Louis Howe and James Farley, that he should protect his lead by avoiding controversy and the Brains Trusters, who pressed him to use that lead to build a mandate for planned reform that his loosely aligned followers couldn't then weasel out of. The most egregious instance of Roosevelt's uncertainty about how to balance caution and boldness was reflected in his handling of the tariff—always a source of consternation for the New Deal. Roosevelt blithely told a smoldering Ray Moley to take one speech in favor of maintaining protective barriers and another advocating new initiatives for free trade and "weave them together." The trick in such attempts at reconciliation was to balance what seemed necessary to achieve a short range objective—such as landslide election or enough breathing room to ready the domestic economy for increased imports—while leaving the way open for a planned cooperative commonwealth in the long run.

Counterpointed with familiar bromides, then, were several key announcements of what the New Deal sought to be. In Topeka, Kansas, on September 14, Roosevelt enjoyed favorable reaction from the farm community when he spoke well of Wilson's crop reduction scheme—indication that both Hoover's cooperative line and McNary-Haugenism had lost favor. Then on the west coast Roosevelt delivered his most sustained series of progressive speeches. In the very shadow of the Rockies' great hydroelectric potential, Portland, Oregon, was the scene for Roosevelt's call for public control over power sources. From there he traveled to California for the high point of his campaign—the address to the Commonwealth Club of San Francisco on September 23.

The long speech, written mainly by Berle, concentrated on the need for planning imposed by the closing of the frontiers. No longer was there a safety valve through which the dispossessed could escape to open land and opportunity. In what might seem rather quaint or fainthearted in light of how the gross national product and per capita consumption have grown since 1932, Roosevelt urged Americans to rely on ever increasing cooperation to ensure that the country's natural wealth would not run out. Conservation and redistribution of resources were the key to decent security for all.

The Commonwealth speech and the campaign themes it highlighted showed that the problem of blending the wisdom of the heroes of his youth still preoccupied Roosevelt. He continued to use Theodore Roosevelt's "rule of reason" to determine which large economic concentrations deserved to survive while echoing Wilson's "New Freedom" ideal of decentralization. As always, the proof of a workable synthesis was its ability to bring social justice and security. "As I see it," Roosevelt told his San Francisco listeners, "the task of government in its relation to business is to assist the development of an economic declaration of rights, an economic constitutional order" that would blend both nationalist direction and democratic choice. Roosevelt made the partnership between collectivism and individualism more explicit with a proposition that echoed (and may well have been drawn from) John Dewey's *Individualism Old and New* (1929). One should recognize, Roosevelt urged, that people are social by nature and can only develop their individuality through association with others. The laissez-faire idea, which had flourished on the lost frontier and pitted individuals against each other, against government, and against social institutions, was not only obsolete, he insisted, but wrong in its conception of human nature. Modern society in its complexity had sound scientific reason to stress cooperation between people who depended on one another.

The address was stitched together with calls for self-sacrifice in accord with Berle's and Roosevelt's autumnal view of the republic's diminishing resources and the need to curb free and unaccountable enterprise. In recent years, Roosevelt contended provocatively, the nation's entrepreneurs "have undertaken to be, not business men, but princes—princes of property." Now "the responsible heads of finance and industry instead of acting each for himself, must work together to achieve the common end. They must, where necessary, sacrifice this or that private advantage; and in reciprocal self-denial must seek a general advantage. It is here that formal government—political government, if you choose—comes in." Not only does the government need to intervene when free enterprise becomes cutthroat; on a day-to-day basis government should aspire to newly responsible wisdom, taking on "the soberer, less dramatic business of administering resources and plants already in hand, of seeking to re-establish foreign markets for our surplus production, of meeting the problem of underconsumption, of adjusting production to consumption, of distributing wealth and products more equitably, of adapting existing economic organization to the service of the people." In words that resonated with the New Deal's commitment to planning, Roosevelt concluded with a declaration that "the day of enlightened administration has come."

Roosevelt's exuberant campaigning was more than a match for Hoover's attempt to pin his challenger underneath a mountain of ever more irrelevant facts and figures. Roosevelt could capitalize on the best of both worlds. With his calls for collective planning, he managed to seem progressive; at the same time, his support for conservation and balancing the budget appealed to conservative instincts. Overall he eloquently cast a vision of a compassionate, activist, orderly federal government without committing himself to any particular legislative program. The result was an overwhelming Democratic victory. Roosevelt received 22,815,539 votes to Hoover's 15,759,930 and lost votes in the electoral college only in Delaware, Pennsylvania, and the thinly populated Republican stronghold of northern New England. Hoover emerged as the victim of the greatest switch in presidential election history. Both in total numbers and percentage of the vote gained, he had gone from a landslide triumph in his first run for the presidency to an even larger landslide defeat in his second. Central to Roosevelt's victory was his success in attracting progressive Republican votes in the west while building on the urban revolt Al Smith had led. In 1920, the ticket on which Roosevelt ran for vice president won none of the twelve largest cities. In 1932, he swept all of them by a wide margin.

With a large coalition of the newest, poorest, and most marginalized voters thus drawn to the promise of a New Deal, electoral challenges from the left fizzled for lack of a constituency. The Socialists and Communists had gained notice during the campaign by attracting articulate intellectuals to their respective causes and seemed ready to benefit from the influence of the Russian Revolution. But on election day the voters showed themselves to be what Roosevelt's shrewd judgment expected: eager for robust leadership that would try some new tactics but not willing to throw away their capitalist heritage—the sole anchor to windward—for a radical adventure. Work and security were indeed, as Moley and Tugwell had seen, the right watchwords. His tactics proved, Roosevelt buoyantly prepared to enact his pledge of a "New Deal for the American people."

CHAPTER FOUR

The Struggle for Financial Stability

The long interregnum between Roosevelt's victory in November and his inauguration was such a ghastly time of uncertainty that on February 6, 1933, an amendment to move up the inauguration of presidents in future years from March 4 to January 20 was swiftly ratified. In the gloom of late 1932 and early 1933 it was rumored that Hoover might resign so that a new broom could start sweeping everything away sooner. But this expectation did not reckon with Hoover's grim belief that he was the last bulwark against socialistic experiment. Roosevelt, sensitive as usual, sought to evade the grip of Hoover's martyrdom through a strategy of cheerfully noncommittal preparation for a New Deal that would be free of ties with Hoover's American System.

Roosevelt's preparation for harnessing the coalition stressed the progressive emphasis on planning he had assured Tugwell was his ultimate goal. An article in *Liberty* magazine, written by Moley under Roosevelt's name, outlined the aims of the New Deal in accord with Moley's April 19 memo and Roosevelt's declaration in *Survey*, the social work journal, that he had advocated long-range planning for some twenty years. The New Deal, the article announced, would make good Roosevelt's campaign promises on a broad front. It would consolidate the nation's transportation, oversee the power industry, establish a farm rehabilitation program, and bring balance to foreign trade through reciprocal trade agreements. Still to be decided upon were programs of recovery for banking, social insurance, and industry.

The administration's set of aims indicated a fairly well-knit New Deal conception. The details for implementation of what Roosevelt called "a new period of liberalism and of sane reform" were another story, however, and the turbulent trial and error maneuvers that ensued were to give the launching of the New Deal a deceptive appearance of indifference to planning.

Roosevelt was quick to seek congressional support but shrewd enough to know that he could not expect much. Since 1930, when the seriousness of the Depression began to sink in and increased numbers of Progressives and Democratic reformers were sent by voters to Washington to challenge the old guard, Congress had become increasingly deadlocked. The leadership of both parties sought to mollify what they considered radical discontent by entering into what one member described as "fearful cooperation" with Hoover's efforts to stop the bleeding. But ideological differences also hardened in the face of crisis. As a result, three major legislative efforts from three very different perspectives—unemployment relief championed by progressives; a national sales tax to balance the budget, proposed by Hoover; and a bill to protect against bank failure, representing the conservative views of Virginia Senator Carter Glass—were all stymied. By the beginning of 1933, the major political figures outside Congress—the president, president to be, and newly elected Democrats eager to get inside and start sweeping—concluded that the best thing would be no congressional action until after Roosevelt's inauguration.

A constructive relationship between the two presidential rivals never emerged. Promoter of voluntary cooperation, Hoover was in no mood to cooperate with his successor. He preferred to go down with the ship of his convictions rather than compromise with the threat to liberty posed by the Brains Trust ideas of governmental planning. The testy actions of the embittered president thus greatly complicated Roosevelt's tightrope walk through the interregnum. On a mid-November Sunday afternoon a telegram from Hoover penetrated Roosevelt's retreat in Albany. It was urgent, the president stated, that he confer with Roosevelt about the international situation so that an answer could be framed to a British request for suspension of her debts to the United States. Indeed, Hoover warned, similar requests from other nations were imminent and Hoover needed assurances that his response could be counted on to stretch into the next administration.

The request was the opening wedge of a campaign to enlist Roosevelt behind Hoover's policies—including collection of foreign debts, retention of the gold standard (that "Gibraltar of stability in the world," as Hoover put it), and new taxes to balance the budget. Although Roosevelt cheerily asserted his wish to cooperate, he also avoided any endorsement of the Hoover approach. It was essential, Roosevelt and his advisers reasoned, to retain the options that had been so carefully cultivated during the campaign. Had Hoover been willing to accommodate his views to those of Roosevelt and to the campaign pledges accepted by the voters, cooperation might have been possible. But Hoover remained lashed to the mast, his rudder locked on course, unable to distinguish his own views from national destiny and economic law. Indeed, Hoover all but acknowledged the arrogance of his intent in a letter to Senator Reed of Pennsylvania: "I realize that if these declarations be made by the President-elect, he will have ratified the whole major program of the Republican Administration; that is, it means the abandonment of 90% of the so-called 'new deal.'"

Roosevelt demurred as affably as possible, but to no avail with Hoover, whose rage against a successor he considered ignorant and untrustworthy—a "madman," even—became obsessive and lasted for the rest of his long and outspoken life. When Roosevelt visited the White House a short time before his inaugural, Hoover displayed his morbid alienation. To Roosevelt's polite insistence that there was no need for the president to return the call, Hoover responded balefully: "Mr. Roosevelt, when you are in Washington as long as I have been, you will learn that the President of the United States calls on nobody." Soon afterward, Hoover accompanied Roosevelt to the inaugural through the rain in an open car, stolidly rebuffing attempts at small talk. His silence served to dramatize that the American System had nothing more to say and that the New Deal was entering the void of great opportunity.

Before the New Deal could proceed on its unprecedented way, it had to resolve a desperate financial situation that threatened to bring down the entire economy. By the time Roosevelt was inaugurated, the withering of economic opportunity had forced over half of the nation's banks—some 5500 in all—to close their doors. The situation revealed basic weaknesses, especially in the Federal Reserve system. Hailed when it became law in 1913 as a progressive triumph over years of banking chaos, the Federal Reserve Act set up a coordinated balance between private banks and the federal government, which would regulate interest rates to ensure that money remained available for investment. Widespread belief, especially among economists and the leaders of financial institutions, that the "Fed" was guiding the system through the perils of boom and bust diverted attention from the way bank failures rose relentlessly after 1913. Essentially, the greatest source of trouble was not in the design of the system but in the choice of about 65 percent of the nation's banks not to join it; these were mostly small outfits for whom the membership fee was not as well offset against returns as was the case with large banks, who could use Fed backing for big transactions. Often located in declining rural areas, small banks tended to be underfinanced and amateurishly run by local leaders with more interest in status than competence. When

such small ventures failed, the large banks, which controlled two thirds of all deposits even though they were only one third of the total number of banks, were not
much inclined to notice—except to withdraw their support capital and muse on how
Darwinian free enterprise acts to build up the strong by weeding out the weak.

Thus accustomed to an unstable system where failure was common and viewing themselves as the surviving fittest, large banks tended to be blind to their
own vulnerability. In accord with the high public esteem in which bankers were
held, the Bankers' Association Code of Ethics declared that "a certain noblesse
oblige, an obligation of honorable and generous behavior in the sight of God and
man, is impressed upon all those who bear the name of [banker] and wear the
badge of this profession." From that lofty perspective, leading bankers were able
to evade the question of why, as prosperity flowered, bank failures had risen to
an average of 691 per year between 1923 and 1929, some seven times the failure
rate during the first twenty years of the century. Bank money, often unsecured by
hard assets, flowed into loans for risky real estate ventures in Florida and California, for luxury purchases by those flaunting their prosperity, and, most significantly, for speculation in stocks and bonds. As one repentant banker put it after
the crash, banks "provided everything for their customers but a roulette wheel."
Still, so strong was the image of bankers as trustees of communal prosperity that
only a series of heavy blows were enough to undermine public confidence and
reveal the fragile nature of the speculative economy.

The first blow came like a thunderclap. In 1930 the fall of the imposing Bank
of the United States in New York—by far the largest bank failure in American
history—made it plain that size and prestige were not necessarily proof of fitness. Indictments of the bank's officers for misuse of funds made a mockery of
the high-flown Bankers' Association Code of Ethics. Instead, in its fall from grace
the bank, with its imposing neo-classical facade and easy credit for Wall Street
insiders, showed an increasingly attentive public the perils of a system where uninsured funds of ordinary depositors were skimmed by speculators rather than
producing something of tangible worth.

Critics of the debacle divided between individualists, who blamed the Federal Reserve oversight for preventing automatic corrections through free competition, and collectivists on both the right and left, who pointed out that other
nations with centralized systems did not suffer such bank failures. But bankers
and government officials were reluctant to move very far toward one pole or the
other. They feared, on the one hand, that letting the crisis simply play itself out
in the marketplace would inflict too much pain along the way, if, indeed, recovery would come by itself at all. Centralization, on the other hand, was too much

against the American grain of open opportunity to draw much of a following. The specter of authoritarian regimes abroad increased resistance to centralization; as well, the crumbling of state banks in Austria and Germany undermined arguments that a centralized system was less vulnerable to economic shocks than the American mix of public and private control.

Hemmed in by disaster and uncertainty, bankers and governmental officials were able to offer little beyond calls for better management and the elimination of weak banks. Even Roosevelt as governor of New York fended off proposals for legislative change by urging greater probity. When the spiraling rate of failures finally stimulated direct relief, the concept of aiding banks by strengthening the bankers remained in force. Loans from Hoover's Reconstruction Finance Corporation (RFC) mostly ended up at the largest banks; even the millions from that source were little more than a sandbag in a doomed dike.

The ultimate crisis broke when Governor William Comstock of Michigan, faced with the collapse of the Union Guardian Trust Company, the state's largest bank and a bulwark of the automobile industry, agreed to suspend all banking operations in the state. That occurred on February 14, 1933, after a frantic month of talks between Hoover, the Senate Banking Currency Committee, and Michigan officials had disclosed shady banking practices and the inefficacy of large RFC loans. Shocked into an awareness of weakness and corruption, other states also declared moratoriums. By the time Roosevelt took office, the nation's banking system was almost paralyzed and discredited. People smiled through their tears at a new response to the popular song of those hard times, "Brother, can you spare a dime?": "No, but I can write a check." They could ruefully agree with the man who, informed that the thirty-eighth statewide banking moratorium had just been declared, replied: "Well, that ratifies the Depression."

Roosevelt entered the crisis with a long-steeped antipathy to the selfish arrogance of bankers that inclined him to blame them for their plight and side with the general public as victims. His inaugural address first drew applause from its anxious audience when it attacked "the unscrupulous money changers" who had been thrust from "their high seats in the temple of our civilization." On that biblical plane he proclaimed that "restoration lies in the extent to which we apply social values more noble than mere monetary profit."

Action came on March 6 when Roosevelt dusted off the emergency powers granted by the wartime Trading with the Enemy Act of 1917 and declared a "bank holiday" to keep banks closed until they were safe from a ruinous run on their inadequate assets. Soon an Emergency Banking Act was readied, whisked through Congress in forty minutes, and signed by the new president on March 9. Its provisions forbade transfer of any gold assets—in effect taking the nation off the gold standard. The threat of prison terms for hoarders, who were squirreling away some $20 million in gold each day, brought most of the gold back to the Treasury in a hurry.

The stability needed to reopen shaky banks was provided by appointment of conservators to reorganize the banks and by authorization for the RFC to buy preferred stock from state banks and the Fed to issue bank notes backed by federal securities and similarly sound assets. With these reassuring reforms in place, the banks were able to reopen on March 13 without incident. In a display of confidence, the public returned to the vaults what they had stashed away under mattresses and buried in the backyard. And bankers, despite the loss of much of the autonomy they had been pleased to ascribe to noblesse oblige and natural law, generally endorsed the new legislation. Well they might. The bank holiday enabled them to throw in a very weak hand—only $6 billion in assets to meet a potential call for $41 billion in deposits.

To buttress that stability the Banking Act of 1933, passed on June 16, created the Federal Deposit Insurance Corporation to insure savings against future failures, thus protecting average depositors from their greatest fears. The act similarly shielded banks and their depositors from speculative adventures of the sort that had ruined many of them during the Great Crash by separating deposit banking from investment banking and forbidding commercial banks from underwriting securities. In keeping with these new federal protections, the act moved the Federal Reserve System significantly further toward centralization, such as prevailed in other modern countries, by giving control over open market operations to the Federal Reserve Board, a move that not only subordinated Federal Reserve banks to the Board but also had the crucial effect of shifting the center of monetary policy from New York to Washington.

Roosevelt had reason to feel proud of the New Deal's first swift accomplishment. The longstanding decline of a faulty banking system had been stopped at the critical moment and was done, as Will Rogers put it, in terms so simple even the bankers could understand them.

Roosevelt completed immediate control over the domestic financial crisis by reforming the stock market. Although Wall Street had suffered appalling damage and a number of stockbrokers had, indeed, jumped out of windows or taken to selling apples, the leaders of the Exchange put up some spirited opposition to regulation in the name of free enterprise "confidence." Richard Whitney, president of the New York Stock Exchange, went so far in opposing the New Deal call for regulation as to declare that "the Exchange is a perfect institution." Unfortunately, Whitney at the time was embezzling from brokerage customers, as well as from his private club and a long-suffering brother, in a failing effort to recoup his own losses. When he was caught toward the end of the decade trying to rescue his last holdings in a New Jersey apple-jack distillery and sent to Sing Sing, he became the symbol of the Stock Exchange's lost dignity—the man who was struck by "Jersey lightning."

In the wake of Wall Street's fall from grace the Securities and Exchange Act of 1934 created a commission to keep the game honest—to check the advantage of those with insider tips, to ensure that all transactions were what the brokers represented them to be, and to curb the amount of stock one could buy on credit. Here, as in other successful New Deal actions, the force of cooperative compromise asserted itself over criticism from the wings. Bankers and businessmen on the right warned of interference—even socialism. On the left, critics like Tugwell, who wanted a government agency to control investment directly, deplored the bill as a relic of prewar Progressive belief in the honest referee. But the day belonged to Felix Frankfurter, who at Moley's behest came to Washington from his teaching post at the Harvard Law School to help infuse the bill with Wilsonian idealism and oversee the key drafting by two brilliant former students, Thomas Corcoran and James Landis. Henceforth, Frankfurter, as a bearer of the Wilsonian preference for regulated small enterprise over larger planned units, advocated most forcefully by Supreme Court Justice Louis Brandeis, would be a power to reckon with in New Deal circles. And the SEC would stand as a prime example of the regulatory side of the New Deal program.

In the midst of the domestic financial crisis, Roosevelt also undertook to carry out arrangements Hoover had made to attend an international monetary conference in London on ways to combat the world depression. For Hoover and many other sponsors, that had meant stressing the importance of the gold standard. Roosevelt's priorities, in keeping with his noncommittal stance while preparing to take over the presidency, were not forthrightly expressed. Judging from the diversity of the delegation he eventually chose, Roosevelt wanted a group that would be pleasingly representative of all viewpoints rather than the bearer of a unified policy. Cordell Hull, the rather stiff-necked senator from Tennessee who had just become secretary of state, was the logical choice to head the group and press his ardent belief in reciprocal trade agreements. Most significantly flanking Hull were vice chairman James Cox, Roosevelt's old running mate, who preserved a link to Wilsonian internationalist idealism; James Warburg, a young New York financier from a famous international banking family, who brought to the group expert advocacy of a stable order based on a restored gold standard;

and Key Pittman, senator from Nevada, who staunchly represented farmers and silver mining interests from his region and, as chairman of the Senate Committee on Foreign Relations, had to be included.

The instructions Roosevelt gave to the delegation aimed vaguely at balancing nationalist and internationalist issues. He would have them work for a tariff truce, with gradually lowered rates; coordination of monetary fiscal politics with the goal of raising prices; agreements on the production of basic commodities so as to avoid surplus; and gradual restoration of the gold standard. Considering the priority Roosevelt had given to domestic recovery ever since the campaign, it seems clear that he hoped to establish a firm domestic base before having to commit the United States to any international stabilization. That way a world balance could be attained that would favor American interests and security, yet not so lopsidedly that it would risk further depression or war.

Roosevelt's obscurely complex aims proved beyond the grasp of an American delegation that was divided against itself. Some of the delegates also proved inadequately informed and even eccentric. The protocol officer went about with a monocle and enigmatic smile that made him, his wife liked to say, the "mystery man" of the conference. The loosest cannon was Key Pittman, who tuned in only to support remonetization of silver and otherwise played the hard-drinking westerner on a spree in foreign lands. He flouted protocol with his hearty hallooing of the king and queen, shot out street lights with a six-shooter, and one wild night was extracted naked from a sink at the Hotel Claridge, where he claimed to be a statue in a fountain.

The confusion in the American delegation was matched by the ambivalence of their British hosts. Led by Prime Minister Ramsay MacDonald, who had abandoned his role as Labour Party leader in 1931 to become the head of a new national coalition, the British delegation was conflicted by the fact that, although their country had gone off the gold standard in 1931, all their instincts inclined them toward that traditional monetary polestar. Tradition aside, it also served their interests to have other nations remain on the gold standard so that devalued British goods would continue to enjoy an international price advantage. The British position was reinforced by the way their old rival, France, had become the main pillar of the gold standard orthodoxy, largely because the recall by French banks of loans to shaky central European nations had produced vast gold reserves.

The roles of two other key nations were less clear-cut or orthodox. Soviet delegate Maxim Litvinoff sought to counter the fact that his country was regarded as an outcast—not even formally recognized by the United States—by acting as an agent of good will and free trade. But the precise plans of the Russian state remained a mystery. The Germans were also enigmatic and were looked upon with suspicion because of Hitler's brutal rise to power and Germany's failure to pay reparations.

A prickly tone set in at the beginning when MacDonald violated the general understanding that the subject of international debts was not to be mentioned. The delegates were embarrassed and Hull, representing the main creditor nation, was outraged for the first of many times by what seemed to him pressure to have the debts eased.

But it was not only the specific topic of debts and the gold standard that proved sensitive. The participating nations, caught in the throes of depression and a rising trend toward strongman rule, were inclined toward self-protection, not cooperative effort on long-range international problems. The wary atmosphere was exemplified by an exchange between Cox and Georges Bonnet, French minister of finance, as they vied for a leadership position. Regarding Cox narrowly, Bonnet commented: "France will not look with favor upon the selection of someone to head the Monetary Commission who comes from a country which has recently gone off the gold standard." Miffed, Cox retorted, "Nor will the United States look with favor upon the election of a man by a country which has repudiated its debts."

This state of irritated stalemate prepared the conference for the entry of some help to break the impasse. Into that vacuum Raymond Moley made a fateful entry as a special envoy from the president. Although Moley always claimed that he shrank from the task, he used conspicuous means to carry it out—beginning with a navy flight and a ride on a destroyer to reach Roosevelt's yacht cruising off Nantucket. Roosevelt instructed Moley on the "nasty chore" of bringing the American delegation into line, which really meant keeping them from making any commitments until Roosevelt could decide what to do. Then it was off on the liner *Manhattan* for Plymouth, England, and a highly publicized trek to London. Some observers parodied the journey as akin to Jesus' palm-strewn entry into Jerusalem by chanting "Moley, Moley, Moley, Lord God Almighty," and Cordell Hull was livid at the way he was being upstaged. Only the intervention of friends, who at the crucial moment took Hull off for a pleasant weekend in the country, kept him from resigning.

Roosevelt soon ended the melodrama by dropping a Fourth of July bombshell in the form of a message to the conference. Rather than praising the efforts of the statesmen to rescue the established system, Roosevelt spoke out bluntly against "the old fetishes of so-called international bankers": "I would regard it as a catastrophe amounting to a world tragedy if the greatest conference of nations, called to bring about a more real and permanent financial stability and a greater prosperity to the masses of all nations, should, in advance of any serious effort to consider these broader problems, allow itself to be diverted by the proposal of a purely artificial and temporary experiment affecting the monetary exchange of a few nations only."

Roosevelt was announcing his planning vision to the world and explained how he would have gold-backed money replaced by a "commodity dollar," based on the value of usable goods: "Let me be frank in saying that the United States seeks the kind of dollar which a generation hence will have the same purchasing power and debt-paying power as the dollar value we hope to attain in the near future. That objective means more to the good of other nations than a fixed ratio for a month or two in terms of the pound or franc."

The reverberations of the message were considerable. Decried as a "Manifesto of Anarchy" by the *Manchester Guardian* and as a new Declaration of Independence by the more anti-establishment and anti-foreign American press, the pronouncement made it clear that Roosevelt was a free spirit. He would not let monetary pieties, which largely served banker interests, nor international considerations, when they meant sacrificing domestic policy, interfere with recovery. MacDonald was beside himself that America should undermine the old order he sought to re-sanctify, and Hull elicited sympathy from the delegates because they knew that he, too, wanted stable international trade agreements and was stunned by the president's gauntlet. The conference refrained from formally condemning Roosevelt. But this achieved only a decent exit; the traditionalist delegates were not prepared to accept an international system that did not include the gold standard, which Roosevelt had correctly renounced as a contributor, rather than a solution, to the depression. Amid the confused din, one voice of support for the president stood out. John Maynard Keynes, England's most famous economist and a genius at stock investments, looked over the wreckage of the conference and declared in words that were to beguile economists long afterward: "Roosevelt is magnificently right!"

In Washington the sound money men reacted as had their brethren in London. Lewis Douglas, director of the budget and rugged southwesterner who charmed Roosevelt into regarding him as one of the brightest finds of his administration, wrote Warburg in London to assure him that he, Secretary of the Treasury William Woodin, and a chastened Raymond Moley were prepared to work for restoration of the gold standard and a stable balanced budget. Roosevelt, however, was not to be deflected from his nationalist course. Soon the resignations of Douglas and the other counterinsurgents were on his desk.

The early New Deal adventures in rescue of the banks, securities regulation, and dispatch of the London conference cleared the decks for novel forms of experimentation. In retrospect, most analysts agree that the United States could not possibly have removed itself from the world scene for the purpose of concentrating on domestic recovery as fully as Roosevelt proposed. America's actions would inevitably affect other nations. Nor does there seem cause to conclude that the degree of abstention from world affairs Roosevelt did achieve blighted opportunities to construct a world system capable of staving off totalitarian aggression and war. There is little indication that the world's statesmen would allow the bold departures a new system required. The London conferees clung in the main to protective tariffs, exclusive nationalism, and a rigid gold standard that would protect business and banking investments without much provision for international amity or for those at the bottom of the economic scale.

Comparison with the pariah nations—Germany, Italy, and Russia—indicated a preference among the more democratic nations for orthodoxy over recovery through experiment. By planning, barter arrangements, and money based on goods rather than gold, Germany and Russia managed to begin a recovery from the Depression while other nations continued to decline. But their overtures were rebuffed and their novel ways discredited; their violations of capitalist taboos could be rejected out of hand because they were associated with outlaw regimes using brutal political methods. Italy, on the other hand, though also poverty-stricken and given to repressive violence, gained a more respectful hearing. Her loyalty to the orthodox economic creed helped divert attention from the findings of the International Labor Organization in 1930 that Italian workers were paid the lowest of any in Western Europe, wages having declined almost by half between 1928 and 1932, even though the eight-hour day in 1926 lost out to the desire of the corporate managers for higher productivity and profit. Mussolini was shrewd enough to know that he could beguile visitors by having the trains they took run on time, the streets they frequented cleaned, and beggars kept out of the way. The image of efficiency and self-denying discipline appealed to the depression-wracked world's yearning for order and to the classical economic view that the bust end of the cycle should be borne with fortitude so that the boom end could appear on its own schedule.

A massive shift of opinion against fascist Italy did not come until long after the monetary conference, when the meaning of Mussolini's doctrine of action—repugnant to the orthodox belief in a marketplace balance of supply and demand that worked best under peaceful conditions—began to sink in. The most conservative of believers in braving the hard times recoiled from Il Duce's conception of how to maintain morale under the circumstances: "Perpetual peace would be impossible and useless. War alone brings all human energies to their highest state of tension, and stamps with the seal of nobility the nations which dare to face it."

Roosevelt shared in the recoil. He rejected the idea that the poor must stoically accept misery and decried the link that fascists made between hardship and brutal force. Thus Roosevelt approached the stalled economy with an urgency born of compassion and national interest and was irritated by any complacent or callous disposition just to ride out the storm. Something had to be done to save people before their democratic faith eroded. In that spirit he wrote to Ramsay MacDonald, as the monetary conference was foundering, that he was more concerned about appeals to war, like those of Mussolini, than about gold, to which MacDonald wearily replied that the United States had more room for experiment than had desperate Britain.

Having dismissed the London conference as too archaic and slow-moving, Roosevelt turned to theorists who would manipulate money as a tool to raise prices and improve distribution. He appreciated those who had been pressing such a policy on him because their attempts to find simple, direct answers mirrored his own impatience. In that mood he welcomed a letter from Professor Irving Fisher, an eminent Yale economist who spoke for the Stable Money League and its campaign to base the money supply on the nation's commodities rather than gold or silver. Fisher urged "reflation"—a coinage of his to describe a deliberate boost of the dollar value and prices toward their pre-crash level by careful expansion of the money supply on a commodity basis.

Fisher touched a sensitive Roosevelt nerve when he argued that continued inaction, in the hopes that the old system would revive itself, would breed "injustice, discontent, violence, and Bolshevism." They shared an ironic belief that the main obstacle to heading off the danger of totalitarian radicalism was the obduracy of the economic conservatives.

The forlornness of orthodox economists in the face of such convictions and the monetary conference demise was well expressed in Warburg's recollection in September 1933 of his last attempt to steer the president away from money manipulators like Fisher. To Warburg's entreaties for a meeting with the experts straggling back from London in order to get the details of a long-run solution, Roosevelt responded that the vision of ultimate stability was "very pretty." But, meanwhile, how does one arrange to make prices advance? How does one relieve the crushing debt burden? What is one to do about the farmers who, in their desperation, threaten open rebellion? Warburg wilted before such urgency:

"I realized with a sense of finality how impossible it was to combat successfully a group of advisers who had ready answers to all these questions, while the only answers those of us could give who felt that the cure could not be a purely monetary one involved a slow and more or less painful process of rebuilding."

To implement his new monetarist policy Roosevelt consulted James Harvey Rogers of Yale and the team of George Warren and Frank Pearson—all specialists in monetary statistics. Warren was the key figure, for both professional and personal reasons. An agricultural economist at Cornell and Secretary of the Treasury Henry Morgenthau's revered mentor, Warren was sympathetic to the farm bloc's economic plight and inflationist arguments. He gained wide influence through association with the Committee for the Nation, a group of business and farm leaders who appreciated the money manipulators' interest in raising prices. From this base Warren spoke with confidence as the new Administration took shape: "So far as the writer has observed, no person who has studied the statistics of production has found any evidence to support the thesis that overproduction caused the Depression, nor has he found any record of a person who now explains the Depression on the basis of production who foresaw the Depression. Correct forecasts were made on the basis of monetary factors."

These were correct forecasts, Warren argued, because they understood the nature of prices and their precarious state as the Great Crash approached. It followed that "The economic catastrophe in which we find ourselves is due to a fall in commodity prices." To arrive at a remedy, one must realize that "our whole tax and debt structure rests on commodity prices. If this structure is to be kept sound either for the creditor or the debtor, it is commodity prices that need to be kept stable, not the weight of gold for which a dollar will exchange."

Thus, Warren concluded in his most famous statement, "The dollar has to be rubber either as to weight or as to value. It cannot have a fixed weight and also have a fixed value." In this formulation, "Rubber Dollar" Warren was echoing Fisher's plea for a scientific relationship between the dollar's purchasing power and its declared value that would avoid the roller coaster effect that afflicts money when it is tied to a fixed standard, unable to cope with the vagaries of the marketplace, weather, and other conditions. No invisible hand or natural law had any place in this conception. Warren was a firm institutionalist, and the crux of a sound economy came down to this proposition: "The price level must be raised to the debt level, or the debt level must be lowered to the price level. This is a matter of grim reality that cannot be cured by psychology, confidence, or government lending."

Warren had considerable ability in demonstrating the grim realities. Warren and Pearson's book *Prices* (1933), followed by Warren's pamphlet, "Some Statistics on the Gold Situation" (1934), emphasized the close links among prices, production, and fluctuation in the world stock of gold. If production expanded faster than gold supplies, prices fell; if gold supplies mounted more swiftly than production, then prices rose. This formula was closely tied to the logical fact that gold was only available to back high prices when it was plentiful. Thus, gold standard nations yearning for higher prices were left to hope and prayer that more gold might be discovered—as happened in the nick of time in the depression of the 1890s. But the *effect* of a greater supply of gold might be simulated. Irving Fisher suggested the creation of a "compensated dollar"—one whose gold exchange value was reduced without a corresponding reduction in its value in commodity terms. Alternatively, the government could sequester the available supply of gold and decree its value by agreeing to purchase gold at an arbitrary price. That was Warren's suggestion and the cause of much conservative consternation over tampering with the mystery of "true" value by the most dangerous of agencies—the government.

Events in early 1933 bolstered the Fisher-Warren case. In the three days after Roosevelt halted the export of gold in April, the scarcity of that metal caused the London exchange price to rise 12 percent. Most heartening to the commodity dollar case, the price of cotton rose by exactly the same percentage, with wheat following close behind, indicating a link between the value of a nation's commodities and the currency to which that value could be converted. As realization of the link was registering, commodity prices seemed to break loose from their Depression chains. Gold climbed 23.2 percent between April 20 and June 10, and the prices of seventeen basic commodities shot up 45 percent. On May 12, in the midst of that surge, Congress, bowing to pressures from rural constituents for a "rubber" currency, empowered the president to expand the silver backing for the dollar as he saw fit.

At summer's end, however, commodity prices fell. Roosevelt concluded that the departure from a rigid international gold standard and the rescue of the banks were not enough. Calling Warren in to confer, Roosevelt decided to move to the outright monetary management Warren urged. Warren's concept was that monetary gold stocks should increase by approximately the same amount as commodity production in order to maintain stable prices. Because gold production since World War I had not kept pace with commodities, the latter had lost ground in price. To redress the balance, Warren estimated that gold needed to gain about 75 percent in value. That would mean a price for gold of $36.17 per ounce.

By pegging the price of gold above its value on the open market, Roosevelt drew all loose supplies to Fort Knox. From the $20.67 per ounce that prevailed for some time prior to March 1933, gold rose to the $35 Roosevelt had fixed for it at the end of his monetary manipulation in the Gold Reserve Act of 1934. The passage of the Silver Purchase Act in June 1934 further swelled the desired excess of monetary reserves.

Here the policy was expected to bear fruit in productive loans and investments as bank reserves rose beyond deposit insurance requirements. Instead the economic system remained frozen in the dive position. Excess reserves mounted from $256 million in 1932 to $528 million in 1933 and all the way up to $1.6 billion the next year, but productive business investment did not advance accordingly. Faced with these discouraging results, Roosevelt ended the rubber dollar project and turned restlessly away from monetary experimentation altogether. And yet, however disappointing the rubber dollar experiment was in immediate results, it did not leave behind conclusive evidence that the monetarist case lacked merit, and the argument over the Fisher-Warren approach continued throughout the remainder of the New Deal. For one thing, an increase in the amount of money available for productive investment was clearly necessary in order for prosperity and higher prices to have a chance to occur. And, as monetarists have continued to argue, the New Deal may have backed away from the experiment too soon, balked by the same sort of timidity that kept orthodox bankers and businessmen from taking advantage of novel opportunities.

CHAPTER FIVE

The Recovery of Industry

With the banking system drawn safely back from the abyss, the New Deal could focus on the revival of America's stalled industrial progress. In undertaking that huge task, the administration showed a balanced concern about both the sources of power and materials and their conversion into goods and services. Roosevelt in his Commonwealth speech had expressed his belief that, with the frontier having reached its limit, continued prosperity required the carefully measured use of finite resources. In accord, the debacle of a vast industrial complex, once the envy of the world and now only able to function at a low level, the workers and consumers dependent on it, sunk in hardship—the situation seemed to call for comprehensive new plans that would combine conservation, efficiency, and fairness.

On the threshold of the search for economic stability was a controversial proposal that had for years appealed to Roosevelt's abiding interest in conservation and was to become the most successful and permanent large-scale New Deal planning venture. The proposal, led by Senator George Norris of Nebraska and supported by an array of visionary planners, engineers, and progressive politicians, would create a federal agency to develop the resources and tremendous potential for hydroelectric power of the Tennessee River Valley into a kind of arcadia of prosperity, beauty, and utility. The original impetus for development arose after World War I when the plant in the Muscle Shoals region used for making nitrates for munitions was closed. The project for completing a dam on the site was carried to completion in 1925, but there remained no clear governmental stake in the possibility some saw of converting one of the most destitute areas of the country into a beautiful and thriving center of hydroelectric power, with ir-rigated farmland that would support the preservation of picturesque folk crafts and customs.

The Tennessee Valley had served as the focus for a test of strength between ad-vocates of private and public development for some time. On behalf of the public tradition, alongside Norris, stood such key defenders as Gifford Pinchot, once Theodore Roosevelt's chief forester and later the reformist governor of Pennsyl-vania, and Harold Ickes, destined to be secretary of the interior under Franklin Roosevelt. The private sector made its most concerted thrust under the leader-ship of two of the era's most prominent folk heroes, Henry Ford and Thomas Edison. In 1919 Ford sought to purchase the abandoned government facilities at Muscle Shoals and promised, with aid from Edison's genius, to build a commu-nity there that would be a model of reform and technological advance.

The Ford plan energized the public sector. Norris combined dissatisfaction with the low price Ford was offering with his conviction that public ownership was necessary if the development of power was ever to go beyond the mere tap-ping of ready customers for quick profits to the full realization of the electric age. To reach that happy end—a dream made especially alluring by an almost complete lack of electric power in farm country of the sort which had sent him to Washington—Norris introduced legislation to create a manufacturing and re-gional conservation complex at Muscle Shoals. The proposal ushered in years of frustration that was important in driving Norris and other progressive Republi-cans away from their party mainstream, eventually toward support of the New Deal. After finally persuading Congress of the value of such public enterprise, Norris saw his pet project vetoed, first by Coolidge and then by Hoover. The Great Engineer's language, complete with unintentional pun at the end, cut to the quick: "I hesitate to contemplate the future of our institutions, of our govern-ment, and of our country if the preoccupation of its officials is to be no longer the promotion of justice and equal opportunity but is to be devoted to barter in the markets. That is not liberalism, it is degeneration."

Hoover's appeal to justice was confounded when investigations by the Fed-eral Trade Commission disclosed massively misleading advertising, inequitable rates, and poor service on the part of private power companies. The Interstate Commerce Committee of the House of Representatives brought outrage to a head with the revelation in 1930 that Samuel Insull, as head of the world's larg-est combine of electric and gas companies in control of nearly 15 percent of the American market and widely touted as a champion of progress, was a swindler and his empire an unstable pyramid of holding companies rigged to siphon money to the manipulator at the top. When Insull fled the country to escape prosecution, public opinion swung toward the Norris position on public power.

Roosevelt was just the person to oversee the change. His ardor for conservation had always been strong, enough so that the course in public utility law at Columbia Law School roused the otherwise indifferent student to achieve one of his rare Bs. And in his subsequent legislative career Roosevelt showed special keenness over the problems of power development and its logical counterpart, conservation. Roosevelt's mentor Al Smith long advocated a St. Lawrence River hydroelectric power project; for emphasis he pointed to the Ontario public utility, which produced electricity at rates embarrassingly lower than across the border in New York. Roosevelt used that comparison frequently, with impish delight, to make a case for broad civic cooperation against irresponsibly selfish business. Roosevelt buttressed the invidious comparison with a concept he claimed to have invented while he was assistant secretary of the Navy. In a debate over the wisdom of constructing a wartime steel plant, Roosevelt had suggested setting up a smaller "yard-stick" plant to determine what, exactly, was needed for the overall war effort. The success of the experimental measure stayed with Roosevelt and was most frequently invoked in connection with TVA—as befitted the most precisely framed experiment of the New Deal. This concept was in line both with Roosevelt's planning instinct and with his partiality for taking advantage of America's unique federal system by using states as legislative and policy laboratories. Thus, like Norris, he had to endure frustration when the Hoover administration blocked his dream for the St. Lawrence River as an encroachment on private initiative.

As Roosevelt's election to the presidency neared, his campaign stressed the potential for regional development under government auspices. In the fall of 1932 he spoke in Portland, Oregon, not far from the great Columbia River, about electricity as a fundament of modern life. The public need, he asserted, would act as an "essential 'birch rod' in the cupboard" to spur private development and prod government to "transmit and distribute where reasonable and good service is refused by private capital."

To announce one of the few commitments he was willing to make during the interregnum, Roosevelt went with a tearfully overjoyed Norris to Muscle Shoals on New Year's Day 1933, where he reiterated the general principle he advanced during the campaign of government as the supplier of last resort as an endorsement of Norris's dream. The ownership of the area, Roosevelt went on to say in a message to Congress in April 1933, "leads logically to national planning for a complete river watershed involving many States and the future lives and welfare of millions. It touches and gives life to all forms of human concern." In conclusion Roosevelt asked Congress to support development of the Tennessee Valley and was rewarded in May by the Tennessee Valley Authority Act granting broad executive powers to develop power and irrigate.

The TVA provided a stage for the interplay of concepts as well as strategies. Chairman Arthur Morgan brought to the task an inclination toward utopian planning, inspired by his youthful reading of *Looking Backward* (1888), the classic novel by Edward Bellamy about an engineered utopia in late twentieth-century America. As an engineer and then president of Antioch College, which was dedicated to the principle of integrating academic study with productive labor, Morgan was able to pursue the fusion in Bellamy's communal vision between technological progress and revolutionary consciousness. Once people are educated to see how knowledge properly fits with a high standard of life, they would simply withdraw from a system that makes a few rich while despoiling the landscape and condemning the majority to misery and immorality. Loyal to that belief in peaceful transformation through right-thinking consensus, Morgan set out a code of ethics for TVA personnel stressing the "general and enduring" interest over special and temporary interests, modest incomes that would eliminate class differences, moral uprightness in the high Victorian sense, and an overall commitment "to the project of helping build a new social and economic order." Guided by those precepts, Morgan built the model town of Norris at Muscle Shoals as a pure example of the good community, complete with the eradication of alcohol, tobacco, and other vices.

That utopian consensus did not prevail, however. After a bitter fight, Morgan was replaced as chairman by David Lilienthal, a lawyer with impressive credentials and connections. Lilienthal had been a protégé of Felix Frankfurter at the Harvard Law School and afterward distinguished himself by assisting in the prosecution of Insull and then as a member of the Wisconsin Public Service Commission under leading progressive governor Philip La Follette. Lilienthal, in line with Populist-Progressive belief in public control of resources and utilities, favored developing the Tennessee Valley as a test case of planning along the experimental, yard-stick lines favored by Roosevelt. His individual style of management, in contrast to Morgan's ideal of selfless consensus, was summed up in the credo he announced as a young lawyer in Chicago: "Our government is and must be a government of *men* and not of laws." That conviction developed into the skepticism he showed on the TVA board about any plans that threatened to subordinate people to abstractions—as Lilienthal thought Arthur Morgan's utopianism often did.

Lilienthal's individualism was not Napoleonic, as Morgan later charged. Instead, Lilienthal spoke out for decentralization, for small "grass roots" units of decision, where the special characteristics and experiences of particular persons and cultures could prevail. Lilienthal had "no confidence in progress that comes from plans concocted by supermen and imposed upon the rest of the community for its own good." The crux of effective management—technical, political, and social—was to learn what the people want, rather than what the experts prescribe, and to induce productive activity by explaining to laymen the "why" as well as the "what." The decentralizing tendency, however, Lilienthal warned, must not allow government to become fragmented in the face of big business. Lilienthal believed that business was a self-aggrandizing force that needed to be faced down by even stronger representative government. The success, therefore, of TVA and any other New Deal effort to stimulate the economy meant that "future responsibility will have to be assumed by the central government to deal with national issues which centralized business inevitably creates." In short the success of decentralization ironically created a need for greater centralized authority. Lilienthal's ideal commonwealth turned out to be less a cooperative entity than a careful balance of power in the ultimate interests of what the "grass roots" folk had been able to convey to an attentive national power center.

To the oft-repeated insistence of the power companies that there was already an excess of generating capacity, Lilienthal charged that the market had been deliberately constricted by power companies interested in preserving their monopolies. The electric age, Lilienthal proclaimed, had hardly reached the threshold of its potential. For all the highly touted increases in power production and technology, the wonders of electricity barely penetrated beyond city lines. During the twenties the Great White Way in New York City symbolized the correspondence of human happiness and the electrification of about three quarters of nonfarm residences. But the prices of power and appliances were high, and almost all farms remained without electricity—a demonstration that the relatively high costs of running transmission lines into the countryside made bringing rural America into the electric age hardly seem worthwhile to private power companies. Lilienthal concluded it would take a broad commitment to the general good of the sort that only national government can orchestrate to create the market for all the uses of electricity that progress could absorb. Accordingly, Lilienthal led the way in setting up the Electric Home and Farm Authority, which granted low-interest loans for the manufacture and purchase of appliances. The electric cornucopia Lilienthal thus stimulated—with many vibrant words, as well as deeds—took its place near the center of the New Deal's characteristic definition of recovery in the form of an abundance of things: of housing, most prominently, along with stoves, refrigerators, radios, and other such electrified milestones in the pursuit of happiness.

Lilienthal's primary concern for efficient prosperity in the Tennessee Valley region brought his advocacy of grassroots democracy into a managerial paradox, compounded by the paradoxical recommendation of expanding federal authority in the service of decentralization. The pattern developed in a standard way: First, a local jurisdiction of the Authority's regions would apply for TVA power. This appeal would follow democratic methods of gaining citizen support and then would develop the grassroots principle by the formation of cooperative and municipal distribution systems. But once the transmission facilities were in place, the need for local participation fell away and the local agencies of the TVA became about as autocratic in managing their affairs as the boards of any private company. What remained was the *aura* of grassroots participation, born of the original impetus for the local systems and sustained by the spirit of innovative uniqueness. One is left to ponder how influential this aura has been, especially in terms of the conviction it encourages that the formation of any local power base should be done only at the behest of the citizenry to be affected. Against this ethic stands the far commoner argument that the drives within modern business toward efficiency, growth, and managerial control meant that centralization was virtually predetermined. The gloomy Austrian refugee economist Joseph Schumpeter was the most forceful defender of the view that state socialism would eventually prevail. But trends more fully bore out the analysis of the leading authority on corporate structure and history, Alfred Chandler, who in *Strategy and Structure* (1962) and *The Visible Hand* (1977) described how oligarchies highly resistant to local and political pressures were the logical outcome of the tumult of the American economy. Still, the progressive hope of fitting business into a democratic framework persisted, and the publicists surrounding Lilienthal were right in declaring the importance of TVA as an idea—even as it stands in retrospect as a symbol of the early aims and growing self-confidence of the New Deal.

These defining struggles over resources and community values signaled the New Deal's main focus on the Depression as an opportunity to recast domestic policy in a planned, cooperative mode, away from the dangers of international entanglements and the isolating abstractions of conventional economic theory. The failure of the loftier hopes for a managed economy and utopia in the Tennessee Valley did not so much dampen enthusiasm for communal reform as indicate that successful planning could not be isolated in any particular region or industry but required that the entire economy be subject to planning designed to bring all interests into a just and efficient balance.

Alongside the TVA experiment, the New Deal instituted a plan to revive business that would become the ultimate test of the ideal of security and prosperity through cooperative planning. The onset of such deliberate action raised the old debate between the New Freedom and the New Nationalism: Should the system be saved by breaking up the ailing giants into smaller units, presumably easier to regulate by modest-sized governmental agencies operating on a regional basis? Or would the best remedy be to determine the size of planned enterprises according to what would be most efficient?

These issues of planning roused many ideas from private and public sector alike. Once again, the innovative electric power industry was at the center of the ferment. Of all the plans presented, the most influential came from Gerard Swope, the remarkably successful president of General Electric. Swope was the son of prosperous German Jewish immigrants and had seen both sides of the economic divide by working in the social settlement movement while rising to industrial eminence. Alongside such other socially conscious businessmen as his corporate counsel at GE, Owen Young, and department store owner Edward Filene, Swope promoted a vision of American life in which efficiency and a wide dispersal of corporate stock would produce both general prosperity and a sense of partnership in the nation's welfare. This conception promoted councils comprised of all elements of business—workers and managers alike—to make industry more productive and its workers more secure, in part through the chance to have their views heard. The urgency Swope felt to do something about the ominous state of business built up through frustrating inability in two meetings with Hoover to convince the president of the need to counter unemployment with public works programs. Swope had already made a reputation for the way he had kept GE workers off the Schenectady welfare rolls by providing them with contributory unemployment insurance. Yet, unlike Hoover, Swope realized that the economic situation was too severe for business to handle alone. Unable to keep thoughts of the deepening woes off his mind even temporarily, Swope conceived of his plan on the annual vacation he and his wife took in January 1931. A bundle of nervous energy in the best of circumstances, he began to organize his thoughts as he cruised through the Panama Canal and eventually made them public in a speech to the National Electric Manufacturers Association in September.

The plan centered on two major provisions, both drawn from GE's worker benefit plan: first, all industries and commercial businesses should be allowed to join trade associations under the direction of the Federal Trade Commission;

second, a national workmen's compensation law should be passed, based on the best state laws in force, to provide life, disability, and unemployment insurance and pensions for retired workers. Immediately, the national Chamber of Commerce and Hoover's rival in the presidential campaign, Franklin Roosevelt, endorsed the plan. Both expressed an anxious desire to rescue a crumbling economic order and its victims. For the Chamber of Commerce, there was also the alluring possibility that the Swope plan for trade associations with the authority to set uniform standards might mean that the campaign business had waged since World War I to relax antitrust laws would finally be won.

Hoover, who held fast to his belief in free enterprise competition, kept a public silence, but in private he denounced the plan as "the most gigantic proposal of monopoly ever made in history"—a vivid expression of Hoover's fear that tightly coordinated enterprise under government authority would lead to fascism.

Roosevelt and his advisers, however, were inclined to see such an appeal to joint planning for the national benefit as a welcome revival of the great mobilization effort of World War I, this time to generate a peacetime cooperative commonwealth rather than a war machine. In that spirit they enlisted many who might contribute to victory. Just three weeks after setting up the Temporary Emergency Relief Administration (TERA), Governor Roosevelt summoned Swope to Albany to help design a plan that would gain the support of Swope's business colleagues. For wisdom on regulation to make the economy more efficient and public works to rescue the unemployed, he looked to Bernard Baruch, who had headed Wilson's War Industries Board, and Senator Robert Wagner of New York, a champion of the working man who suggested codes that would give workers shorter hours, minimum wage protection, and collective bargaining to determine working conditions. Soon after the Brains Trust was formed in 1932, Rexford Tugwell added an appeal for comprehensive planning that would subordinate the antitrust relief business wanted to a design that would balance all major interests—business, labor, and consumer. In that way, Tugwell maintained, recovery would come through efficiently increased productivity and the purchasing power to absorb the increase.

The National Industrial Recovery Act (NIRA) that became law in June 1933 on the basis of enthusiasm for planning a cooperative way out of the Depression contained three separate titles. Title I set out the high purpose of the NIRA to establish federally supervised codes that would "eliminate unfair competitive practices" through the "united action of labor and management." Title II provided $3.3 billion for public works that would engage the unemployed in projects that served the cause of conservation and the development of natural resources.

Under the determined leadership of Harold Ickes, a progressive Republican from Illinois, the Public Works Administration (PWA) that resulted established the New Deal as the vastest promoter of relief efforts in American history. During his tenure as public works czar, Ickes spent more than $4.25 billion on 34,000 projects that displayed his preference for monumental, permanently useful landmarks. Title III provided the National Recovery Administration (NRA) the power to amend its authority and, by transferring to it a significant share of the funding and power of the RFC, demonstrated the New Deal administration's intent to make the NRA its primary agent of economic reconstruction. The excitement these developments aroused among the reformers just emerging from the shadow of the conservative, laissez-faire 1920s into the light of possibilities for social planning was captured early by the leading progressive historians, Charles and Mary Beard. As soon as the Swope plan was announced, they pointed out buoyantly that this first salvo in the drive to reengineer society, which would culminate in the NIRA, "had shaken the pillars of respectability for the season and thrown a burning brand of thought into the very center of complacency."

To head the NRA Roosevelt found a very brightly burning brand, General Hugh Johnson, who as a member of the War Industries Board had impressed Roosevelt during World War I with his forcefulness and ability to write persuasively. Johnson's Democratic connections helped, too. After campaigning for Al Smith in 1928, Johnson was hired by his former WIB boss, Bernard Baruch, to help run Baruch's far-flung financial and consulting ventures. In that strategic post, amid deepening Depression, Johnson helped Baruch devise policy advice for the New Deal.

The old general's hard-drinking volatility roused serious misgivings. Baruch cautioned Roosevelt that Johnson would make a fine second in command but did not have the stability to be in charge. Once he took over, Johnson's bellow and bluster alarmed some observers who saw him as a kind of frontier Mussolini. Yet, as Roosevelt hoped, Johnson's vigor was an important advertisement for the New Deal's effort to restore the nation's confidence and fighting spirit. Indeed, Johnson's life expressed the pioneer epic. He grew up in the Cherokee strip of Oklahoma, where he soon got used to hardship and the taints of violence. A tough campaigner who was part of the cavalry pursuit of Mexican rebel raider Pancho Villa just before World War I, Johnson found time while carrying out his army duties to write boys' adventure stories and gain a law degree. War service knit these experiences together into a firm outlook on public policy. In 1918 Johnson declared from his vantage on the WIB that "efficiency is attainable by cooperation." In 1930, at a reunion of old WIB executives, just when realization of the Crash was fully registering, Johnson, reflecting both his military and business background, insisted that the antitrust laws needed an overhaul so as to replace "uneconomical competition" with efficient self-government under the supervision of what he termed the High Court of Commerce.

By the time he arrived at the Democratic convention in Chicago that nominated Roosevelt, Johnson in his bumptious way had distilled his fervent thoughts on public duty into a mock manifesto, signed by "Muscleinny, Dictator pro tem." Within the satire was an earnest plan for coordinated economic recovery that served as the core of Johnson's ferocious devotion to the NRA cause. His "Muscleinny" program reflected the moderate center of the Democratic Party. It called for increasing farm income by paying farmers not to plant on some of their land, suspension of the gold standard to facilitate trade and debt payments, higher income taxes on upper brackets to balance the budget, and a shortened work week to spread employment to the jobless. Closer to the business and financial elements within the Democratic Party than to the reformers, Johnson nonetheless was aligned with Roosevelt in seeking a balance of New Nationalist planning and New Freedom free enterprise—envisioning them enmeshed by the general public's cooperation. In that sense he was in agreement with Swope's desire to release business from the restrictions of the Sherman Antitrust Act and called on Swope to help write the final NIRA draft emphasizing the benefits of industry planning. The private sector and government, relying on common interest, would arrive at a consensus, which would then be mobilized under government auspices. As the new administration was getting underway, Johnson proclaimed that the patriotic fervor necessary to get voluntary cooperation was in place: "Almost every individual has either suffered terribly, or knows of friends and relatives who have; so there is waiting here to be appealed to what I regard as the most fertile psychology that you could imagine. "

Organized labor also found a significant place within the code-making process. Section 7, reflecting union support of NRA and its promise of a "new order" of managed prosperity, required that every code must specify maximum hours, minimum wages, and a ban on child labor. A guarantee that those negotiating for workers would be truly representative was included in the endorsement of the right of collective bargaining found in Section 7(a). Its provisions, giving workers novel support from government, helped to realize the New Deal goal of "balance" ensuring that all the elements of an industrial "concert of interests" might have an effective voice in deciding their fates. That approach fitted the longstanding inclination of Roosevelt and Secretary of Labor Frances Perkins to seek accommodation rather than battles of opposed interests. Within that ameliorative framework they both had long supported unions. During World War I Roosevelt stood up for the rights of the workers within his Navy Department jurisdiction to organize, provided they did so in a spirit of cooperation with the war effort. Even earlier, in 1913, he had set out that position to the International Association of Machinists: "We want cooperation. We want to get down and talk across the table with you and to right your wrongs. . . . If I had my way we would create a board composed of the heads of departments and some of the men and would send them to Europe to look into shop conditions there, with the idea of benefiting men here."

Perkins had a similarly benevolent approach, drawn from her many years as a social worker and reformer. She had battled for improved conditions of health and safety and had laid the groundwork for much of the welfare legislation Al Smith's administration enacted. Perkins's reform stature was secure—but it was as a champion of downtrodden persons, not as a partisan of unions or other special interests.

The progressive experience and cooperative ideal common to Roosevelt and Perkins were not enough to guarantee success. As ever, there was the problem of gaining voluntary agreement from businesses to act for the general welfare rather than in the traditional ways of self-interest. Another basic difficulty was the matter of scale. The act was given a two-year trial period by Congress to make complex arrangements for hundreds of different industries. At the end of the decade, Mordecai Ezekiel, one of the most accomplished New Deal planners, declared with some justification that it would ideally have taken about ten years of preparation before the NRA administrators were in a good position to begin implementing the act. Even that long estimate may have been conservative. Exhortations by New Dealers for businessmen to take the ethical high road to recovery by cooperating in a grand moral revolution to democratize industry at first resulted in earnest efforts by businesses to make the NRA work. But insoluble problems leading to backsliding soon emerged. The long-recognized problem of the "race to the bottom" began to play a role: when some businesses gained an advantage by not abiding by the codes, their rivals were faced with the choice of following suit or else failing to compete. Thus cheating tended to snowball. The other side of the coin was that strict enforcement of the rules was not a viable option for the New Deal administrators. If it were taken too far, overly aggressive compliance would cost the NRA the will of business to cooperate, an ethos on which the NRA very much relied. Establishing codes, then, that were well designed and used fairly for recovery remained crucially beyond the grasp of the NRA planners.

In the labor sector, a comparably knotty dilemma balked the implementation of employee rights supposedly guaranteed by the NRA. Section 7(a) declared that employees should have "the right to organize and bargain collectively through representatives of their own choosing." But what actions were to be sanctioned as undertaken by the workers' "own choosing"? Did the act endorse the union shop concept, in which a majority vote would obligate the minority to join the union? Or should each worker have the right to choose his or her own bargaining agent? Industrialists, even liberals like Gerard Swope, favored "proportional representation," which would allow company unions to exist alongside independent unions. Roosevelt and Perkins were also inclined toward proportional arrangements, in accord with the inclusive character of the cooperation they favored. Organized labor, on the other hand, favored workplaces limited to union members, realizing from past battles that worker solidarity was necessary to counter the unified structure of corporations. In approaching this disagreement, the National Labor Board, created by Johnson in August to mediate labor disputes, was handicapped by the ambiguities of the wording on labor organizing and by the lack of definite sanctions it could attach to its rulings. Soon after the NLB was created, Johnson declared that no references to union or nonunion status were to appear in any NRA directives. Roosevelt airily justified Johnson's determination to keep both corporate and labor union coercion at bay as a simple matter of free choice: workers could swear allegiance to any bargaining agent—to the "Ahkoond of Swat" or the "Royal Geographic Society," if they wished. But that blithe answer, however useful in deflecting questions of government regimentation, left the NLB in a quandary as to the proper way to achieve labor and management cooperation at a point somewhere between what each side most wanted. The NLB and the NRA planners endorsed the "Reading Formula" hammered out in the Reading, Pennsylvania, hosiery strike that called for a majority vote by workers to decide what single union would represent them. Many employers, however, would not give up their attempts to weaken union opposition by allowing employees in a single workplace to be represented by several different organizations, including company unions.

In the course of trying to overcome evasion and union issues, Johnson and his aides, many of them fellow WIB veterans, ran themselves ragged. Johnson organized parades and rallies and spread the emblem of compliance, a blue eagle, throughout the countryside for display on shop windows. In the end, 775 codes were approved, but the problem of cooperation between government and private enterprise was not solved. Businessmen, especially through the administration's own Business Advisory and Planning Council, greatly influenced the

code-making in the direction of vested interests. What emerged was an ill-coor-
dinated aggregate of protective arrangements and massive confusion. Although
the economic indexes rose and unemployment declined during the period of the
NRA's existence, precious few codes achieved their intended effect of creating equitably shared prosperity. Despite talk of the mutually reinforcing concerns of all
segments of society, for example, only slightly more than 100 of the code authorities had consumer or labor representatives to temper the promotion of business
interests and the general resistance of business to governmental planning.

The NRA hastened its own demise when it hired the famed lawyer for the underdog, Clarence Darrow, to study the relationship of the NRA to consumers. In
his usual flamboyant style Darrow reported that consumers were being victimized by the drift of NRA practices toward monopoly. These revelations, fired by
Darrow's old-fashioned moral preference for small business, helped force Johnson out in the summer of 1934. The NRA was then run by a five-man National
Industrial Recovery Board, representing the major factions of business, labor,
and consumers. Although it attained greater representative breadth, the Board
could not duplicate Johnson's galvanic attempt to secure common purpose and
move forward. The ideal of full cooperation was abandoned in favor of trying to
keep a patchwork compromise afloat without too many complaints.

Under those circumstances, the final blow against NRA came as a kind of
euthanasia. It occurred when the four Schechter brothers who ran a family poultry business in Brooklyn succeeded in persuading the Supreme Court that the
NRA was an unwarranted invasion of commercial rights. The decision, handed
down on May 27, 1935, less than two weeks after the Senate agreed to extend the
life of NRA for another two years, greatly restricted federal reform. Chief Justice
Charles Evan Hughes declared for a unanimous Court that "extraordinary conditions do not create or enlarge constitutional power." Thus, the code authority
lacked precedent and was "an unconstitutional delegation of legislative power."
Setting strict constructionist boundaries, the Court ruled that Congress could
not confer discretionary powers on the president but only those spelled out by
definite legislative guidelines. Further, the decision specified that federal powers
under the commerce clause of the Constitution extended only to undertakings
that have a direct effect on interstate commerce. All other enterprises, such as
processing poultry in Brooklyn, were deemed immune even though they might
be part of a national economic whole.

Because one of the government's complaints with the Schechters was that
they dealt in diseased meat, wags were able to describe the NRA case as the
triumph of a "sick chicken" over the Blue Eagle. In the midst of such derision,

the NRA ground to a halt, leaving behind a legacy of doubt about planning. Unless the New Deal could find a way to reverse the Court's position, it could only hope to influence industrial recovery by such indirect means as public works, taxes, and regulation of the money supply and interest rates. This weakened the administration's grip on industry at just the time when a brightening economic climate gave business renewed confidence in the old free enterprise case against attempts of the state to "regiment" capitalism.

Even the use of Hoover's Reconstruction Finance Corporation, headed by an orthodox pillar of the Houston, Texas, business community, Jesse Jones, to aid in the formation of investment capital through quite conventional loans and advice ran into reflexive aversion to government involvement. Typical was the president of the Manufacturers Trust Company of New York, whose horror of being seen in a government office was so great that, despite the firm's desperate condition, he would only agree to a secret meeting with Jones in a hotel room.

As the awkward standoff between the New Deal and business interests unfolded and the NRA approached its inglorious end, the economy rose out of the depths. From its low point in July 1932 production rose to 57 percent of its pre-Crash 1929 level by 1935. To some extent this was a natural recovery, in keeping with previous boom-bust-boom cycles. Doubtless, also, the stabilization of the financial system, which had seen investment drop by 87 percent between the Crash and the onset of the New Deal, had been helpful, as had the creation of unemployment relief, the investment of state capital in support of farm prices, and the development of natural resources through the TVA and other conservation projects. In the absence of a consensus on cause and effect, those on the scene tended toward opposing poles with increasing antagonism as confidence was renewed.

In 1934 a group of economic conservatives formed the Liberty League to reinvigorate free enterprise principles and serve as the focal point for anti–New Deal propaganda. Into its membership flocked businessmen embittered by their loss of power and prestige, political opponents of Roosevelt (including even his erstwhile ally, Al Smith), old progressives who saw in New Deal collectivism the undermining of individual conscience as the basis for reform, and those further to the right who decried the administration as inspired by socialism or even communism. Although Herbert Hoover did not join the Liberty League, partly because it harbored former Democratic rivals, he contributed to the anti-statist mood by publishing a collection of his speeches against the New Deal, pointedly titled *The Challenge to Liberty* (1934).

For New Dealers the question was whether the rising economic tide meant that the basic problems of the Depression had been addressed and that emergency measures could be phased out or whether success endorsed the New Deal efforts to transform the system and should be used as a basis for pressing on toward a fully realized cooperative commonwealth in which all shared a decent standard of living, just working conditions, conservation of resources, aesthetic fulfillment, educational attainment, and the full rights of citizenship. This debate and the polarization of society within which it proceeded was most vehemently acted out in the struggle of organized labor to break from its feudal past and lay claim to the democratic equality that the New Deal and more radical champions on the left proposed as the proper outcome of the Depression and a just response to the oppressive business class that caused it.

In the effort at industrial recovery the New Deal found itself drawn away from preoccupation with producer and consumer issues of price and purchasing power and toward the troubles of those in the fields and factories. That shift fitted easily within Roosevelt's original vision of a cooperative commonwealth in which farmers would remain on their land and jobless city dwellers would either find their way back to farming or else be absorbed by a revived industrial sector. Yet the painful clashes that marked the consequent working out of labor's fate belied Roosevelt's hopes of attaining harmony through the integration of related interests.

As the NIRA was being devised with such planned mutuality in mind, efforts to alleviate labor's troubles concentrated on reviving interest in two approaches that had been tried before. During World War I, always a key point of reference for crisis management, the federal government had established the United States Employment Service (USES) to find workers quickly to aid the war effort. Allowed to wither during the 1920s, USES was revived in 1933 under the auspices of labor's perennial champion, Senator Robert Wagner of New York, in the Wagner-Peyser bill. Through a coordinated network of state offices, USES proved helpful in tracking down those eligible for relief and then moving them on to employment opportunities. The main problem, however, was not to find jobs but to produce enough of them to go around and to ensure that working conditions were fair and decent. Predictably, conservatives advised that the free marketplace would eventually provide optimal results. Organized labor, led by United Mine Workers president John L. Lewis, countered with suggestions for a government program of price and wage supports of the sort he had long sought for the chronically depressed coal fields. At the center of the debate was the puzzle that also beset agriculture of how to strike a balance among employment, production, and consumption.

Labor's major component, the American Federation of Labor (AFL), drew upon a traditional skilled craft view of progress by arguing that unemployment was to a great extent the result of technological advances that had increased the productivity of some workers and replaced others with machinery. Rather than being punished for their achievement by being laid off, which made the loss of their livelihood profitable for owners, greater productivity should entitle workers to earn the same pay for proportionally shorter hours. Moving beyond Calvin Coolidge's fatalistic truism that when there aren't enough jobs, unemployment results, the AFL contended that the proper balance between production and consumption would occur when hours of work were shortened enough to absorb the jobless. Accordingly, the AFL endorsed the bill introduced by Senator Hugo Black of Alabama in December 1932 to limit the work week to thirty hours.

The Black Bill, passed when the New Deal planners were in the midst of putting together the NIRA, posed a challenge of how to deal with a proposal that promised short-term benefits at the expense of a good long-term solution. Roosevelt and Secretary of Labor Perkins, along with the reformers advising them, believed that the real answer to labor's woes was to expand the nation's ability to consume what a fully employed workforce could produce. An abnormally short work week would slow recovery by adding greatly to production expenses; that, in turn, would raise prices and so make it harder for the general public to buy what it needed. Further provoking resistance by the administration was the lack of minimum wage protection in the Black Bill, excluded at the insistence of the AFL because of its long-held fears that a required minimum wage would soon become the standard wage.

With Roosevelt insisting on swift action to head off the Black Bill threat, the NIRA drafters came up with several ways to appeal to labor. Section 7(a) was of prime importance. In addition, a catch-all code called the President's Reemployment Agreement required those who signed on to forswear hiring children under the age of sixteen and agree to weekly white-collar wages of at least $12 and blue-collar wages of 40¢ an hour for a thirty-five hour week. The enticements drew support away from the Black Bill, and organized labor's praise of the outcome seemed justified by the 50 percent increase in production and the reemployment of 2,500,000 workers in the ensuing three months. Union growth under 7(a) also boomed, especially for the nation's hardest-pressed workers. The United Mine Workers union, for example, increased its membership fivefold, and both the United Textile Workers and the Amalgamated Clothing Workers did almost as well. Organization proceeded so rapidly within automobile, steel, rubber, aluminum, and other mass production industries that the buried dream of the defunct Knights of Labor and Industrial Workers of the World (IWW) to unionize unskilled as well as skilled workers gained new credibility. John L. Lewis, the long-embattled head of the United Mine Workers (UMW) who had helped write the 7(a) labor proviso, was effusive in his praise of the NRA's new deal for labor. That historic legislation, he declared in the *United Mine Workers Journal,* "has given labor the greatest opportunity it has ever had to work out its own destiny." Labor's new lease on life, Lewis insisted on another occasion, represented the "greatest single advance for human rights in the United States since Abraham Lincoln's Emancipation Proclamation."

Lewis's euphoria spread among the most neglected and least organized workers, who seized upon 7(a) as the way out of their exploited misery. On their own the rank and file in numerous mass production industries created unions and engaged in 2000 work stoppages affecting more than 5 million workers by the end of 1934. Success most jubilantly bloomed in the rubber factories of Akron, where a sevenfold increase in unionized workers led to markedly improved working conditions. In her firsthand report, *Industrial Valley,* Ruth McKenney marveled at how these long downtrodden rubber workers now "believed, blindly, passionately, fiercely, that the union would cure all their troubles . . . make them rich with wages." The first weeks of their uprising seemed to her "something like a cross between a big picnic and a religious revival."

As the year wore on, however, and New Deal measures seemed to be saving the country from chaos, employers became less fearfully inclined to go along with these concessions to labor. Practice drawing up codes and a growing awareness of the ineptness of the NRA's Labor Advisory Board in preventing, or even recognizing, violations of labor rights, emboldened many employers to reimpose the old feudal conditions that had prevailed before the Crash: long hours, no minimum wage, and company unions or no union at all. By mid-decade less than a third of American industry had independent unions; NRA administrators tacitly endorsed the situation by recognizing company unions as bargaining agents, even in certain cases when competing independent unions in the same industry had more members.

Difficulties were intensified by growing apprehension in the South that economic and labor reform would disturb race relations. By trying to enact codes that would give workers higher wages, the NRA ran into criticism that it was the "Negro Relief Association," bent on raising the cost of picking cotton and harvesting crops. Likewise, union formation posed the threat for alarmed southerners of breaking the historic pattern that kept blacks unorganized and subservient. Resisting the provocative assertion of Clark Foreman, a Georgia liberal appointed by Harold Ickes as "Special Advisor on the Economic Status of Negroes," that Section 7 of the NIRA was "a second emancipation proclamation for southern workers," the Southern States Industrial Council and allied politicians kept the NRA from doing much to challenge the segregated, anti-union climate of the South.

The regressive situation soon drew complaints from unionists and we-told-you-so reiteration from the left of its original criticism that the NRA was a form of fascism designed to regiment the working class for the benefit of nationalized monopolies. Alongside the turn against the NRA, a militant spirit of confrontation arose. The response of the NLB to these warning tremors showed the NRA's lack of enforcement power. Although the provisions of Section 7(a) giving workers the right to have collective bargaining agents of their own choice and not to be forced to join a company union were definite enough so that unions won about 75 percent of the election disputes handled by the NLB, very little clout went with the power to judge. By June 1934 only four Blue Eagles had been removed from recalcitrant employers; on the eve of the Supreme Court decision knocking the NRA out of commission, compliance with the board's rulings against industry was only obtained in 34 of 86 cases. Because the Justice Department demanded that NLB complaints against business firms be complete in all legal details, despite the board's lack of power to compel the appearance of witnesses and documents, only one case out of the 33 presented to Justice for action had actually been tried in court.

Relations between the New Deal and unions were further complicated by Hugh Johnson's hard-driving insistence on getting results from the NRA, especially when he declared his willingness to accept equitable labor codes even if they had not been created through collective bargaining. Pressure from organized labor and the presidential Labor Advisory Board caused Johnson to ease his position, but he could never gain the confidence of labor thereafter.

The failure of the NRA to bring industry and labor into harmony lent weight to the determination of labor to take matters into its own hands. By the summer of 1934 the International Longshoreman's Union had gained enough strength in the West to stage a strike that shut down the port of San Francisco, thus touching off a major crisis for coast cities and their vast inland supply network. A few weeks earlier, workers in the Autolite plant in Toledo and in an array of teamster industries in Minneapolis launched strikes that, given the central role of the enterprises affected, constituted virtual class war against the capital interests of those cities.

The strife surged with radical energy. On the wings of victory in San Francisco, Australian-born radical Harry Bridges, director of west coast longshoremen's locals, brought maritime and warehouse workers together into a powerful

Maritime Federation of the Pacific and aimed beyond that to forge alliances with industrial transport workers that would exert control over much of the flow of commerce in the West. Midwestern insurgents added Marxism to an explosive mix of ethnic differences and populist suspicion of wealthy elites. To help guide the movement, the American Workers Party entered the fray in 1933. The party's emissary to Toledo, A. J. Muste, had been a leader at Brookwood Labor College just outside New York City, where the AFL since 1921 had educated workers about their history and social role. Under the goad of the Depression, Muste had concluded that the true common concern was the class solidarity Marx had preached and that the time had come to lead a contingent out of the Brookwood retreat into the vanguard of a new radical age.

Muste's class war idea found ripe occasion in Toledo. When a coalition of AFL unionists and Muste's Unemployed League on May 24 jammed the sparkplug factory gates in defiance of the armed guards and deputies who flourished an injunction against more than twenty-five picketers, the notorious "Battle of Toledo" erupted. A fusillade of bricks through the barricaded factory windows preceded a melee inside, as workers breached the walls for hand-to-hand combat. Tear gas shrouded the area until the next morning when National Guard infantry lifted the siege. In the gray aftermath, company and workers hastened to sign an agreement that would prevent another outburst. Yet the battle-hardened strikers retained their militancy; the agreement of June 4 began with the radical declaration that "a struggle is going on in all nations of the civilized world between the oppressors and the oppressed." To rise from degradation oppressed people must strive to meet on common ground.

The uprisings in Minneapolis and St. Paul carried the radical wave to its highest and broadest stage. Once imperial gateway to the northwest, the Twin Cities had fallen on even harder times than most other cities during the Depression. Their role as transportation hub for the West had been eroded by the Panama Canal, lumbering had departed for the far northwest, and the principal iron ore industry connection was beset from both sides—the Mesabi range mines were locked into one of the most militant labor struggles of the era, and the demand for steel had drastically declined. The city was also ringed by farmers facing ruin who reacted bitterly, sometimes violently, against the bankers and suppliers whom they held responsible for their plight.

Within the beleaguered city, longstanding ethnic and class divisions came to a head. The stature of the WASP elite sagged when Wilbur Foshay, utility magnate and leading citizen, was sent to the federal penitentiary in 1929, leaving in the trail of his bankrupt frauds both unemployment and a widespread convic-

tion that the old regime had to go. The next year Floyd Bjornstjerne Olson carried the banner of the poor Scandinavians and Irish into the governorship, vow-
ing with exceptional eloquence in English, Norwegian, Swedish, and Yiddish to
make whatever radical changes were necessary to end a bleak period for Minneapolis as one of America's most violent and despairing cities. As Olson worked to
create the Farmer-Labor Association to unite the dispossessed, union forces prepared for a showdown under the remarkably able and disciplined leadership of
a group of anti-Stalinist Marxists. Earnest and amiable Swedish immigrant Karl
Skoglund and the three Dunne brothers, Vincent, Miles, and Grant—representing the other major ethnic enclave, Irish Catholics—organized Teamsters Local
#57 into the spearhead for a citywide movement and surrounded themselves
with a legion of hard-bitten shock troops from the outside, including members
of the Stalinist Trade Union Unity League (TUUL). With orchestrated precision
thousands of strikers blocked the major roads and prepared for counterattack
from a "Citizen's Army" of vigilantes designated "special deputies" by the city for
the occasion. As the rival forces surged toward the public market for a decisive
struggle, crowds of onlookers rolled along with them, and an enterprising radio
station prepared for a play-by-play account as though the Little Brown Jug was
at stake. When the workers routed police and the Citizen's Army, fears mounted
among the respectable that a midwest version of the Paris Commune was about
to engulf the city. Instead, as had happened in Toledo, the aftermath of battle
brought the sober combatants to agree to a truce on May 25.

   This time, however, divisions were too deep for the agreement to hold. Employers refused to relinquish their long opposition to unions. On the other side,
assurance of a food supply by alliances with growers and the encouragement of
the top Communist League strategists, who had moved into Minneapolis for the
duration, gave the unionists a sense of strength. So the contest reopened in July
on a larger scale. After a convoy of police fired shotguns into a crowd of strikers
trying to block passage of a truck, enraged militants headed for city hall threatening to lynch Mayor Bainbridge and Police Chief Johannes. Only action by Olson
calling in the militia stayed the crowd—but the troops also opened the way for
owners to dispatch enough truckers to endanger the strike. After a tongue-lash-
ing by union leaders, Olson cracked down on the trucks permitted to move and,
under further goading from both sides and rising tensions, declared martial law.
A fortuitous visit by Roosevelt to the Mayo Clinic in nearby Rochester gave Olson a chance to confer with the chief executive and, as it turned out, gain some
jawboning support. His position held against an attempt of the Citizens' Alliance
to serve an injunction, and at that impasse employers in numerous concerns

signed union contracts. Minneapolis organizers stood triumphant at the head of radical labor insurgency.

But the most difficult terrain for labor still lay ahead. The arduousness of labor's challenge was most poignantly displayed by the fate of the largest strike staged up to the midpoint of the 1930s, which occurred in the long-troubled textile industry. Located mainly in staunchly conservative New England and southern towns, textile manufacture was in autocratic hands, reinforced by intense communal loyalties to clan and locality that tended to root workers and elites alike in their accustomed circumstances. Management was duly astonished when the United Textile Workers under Francis Gorman staged a protest walkout on Labor Day of 1934 in the Gastonia, North Carolina, region. Smoldering discontent in textile centers elsewhere broke out in a ground fire of violence while the government and officials on both sides groped for some semblance of control. Under the auspices of the NRA, Roosevelt convened a board of inquiry. Although New Hampshire Governor John Winant presided with a craggy, Lincolnesque integrity that gained great admiration, the textile manufacturers refused conciliation. The board could do little but note that recognition of the union was not feasible and that the NRA was limited to studying conditions and making recommendations. Having exhausted the resources available to him, Gorman had to ask union members to abandon their cause and return to mostly unchanged conditions. From that humiliation on, textile workers and the very word *Gastonia* stood as symbols of oppression for all those who would raise labor from the depths. And under the stigma of its failure to help the most helpless, the NRA sank even lower.

The crescendo of labor disputes and the failure of the NRA swung the New Deal toward firmer sympathy with organized labor's traditional strategy of adversarial bargaining. Senator Robert Wagner, the prime sponsor for the labor rights clause in the NIRA, introduced a bill on February 21, 1935, that would provide the teeth missing in the NRA. Rather than calling on industry to bargain in "good faith," Wagner's National Labor Relations Act established industry's duty to bargain; it conferred on the National Labor Relations Board the power to subpoena witnesses and documents and to enforce its decisions.

Although a massive lobbying campaign set in against a law that would revolutionize the balance of power between labor and management, the Wagner Act passed with surprising ease. The bill's proponents had refrained from consulting with Roosevelt, Perkins, or the NRA in order to avoid disapproval of an adversarial approach over a cooperative one. Yet in May, just three days before the Schechter brothers decision, Roosevelt showed that he could read the handwriting on the wall by announcing that the NLRA was "must" legislation. Later in July, when he signed the act, Roosevelt sought to salvage a measure of his cooperative ideal by announcing that "a better relationship between labor and management is the high purpose of this Act." But the crux of the bill was, as Roosevelt correctly put it, the right of "independent self-organization." Armed with that power, labor was prepared to develop into a large, autonomous special interest bloc. The New Deal retained great power through fiscal and monetary policy, jobs programs, industrial regulation, and the like to influence the situation of labor. But in the field of labor-management relations, the New Deal, despite its great public mandate in 1934, could only move to the sidelines with the downed Blue Eagle and await whatever chances might come its way to offer aid and comfort.

Before organized labor could mount its decisive campaign, however, it was necessary to settle some crucial issues of leadership and strategy. The great campaign of 1934 had opened painful breaches between the old AFL "labor barons" and the militant strikers, most of them in positions that did not meet the AFL standards of skilled labor. AFL President William Green was a paternal exemplar of orderly small-town virtues and a protector of traditional crafts occupations against what his cohort and chief representative to the New Deal from organized labor, Dan Tobin of the Teamsters, called the "rubbish" of industrial workers. Characteristically, Green would offer charters to the striking factions that would put them under his thumb. If the insurgents refused the charters, they would be cast adrift; if they chose the charters in order to gain AFL security, their ranks would be divided so that workers could be assigned to established craft unions. Weakened by the division of persons working together in regimented conformity, the militants were further deprived of strength when the AFL pronounced anathema on any groups that smacked of red revolution, like the American Workers Party and the TUUL. As a result, the hold of the AFL on the nearly 500,000 workers who had joined its ranks since Roosevelt took office was shaky. The trouble with the rubber workers, whose strike in Akron was one of the most heroic of the era, was instructive. After inducting some 40,000 rubber workers, the AFL leadership began its usual process of dividing them into crafts divisions and promptly lost all but 3,000 of the new members.

In this mood of tension and uncertainty, the AFL gathered in Atlantic City in October 1935 for its annual convention. Although the most militant of unionists were not present, AFL adherents carried banners for all of the contending positions short of Marxism. Especially at issue was the promise the AFL leadership had given under duress in 1934 to grant some federal charters to unskilled workers. But the old guard hung back. Imbued with belief in the superiority of skilled craftsmen and the value of aspiring to respectable middle-class status, AFL leaders were vulnerable to suggestions of taint by association with the proletarian mass of industrial workers. At the same time, the AFL chieftains harbored fear of the new unionists. John Frey of the Molders Union was especially provocative in discussing the menace of the industrial unions. The failure of earlier efforts at mass unions, Frey proclaimed, had been absolute: "There is only a tombstone now to mark the fact that they existed." From the Knights of Labor, with their benign vision of harmonious business and labor interests, to the Industrial Workers of the World, who postulated the absolute opposition of the interests of labor and owners and specialized in confrontation and sabotage, industrial unionism had been a disaster. The partial successes of the 1934 insurgency by mostly unskilled workers could only be cemented, in the AFL view, by organizing the various tasks of production line industries into their separate components of workmanship. The last argument had ambivalent implications. On the one hand it represented a concession to unskilled industrial workers: from wholesale neglect of this segment of labor, the AFL had moved to stating a policy for including them. On the other hand the policy restated the old restrictive craft-related position that the AFL had always insisted was unsuitable for industrial workers. Nothing had changed to make it more suitable.

AFL leadership made the prospect even dimmer by denouncing the leadership of the 1934 strikes for their left-wing associations. Anti-radicalism had been a special sideline for AFL leaders, who both in print and before congressional committees often appeared as proletarian character witnesses against international socialism and subversion at home, especially when it arose in the ranks of industrial unionists.

In his Atlantic City speech, Frey courted the fearful by invoking specters from both left and right:

> When the Bolsheviks gained control and formed the Soviet they destroyed . . . trade unions, they assassinated most of the officers, and in their place the government created twelve industrial unions. . . . When Mussolini gained control in Italy he destroyed all the free trade unions, and in their place organized three industrial unions to which every one must belong who worked for wages. And I submit to you . . . that the only thoroughly industrial unions in the world are the company unions or the type of organization forced upon the workmen in Russia, in Italy, and recently in Germany, by dictators brought into existence only after free institutions and free expression had been suppressed.

For the have-not workers themselves, however, radical agitators were not so easily demonized. Dedicated and tough, the leftists who appeared on the scene

of the 1934 upheavals were an invaluable help in lifting combat morale and preparing the practical details of battle. Denouncing Reds in the name of law and
order, private property, and the sanctity of democratic free choice seemed a dubious virtue to those beset with dire poverty and harsh working conditions.

When the AFL convened in Atlantic City, it included for the first time a significant number prepared to breach the party line. The group consisted of a coalition
of the most chronically hard-pressed unions and the most traditionally idealistic
and intellectual. The first contingent was led by United Mine Workers chief John
L. Lewis with significant support from able Communist and Socialist organizers
from mass production industries. On the more meliorative side were Charles P.
Howard of the typographical union and veteran Socialist leaders of the needle
trades, David Dubinsky and Sidney Hillman.

Lewis, a great shaggy-browed bear of a man with a booming voice and fists to
match, took command. A veteran of losing battles during the 1920s in the roughest
of anti-union territories, Lewis smoldered with rage at the comfortable leaders of
AFL trades. The elevation of carpenters, teamsters, tool and die makers, and similar groups of craftsmen into virtual partnership with management had, in Lewis's eyes, helped entrench the conservative laissez-faire views that had mesmer-
ized press, pulpit, courts, and legislatures and kept the mass of workers down.

Of primary concern to Lewis and his widely beloved lieutenant, Philip Murray,
was the organization of steelworkers. After the defeat of their 1919 strike, steelworkers were in almost as abject a position as textile workers. If steelworkers could be lifted up, Lewis and Murray reasoned, industries tightly bound to
them—especially mining and machine manufacture—would follow in their
train. That way the promise of the 1934 strikes would be fulfilled.

The vision was a spacious one, enough to rouse even William Green's assent.
The way Green phrased it, however, revealed old trade union condescension
more than helpful support. Maybe amalgamated unions were all right after all,
Green conceded: since workers in mass production industries all became part of
one mass mind, anyway, why not herd them into a mass industrial union?

Green balked, however, at acting on the supposition. Instead the active allies
of Lewis and Murray came mainly from the clothing workers headed by Sidney
Hillman and David Dubinsky. Hillman's Amalgamated Clothing Workers and
Dubinsky's International Ladies Garment Workers arose primarily out of the
immigrant ferment of New York City. Their mainly Jewish aspiring members
traded heavily on the advantages of socialist brotherhood as a counterpart to their
beleaguered ethnic solidarity. Their sympathies with reform and tight-knit community made them view the plea for inclusion of industrial workers favorably. At

the same time their belief in brotherly harmony made them more reluctant than pugnacious John L. Lewis to fight with fellow AFL members who opposed industrial unionism. On behalf of principle, the needle trades would go with Lewis—but they wavered with regret. It was up to the mine workers' chief to mount the charge.

Lewis confronted the old guard with the simple fact that, for all the recently heightened talk about including industrial workers, almost none had been accommodated. Knowing that an appeal to compassion for the lesser breeds on the production line would not get very far, the mine leaders hammered on the ever-present fears about security. Where the old guard exclaimed about mass unionism and the general strike as characteristic of totalitarian countries, Lewis countered with the argument that a labor movement that did not include all suffering workers ran the risk of being eliminated by fascists who would vie for the support of the disaffected. For a time Lewis tried his unique brand of rhetoric—likening his plea to a "cry from Macedonia" and warning that "high wassail will prevail at the banquet tables of the mighty" if the AFL failed to heed the industrial workers. When that didn't work, Lewis declared war—first by decking Big Bill Hutcheson of the Carpenters Union with a right cross as a way of ending an argument and then, in October 1935, by leading in the formation of the Committee of Industrial Organizations as an umbrella structure within which unskilled labor could form unions. The CIO made a brief effort in January 1936 to gain industrial charters from the AFL, but, when their request was rebuffed as "effrontery," they set out on their own.

The walkout by Lewis and his cohorts dramatized the passage of labor to a new era and added momentum to the tilt of circumstances against the feudal advantages management had always enjoyed. The ill-fated NRA gave lip service to collective bargaining and at least tried to rid the workplace of child labor and sweatshops; the Wagner Act granted workers the freedom to be represented by unions of their own choice. Now, with the breakout of the CIO from its parent AFL, there was a militant force on the front lines, eager to lead a decisive test of labor's new autonomous powers.

CHAPTER SIX

Saving the Farms

While most of the opinion-makers and the general public focused their Depression anxieties on the plight of industries and the cities, Roosevelt, as his expansive enthusiasm for the TVA indicated, was drawn most wholeheartedly to the countryside. He showed his personal preference by listing himself in *Who's Who* as a tree farmer—but he also drew from his hero, Jefferson, the belief that the quality of farm life was the key indicator of American character and crucial to recovery in all areas. Yet, in facing the farmers' worst plight of the century—their average annual family income of about $900 in 1933 represented half of parity—Roosevelt contributed to the ambivalence that had long deadlocked progress. As he had done while governor, Roosevelt praised the yeoman ideal in obsolete terms. "We have got to restore the balance of population," he declared in January 1933, echoing the alarm he expressed more than a decade earlier, when the census of 1920 showed that for the first time the urban population had become larger than the rural, and "get [the unemployed] out of the big centers of population, so that they will not be dependent on home relief." But how would city people gain the skills needed to survive on the land? he was asked, especially by Rexford Tugwell, the Brain Truster who had become assistant secretary of agriculture and had grown up on a farm. And what would having more farmers do to the problem of surplus? Was there not a greater need to get people off submarginal land than to shift more into farming? Should one not look to the other side of the rural situation and see that greater managerial and scientific expertise, not self-reliant subsistence farming, was the answer?

Behind this policy debate lay a long history of unrequited agrarian protest seeking to redress the way the Industrial Revolution following the Civil War had shifted wealth and status away from farmers to a growing urban elite. In the 1880s and 1890s a populist movement of aggrieved farmers and reform allies arose to redress the balance. Through its People's Party, the insurgents scored some local electoral victories and nationally sought alliances with reform Democrats and labor unions, especially the Knights of Labor, who espoused similar communal ideals. In order to reduce economic burdens, which they thought a conspiracy of financial and commercial interests had heaped unfairly upon farmers, Populists formulated plans to place banks, railroads, and utilities under governmental control and to eliminate tariffs designed to raise the price of goods farmers had to buy. Balancing that defensive tactic were proposals to raise farm income through scientific education and assistance in marketing surplus produce, especially through export. Though their success at the polls was minor, the Populists influenced progressives at the turn of the century to enact railroad regulation, anti-monopoly measures, the graduated income tax, and, through the land grant colleges, extension programs to bring scientific agriculture to the hinterland.

A season of prosperity just before and during World War I raised farm morale. But the war itself, though it benefited farmers through high demand for food to feed the troops and starving Europe, also roused reaction against collectivist—and thus seemingly alien—dissent of the sort Populism had embodied. Instead, farmers exuberantly returned to older ideals of individual success. As suppliers to an embattled world, wheat farmers grew more and doubled their prices. Speculation followed prosperity. As the leading farm publication, *Wallace's Farmer,* put it, a lot of farmers were "sitting around the livery stable and playing games with options" rather than working the land they had bought with borrowed money. Farm debt skyrocketed; by 1920 it was nearly three times what it had been in the good crop year of 1910—$8.4 billion as compared to only $3.2 billion ten years before.

As in the great nineteenth-century westward movement, not all of those seeking their fortune on the land had any experience in farming. In 1922 an economist studying newcomers on the land in Montana found among them "two circus musicians, a paper hanger, a sailor, a sea-going engineer, two wrestlers, two barbers, a cigar maker, a race horse man, a bricklayer, a deep-sea diver, six old maids, a milliner, and a professional gambler." Nothing united them but a common euphoria over the presumed bounty of nature.

Then the mortgaged roof fell in on them. With the end of the war and voluntary government price supports, wheat plummeted from $2.19 per bushel in 1919
to less than a dollar three years later. Though a modest recovery followed, by 1929
wheat was still selling for only $1.05. In that last year of the most prosperous de-
cade America had ever enjoyed, the annual income of farmers was only $273, as
compared to $750 for people nationwide. The apparent inconsistency of Repub-
lican administrations building high tariff walls for industry, which raised the prices
of goods for farmers, while invoking free market precepts to reject market protection for agriculture, roused suspicion among rural Americans that their thwarted
hopes were the result of a new industrial society that was rigging the game in violation of America's agrarian virtues. Against the voluntary cooperation Coolidge
and Hoover advocated, and the lack of a strong Democratic alternative, insurgents
from the thinning ranks of farm-labor third parties and the Farmers' Union gave
a last hurrah for populism. In the 1924 presidential election they gathered behind
the battered champion of progressive reform, Senator Robert La Follette of Wisconsin, in a futile challenge to conservative Democratic and Republican candidates that spelled the end of organized Progressive party politics.

After the Great Crash of 1929 a new flurry of farm insurgency arose in the
form of scattered rebellions against oppressive measures, especially foreclosures
of defaulted mortgages, that went with hard times for farmers. The most flamboyant rebel was Milo Reno of Iowa, who whipped up a campaign in 1931 to boycott food production and distribution until farmers won a greater share of the rewards. Reno carried on the colorful, idiosyncratic tradition of farm belt agitators.
A spellbinding stump speaker who also played the fiddle at barn dances decked
out in his trademark ten gallon hat and flaming red necktie, Reno aimed for
maximum excitement. His denunciations of oppressive eastern financiers and
politicians inspired John Simpson, president of the National Farmers Union, to
tell the Senate Committee on Agriculture that "the biggest and finest crop of rev-
olutions you ever saw is sprouting all over this country right now," to which the
president of the American Farm Bureau Federation, Edward O'Neal, added in
another context, "Unless something is done for the American farmer we'll have
revolution in the countryside in less than twelve months."

Reno organized a timetable for a national farm strike to occur on May 13, 1933,
unless crop prices by then enabled farmers to break even. Along the way were
various flare-ups: embattled farmers threw up road blocks around Sioux City,
Iowa, and dumped truckloads of milk, in the manner of the Boston Tea Party, by
the side of the highways. Before long the movement encircled Des Moines and
Council Bluffs and then invaded Nebraska and Wisconsin. A tactic for thwarting

mortgage foreclosures also took hold. When auctions of defaulted property were announced, neighboring farmers shouldered bidders aside and brought back the victims' possessions at a token fee. To underscore the message, several lawyers and judges were intimidated, sometimes violently.

The uprisings proved a boon to New Deal aspirations for change. Farm belt anger and violence alarmed political leaders and the public alike and thus gave credence to New Deal emergency action. Roosevelt's whirlwind stabilization of the banks also helped significantly to ease the pressure and instill confidence that a more empathetic group had taken charge in Washington. Only a few of the most militant protesters remained committed to independent political organizing. At the 1933 convention of the aptly named League for Independent Political Action, the newly formed Farmer Labor Political Federation locked arms with the Farmers' Holiday Association, endorsing the strike idea; in return, Milo Reno endorsed the call for a new national party. But the attempt at solidarity fizzled and, in doing so, demonstrated the essential division within the diminished ranks of farm radicals. John Simpson and the National Farm Union he headed, many of whose members were impressed by democratic socialist movements in Europe that had brought benefits to farmers, especially in Scandinavia, favored a union between farmers and workers. But most insurgents were suspicious of such foreign doctrinaire thinking. Reno exemplified the majority of agrarian agitators who were essentially looking for the status and security they associated with a lost golden age. He was proud of his membership in the Masons, the Odd Fellows, the Christian church—and the Republican Party (though he cast protest votes for Smith in 1928 and Roosevelt in 1932). In his fulminations against the smart-aleck college professors and city operators, Reno resounded to the drum of old-fashioned resentment rather than radical change.

As the right and left wings of farm radicalism diverged, the New Deal gained ever more territory in the middle. John Shover in *The Cornbelt Rebellion* expressed the essence: "Reno spoke for a day that had been; the radicals . . . spoke for a day that never came. The New Deal was the catalytic agent of time and change that defeated both of them. The agricultural program removed the rural discontent which provided Reno's ideology with the only driving force that could sustain it; benefit payments and price supports rendered the steady force of social and technological change that absorbs and destroys the family farmers far more painless than the radical left could have imagined possible."

To anchor New Deal farm policy within the progressive legacy of scientific agriculture, Roosevelt chose Henry A. Wallace of Iowa to be secretary of agriculture. Son of a former secretary of agriculture under Harding and Coolidge, Wallace was serving as the third-generation editor of the widely respected journal, *Wallace's Farmer*. When it became his turn in the 1920s to succeed father and grandfather as editor, young Henry wryly announced that his ambition was to "make the world safe for corn breeders." By that time he had become one of the world's leading corn geneticists. He was also a painstaking student of economics and in 1920 published a book on agricultural prices that anticipated his commitment to New Deal reforms. Deploring the decline in farm population while agricultural productivity was rising, Wallace drew the unpopular conclusion—on the eve of the Republican boom—that there was an inescapable need to curtail production through the cooperation of farmers and economists. Only planning would assure the "federal guidance, collective action, and application of science to agriculture" needed to end the woes of overproduction.

During the 1920s Wallace instilled a many-sided idealism into the campaign of *Wallace's Farmer* against the domination of Big Business. As a youth he had discovered the writings of the great iconoclast of the plains, Thorstein Veblen, adopting his explanation of how in the prevailing "free" enterprise system financiers and businessmen were able to gain special favors from government while farmers were expected to remain at the mercy of the "natural laws" of the marketplace, even though they were often manipulated by absentee owners. By accepting Veblen's lesson that one should look for explanations in the actual workings of institutions, rather than in abstract theory, Wallace was of the same mind as the Brains Trusters and went on to the same conclusions about what to include in New Deal farm policy as those drawn by Tugwell.

Wallace enlarged his vision to internationalist scope by accepting Veblen's contention in *Imperial Germany and the Industrial Revolution* (1915) that the pairing of industrialism with autocratic government made Germany and Japan threats to the peace and the complementary concept in Veblen's *The Nature of Peace* (1917) that such threats could be headed off by making the nations of the world more interdependent as well as more democratic. By removing tariff barriers, Veblen and Wallace believed—thus siding with traditional free trade agricultural beliefs against the more "businesslike" protection of farm interest groups like the American Farm Bureau Federation (AFBF) and the Grange movement—cooperation would grow, and no nation would be self-sufficient enough to risk war. Wallace also favored a devalued dollar, which would make American goods cheaply saleable abroad and finance farm operations with a minimum of squeezing by tight-fisted bankers. In that spirit he followed his father's adviser, George Warren, into the Stable Money League and then onto sympathy with Roosevelt's internationalist monetary experiment.

Wallace's strong religiosity, so characteristic of the agrarian reformers of his youth, added a final dimension that sometimes caused critics to dismiss him as a mystic but also provided a stabilizing moral framework for his cooperative approach. In his most famous reference to religious tradition, Wallace combined two disparate tales. The first was the Old Testament story of Joseph in Egypt, combating an unjust marketplace by withholding his crops; the second was the Chinese plan found in Confucius's writings of maintaining a "constantly normal granary" filled with surplus crops in fat years to be marketed in lean. As secretary of agriculture, Wallace gained the chance to try stabilizing the market with his own "ever-normal granary."

A few days after the inauguration Roosevelt and Wallace convened about fifty farm organization leaders and rural editors to discuss a program that would be broad enough to encompass the long accumulating needs and hopes of the farmers. Fresh from the discussion of price stabilization and production control, Wallace and Tugwell presided over the creation of the Agricultural Adjustment Act and its May 12 passage by Congress.

All through the lame duck session of Congress before Roosevelt's inauguration, farm organizations had been pressing their views alongside the efforts of the New Dealers to hammer out a position. A meeting of the AFBF leaders just after the inauguration drew together several basic contentions, which were promptly wired to the new president. They called for support of rural banks, monetary inflation along the lines proposed by George Warren, price parity between agricultural and industrial commodities, and mortgage relief for farmers. The Farmers Union urged that price goals be based on the cost of production so that farmers might gain the same measure of recovery from the New Deal as other workers. More aloof from direct governmental intervention, the National Cooperative Council stressed the value of mutual aid in a way that prefigured the later New Deal interest in building communities out of farmers too helpless to make a go of it alone.

The bill that emerged ranged widely. Authorization for refinancing mortgages and loans spoke to the dire need farmers had long expressed for help in dealing with creditors. And by 1936 the administration had channeled $2.5 billion to buttress farmers' land holdings. A more controversial effort to help farmers financially was the proposed amendment by Senator Elmer Thomas of Oklahoma empowering the president to reduce the gold backing for dollars and to print bills with silver backing alone when money became depressively tight. When Lewis Douglas, Roosevelt's conservative budget director, learned of that desecration of the gold standard, he walked the night and lamented to friends that it was "the end of Western civilization." But Roosevelt made sure there was a provision included to tame the amendment: he was given discretion as to when he would invoke its provisions, and with that in hand did little to stimulate the wild inflation some feared, once his experiment with manipulating the value of gold was over.

The crux of the bill was its adaptation of M. L. Wilson's domestic allotment plan designed to reduce the surplus and give growers higher prices. It authorized the secretary of agriculture to sign agreements for the reduction of acreage under cultivation. In return, the producers would be paid a price as close to parity as the general welfare warranted, with funds being obtained through a tax on processors.

To gain support and determine how a commodity adjustment would affect farm income, the Department of Agriculture set up a series of regional conferences. A triumvirate of county agents, Farm Bureau representatives, and state college faculty coordinated the work—thus giving powerful governmental endorsement to the quasi-official representatives of the farm belt status quo. Uneasily, with Tugwell opposed to the power the act would bestow on wealthy farmers and the virtual exclusion of those who owned little or no land, the Agricultural Adjustment Act went on to establish more than 4,200 county associations by the end of 1934—all heavily involved with the Farm Bureau and its conservative Alabama plantation owner president, Edward O'Neal.

To serve as chief administrator of the AAA, Wallace enlisted George Peek, who had become prominent as coordinator of farm policy for the War Industries Board in World War I and afterward as head of the Moline Plow Company in Illinois and lobbyist for the failed attempt of the McNary-Haugen bill in the 1920s to raise farm income by dumping surplus crops abroad. The choice was undoubtedly a boon for cementing relations with the traditional farm bloc. But relations within the Department of Agriculture—that was another story. The planning group attached to Tugwell, now undersecretary of the Department of Agriculture and its chief planner, had a concept of welfare that extended beyond established farmers to a concern for the tenant farmers and sharecroppers who toiled on the margin. Peek considered such collectivist disturbers of the status quo, especially those with an urban background, like Tugwell and counsel Lee Pressman, as "reds" and could never reconcile himself to their role in replacing his cherished McNary-Haugen dumping scheme with the more tightly regimented domestic allotment plan or to their interest in doing more than raising farm prices. Obstinately determined to be the successful farmer's advocate and opposed to the sin of curtailing the Lord's bounty, Peek resisted the logic of crop reduction in favor of finding foreign markets for whatever farmers might grow. After seven months of raising havoc over trade policies that did not include disposing of the surplus (or the "reds"), Peek had to be replaced and, at Tugwell's suggestion, was exiled to the State Department, where he promptly got into another losing war with Secretary of State Hull over his efforts to circumvent reciprocal trade agreements by trying to make a special barter arrangement with Germany.

Before he left the Department of Agriculture, Peek warned his successor, Chester Davis, that true-blue farm belt veterans like themselves could only expect trouble from left-wing theorists from the city. But Davis, though Peek's main cohort in the campaign for McNary-Haugen, was more patient and keener about the objectives of the AAA as well. He surrounded himself with able farm economists and set about to continue the evolution of New Deal policies while Peek was left to grumble, in his subsequent testament to the old self-sufficiency, *Why Quit Our Own?* (1936), that "I eventually found that I was not in a Democratic Administration but in a curious collection of socialists and internationalists who were neither Republicans nor Democrats."

Davis entered the scene at a trying moment. Because the AAA was not even passed until after planting season, putting acreage out of commission involved plowing under crops already growing—some ten million acres of cotton alone—an act that, in Wallace's words, "goes against the soundest instinct of human nature." But the most notorious act was the killing of several million sows and piglets, much to the horror of a squeamish public which seemed to have forgotten, Wallace remarked, that execution was the inevitable fate of the porkers anyway.

Farmers did not mourn the lost crops and pigs. Support for the AAA was cemented by the remarkable recovery of prosperity. Prices increased from the time of the first crop reduction contract until by 1936 they nearly reached the ideal of parity with the boom years before World War I, and farm income had risen to double what it had been when Roosevelt took office.

There was, however, a "forgotten man" in the midst of these rising fortunes. As Tugwell had feared, tying the crop reduction arrangements to established state extension agents and their AFBF allies gave the more powerful farmers an inside track on subsidy benefits. That left the small family farmer and hired hands in limbo. Most painful was the situation of southern tenant farmers. Over half of the farms in the South were operated by these dependent people—some 5.5 million white and over 3 million black, mostly in the depressed cotton sector. Through a system of credit advances for their homes, land, and supplies at interest rates up to 28 percent (because they were "bad risks"), tenants had been reduced to penury. Federal studies at the time revealed that in the Black Belt region of Alabama, South Carolina, Mississippi, and Texas, many tenants had had no cash incomes since 1921. Those with money to show for their labors in 1933 only brought the family average up to $105.

Although the crop reduction program raised the price of cotton closer to parity, most of the windfall went to owners of large spreads. To induce participation by cotton growers, the contracts drawn up in the fall of 1933 for the following two years awarded 89 percent of the governmental rental fees for land out of production to owners and only 11 percent to tenants. To make up for the destitution of croppers left on retired land, the contract laid a moral obligation—a legal requirement was too much to get through a Congress heavily larded with southerners in seniority leadership positions—on owners to retain tenants no longer farming and allow them to grow food and cut wood on unused land. A significant number of tenants were nonetheless displaced, adding to the hapless throng whom the Depression had earlier cut adrift.

The desperate situation demonstrated that the farm problem was a dual one, involving the need for higher prices on one hand and subsistence through redistribution of land profits on the other. Pricing called for bold adjustments within the system; providing for the dispossessed seemed to require changing the system itself.

The oppression of poor farmers became a prime issue for the left. Socialist Party leader Norman Thomas agitated eloquently for government action to free tenants and provide them with land, giving evidence of woe that humane reformers could not dispute. But the appeals of Thomas and his allies for social justice failed to move Wallace and Davis, who regarded the plight of the landless poor as deplorable but were not willing to jeopardize the larger aims of the AAA by an attempt to help the most abject group, which they believed would be futile anyway. The painful issue of how to temper the AAA program with mercy came to a climax in February 1935, when the mostly city-bred legal staff gathered by Tugwell decided to take a stand on how the good faith agreement designed to protect tenant farmers would be implemented. The insurgent staff members artfully chose a time when both Davis and Tugwell were out of town to issue a declaration that owners of land were to retain all tenants who had worked on land taken out of production.

When Davis returned, he found sharp conflict between his section and aroused growers. Miffed, Davis prevailed upon Wallace to fire the insubordinate group in what was portrayed in the newspapers as a "purge," thereby linking the dismissed malcontents, some of whom were known to have leftist sympathies,

with the victims of the sensational treason trials going on in Moscow to eject undesirable elements from the Communist Party.

Wallace had little practical choice. To gain crucial support for the subsidy program in the Deep South, the New Deal had to place the program under the control of southerners aligned to the leading cotton growers and the Farm Bureau,
whose president, Edward O'Neal, was himself a large plantation owner with
many tenant farmers on his land. Cully Cobb, editor of the *Southern Ruralist,*
published in Atlanta, was in charge of the Cotton Section of the AAA, and Oscar Johnston, head of the vast Delta and Pine Land Company in Mississippi, ran
the USDA cotton pool. Both men were sympathetic to improving the economy
of the South through modern planning, but they linked their hopes mostly to
the fortunes of the white ownership class. Reform of the situation for the landless, many of them black, had to follow a cautious line that southerners would
not see as a threat to traditional social and economic arrangements, even to the
point of overlooking defiance by owners of the legal requirement that they share
subsidies for tenant land put out of production. Why share payments for land
policies with people who don't own the land, the rationalization went; indeed,
why pay tenants at all, or even let them stay on the property, when they are not
earning their keep by raising crops? To ease the plight of those caught in the vise
of such figuring, Senator John Bankhead of Alabama sponsored a bill in 1934
that would provide loans for establishing dispossessed farmers on small farms.
Wallace was doubtful that such undertakings would be limited to subsistence
and feared that their cash crops would interfere with the effort to eliminate the
surplus. The measure would also do little to help African Americans, who were
most heavily victimized by the evictions and not apt to be considered for loans
in the segregationist South. Nonetheless, Wallace went along with the Bankhead
Bill as the best way to mitigate a sad dilemma while leaving control of the Department of Agriculture's policies thereafter in the hands of large interests and white
supremacists. Thus it was able to remain steadfast as the department with the
fewest black employees and virtually no relationships with organizations representing the views and interests of African Americans. It wasn't the kind of place
where you'd take a Negro to lunch, was the way New Deal farm expert Will Alexander once put it.

In April 1935, with the Bankhead Bill stalled, Roosevelt created the Resettlement Administration in order to consolidate the several types of rural relief
programs into a coherent plan for relocating people who were landless or on
submarginal land. This agency would encompass the tenant problems within a
larger nationwide framework. Its charge was to resettle the destitute, rural and

urban; to help the land conservation movement, which was closely related to the task of moving people from marginal to productive land; and to give technical and financial assistance so that families on relief might become self-sufficient. The ambitious RA acted as a meeting ground for many ideas about farm reform that reflected Roosevelt's old desire to turn the downtrodden into self-sufficient farmers. Tugwell's interest in expert planning—what he called the "Fourth Power" of government—gained expression in the building of model communities. Folk traditionalists had a brief chance within the Special Bills Division to promote rural arts and crafts. And the steady reform aim of getting farmers out of debt and onto their own land was advanced through the program of rehabilitation loans.

Criticism from centers of status quo power, including Congress, steadily beat upon the RA enterprise. Conservatives derided it as impractical and utopian and huffed at it for wasteful spending. From the left, Norman Thomas and the Socialists attacked the RA for being too slow to step in with aid for aggrieved tenant farmers. Throughout, Tugwell, who was named to head the agency, and his staff counseled moderate advance between the two rocks of criticism. But the contentious situation cost him too much. In December 1936, Tugwell resigned to reenter private life, partly having served as the lightning rod for criticism of "radical" experimentation to such an extent that he had become something of a liability to the New Deal. The Resettlement Administration he left behind had begun a number of model communities whose roomy new white houses contrasted with the usual tenant farmer shack in a way that starkly brought the plight of the rural poor to public attention.

By mid-decade, the final outcome of New Deal farm policy was very much in doubt. Although farmers had advanced toward parity, farm sales and prices had not recovered to their 1929 level. Nor had the battle against surplus production checked the drive of farmers to apply improved techniques toward increasing yields, as the Department of Agriculture had long taught them to do. During the 1930s the annual population rise slowed to 7 percent, but agricultural production rose 12 percent. Recognizing this adverse trend, the New Deal created the Commodity Credit Corporation in 1933 with provisions for storing surplus goods, even though the horrible example of Hoover's Farm Board getting stuck with mountains of leftovers moved New Deal planners to try to avoid the pitfall of surplus storage.

The figures would have been even more daunting had it not been for the severe droughts that afflicted large portions of the West and Southwest, beginning in 1934. As crops withered and powder-dry topsoil vanished in huge dust storms, prices for remaining foodstuffs rose until the drought subsided in 1938. Once again the elements proved that calculation of farm policy is always at the mercy of nature. In ironic sequence the very technology that was designed to lessen risk led first to overproduction on plains that had originally been called "the great American desert" and then, by removing much of the grass that bound the plains together, made it easier for the dry winds to blow away the overproduction along with illusions of a garden paradise.

In the midst of hopeful experiment and dire distress, the New Deal confronted a crucial challenge. From the beginning New Deal agricultural planners had realized they would be tested in court, and so they had tried to build safeguards into the unorthodox AAA and also frame alternatives in case the conservative Supreme Court should reject their case. When in 1935 a processor named Butler contested the fees levied against him, Attorney General Homer Cummings felt confident. The voluntary nature of the AAA agreements along with the federal power to levy taxes for the general welfare seemed to protect the farm legislation. But in January of 1936 a 6-3 majority of the Supreme Court delivered a judgment against the AAA that denied the sort of federal activism on which the New Deal depended. Conceding that Congress had the right to tax for welfare purposes, Justice Owen Roberts insisted that taxes must be designed to raise revenue. Taxes aimed at affecting the public in other ways were impermissible—otherwise what was to stop one class of enterprisers from getting government to rig taxes for their benefit at the expense of other classes, just as the farmers in this case were profiting at the expense of the processors? The key, Roberts insisted in a famous passage, was strict construction: "All legislation must conform to the principles it lays down. When an act of Congress is appropriately challenged in the courts as not conforming to the constitutional mandate the judicial branch of the government has only one duty—to lay the article of the Constitution which is invoked beside the statute which is challenged and to decide whether the latter squares with the former."

This concept, aptly derided as "slot-machine law," boded ill for any innovative programs. Thus hemmed in, the New Deal responded with the Soil Conservation and Domestic Allotment Act of 1936. The law skirted the case against the first AAA in a way that preserved the original substance. Price supports were now provided out of general revenues, and the authority to preserve land by removing it from cultivation made it possible to continue crop controls.

But in an important way the new act also furthered a change of direction. Where the original New Deal farm policy had concentrated almost wholly on producers' interests, the substitute act, written under a black cloud of swirling dust and at a time when farm prices had risen out of the catastrophe zone, paid more attention to honoring the land and the humbler folk living on it. In concert with the Resettlement Administration and rising public concern over the downtrodden, the farm bill encouraged departure from the notion of farming as another business to be made ever more profitable through large-scale technology. The way was prepared to test the spirit of Roosevelt's cooperative commonwealth and rural ideal.

CHAPTER SEVEN

Launching the Welfare State

In addressing the dilemma of why there should be Depression in a land of bountiful resources, the New Deal necessarily had to adopt a double focus. On one side it looked for ways to revive an economic sector that was lagging but still operating. At the same time the administration had to deal with those who had succumbed and were out of business—the victimized "third of a nation," as Roosevelt would call them in his second inaugural address. To aid surviving enterprise, New Dealers drew upon wartime planning experience, regulation, and a network of loans and other financial props. For the dispossessed, however, a crucially different approach was needed..

The first problem to be solved was that of justification. While the public could applaud a helping governmental hand to balance productivity and prices for businessmen and farmers and protect the rights of labor to organize, they were inclined to look askance at aid to the destitute as a form of indulging idleness. Britain's desperate tactic during the interwar years of supporting a large number of unemployables prompted critics to warn against robbing Americans of their initiative by putting them on the "dole." Yet vital considerations kept the jobless from being abandoned. Stories that Americans had actually starved to death horrified the public conscience and buttressed a general resolve to find emergency aid. America's characteristic faith in the improvability of human nature fed hopes that material encouragement could provide just the lift needed to get the jobless out fending for themselves. Moreover, the great magnitude of the Crash indicated that many people had been thrown out of work by forces beyond their control. Was not the government—the people's representative—the sole power great enough to overcome those forces and lift the victims to their feet?

That concept of benevolence had to contend with a harsh tradition of individual responsibility for salvation or damnation. The Puritan view of innate human sinfulness, coupled with belief that opportunity in America was limitless, led to a general conclusion that the poor were so because of their own failings. The best policy, it seemed, was to avoid indulging such weakness and to disturb the dynamic of the free marketplace as little as possible in aiding those who had stumbled in the competitive race.

Thus, private and public provision for the poor in America had been marked from the outset by a stringent approach. Through hard work, the poor should be brought to realize their possibilities and then released into society. Relief work ought not be satisfactory in itself, for that would tempt the poor to remain on the dole; nor should it be highly productive, for that would put relief agencies in competition with private enterprise. So delicate a balance was always in danger of going awry. An ethic designed to strengthen the weak all too often lapsed into contempt for relief recipients who seemed perversely mired in want despite the many chances to get ahead.

In the late nineteenth century, the drive to discipline the poor was intensified by a pseudoscientific appropriation of Darwin's evolutionary concept that only the fittest survived in nature. To be sure, scientific reformers were piously devoted to helping the weak become fit; yet there is a chilling quality to the statement made by one of their leaders that it must be done with "not one cent" given to the poor directly. John Boyle O'Reilly, poet of the Boston Irish and himself an escaped convict from Australia, conveyed the chill with a shudder in his ironic verse:

> The organized charity scrimped and iced,
> In the name of a cautious, statistical Christ.

Only Civil War veterans prior to the New Deal had been able to gain substantial help from a grateful nation in the form of pensions. In a magnificent forecast of the welfare state, a Renaissance-style palace—complete with frieze around the top depicting military exploits—was built in Washington to staff the bureaucracy that would run the pension system; with it went a huge monetary outlay, approaching half of the federal budget in the late nineteenth century. But, though the pension system demonstrated the willingness of Americans to have the government provide welfare to deserving patriots, it faded as the Civil War generation passed away in the early twentieth century. A related indication of a bygone era was the fact that most of the Civil War pensioners were farmers and small townsmen of old stock background, whose lives were remote from the hard-pressed immigrants and new industries at the center of the very different and far more urban social realities of the Great Depression.

The basis for a collective response to those new conditions was laid when the Social Gospel movement eased the grip of Puritan stewardship by stressing the compassionate spirit of the Sermon on the Mount. That appeal to shared responsibility for social ills gave rise to the settlement movement, most famously exemplified by Jane Addams's Hull House, begun in Chicago in 1889. As havens of welcome and progressive reform, rather than stark places where the poor would do penance, as the old workhouses and poorhouses had been, the settlements caught the imagination of a public newly eager to find kindly means toward progress.

One of the most important fruits of these "outposts in the slums" was the study by Hull House veteran Robert Hunter called, simply, *Poverty* (1904). The book presented a mass of facts that refuted the old theory equating poverty with sin and the slightly newer, but even bleaker, "scientific" linkage of poverty with hereditary weakness and economic law. The hard core of poverty, Hunter declared, was not the few ne'er-do-well paupers who had ceased worrying about their plight but the many working poor whose efforts could never lift them out of a pit dug by upbringing, illness, geography, and, most immediately, the refusal of employers to pay those at the bottom a living wage. This large mass—most of the ten million Americans Hunter estimated were living in poverty—did not even qualify for public assistance and so were hardly noticed by those who gave to, much less decried, charity. Yet, they had wants of the body and spirit that could only be met by outside help.

Hunter's demonstration of widespread suffering and his conclusion that the mental anguish of defeat was a large share of it spurred a drive to establish a scientific profession of social work. In the wake of Hunter's findings and the rise of interest in psychology, a new individual casework approach developed that dealt with poor clients in terms of social maladjustment. That approach reached its height during the 1920s, in harmony with the contemporary message of voluntary association—of "fitting in." Within this framework the ability to redeem the poor was assumed, and the emphasis, in theory, was on a constructive response to the complaints and needs of clients.

But psychological casework, for all its revealing penetration into the private hell of social deprivation, often hindered reform by diverting attention from the material causes of poverty and assuming social pathology on the part of recipients. It sided with the purblind individualism of 1920s leadership that left the nation unprepared to make a concerted response to the nationwide scale of the Crash. In 1929 the poorhouse, with all the old stingy piety surrounding it, was still the chief means of tending to the poor. Many districts let out unemployed to the highest bidder, and in some instances destitute children were indentured away from their parents. To gain relief funds a pauper's oath was customary, with relatives likely to be forced to sacrifice their own means for the paupers or be jailed.

Before the Crash, a resolute few reformers and advocates of social planning warned that reliance on individual initiative was inadequate. The specter of unemployment prompted the National Federation of Settlements to make a study in 1928 of its adverse psychological effects. The alarming findings—defeatism, depression, lowered horizons, and destructive behavior—later became the basis for Clinch Calkins's classic plea for a compassionate solution in his ironically titled study, *Some Folks Won't Work* (1930).

Events then forced the issue. New York took the lead, in accord with its progressive reform and social work tradition, when the settlement house champion, William Matthews, founded the New York City Emergency Work Bureau in 1930. The Bureau helped establish liaisons between private and public agencies, paving the way for Governor Roosevelt in 1931 to establish the New York Temporary Emergency Relief Administration (TERA). Under Harry Hopkins's energetic leadership TERA became the prototype of New Deal relief measures and stressed the need for public acceptance of government spending on useful work projects as the best way to restore the dignity of those cast into idleness. "Give a man a dole," Hopkins proclaimed, "and you save his body and destroy his spirit; give him a job and pay him an assured wage, and you save both the body and the spirit."

The fine line Hopkins drew indicated his understanding that TERA's acceptance depended heavily on public reaction to the way widespread unemployment challenged old ways of thinking about initiative and opportunity. The accession of Roosevelt to the presidency took place within a shudder of concern throughout the western world over both the soul and body of the unemployed. In 1933 E. Wight Bakke's pace-setting sociological study *The Unemployed Man* appeared. The year of New Deal advent also produced influential works of fiction with a Depression victim at the center: Walter Greenwood's *Love on the Dole*, written in America about conditions in Britain, and two German novels: Hans Fallada's *Little Man, What Now?* and Rudolf Brunngraber's *Karl and the Twentieth Century*. None of these pitying looks at the "little man," crushed by unfathomable and uncontrollable social forces, offered solutions, but they shed important light on the tendency of material want to crush the spirit and so lead into a vicious cycle where poverty and lack of initiative reinforced one another.

The problem was how to institutionalize compassion and still honor the tough-minded competitive initiative Americans thought they should follow. TERA grappled with the problem inconclusively, dispensing most of its help in hastily devised tasks of the sort that brought new notoriety to the old Appalachian word *boondoggle*. But when the New Deal entered the scene, the atmosphere of opprobrium was significantly lifted from those who needed relief. The magnitude of immediate need swamped the tendency of the secure to peer closely at the insecure for signs of profligacy. Further, it was demonstrable that most of the thirteen million unemployed—estimated at 25 percent of the work force, there being no official figures—had been self-supporting before the Crash swept their jobs away. More persuasively than ever, the unemployed could be depicted as victims. There was room, too, for easing the strictures against putting the unemployed to work in profitable enterprises; with the capacity of the nation so obviously underused and so many people in need of work, government-run industry began to seem a reasonable idea.

Consequently, the New Deal relief effort set off in two directions. The Federal Emergency Relief Administration (FERA), the first agency, dispensed funds to meet immediate needs. Following TERA's lead, the Civilian Conservation Corps (CCC), the Public Works Administration (PWA), and the Civil Works Administration (CWA), formed by taking $400 million out of PWA funds to provide emergency work relief for the first harsh winter of the Roosevelt administration before the PWA was scheduled to begin its operations in the spring of 1934, employed over four million persons and spread their energies widely into building or improving about half a million miles of road and thousands of schools, airports, and playgrounds—and even into excavating prehistoric Native American mounds for the Smithsonian Institution.

The CWA was the most imaginative, best paying, and least restricted of New Deal relief programs. Among its many unconventional deeds it arranged to get all of Boston's unemployed teachers on the payroll, hired 3,000 artists and writers, and sent a group of destitute opera singers to the Ozarks to ply their art in the healthy outdoors. Yet, despite the contention of enthusiastic analysts that the $718 million spent in 1933 and 1934 produced new employment, productivity, and consuming power worth $9 billion, the program roused fatal opposition. Both Roosevelt and the Congress were averse to deficit financing. CWA also strained the new tolerance for relief agency entry into useful economic enterprise and for free market level wages. In early 1934 the experiment was abruptly terminated, and the New Deal reverted to the more traditional welfare style of self-liquidating public works with "maintenance" pay set below prevailing wages so that relief recipients would return to the private sector as soon as possible.

The retreat to a more conservative approach favored the Public Works Administration. Harold Ickes, the new secretary of the interior, took charge of the operation and directed it toward such massive creations as the Boulder Dam (what we today call the Hoover Dam). As a deeply committed veteran of progressive reform in Chicago and a leader in the NAACP, Ickes wished the PWA to display social justice as well as engineering prowess. Despite resistance from labor unions and local officials, especially in the South, Ickes's attempt to build facilities for blacks in accord with their percentage of the population resulted in far more benefit for the black community than it had ever received from a government program. PWA spent $45 million on schools, hospitals, and other structures for blacks, and fully 31 percent of the PWA payroll went to blacks in the fullest demonstration by any New Deal program of their disproportionate plight. Yet the principled effort was little more than a demonstration of what needed to be done. With a style as ponderous as his projects, because of his stickler's concern for precision and his fear of competition and corruption, "Honest Harold" never took on more than 500,000 workers at a time. That prevented PWA from being a significant instrument of unemployment relief, even though the agency's virtues and finely wrought works greatly burnished the New Deal's reputation.

Of all the New Deal programs for work relief, the Civilian Conservation Corps gained the most lasting public approval. It appealed to educators and social workers for the way it took youths off the city streets and to conservationists worried about eroding resources. Roosevelt was a strong partisan because CCC met his ideal of drawing defeated city-dwellers back into fruitful contact with the land. With that support behind it, the CCC by 1935 had 459,000 persons on its rolls at a cost of $332,851,000—thus taking up a good share of the slack from the defunct CWA and the declining FERA.

The need for a much larger effort, however, was manifest. There were still ten and a half million unemployed in 1935—20.1 percent of the workforce. To meet the need Hopkins sought to reinvigorate the spirit roused by the CWA. On the flood tide of the smashing endorsement given to Roosevelt by the Democratic sweep of the 1934 congressional elections, Hopkins exulted to his associates: "Boys, this is our hour. We've got to get everything we want—a works program, social security, wages and hours, everything—now or never. Get your minds to work on developing a complete ticket to provide security for all the folks of this country up and down and across the board." The subsequent push culminated in the Emergency Relief Appropriation Act of 1935, which committed $4.8 billion, the largest single appropriation for the purpose ever raised. Roosevelt in his annual message in January of that year prepared the ground. The forthcoming relief measure, he insisted with a bow toward traditional practice, would leave the unemployables in the hands of the states, while the employables would be shepherded by a new agency, the Works Progress Administration. The WPA would also be orthodox and rely upon means tests and investigations for the noncompetitive jobs and wages it offered. Private business need not fear. "I ask you," pressed Hopkins, who was named to head the agency, "is it reasonable to suppose that an American worker . . . will reject private employment to remain in such a situation?" In 1936 faith in the traditional doctrine of justification through work was made the centerpiece of the WPA's *Workers' Handbook*. To drive the point home, those coming onto the payroll were greeted with a brief litany:

What happens to us when we are on the dole?
We lose our self-respect. We lose our skill. We have family rows.
We loaf on street corners. Finally, we lose hope.

Unfortunately, the New Deal was not able to extend hope to everyone. Every month there were between 600,000 and 1.3 million qualified applicants who had to subsist on widely varied, but always meager, local aid while waiting on street corners or in tense households for word of openings on the WPA rolls, word that for some never came.

For the favored majority Hopkins set out with a blaze of expensive and bold action that caused the WPA to take the lead from the Public Works Administration and incited curmudgeonly Harold Ickes to turn against Hopkins in one of the most notorious feuds within the always turbulent New Deal. By the start of 1936 the WPA had taken on three and a half million people. The WPA's hallmark was both vast scope and spartan administrative cost. When the program had almost run its course at the end of the decade, more than eight million persons had been helped, and their benefactors could boast that of the $10 billion appropriated for the task, some 86 percent was made available for wage payments. In its wake the WPA left a permanent legacy of public buildings, sometimes decorated with murals by artists rescued by the agency, as well as dams, bridges, roads, parks, and other public amenities.

The WPA was hardly the boondoggle that budget cutters and conservative critics made it out to be. Wages were meager, costs were kept low, and the program as a whole was tightly run, following sound administrative principles. Essentially, the WPA and other New Deal work relief programs were instances of the government itself performing as the rational economic actor of classical liberal theory: it took advantage of a period of labor surplus and low labor "prices" to build socially useful infrastructure at bargain basement costs, thus offsetting the expense of attending to unemployment and social distress.

Public response to the great and efficient relief campaign was ambiguous. Only a halfway revolution of attitude affected the old ideas of self-reliance. Polls showed that the WPA was rated throughout its existence as an agency that should be continued by majorities ranging from 54 to 90 percent; yet it also aroused vehement opposition for its alleged waste, corruption, and sapping of initiative. The complaints had some merit. Since Senate approval was required for the appointment of any official in the WPA earning over $5,000 and since local authorities determined most of the projects to be funded, there were temptations for undeserved patronage and payoffs not resisted by all in charge. Tapping into this ambiguity, the Gallup poll of 1939 on "Relief and the WPA" showed that of all of the programs promoted by the New Deal, relief work undertakings ranked first in both "greatest achievement" and "worst thing"!

New Deal efforts to aid the jobless existed within the larger vision of a cooperative commonwealth in which there would be full employment and all in the nation's family would be well housed. The collapse of banking and the skilled trades made it plain that the housing industry was in a grim predicament. Even before the Depression, the American dream of owning a home was far from complete, with stringent loan conditions keeping all but about 40 percent of the population from reaching that goal. Buyers normally had to present a down payment of 30 to 35 percent, and loans carried interest rates of about 8 percent, well above usual market rates. Even with such burdensome terms, borrowers had only five to ten years to repay their loans. Little wonder, then, that in 1928, at the height of prosperity, only 5,778 mortgages were issued nationwide.

When hard times came and the nation's banks nearly all collapsed, there was sparse mortgage opportunity. By 1931 home construction had fallen to only 5 percent of its 1929 numbers. A meager 864 new mortgages were granted in 1933, the year Roosevelt took office, and fully 49 percent of the $20 billion mortgage debt on the books fell into default. Throughout this debacle Hoover's Federal Home Loan Bank Board pursued an ineffectual strategy of directing its monetary aid to lending institutions, rather than to consumers, who were left to exercise the self-reliance Hoover continually vaunted as the great American virtue.

The New Deal approach to fulfilling the American home-owning dream came at things the other way around. The Home Owners' Loan Act, passed in June 1933, set up the Home Owners' Loan Corporation with $2 billion, which was used to recast the mortgage industry to the advantage of people with moderate incomes. Down payments were lowered to 10 percent, and borrowers were given up to thirty years to repay at interest kept at no more than 5 percent. These favorable terms, alongside the New Deal rescue of the banking system, prompted a surge of home loans that went mainly to breadwinners in the $50 to $150 a month income range, who had formerly been excluded or were at greatest risk of losing their homes to foreclosure.

As banks and the housing market revived, Congress passed the National Housing Act in June 1934 in order to regulate the construction of new housing and modernization of old stock. Its provisions, superseding the hodge-podge of local rules that had always prevailed, brought permanent standardization to the building industry. All together, the framework was created within which a majority of Americans would eventually own their own homes.

In other areas, the crisis roused more inclusive concern for those unable to attain such success. Awareness that helplessness crushed the spirit spread from issues of work to health and old-age insurance. The shock of the Depression had forever undermined the notion that individual prudence and local charity could suffice. Inexorably, the new concept of governmental welfare widened; at Roosevelt's behest, in the summer of 1934 an exhausted Harry Hopkins embarked on a tour of Europe to survey welfare measures developed earlier and more broadly elsewhere. On the urging of his old New York social worker colleague, John Kingsbury, Hopkins went to see Beatrice and Sidney Webb. Those venerable relics of socialist causes argued eloquently that America should depart from her voluntaristic local tradition—just as Britain's far more elaborate private charity and labor union mutual aid arrangements had been forced to yield to comprehensive government programs. Hopkins decided to expand his horizon accordingly and redesign federal strategy to meet the unprecedented need. For most of those whom the Depression had set adrift, his objective remained to place them in paying jobs, but Hopkins realized that the helpless—the old, the very young, and the sick—would not benefit from that rugged strategy.

When Hopkins returned, he acted on his broadened awareness by sending a team of observers all over the country to gather information on living conditions, to be used as the basis for an expanded welfare system. Hopkins especially sought advances in three key areas: aid to dependent children that would include children of unemployed parents; old-age and insurance benefits to include workers in agriculture and domestic service; and, most sweeping of all, a compulsory health insurance program.

Although his team of experienced writer-observers, including project chief Lorena Hickok, a gifted journalist who was also a close friend of Eleanor Roosevelt, compiled evidence of unbearable misery, Hopkins's proposals still ran into formidable opposition, especially from the well-entrenched attitude that looked askance at any government aid that was not "temporary" and did not defer to private enterprise. Eventually the power of southern Democrats defeated all attempts to change the traditionally subservient status of farm workers and domestic servants, many of whom suffered a double stigma of being black or Hispanic as well as menial, and the American Medical Association, armed with high prestige and the sanctity of the American's presumed right to a free choice of physician, lobbied successfully against all efforts to impose "socialized medicine." The issue of whether and how the New Deal would institutionalize a welfare system was thus played out on the remaining, long-contested terrain of workmen's compensation, and social insurance to cover unemployment, old age, and dependent children.

Hopkins had at least a meager American tradition of social insurance thought on which to draw, most notably in the area of workmen's compensation. In 1908 Theodore Roosevelt had followed the urging of progressive reformers and signed into law the first federal program to compensate for injuries suffered in the workplace. The act was hardly a vigorous blow against the old rugged individualist view, however—it actually gave fewer benefits than its counterpart in impoverished monarchical Spain. But it signaled a new trend. The following year the first state employee liability commissions, in Minnesota and Wisconsin, opened the way to compensation legislation that was decidedly more generous. New York soon followed suit and then other states, until by 1920 forty-three of them had workmen's compensation laws. The trend was accelerated by court decisions that Roosevelt's successor as president and eventual chief justice of the Supreme Court, William Howard Taft, reproved as "undue emotional generosity on the part of the jury." Especially galling to Taft and other anti-welfare state conservatives was the phasing out of the "fellow-servant" doctrine, which made those working alongside accident victims liable before employers, in favor of the progressive insistence that owners bear the primary responsibility for what happens within their workplaces.

More problematic were benefit issues not governed by liability. For a time early in the century the vogue of welfare capitalism within private industry sought a cost-benefit balance that would serve the interests both of owners and workers. Pension funds drawing contributions from both sides, savings plans, stock options, and unemployment insurance for workers subject to seasonal layoffs were the most prominent innovations. They were stymied, however, by circumstances and competing interests. Employers, especially in labor-intensive mass production industries, favored benefit packages that would tie workers to the success of their employers and require that they not unionize. As officials of the Endicott-Johnson Shoe Company rather smugly pointed out to workers who used company benefits, "your own selfish interest, now, demands that you protect this business."

Organized labor was inclined to resist such paternal welfare capitalism, either private or governmental, on the grounds that all terms of employment should be bargained rather than imposed. In the view of the AFL's Samuel Gompers and his successor, William Green, providing labor with the opportunity to organize was the key to labor's advance. The social insurance approach would reinforce social stratification, creating a permanently inferior class of those dependent on private or governmental largesse. Thus, ironically, unions largely echoed the argument for the equality of the workingman and the tycoon at the bargaining table that had always been used by laissez-faire conservatives to oppose the very improvements in living standards unions were formed to bring about. Welfare plans were further destabilized by strikes, especially the thousands that ravaged the industrial scene in 1919, and by the recessions of 1921 and 1923 that raised welfare costs to such an alarming degree. Finally, the majority of businessmen resisted unions and worker benefits in the belief that firms not saddled with such luxuries would be able to outcompete their more benevolent rivals.

Accordingly, the fruits of welfare capitalism were meager and carefully hedged. Of all the private pension plans in effect at the time of the Great Crash, for example, only 10 percent obligated the companies to pay. Private unemployment insurance plans had similar escape clauses. Under the circumstances, assurances to workers that they were well protected had the sort of hollow sound that could be detected in the boast of a corporate executive in the spring of 1929 that his company's plan would surely prove secure—"unless a Depression came upon us very suddenly."

As the private sector faltered at the close of the 1920s, pressure mounted for the states to take on the nation's welfare burdens. Essentially, the campaign divided proponents of social insurance into two camps. One side, led by John Commons, the prominent labor historian and champion of progressive reform in the "laboratory" state of Wisconsin, included those who favored incorporating traditional American free enterprise values into a social safety net. Commons offered a plan requiring an unemployment reserve funded by employers and government together. Calling his concept the "American System," Commons argued that joint contributions would be commendably "individualistic and capitalistic." The plan would give employers an incentive to maintain jobs and productivity, since they would have to bear part of the cost of unemployment. By the same logic, he believed that the plan would appeal to the "individualism of American Capitalists who do not want to be burdened with the inefficiencies or misfortunes of other capitalists, and it fits the public policy of a capitalistic nation which uses the profit motive to prevent unemployment." On that basis Wisconsin enacted an unemployment insurance bill in 1921 that stimulated passage of similar "American System" legislation in other states, including Massachusetts, New York, Pennsylvania, Minnesota, South Carolina, and Connecticut. Especially persuasive for that era's sensibilities were the emphases on efficiency and enlightened self-interest. Commons successfully appealed to the "modern businessman" as "the only person who is in the strategic position and has the managerial ability capable of preventing unemployment."

For all its momentum, however, Commons's "American Plan" approach ran up against the second major camp—that is, strong advocates for social insurance benefits on the European model of total governmental liability. The general notion of "social insurance" as an entitlement of all citizens was first developed in Europe, particularly in Germany, in the late nineteenth century. European plans shared with Commons's American System the clear separation of social insurance as an earned right of working people from the more socially stigmatized relief or "dole" for the uninsured poor. European plans, however, generally provided broader and deeper coverage with a higher proportion of social wealth distributed as governmental benefits. While Commons's American System was to be funded solely by employer and employee contributions, European plans, while often including a contributory component, required yearly subsidies from general tax revenues.

By the time the 1930s made their dismal appearance, the Ohio Commission on Unemployment was preparing a plan that would provide public insurance without devices to stimulate worker thrift and employer liability for the causes of joblessness and injury. The Ohio Commission contended simply that "insurance is based on the assumption that the risk itself is inevitable, however much it may be reduced" and that insurance was "soundest and most economical when it covers the widest spread of people subject to the risk." The Ohio plan did make a concession to the popularity of the American System by giving an incentive to employers to keep jobs open and safety standards high in the form of variable employer contribution rates. But this gesture did not save the bill or the commission from attack by the Ohio Chamber of Commerce as a socialistic threat to self-help and the charity of family and neighbors. Criticism from partisans of the American System were far less abusive yet still provoked one advocate of the

European approach tried in Ohio to describe the rival plan as the "most stupid undertaking that has ever been suggested."

Aside from the rivalry between advocates of social insurance, the great differences among states in economic resources and willingness to reform worked against any uniform approach. States offering relatively good benefits, all of them in the North, were vulnerable to the migration of jobs to southern states with cheaper labor costs. As the interwar period wore on and welfare plans were tried out, these regional disparities grew ever larger. Between 1919 and 1927, for example, employment in manufacturing decreased by 9 percent nationally but rose by the same percentage in the South. Wage rates revealed what drove the move southward; in that period wages in the South dropped from 73 percent of those in the North to only 60 percent, a gulf greater than had existed before World War I had presumably raised the southern economy to a higher level.

Faced with such handicaps to state action, only Wisconsin offered unemployment insurance of a limited sort, although plans in other states, notably Massachusetts, New Jersey, and Pennsylvania, were moving toward passage on the eve of the New Deal. The movement for pensions fared somewhat better, with seventeen states in the North passing laws providing some slight coverage. Agitation for something more generous as conditions worsened, however, was at fever pitch. The scores of state bills emerging between 1930 and 1933 created a crazy-quilt variety of coverage that set the stage for the entry of the federal government, which, it was increasingly conceded, was the only agency able to provide uniform standards and administration.

Franklin Roosevelt came into the complex and often bitter debate over social insurance well before his presidency. In 1910, as a state senator, he backed workmen's compensation laws, much to the satisfaction of his more socially conscious wife. Before then, his uncle Frederic Delano, an expert on civic structure, and the famous English observer of American institutions, Lord Bryce, had impressed upon him the view that the cooperative spirit among the states and their usefulness as laboratories for government policy gave a unique advantage to the American political system. That idea, alongside his experience with New York state reform, made Roosevelt receptive to the system for social welfare emanating from Commons's Wisconsin. With enthusiasm, Governor Roosevelt in 1930 signed an old-age pension law that concluded many years of strife; at the governors' conference the next year Roosevelt took the lead in arguing for state unemployment laws throughout the country.

In line with the American Plan, Roosevelt hesitated to call for vast federal expenditures traditionally met by families and local communities. Bound by that tradition, the party platform on which Roosevelt had run for president stated: "We advocate unemployment and old-age insurance under state laws." After the election he was further dissuaded from federal initiative by pressure from physicians' lobbies, insurance companies, and business associations. Prior to the entry of the WPA in 1935, the federal government offered no insurance for job loss and even avoided keeping statistics on unemployment, which many considered a private embarrassment best left to the individual to work out, away from public scrutiny.

In the end the administration was jarred into action by a highly unlikely 67-year-old agitator who wielded the authority of age and classic American evangelical fervor. Dr. Francis Townsend of Long Beach, California, also had another asset resonant to Americans: a sure-fire gimmick. Townsend's formula, which occurred to him when he saw an old woman clawing through a garbage can, linked concern over the impoverishment of the aged with a share in the era's fascination with monetary manipulation. In a letter to the *Long Beach Press-Telegram* on September 30, 1933, Townsend proposed that the federal government retire everyone at age sixty on a pension of $200 a month or more with the provision that all the money be spent by the end of the same month. The tremendous stimulus to the economy would benefit the national economy while coming to the rescue of the elderly. Moreover, the jobs otherwise held by persons over sixty would be released to younger workers desperately in need of work.

Behind Townsend rose a mighty chorus of old people and panacea seekers, who formed Townsend Clubs and lobbied for the enactment of the Townsend Plan. More orthodox advocates of social insurance reacted in alarm and helped Congress and the New Deal administration repel efforts by Townsend's supporter in Congress, Representative John S. McGroarty of California—the state's populist poet laureate—to have the plan legislated. Opponents hammered home the point that paying $200 a month to the eight to ten million recipients Townsend foresaw would cost the budget over $20 billion a year—about twice as much as all federal, state, and local tax revenues combined. Indeed, that sum was approximately half the total national income. Were there some way to extract such a ransom, it would mean taking by demand half the national income for payment to about 9 percent of the population—a comment on both the grandiosity of Townsend's scheme and the meagerness of most people's means. The second problem was the insistence that each pensioner spend the entire $200 each month. To make sure this was done in each and every case—on penalty of fine or imprisonment—would require a vast, prying police force. This gave the Townsend movement unwanted power to conjure up images of national ruin and a fascist police state.

Unwisely, Townsend cultivated a Messiah image tinctured with anti-intellectual resentments against his critics. Questions from a congressional committee provoked Townsend into a walkout, which only a pardon from Roosevelt prevented from leading to jail time for contempt of Congress. As he stalked out, Townsend growled, "Every time a brain truster says this plan is crazy a hundred thousand new converts come to our banner. . . . I myself am not an economist, for which fact millions of people have expressed thanks. . . . God deliver us from further guidance by professional economists!" Townsend's ally, McGroarty, pressed the point further: "I refuse to talk to college professors. Give me the names of some practical people."

These flareups occurred in early 1935, close enough to the next year's presidential election to mobilize New Deal concerns. Roosevelt urged the Committee on Economic Security to devise an alternative to the Townsend plan. In doing so he showed his partiality to the state laboratory approach by appointing two veterans of Wisconsin welfare planning: Arthur Altmeyer, a Commons student, as head of the committee's technical board and Edwin E. Witte, a professor at the University of Wisconsin, as executive director of the committee's staff. With Frances Perkins chairing, the committee was strongly inclined toward the balance of responsibilities favored by the American System and by the tradition of social reform in New York, so importantly advanced by Perkins.

Predictably, the committee endorsed the bill sponsored by New Deal stalwarts Senator Robert Wagner of New York and Representative David J. Lewis of Maryland. The bill followed the American System plan, with the enactment of Roosevelt's belief that employees should acquire a personal stake in their own welfare by contributing through payroll taxes to an unemployment fund designed to equalize differences in state benefits. Despite sharp opposition from Perkins, Tugwell, and lobbyists for the European plan, who wanted uniform national standards, the bill also gave states the right to set unemployment insurance rates beyond the basic level of federal grants.

Unlike unemployment insurance proposals, the provisions for old-age insurance and aid to dependent children and the blind did not have to contend with a Wisconsin plan legacy, however, and were drawn on a wholly national basis. The anxiety to eclipse the Townsend Plan added resolve, and on the most practical level, the mobility of retired people—a point strongly raised in opposition to private pensions—would make it virtually impossible for states to determine which persons were their rightful responsibilities. Still in place, however, was Roosevelt's concern to have a contributory feature. He was willing to concede the economic arguments raised by Tugwell and others that such contributions constituted a regressive tax that hit hardest those whose meager incomes left them most in need of social security, but he clung to the view that the political benefits were worth the price. Roosevelt realized, shrewdly, that citizens who believed they had earned the right to social security through their own investment would never allow the system to be scuttled; in the bargain, the more helpless beneficiaries, children and the blind, would be secure. Years later Roosevelt reassured himself in a note taken at a conference to review Social Security that "with those taxes in there, no damn politician can ever scrap my social security program."

Great windy gusts of hosannahs and horror surrounded the subsequent debate in Congress over the social security legislation. Business leaders resonated with the warning of the president of the American Bar Association that the fall of Rome also started with welfare. Republican congressmen opposed to the legislation spoke of the tyrant's lash and fingerprint tests for 5 million citizens. But friends of social security carried the day with their argument that a basic humane advance had been devised and that the Townsend menace could be headed off; Republican opponents prudently voted with the wide majority in favor of the bill reported out of the House Ways and Means Committee as the Social Security Act of 1935. In its final form, the bill contained most of the recommendations of the committee Roosevelt had appointed. That all categories of aid in the bill, except for old-age insurance, were to be administered on the state level bespoke the persuasiveness of Commons's American System and left the federal government an agent of last resort for most issues of social welfare.

Pressure from business interests and conservatives exacted a toll, however. To appease agricultural interests in the South, whose representatives in Congress were vital to maintaining the Democratic majority, and cautious and frugal Secretary of the Treasury Henry Morgenthau, who worried about the difficulty of collecting the contributions of casual workers, the final plan exempted small business employees, agricultural laborers, and domestics from coverage. The administration also yielded on its plan to have uniform state welfare benefits, thus arranging for the disproportionately large share of exempted workers living in poor states to be joined by a pool of cheap labor with coverage. These exclusions most severely disadvantaged those who were already victims of discrimination and low pay rates. Although they often had to contribute to Social Security, the half of the population who worked only intermittently or for a few years, such as migrant farm laborers, domestic servants, women who married at an early age, and housewives earning money on the side—all were denied coverage. That left 60 percent of the nation's women and the same proportion of all African Americans, male and female, outside the Social Security system. Aid to Dependent

Children helped widows whose husbands had had adequate employment, but other women and men with few resources often did not qualify.

Yet, despite its omissions, the momentous change in public policy that Social Security represented roused expectations that society would eventually rescue the helpless and provide a dignified and secure old age for everyone. From there the elderly began their journey from the lowest economic status to the highest, and the attachment of ordinary workers to the New Deal became even stronger. The contributory feature, which Roosevelt insisted on over the objections of such important participants in the creation of Social Security as Perkins, Tugwell, AFL President William Green, and veteran social worker Grace Abbott also proved an asset for the cause of universal coverage.

As Roosevelt always argued, having workers contribute to their own retirement gave them an active interest in the program's continuance, which could not be overridden by any future champions of states' rights or the private sector. The contributory feature was also essential to Roosevelt's aim of erasing the stigma of a dole. His insistence on placing the system on a footing of actuarial soundness has been a key to the system's weathering the years and some epochal demographic shifts. Though the taxes by which the Social Security trust fund is accumulated placed a disproportionate burden on those with modest means, the actual distribution of benefits has remained progressively weighted toward those most in need, especially in terms of aid to dependent children and survivor's benefits. Thus, the Social Security system, designed in the New Deal experimental spirit to grow and incorporate a share of most citizens' faith and fortune, came to combine American and European approaches into a unique prototype for the development of the American welfare state.

Most strikingly, mid-decade social insurance legislation endorsed the conviction that civic society should concern itself with the psychological health of its citizens as well as their financial security. In contrast to the ethic of self-reliant survival, a sunnier, less guilt-ridden spirit of sharing was on the rise, which helped to alleviate the tendency observers had noted from the nation's beginning for Americans to be devoted to the pursuit of happiness in a land of abundance, while often remaining pinched materially and emotionally. Roosevelt owed much of his success to the enthusiasm he aroused when he declared, on many occasions, that the New Deal meant to make life more joyous and that material improvement counted most for the way it lifted the spirit. We have "nothing to fear but fear itself," he intoned at the first inaugural, by which he implied that a secure optimism must be the prelude to rebuilding. Along that line, in a radio address Roosevelt compared the problem of recovery with the question raised after Andrew Jackson's death about whether Old Hickory would go to Heaven. "He will if he wants to," was the answer. So, too, Roosevelt said jauntily about whether Americans would rebound from depression: "They will if they want to." In that spirit of purposeful hope, Roosevelt signed the Social Security Act on August 14, 1935, describing it as the cornerstone of a structure "by no means complete." The welfare it provided pointed toward a broad collectivist change in Americans' conceptions of the good life and, more modestly, in their actual level of security and well-being.

CHAPTER EIGHT

Revival of the Spirit

Although New Deal recovery programs were aimed primarily at restoring material well-being, the effort showed that the emotional response to stress was also a significantly related concern. The fact of so many people being reduced by unemployment to self-accusing despair shocked a nation that had been brought up on the go-getter concept. Clearly, there was a connection between material and spiritual health, as Roosevelt recognized in his campaign against fear. With his blessing, the dispensing of aid to the dispossessed was presented as a key to lifting the public out of despair; recovery programs were to engender a happier, more moral, more intelligent citizenry by freeing them from a demoralizing struggle for survival. As recovery proceeded, it began to seem that attaining a modest level of creature comfort was the keynote of New Deal aspirations for the spirit as well as for the flesh.

There were those who approached things the other way around, however, and chose to give first priority to matters of the spirit that were especially the province of artists and writers. Their expressive sensibilities extended across a wide range of consequences wrought by the Crash upon a people who had generally assumed that continuous progress was supposed to be their destiny. The focus of spiritual concern was mainly on three questions about the meaning of the Depression: Was it the bad end of mistaken American premises? To this radicals answered yes and called for revolution. Or was the Crash the result of a lapse from faith into the orgy of experimentation and self-indulgence that reached its peak during the 1920s? That view appealed more to moralists and critics on the right. Still others, less inclined to find fault, took the third view, that the decline indicated that an era had come to its natural end. The most persuasive argument in that key, endorsed by Roosevelt in his Commonwealth Club speech, was that the continuation of wasteful ways after the end of the frontier, which had always represented the horizon of endless bounty, had brought on the Crash.

As for the artists who might alleviate pain and inspire recovery, they had little cause to lament the passing of the New Era. Most had long felt alienated from a commercial society in which they had little stake. A substantial group of artists and writers who subscribed to the view that the Crash had brought a discreditable system to earth signed a statement in support of the Communist Party candidates in the 1932 election. They could readily agree with the discerning photographer of Depression life, Walker Evans, that the "awful society damn well deserved [the Crash]." Evans recalled how "I used to jump for joy when I read of some of those stock brokers jumping out of windows! They were really dancing in the streets in the Village the day the banks all closed."

For those with less bitterness than Evans toward the philistine mainstream of the 1920s—"women's clubs, fake culture, bad education, religion in decay"—the mood was more one of liberation than vengefulness. Literary and social critic Matthew Josephson remembered in his *Infidel in the Temple: A Memoir of the Nineteen-Thirties* how "this dismal year 1932 became for many of us a time of hope. . . . Here I would like to cross my heart and deny that the mood of the intelligentsia of the 1930's was in any way . . . melancholy or grim." Josephson's fellow critic Malcolm Cowley extended the upbeat argument by contending that "The 1930's were a vigorous age for criticism, an experimental age for the drama, a really brilliant age for the realistic novel." It was, Cowley concluded, an "age of faith" that encouraged artists and writers to believe that they could express a vision that would draw the general public up into "the golden mountains" where "a revolutionary brotherhood" would usher in a new society of social justice and beauty.

That faith, following in the wake of discredited conventional wisdom, concentrated on the creation of new values. For a time, Josephson, Cowley, and many others sought guidance from the fashionable Marxism of the day. "The secure world of their childhood had fallen apart," Cowley recalled. "They were looking for a scheme of values, a direction, a skeleton key that would unlock almost any sort of political or literary situation." But, as Cowley wryly acknowledged, he only *thought* of himself as a Marxist. Later he and other veterans of the left discovered that they were really Emersonians—seekers in the American grain after transcendent spiritual values rather than believers in some determinist formula for revolution.

Adrift and often confused in the search for values, artists and critics during the 1930s reflected the judgment novelist Sherwood Anderson reached after a long journey across the land that the nation was "Puzzled America." It needed to find out how it had fallen so low and what the true nature and fate of its people were. That urge directed attention toward the "forgotten man" Roosevelt exalted. The study of little-known localities and regions enjoyed a vogue, as a new wave of explorers—social scientists, journalists, novelists, and critics—fanned out over the countryside to find clues to the American character and condition that had eluded the nation's leaders and interpreters in the 1920s, with disastrous results. This sense of a need to integrate a broader range of reality encouraged a doctrine of cultural relativism, highlighted by Ruth Benedict's *Patterns of Culture* (1934), which argued that persons were so thoroughly conditioned by their various and distinctive societies that few, if any, traits of "human nature" were universal or inborn. Alongside that anthropological view, the movement called "cultural pluralism" proclaimed American character to be a composite of many ethnic and racial types that need not defer to a WASP ideal. The pluralist view gained great strength from events: in the midst of hardship and witness to brutal aggression abroad, it helped define the ethic that held the New Deal coalition together and governed the idealist resistance to narrow standards of racial, ideological, and national purity. Since all persons are shaped by their culture, the cultural relativists argued, it followed that every person is integrally a part of that culture; none are rightfully outcasts, subject to discrimination and caste distinction.

The search for inclusive and democratic roots and values spurred on the mission urged since early in the century to find a "usable past." Originally intended by cultural critics like Van Wyck Brooks and Randolph Bourne to trigger an "awakening" of the arts and intellect for a revolutionary overthrow of commercialism, the idea of a "usable past" came to have a more conservative thrust in the "Puzzled America" of the 1930s. Critics who were troubled about what the Depression fall from grace indicated about the American character and purpose looked to the "usable past" for an indication of how to recover old truths. History and biography came back in vogue, and figures from the American past, like Mark Twain, Benjamin Franklin, and Ralph Waldo Emerson who had been written off during the skeptical 1920s as shills for materialism and Puritan moralism were rehabilitated as national heroes. To place such heroes in full perspective, a flood of works explaining critical periods and issues of history gave Americans their best means ever to judge where they stood in relation to the past and other cultures—to find, as John Dos Passos put it in a historical study that marked his change from cynic to celebrant of American values, *The Ground We Stand On* (1941).

The first influential proposal to link the new wave of cultural concern to the New Deal came from a wealthy Philadelphia artist and Groton schoolmate of

Roosevelt, George Biddle. In May 1933, Biddle wrote to tell the new president about the artistic achievements of Diego Rivera and his fellow Mexican muralists José Clemente Orozco and David Siqueiros. Their heroic celebration of the triumph of the common man in Mexico's bloody revolution captured the imagination of the Mexican public and indicated how American artists, eager to follow similar inspiration, could express the ideals of social reformation the New Deal wished to advance. Roosevelt responded favorably, and at the more fervent urging of Eleanor Roosevelt and Harry Hopkins, who had pressed Roosevelt during his governorship to aid desperate artists, agreed to sponsor relief for artists.

A logical starting point for federal patronage was the Treasury Department, which had long been in charge of decorations on public buildings. But the National Commission of Fine Arts, presidential advisers since 1910, cast a cold eye on any new proposals. The commission was vintage fogey, dedicated to the Beaux Arts classical style, which they could advocate with a show of plausibility as appropriate for Pierre L'Enfant's Greco-Roman master plan for the capital. Fortunately, the Treasury staff included a trade expert, Edward Bruce, who also happened to be a painter and a defender of the arts. After graduating from Columbia Law School, Bruce had gone to the Philippines and bought the Manila *Times*. An interval in the Asian import-export trade followed before Bruce, at age 44, went to Italy for six years of art study. In 1932, looking for a way to support himself, Bruce arrived in Washington as representative of the West Coast Chamber of Commerce and then joined the Treasury as an expert on international monetary matters. Blessed with that uncommon blend of artistic and bureaucratic experience, Bruce seemed the perfect choice to organize a federal arts program.

But although Bruce had an exotic background, he was no rebel. He chose to serve the artistic establishment by steering a middle course between the classical "ladies in cheesecloth" and abstractionist "tripe," as he described the avant garde innovations of the 1920s. He also, as he put it, intended to halt the "Mexican invasion on the border." Unmoved by revolutionary art, Bruce wanted to inspire recovery and national pride through art that would give "the same feeling I get when I smell a sound, fresh ear of corn"—a feeling well attuned to the premium the New Deal placed on the confidence and good cheer of the Common Man.

Under Bruce's paternalistic direction, commissions were awarded through competitions judged by mainstream experts. Only one quite benign abstract mural was selected for an Ohio post office. Otherwise artworks of slightly larger than life neo-realist character were favored. An aura of excitement attended the mural program nonetheless. Several among the chosen artists expressed kinship with the great Renaissance muralists who also worked in association to express civic values; never before had there been patronage in America sufficient to carry out work of such large scale in public spaces. A sense of historic, even prophetic, mission was also generated by the directive that the murals depict some aspect of the culture of the locale in which they would be displayed. One artist concluded that he had been sent to a certain small town in upstate New York in order to deliver an "article of faith"—a belief in concrete visual terms that such towns embody an essential fusion of unique historical experience with the national values it was the task of the New Deal to discern and promote. For symbolizing that combination of the particular and the general, the mural section's neo-realist style was perfectly suited. Although mural commissions did not often lead to notable art, the effort to link day-to-day life with myth and historical destiny lent the program some cultural significance, while it conspicuously promoted its sponsor's ideal of a cooperative commonwealth that would link local mores with national purpose.

A quite different, more free-ranging, approach to artists was followed by the later and larger arts project sponsored by the WPA. Like all other unemployed persons helped by WPA, artists were put to work in their own specialties. The issue, at least for official consumption, was relief, not patronage of the arts. The artistic results were beside the point for bureaucratic management, and expenditures were not to be decided upon by competitive judging of artists' entries. With fourteen times as much money to spend as the Treasury program and a bias, however inadvertent, toward free expression, the WPA's Federal Arts Project (FAP) shaped the dominant pattern for federal support by giving its relief recipients the right to create as they chose.

FAP's head was Holger Cahill, yet another New Deal enthusiast of unusually diverse background. Cahill had fled his somber Minnesota farm family when he was twelve and panhandled across Canada until, four years later, he shipped out of Vancouver as a coal shoveler. In Shanghai he jumped ship, wandered a while, and then worked passage back to America. Night school to repair his lack of education led to a try at writing for small newspapers. But that job quickly lost its appeal, so he moved restlessly eastward as deck hand on a Lake Michigan iron ore carrier and an insurance salesman in Cleveland before hopping a freight for New York City just after World War I. Content, at last, to be in Greenwich Village bohemia, Cahill listened attentively to Thorstein Veblen's critique of philistine business at the New School for Social Research and joined the quest for a "usable past" in order to advance the cause of modern art and socialism.

Cahill's talents and fervent concern for a distinctive American aesthetic gained him a job at the Newark Museum where, from 1922 to 1929, he assembled a notable collection of contemporary American art and developed an appreciation of folk art. Successful exhibits led to his appointment in 1929 as director of exhibitions at the new Museum of Modern Art in New York. There he made a reputation with displays of American folk art—artistry that corresponded perfectly with the general interest in becoming more aware of the American character in all its variety.

The selection of Cahill to head FAP was a natural for Hopkins, whose New York contacts extolled Cahill's New Deal sensibilities and his relevant experience. Cahill was also content with the WPA concept of placing relief needs first, and he had an appropriate concept of the role art should play in the community, taken from the argument philosopher John Dewey had made in the most important aesthetic text of the period, *Art as Experience* (1934), that art should move out of sheltered "ideal" realms representing aristocratic taste and draw beauty from the common life. Art, Dewey insisted, was the conveyer of society's most important news. It followed, Cahill believed, in accord with a growing contingent of social activists, that the artists themselves should be representatives of the common life —workers and farmers, "girls in boarding schools, old maids, lonely bachelors," people from the neglected, and therefore exotic, outlands and back rooms of society. Buoyed by that spirit, Cahill launched the Federal Arts Project with the explicit aim of using community-based programs to bring "art to the millions" and draw out the talents of the submerged masses.

As Cahill was gathering his forces, three companion programs took shape: the Federal Writers' Project, the Federal Theater Project, and the Federal Music Project. Each of them struck a distinctive balance between creativity and community service by carrying their art into schools, parks, community centers, and mental hospitals, where WPA artists pioneered the use of music and the visual arts for therapy. All of these ventures, sometimes reaching remote areas in caravans like the theater companies and circuses of a century before, converged on a mission: the discernment and celebration of folk roots and shared values. The rise of this mission was a tribute to the campaign to discover a usable past, even as it fed the New Deal aim of unifying the nation through agreement on cooperative planning.

Whatever room there might be to dispute government patronage of the arts, the staggering volume of work done on the WPA program makes it clear that the participants did not lack enthusiasm or a work ethic. During the first four and a half months of Bruce's Treasury art program, for example, 3,749 artists on the payroll turned out over fifteen thousand works of art and craft. The four hundred murals which were included drew the most attention, but they constituted less than 3 percent of the total output. Holger Cahill's larger WPA program declared as part of its final report that its workers had produced 2,566 murals, 17,444 pieces of sculpture, 108,099 works in oil, watercolor, tempera, and pastel, and 240,000 copies of 11,285 original designs in various media. Out of the quantity came a strong measure of quality: WPA muralists won a high proportion of national competitions; FAP artists appeared on every list of Guggenheim awards between 1935 and 1943; in 1937 no fewer than ten FAP print makers were included on the British Fine Prints of the Year list. All this is to say nothing of the indirect benefits to artistic production; for the WPA in 160 locations taught over 2 million students in all phases of art. The aim of finding the sources of artistic inspiration in the common life led to the discovery and exhibition by FAP of folk artists like "Grandma" Moses, who would have considerable influence, and to the compilation of the Index of American Design, which demonstrated in rich profusion that the imaginativeness behind America's practical and decorative crafts created a distinctive American style ranging from folk realism to abstract inwardness. At some point nearly every artist born between 1900 and 1915 and destined to gain a high reputation found rescue on the FAP—including painters who evolved socially conscious symbolism into the abstract expressionism that made New York the art capital of the world after World War II—household names like Jackson Pollock, Mark Rothko, and Robert Motherwell.

The WPA project for writers posed even greater problems of organization than did FAP, largely because writers, in the manner of gods or beasts, as one of them put it, tend to be loners. To find something inspiring for them to do, Hopkins chose another adventurous character named Henry Alsberg. As a young man who could not fit his career as a lawyer in with his anarchist and literary sensibilities, Alsberg traveled to Russia in 1919 to witness the new Bolshevik "utopia," only to flee the repression he actually found in a hail of bullets from revolutionaries he had annoyed with his criticism.

Back in New York, Alsberg became a journalist, occasional play producer, and would-be novelist. But mostly he devoted himself to causes aimed at the sort of social justice the New Deal came to stand for. From various forays into the midst of labor strife and assaults on free expression Alsberg emerged, in the words of one who knew him well, as one of those rare persons "with a public sense, a feeling for broad human movements and how people are caught up in them."

Alsberg's first task for the Writers' Project was to certify who were truly writers and so worthy of inclusion in the support program. Several competing views clamored for his attention. The Authors Guild insisted that a bona fide author had to be a proven professional who had published two or more books; the Newspaper Guild reduced that to anyone whose work had appeared in print; and the

Writers Union—the most radical of the lot—included anyone who had earned a living in the literary world and who could produce a manuscript judged satisfactory by a review committee.

Because the leaders of the Writers' Project never did manage to agree on criteria, it proved hard to settle on suitable recipients and projects beyond makework, such as classifying documents and revising manuals for government agencies. On the side, several literary magazines kept the creativity of project workers alive. "American Stuff" was the most prominent example. But "Frontier and Midland" in Montana, "Material Gathered" in San Francisco, and other such ventures also helped young writers—including many destined for fame, like Saul Bellow, Ralph Ellison, Eudora Welty, and Richard Wright—find their places as creative artists.

The wide variety of approaches gave rein to creative differences, and the diversity fit the turbulent nature of the projects, composed under the press of necessity faced by a motley crowd of hard-luck cases. There were talented writers on the rise, writers converted to a new social consciousness, failed writers, drunken writers, even a few mad writers. They could be only loosely harnessed under the best of circumstances, and the 1930s provided few of those. Alsberg, whose long, drooping face made him look like a tired bloodhound in the midst of frantic improvising, relied on his nineteenth-century optimism, his dreams of a new culture, and his ulcer remedy. One day Eleanor Roosevelt asked whether he would be kind enough to make room in an out-of-the-way post for an old journalist friend who had become alcoholic. "Mrs. Roosevelt," the rumpled director replied, "if we made it a rule not to hire writers given to drink, we would probably not have a Writers' Project."

Fortunately, as the lack of clear direction began to seem chronic, a project worker suggested that a guide to the United States be the central thrust of the project. The idea perfectly suited the prevailing enthusiasm for regionalism; it also met a real need since only the original Baedeker's Guide to the United States, first issued in 1893, was then available. Though the task was never to be fully accomplished, it was a vital spearhead for the New Deal intent to understand what needed to be done by exploring and analyzing local economies, institutions, and cultures. Alsberg proved to be an able and imaginative editor, and his administrative shortcomings may also have contributed to the fascinatingly diverse way the guides were prepared. Throughout the decade guidebooks appeared to critical acclaim—mostly—and took their place as the standard reference to American states and regions. The reviewer who declared that the guides would outlast most books of the era has been borne out, and Van Wyck Brooks was appropriately moved by the guides' service to his concept of a "usable past" to write Alsberg that he should be awarded a Ph.D. by every college in the country.

The emphasis on regionalism led beyond guidebooks to a more thoroughgoing analysis of customs and values. With Alsberg's blessing, two accomplished anthropologists with active sympathies for the forgotten and downtrodden, John A. Lomax and Benjamin Botkin, established a section on folklore. In agreement with Alsberg about the value of supporting more artistic freedom than work on the state guides generally provided, they looked on folklore as a means for combining regional information with artistic sensibility. On that sensitive edge of the guidebook project appeared the *Life in America* series of 150 volumes. With titles like *Hands That Built New Hampshire* and *The Albanian Struggle in the Old World and the New,* the series sought to follow dramatic themes that would honor the rise of the Common Man. The most famous product of the folklore section, however, was Botkin's *Lay My Burden Down: A Folk History of Slavery* (1945), a compilation of interviews taken with ex-slaves whose wide and contradictory memories ignited interest in the complexities of the slave experience that vast research has still not made wholly clear.

Under that impetus a project to gather slave narratives was begun under the Federal Emergency Relief Administration in 1934. Two years later Henry Alsberg appointed as the national editor of Negro affairs a young African American named Sterling Brown, whose inspirational leadership raised the Washington, D.C., guide book to a level of insight into black life never before reached. On the heels of that success the Chicago Writers Project group produced an excellent guide to black life in Chicago, and the New York entry under Roi Ottley won the Houghton Mifflin "Life in America" award for 1943.

The Theatre Project had a more troubled career. In early 1934, as the CWA was unfolding, Hopkins called on his friend from his days at Grinnell College in Iowa, Hallie Flanagan, to devise some sort of drama program, using the argument that half of the theaters in New York City had gone dark in 1933 and that most actors were unemployed. Flanagan, who at the time ran the theater department at Vassar College, was receptive to Hopkins's plea. The basic plains populism she had absorbed in Iowa suited the realist acting style she had recently learned from the world-renowned director Constantin Stanislavsky at the Moscow Art Theatre. The compatibility of her outlook and skills with the New Deal focus on the "common man" was evident in her Vassar production, *Can You Hear Their Voices?* (1931), a dramatization based on an account by a young radical journalist named Whittaker Chambers of the takeover and looting of an Arkansas town by drought-ridden farmers who could think of no other way to feed their families. Since all the elements could be assembled cheaply without the need for highly expert talent, documentary drama was a likely vehicle for an undertaking that placed relief of the unemployed ahead of professional stage production and sought to reach the widest possible audiences with news about what was affecting their lives.

In subsequently developing the WPA Theatre Project, Flanagan took on two major goals: the creation of regional theaters and the development of theatrical means to project basic, even earthy, themes and so make the theater a contributor to social progress. Flanagan called for "relevance" in the charged language of the times: "We live in a changing world. Man is whispering through space, soaring to the stars, flinging miles of steel and glass into the air. Shall the theatre continue to huddle in the confines of a painted box seat?" The enlistment of the theater and the New Deal in a common responsibility seemed equally clear: "In an age of terrific implications as to wealth and poverty, as to the function of government, as to peace and war, as to the relation of an artist to all these forces, the theatre must grow up. The theatre must become conscious of the implications of the changing social order, or the changing social order will ignore, and rightly, the implications of the theatre."

Flanagan hoped that the Theatre Project could contribute to change by ending America's chronic overconcentration of theater in New York and a very few other large cities. Her plan was to draw upon the regionalist emphasis of all the Arts Projects to set up a federation of theaters that could use federal support to produce plays reflecting local issues and distinctiveness and at the same time convey concerns the nation had in common. The federated system would also develop local talent and so have a similarly balanced local and national significance. Blessed with some remarkable members, including the 21-year-old acting and directorial phenomenon Orson Welles, the FTP got off to an exhilarating start. Plays in a variety of languages and presentations of local history in places far from Broadway expressed the governing ideal of folk-rooted diversity. The Federal Theatre group also played an important part in black theater life by granting a reprieve to Harlem's Lafayette Theatre after its closing early in the Depression left the area without a stage. The company that subsequently came into existence grew impressively to a total of about 140 black actors, writers, and stagehands and, with its *Swing Mikado* and *Macbeth,* staged by Orson Welles in a Haitian voodoo setting, became one of the most attention-getting theatrical experiments of the era. Relevance was also served by allegories about union struggles and the fascist menace, climaxing in a dramatization of Sinclair Lewis's best-selling novel *It Can't Happen Here,* about a fascist coup d'état. With perfect dramatic timing the play attracted large audiences and great critical interest by opening in seventeen cities just days before the election of 1936 tested the appeal of the radical Union Party of Father Charles Coughlin and Francis Townsend.

The remaining arts program, for musicians, was the least committed to overt promotion of social reform. The language of music is, after all, relatively universal and formal. Moreover, the director of the Music Project, Nikolai Sokoloff, was a professional with stringent standards developed as conductor of the Cleveland Symphony Orchestra. Yet the Music Project also took up the quest for a usable past and the desire to involve the masses. Sheer need pressed in those directions from the outset. In 1933 the American Federation of Musicians estimated that about 70 percent of formerly employed musicians were out of work, a flood of relief applicants that made it impossible for Sokoloff to audition carefully for quality. His consolations were that music was inherently a democratic art—everyone could take part, even if only to hum or whistle—and that the Depression offered a valuable opportunity to spread music to the provinces and to encourage American composers and performers where previously more attention had been paid to Europe.

The project moved on a wide front to remove the barriers against American music. It commissioned new works, including the 1937 competition winners by William Schumann and Elliott Carter, later recognized as two of the most important American composers. Performances also featured Americans. In his final report Sokoloff included the remarkable item that his musicians had performed pieces by 3,258 American composers, almost 300 of whom had worked on the Music Project. This was not done in isolation. By the end of the decade the Music Project noted that the quarter of a million performances under its auspices had drawn 160 million listeners. Still, in the long run the greatest stimulus to creativity may have come through the music teaching program, which ultimately employed 6,000 teachers and gave instruction to over 17 million students.

As this massive drawing of the public into art galleries, concert halls, and classrooms went on, the Music Project's section on folk art, headed by musicologist Charles Seeger, worked to connect formal American composition with folk customs through a broad study of regional musical cultures. By joining forces with FAP on the Joint Committee on Folk Arts, music project researchers endorsed the proposition that folk art was an organic whole, rather than an aggregate of creative specialties. Out of the pooling of resources came thousands of recordings done in the field, most famously those taken by John Lomax and his son Alan at prison camps throughout the south. By the end of the project in 1945, the Archive of American Folk Song in the Library of Congress had received about 8,000 discs from every corner of the country.

The reformist, inclusive effort to recover folk roots proved especially beneficial to black music. Acute need, as well as interest in finding roots, provided especially strong reasons for helping black artists. After the heyday of the 1920s,
when the worldwide discovery of African art and American jazz excited great interest in black art and life, the Crash came as a devastating reversal. Struggling
black artists, even those in the relatively prosperous "Harlem Renaissance," were
the least able of all groups to absorb economic shocks. They had few reserves
of wealth and were further victimized when white sponsors withdrew in order
to concentrate their dwindling resources on white artists. Without the massive
gathering program carried out by the Joint Committee on Folk Arts, the treasury
of black folk music, jazz, and spirituals would have drifted further to the periph-
ery, some of it to disappear entirely. Instead, black folk artistry became forever
linked with New Deal cultural aims, its historic and artistic meaning interpreted
and its content classified by New Deal preservationists. At the same time, the
Music Project furthered the entry of blacks into the mainstream of concert music. Most importantly, it sponsored composer William Grant Still, who worked
folk themes into his formal compositions, to be guest conductor of the San Diego Symphony. Furthermore, black choruses trained by the Federal Music Project for operatic productions of *Aïda* and Auber's *Fra Diavolo* brought black musical talent to the opera stage.

The gains of black artists exemplified the outreach of the WPA projects. That
even the most disadvantaged element in society should benefit indicated a sea
change against the traditional view that art was the privilege of those who attained
leisure. Impressed by the fall of the old order and by the vast domain of the
New Deal coalition, artists generally agreed with the strategy of diffusing support
throughout all the nation's regions in an attempt to develop new talent and a general awareness of the importance of art in defining a people and raising spirits.

It followed that, though launched independently under distinctly individualist leadership, the WPA projects to rescue artists, writers, actors, and musicians
followed common enthusiasms and encountered common pitfalls. None of the
programs could find the perfect formula for meshing relief with dedication to
artistic standards and so had to accept uneven results and the all too real danger
that the entire program would be judged by some of its more bizarre or amateur-
ish products. Thanks to the make-work image cast in the public mind by WPA's
enemies, after the Arts Projects ended in 1943, they suffered such disdain that
for many years they were written off as a source of true creativity once the enthusiasms of the 1930s for a people's art had cooled.

The movement of the Arts Projects toward a coherent view of the common life was closely paralleled by developments in film and photography. At the time that art was coming to stress realism, photography was enjoying great forward strides in technique and a sense of its own possibilities as an art form, most widely celebrated in the new picture magazines—led by *Life* and *Look*—which promoted the photographic essay as a way of bringing the reader closer to reality than words could do.

Much of the rising interest in the documentary photo that attended these claims was emotional—the shock of recognition of the human comedy and plight, accompanying a certain awe at moods and expressions so directly conveyed. But there also lay behind the documentary concrete support for the progressive belief that knowledge was the best lever for reform and that once the facts were presented, most people—the decent American public—would act accordingly. From the time of Jacob Riis's grim photographic record of New York slums in *How the Other Half Lives* (1891), the value of photography as an instant fact-gatherer and catalyst for reform was earnestly assumed.

And yet, for all the Progressive insistence that hard reality makes its own case, compilers of facts and pictures could hardly avoid selecting and arranging their findings. Trading on the axiom that "seeing is believing," those with a message to give through images were excited by having the best of two worlds: they were able to present viewers what seemed the unvarnished truth while retaining the ability to edit actuality to suit their viewpoints. The documentary was at once a staple of the rising flood of propaganda, which fascinated the era with its ominous implications, and prized by the public as a weapon against propaganda. Thus, to take a prime example, "The March of Time" films awed moviegoers between features with their portentous air of setting the record straight—while drawing little attention to the selective hand of the *Time* magazine editors behind the scenes. The *Annals of the Academy of Political and Social Science* followed suit in its special issue of 1935 on propaganda by treating that phenomenon as essentially a tool created by foreigners bent on repression rather than one used by Americans seeking progressive reform and enlightenment.

As enthusiasm for the documentary made its way into government during the early 1930s, a dramatic shift occurred in the federal bureaucracy's approach to film. As far back as 1908, the Signal Corps and Department of Agriculture used film to convey information in a neutral and unadorned style. Then, in 1934, keen about the possibilities for a new governmental involvement in the arts and the common life, the independent Film and Photo League produced a dramatization of the WPA called *Hands*. Pare Lorentz, a journalistic film critic, turned the WPA film into a theater event by fashioning a script set to music by a champion of the

American cause in the arts, Virgil Thomson, and read on stage by a former Metropolitan Opera baritone.

Lorentz had also edited a book of photographs with Henry Wallace in 1933 called *The Roosevelt Year,* and two years later he accepted a job as publicist for the Resettlement Administration. Almost immediately he agreed to collaborate with Archibald MacLeish, then lending his keen poetic insight to *Fortune* magazine, on a pictorial study of the Southwest, where drought was turning productive farm land into a dustbowl. The result in 1935 was *The Plow That Broke the Plains,* a film depicting how man had upset the balance of nature by plowing up the grass that held the land together. The film impressed a wide and receptive audience with the need for a New Deal program to guard against disaster, whether natural or man-made, by regulating farm methods and patterns of settlement.

Inspired by the success of *The Plow,* Lorentz went on to his greatest acclaim with *The River* (1937). The film's motif, suggested by a conversation with Rexford Tugwell, was to follow a drop of water down the Mississippi to the river's wide-flowing juncture with the sea. En route the film crew found itself in the midst of spring floods and captured their disastrous rampage in an exciting, spontaneous sequence. On seeing the results, Roosevelt enthusiastically agreed to Lorentz's proposal for creation of a separate film service to portray New Deal concerns. The new venture was borne along by international acclaim for *The River*—including first prize at the International Cinema Exposition in Venice in 1938.

Still photography enjoyed comparable success within the New Deal. Once again Tugwell was the catalyst. During his years at Columbia he had developed his progressive belief in the value of experience by sending students out into the streets to witness the socioeconomic whirl for themselves. His graduate assistant, a country-bluff fellow from Colorado named Roy Stryker, took most fervently to the experiment. Stryker's fascination with city life and the arresting photographic impressions of New York by Jacob Riis and Lewis Hine led to a collaboration with Tugwell on a text called *American Economic Life and the Means of Its Improvement* (1925), for which Stryker provided a sample of the photographs he most admired. Later, as undersecretary in the Department of Agriculture, Tugwell chose Stryker to preside over a photographic unit to chronicle the ills of the countryside with the intent, once again, of finding the "means of its improvement."

Stryker made no claims to any picture-taking talents of his own. Long afterward he acknowledged, "I was never a photographer. I was a teacher and gadgeteer. I always had a camera but I had no more business with that damn Leica than with a B-29. I got a hell of an inferiority complex because of it. My aunt and

I once shot a family reunion. Her ten-dollar Brownie got everything while I drew blanks. I never snapped a shutter after that." But Stryker's lack of talent did not hold him back. He had a fervent conviction about the relationship between economics and social mores and about the value of observing that relationship directly. He would berate his Columbia class accordingly: "You want to know about economics? Economics is not money. Economics is people." Then he marched them through the streets and workplaces to show them the truth of it. For a more remote audience, photography was the indispensable substitute for direct observation, and with a brusquely commanding certitude Stryker shaped up a battalion of photographers to carry the New Deal reform truth to the public. As Stryker recalled, "I was one-half editor, one-half papa, one-half hell-raiser, one-half purchasing agent, and occasionally psychoanalyst without portfolio." And he was always the boss, given to referring to his photographic legion as "camera fodder."

Stryker's approach, which produced about 270,000 pictures, including some of the most famous photographs of the era, brilliantly suited Tugwell's charge that the photographic unit should introduce Americans to America. Thus the team became a kind of social science auxiliary—"a bunch of sociologists with cameras," as the great nature photographer, Ansel Adams, rather derisively called it. The massive volume of work formed a rich enough data bank for one of Stryker's photographers, John Collier, to use as a basis for his pioneering *Visual Anthropology: Photography as a Research Method* (1967). Pictures, Collier argued with considerable analytic detail, stimulate understanding—even if only inarticulately through inferences drawn from emotional reactions to what is seen.

Certainly, the many images captured stimulated perceptions of the 1930s that have influenced conscious, even subconscious, impressions of the decade ever since. The haggard faces, the weathered lines, the wistful gestures and anxious body curves—all against a backdrop of parched land and dilapidation—these were the stock in trade of Stryker's effort to convey the New Deal message of a need to reform and to revive the spirit. The Depression victims captured by the lens, helpless though they might be in real life, were seen to have symbolic power to rouse conscience and compassion. Photographers, by using the same sort of sensibilities that had long served socially conscious painters, could make it their mission to reveal the nobility of their subjects and so persuade the nation to see them as worthy of rescue.

CHAPTER NINE

Renewing the New Deal Lease

By mid-decade the New Deal was at a crossroads. The basic elements of its emergency program had been put into practice and were nearing the point where their effects could be evaluated. Along the way certain key divisions over New Deal objectives had formed, centered on the viability of planning for a cooperative commonwealth. In the TVA, for example, the bitter struggle between Arthur Morgan and David Lilienthal raised uncertainty about how much the TVA was to be a model of Brains Trust planning. Would the grassroots experiment advance the cause of planned reconstruction of community life, or was it mainly an exercise in bureaucratic management and resource development? Within the AAA battle, lines had been drawn between large producers who benefited from acreage reduction and the have-not tenants and marginal farmers whom "modernization" tended to force off the land. Would the New Deal be able to champion the self-reliant yeoman ideal and enact a plan to resettle the destitute on small farms that would give them a secure future? Or was the farm program destined to serve merely as a guarantor of high prices for large entrenched interests? On both wings of the NRA, resistance to the New Deal plan for a cooperative commonwealth also arose. As business recovered and regained some of its old arrogance, it rebuffed both government direction and union demands with an attention to self-interest that eventually derailed the NRA. Organized labor, on the other hand, rebelled against codes that favored business and inhibited collective bargaining. The wave of strikes in 1934 were an early indication of organized labor's resolve to be an independent force, despite its affinities with New Deal goals.

The challenges to the New Deal's aim of cooperative inclusion were especially acute in responding to racial divisions. Segregation by law and custom blocked African Americans from receiving their share of opportunity and benefits. In the case of Native Americans, New Deal good intentions faced unique dilemmas that led to a comparably unique policy honoring separateness, rather than inclusion. That anomaly reflected the way pressure for assimilation had long inflamed relations between whites and Native Americans. Under the auspices of the Dawes Act of 1887 federal policy sought the elimination of Indian reservations by allotting tribal lands to individual Indians. The policy gained momentum when Indians who served in World War I were granted citizenship, followed in 1924 by the extension of citizenship to all Indians. At the same time reaction against the materialistic pressures of modern life led reformers, alienated artists, and Native Americans themselves to hail the subtle harmonies of Indian life and argue that contact with whites simply brought exploitation. Led by progressive writer John Collier, a group calling itself "friends of the Indians" pressured Congress to issue a report on Indian conditions in 1928 that revealed how failed policy had left Native Americans in desperate poverty and ill health.

Soon after he took office, Franklin Roosevelt, who saw the plight of Native Americans as part of widespread common man woes, urged Secretary of the Interior Harold Ickes to take action. Ickes responded by making Collier Commissioner of Indian Affairs and charging him to create legislation expanding tribal autonomy. The Indian Reorganization Act of 1934 that resulted provided for self-government, transfer of individually held allotments of land to communal property, and tribal corporations for the management of tribal resources. Elated, Collier predicted that the act would lead to "the economic and the spiritual rehabilitation of the Indian race."

But dilemmas mirroring the unresolved strain between Native American autonomy and New Deal inclusiveness persisted. Opposition from some Indians who feared the imposition of alien ways and, at the opposite pole, from Indians who preferred assimilation, resulted in 77 tribes, including the Navajos, the nation's largest tribe, voting against reorganization. For the 181 tribes who accepted the new order, there were some benefits. Millions of acres were converted from individual to tribal ownership, and with financial assistance from Washington, the consolidated tribes were able to provide better education and health and build a stronger economic base. Reflecting the improved conditions, the Native American population rose from 343,000 in 1934 to 1.9 million by 1990.

On the other hand, greater numbers meant less per capita land and led to an exodus of almost half the reservations' people, while interference from outside government agencies and business interests, along with faulty governance on some reservations, hindered community development. As a result the Indian Reorganization Act failed to achieve its ends, and many Indians languished in poverty and low educational attainment. As with blacks, the New Deal extended hope to Native Americans but was never able to enfold them within its vision of security and prosperity for the common man.

The drive to be independent prompted some critics of the New Deal to form the Business Council as a kind of conservative anti–Brains Trust to devise strategies from the orthodox free enterprise standpoint. Following a similar impulse, the Liberty League gained a large following for its free enterprise opposition to New Deal initiatives. Herbert Hoover still refused to join the Liberty League, but his voice was heard loud and clear within the ranks of New Deal critics. Roosevelt mostly ignored the right-wing barrage but occasionally challenged it with satirical contempt, as when he urged the Liberty League to broaden its high moral tone of outrage to include all ten commandments, not just those supporting private property. Behind the amused facade, however, he realized that the Liberty League and its allies posed a threat that would have to be absorbed by future plans.

Challenges to the New Deal also included a social and psychological reluctance to sustain reform movements. As left-wing journalist John Chamberlain described in his widely read *Farewell to Reform* (1932), bad conditions have occasionally moved the American middle-class consensus toward progressive action, but he argued further that, given the individualism, absence of feudal class divisions, and suspicion of the state that observers since Tocqueville have found in the American character, the urge to reform would abate well short of its original goals once a modicum of the old comfort was restored. The great irony, Chamberlain concluded, was that reformers generated their own defeat: by improving conditions slightly, they gave most of their followers an excuse to return to the old complacency at the same time that they roused the opposition of malefactors against whose interests the reforms were directed. Reform in that reckoning was an endlessly imperfect cycle, nourishing the very enemies it needed in order to exist.

In keeping with the radical spirit of the times, Chamberlain thought that revolution to break the cycle and overthrow the system was the answer. But the New Dealers, who understood that people within complex industrial societies had too much to lose to risk revolution, had to hope that reform momentum could be maintained while recovery went forward. It would be a difficult feat: when a lull in the administration's pace occurred during the first months of 1935, friends and foes of the New Deal alike speculated that the time might have come for it to peter out. As the lull stretched into early spring, a writer for the *New York Times* reported solemnly that the New Dealers had "little faith left." Could it be that the hopes of the architects of the breathtaking first hundred days—such that "a new America could be created"—had become merely "a bitter joke"?

For the faint of heart, "Black Monday," May 27, 1935, the day that the Schechter brothers court ruling gutted the NRA, appeared to signal the end of the great experiment. The concept of a planned society—its blue eagle shot out of the sky—was apparently repudiated; with it, in that view, went the basis on which the Brains Trust had built the concept of an industrial concert of interests.

Characteristically, however, the New Deal spirit proved very resilient under pressure. Black Monday roused the administration to a counteroffensive that was so swift and full it has come to be known as "the Second New Deal," or "the Second Hundred Days." The resurgence involved changes in emphasis, but the New Deal goal of a cooperative commonwealth that would distribute economic and political power equitably remained intact. Within that basic framework, the demise of the NRA helped move the consensus away from the planning favored by the Tugwell camp toward the Progressive regulation favored by Democrats from Jefferson through Wilson.

The chief organizer of the forces committed to the regulatory approach was Harvard law professor Felix Frankfurter, who had gotten to know Roosevelt when they both served in the Wilson administration during World War I. Undergirding Frankfurter were the ideas of his friend and mentor, Supreme Court Justice Louis Brandeis, who had long argued the case he popularized in *Other People's Money* (1914) for decentralizing business and government. Both institutions, Brandeis insisted, had grown beyond the "wee scale" of human understanding and virtue and should be broken down into smaller units, varying in accord with local conditions and customs.

But Brandeis and Frankfurter were not merely harking back to the Jeffersonian self-reliance and localism Wilson had recast in his "New Freedom." They also expressed a modern commitment to efficiency. Brandeis, especially, was a devotee of the scientific management school and insisted that without careful attention to the logical ordering of detail one could not justly fit institutions to the claims of locale and human welfare. By such reckoning, grandiose planning attempts like NRA seemed irresponsible, even wicked, as Brandeis showed in his fervent brief in the Schechter case.

Frankfurter and other Brandeis protégés were more flexible than their mentor, and more modern, reflecting the new consensus among liberals and leftists that maldistribution of wealth was at the heart of the nation's economic difficulties and that federal regulation was needed to rectify that imbalance. Frankfurter supported the emergency planning of the Hundred Days—at least to a point. He expressed a cautiously balanced position, not far removed from Roosevelt's own attempt to balance the collectivist and progressive sides of his nature. "I am not for a planned society *en gros*," Frankfurter explained. "I am prepared to get these [reforms] by *ad hoc* treatment of specific problems." This middle-ground position of piecemeal progress included the influence of John Maynard Keynes, the English economist whom Frankfurter had met while both were serving their governments in World War I. Frankfurter admired Keynes's writings on state activism and monetary management for their elegantly nuanced insights into the uses of the state to advance the public welfare without resort to ideological systems or comprehensive planning. In time, as his own influence and Keynes's fame grew, Frankfurter would press the English economist and his views on a skeptical Roosevelt.

Frankfurter's tireless efforts from his post at the Harvard Law School to influence policy and place his students in strategic government positions raised the hackles of the Brains Trusters. Most of all, Berle and Tugwell opposed Frankfurter's stress on regulation and monetary policy over planning. They saw him as an apostle of old-fashioned manipulation to save the illusion of "free" enterprise instead of understanding that the time had come for the government to step in directly on behalf of the public it represented and to reshape the society along organic, cooperative lines. Tugwell recalled many years later how he and Moley had struggled to keep Roosevelt from accepting Frankfurter's message of "imperious Brandeis objections" to the planning concepts expressed in the 1932 campaign speech at Oglethorpe College. Berle was harsher; in that presidential campaign he complained regularly to Roosevelt about Frankfurter's intransigence: "Typically, F. F. comes in at the last minute with many ideas, some very good, none of which could be got into legislative shape in less than a year or got by this Congress; and would like to do nothing unless he can have everything he wants; but will take no responsibility for getting anything done. . . . Which explains why, in his long and interesting career his opposition has been brilliant, but his ideas have never been brought to fruition—except over his protest." Frankfurter was outraged in return, describing Berle to Brandeis as "almost the most offensive and obstructive egotist I know."

These hostilities became exaggerated in the heat of battle and obscured the complementarity of their approaches to common dilemmas. Brandeisians and

Brains Trusters were each caught up in their own versions of the general New Deal attempt to balance individualism and collectivism. Frankfurter and his followers sought to reconcile the opposed values of small-scale liberty and the regimented precision of scientific management. Even more tortuous was the Brandeisian logic that stricter regulation, requiring a broad network of laws and a phalanx of regulatory agencies, would serve the cause of decentralization and personal freedom. Opposed to the Frankfurter faction, Tugwell and his allies would use central authority to establish an organic society embodying traditional, mostly rural, values of friendly cooperation. In contrasting ways, each side honored old ideals and the expertise of modern technological society. Each sought a balance of individual freedom and discipline for the general welfare. Under the circumstances, onlookers could be excused for their difficulties in trying to locate a single, unified New Deal "ideology," though the full spectrum of labels from communism to fascism was attached to the intense reform activity Roosevelt preferred to call progressive liberalism.

At the center of the "Second Hundred Days" flurry of activity in the summer of 1935 was a bright group of lawyer-bureaucrats, versed in administrative law, who gathered around Frankfurter's protégés Thomas Corcoran and Benjamin Cohen—the "Happy Hot Dogs," Hugh Johnson called them in the disgruntlement of exile from NRA. The legislative blitz they orchestrated used whatever mix of centralized planning and decentralized regulation seemed most apt to advance the cause. The Wagner Act, Social Security, and the omnibus relief bill that created the WPA greatly broadened the protective reach of the welfare state. On the other hand, the new tax and regulatory measures, reflecting the Brandeisian influence, favored localized enterprise over large concentrations by aiding small businesses and narrowing the gap between rich and poor. The Frankfurter group also provided expertise for the Banking Act of 1935, which brought all state banks into the Federal Reserve System. More provocatively, they applied Brandeis's emphasis on ethics to public utilities and their control by holding companies, whose evasion of responsibility for price-gouging utility management caused humorist Will Rogers to liken a holding company to the person a suspect hands the goods to just before being searched. The abundant evidence of deception and inefficiency persuaded Congress to pass the Wheeler-Rayburn Act enabling the SEC to pass a "death sentence" against any holding company not acting in the public interest.

To the extent that the opportunistically mixed style of the second New Deal was a shift in focus from comprehensive planning to an older quest for results within the prevailing system, it meant that the ideal of cooperation would give way to the divisiveness that had characterized progressive reform earlier in the century. In contrast to the emphasis of New Deal liberalism on the rational coordination of interests, Progressivism mounted crusades against injustice that pitted defenders of individual rights against arrogant concentrations of power—the good against the wicked. Brandeis as the protector of *Other People's Money* and dissenter to the Supreme Court's defense of property over humane conditions exemplified that progressive emphasis on virtue. His protégé, Frankfurter, showed much the same combative ethic, most notably in his defense in the 1920s of the condemned anarchists Sacco and Vanzetti, which focused the greatest national outcry during that decade against a prejudiced status quo.

The demise of the NRA and the threat of further court action against New Deal collectivist experiments also indicated that cooperation with business was not attainable. That view was forced upon the administration by the growing inability of its Business Advisory Council to attract members from the business sector and by the increasingly intemperate attacks on New Deal "socialism" by the mainstream Chamber of Commerce and the National Association of Manufacturers and by the fringe groups springing up like mushrooms to vent their hatred toward New Deal reform and "that cripple in the White House."

The poisoned atmosphere thickened in a clash over the distribution of wealth, which had always been the ultimate grievance for populist-progressive reformers and was also crucial to New Deal reform prospects. Ever since the first battles over taxation that led to the Revolutionary War, taxes had been decried as the fuel of overweening governmental ambition. Low taxes and meager treasuries indicated the governmental restraint that enabled free individuals to make the most of their opportunities. With a low-tax tradition in force, the New Deal, unlike European nations developing welfare systems, faced a chronic shortage of funds to pay for its programs. Only a small number of restrictive alternatives were available. Sharing costs and controls with the states was one way of defraying expenses for welfare programs while honoring traditional state authority. Short-term "emergency" sales and excise taxes on nonessentials and last-resort borrowing were other New Deal tactics to support relief efforts. Processing taxes on agricultural commodities and payroll taxes for social security were also employed to keep programs from becoming a drain on the treasury. These strategies offended the New Deal sense of rational planning and fairness because of the stopgap nature of emergency levies and the regressive tendency of sales and excise taxes to load the greatest burdens on the backs of the poorest. For believers in thrift and accountability, like Roosevelt, deficit financing was also unwelcome for the way it benefited present society at the expense of the future.

The wearying struggle over whether to finance Social Security through contributions by recipients or with government funds, or both, brought the issue of
inadequate government revenues to a head. The more the situation was studied
by the Committee on Economic Security, which drew up plans for the Social Security system and favored government subsidy, and by the Treasury Department,
whose head, Henry Morgenthau, urged payroll taxes, the clearer it became that
neither approach could pay for a decent program without either higher general
revenue taxes or prohibitive employer and employee contributions. Fearful that
neither tack would be politically viable, the administration resorted to the desperate evasion of assuring the public that their contributions would entitle them to
benefits and then setting a rate of contribution that would not be enough to cover
future costs when recipients began retiring in large numbers. The tactic rested
on the hope that some future sources of revenue would materialize to keep the
Social Security fund solvent.

The search for revenue led inevitably to the wealthy and to the income tax that
had been designed by progressive reformers specifically to curb the excesses of
turn-of-the-century plutocrats. The prospect suited Roosevelt very well. He had
always doubted the character and intentions of those who accumulated far more
than they needed; he had even suggested at least half-seriously during the debate over the minimum wage that there might just as well be a maximum wage
also—something in the neighborhood of $25,000 would be about right, he sug-
gested—to ensure fairness and a decent general standard of living. Beyond that
animus was the fact that the income tax had played little part during the first half
of the decade. Only about 5 percent of the population at the top of the scale paid
any income tax. Clearly, the time had come to make use of this neglected tool to
serve the general welfare while cutting down the dangerous power of the privileged who had vilified the New Deal.

Out of that determination was created the Wealth Tax Act of 1935. It expressed
progressive disapproval of concentrated wealth and big business ways by seeking to tax the fat out of inheritances and gifts and by levying a graduated tax on
corporate income. Although in the end Congress pulled much of the progressive
punch from the Wealth Tax Act by removing the inheritance tax provision, the
bill's remainder broadened the tax base while making the burden more equal for
rich and poor. As for its direct effect in raising the revenue needed to operate the
fledgling welfare programs, the Wealth Tax was set to generate income roughly
equal to half the amount brought in by the crucial social security payroll tax.

The new tax thrust was carried along past the well-financed opposition by a
groundswell of popular discontent, running the gamut from the Communist

Party on the left to the Distributists on the right, whose manifesto *Who Owns America?* (1935) brought together arguments favored by many conservative spokesmen—and even by Roosevelt in his more bucolic moods—that people be returned to their heritage as self-reliant landowners sharing nature's bounty. At the center of the spectrum lay four massive volumes of the Brookings Institution's study *The Distribution of Wealth and Income in Relation to Economic Progress,* documenting both inequities and the reluctance of certain moneyed elements to use their purchasing power in hard times to help stimulate recovery. In the Senate, progressive Republican Robert La Follette Jr. of Wisconsin carried on his more famous father's role as tribune of the plain people by praising the new tax legislation as a first step in the direction of far more radical populist traditions of raising the poor up at the expense of the rich.

Inevitably, as with all American legislation that has sought to redistribute income, the Wealth Tax encountered staunch resistance. Business and financial forces took the "soak the successful" tax program as the most shocking proof of the New Deal's red tendencies. That and the other "socialistic" actions of the Second Hundred Days would be the focal point for their attacks on the New Deal in the elections of the following year. By the end of 1935 the last vestiges of broad business cooperation with the New Deal had disappeared. The Business Advisory Council had become a hollow shell, its most influential members departing one by one as the Second Hundred Days heated up. When it became evident that the Chamber of Commerce, which had given the New Deal substantial support in 1933, was going to slam the president at its annual convention, Roosevelt discreetly absented himself from the proceedings, noting reproachfully at a press conference afterward that he understood there was not "a single speech which took the human side, the old-age side, the unemployment side." The gauntlet was cast by both antagonists; business bade farewell to New Deal reform, and Roosevelt bade farewell to his hopes of convincing the business community to change its plutocratic ambitions for the sake of the common good.

The Second Hundred Days revived New Deal momentum, but at a cost. The novel device of opinion polling indicated that Roosevelt's favorable rating with the public had fallen during 1935 from 66 to 40 percent. During the same period a whispering campaign against "that man in the White House"—the "insane cripple"—reached depths seldom plumbed in the scurrilous history of American politics. As columnist Marquis Childs put it in May 1936, seeking to explain in the pages of *Harper's* "Why They Hate Roosevelt," it had reached the point where

"No slander is too vile, no canard too preposterous, to find voice among those who regard the President as their mortal enemy."

The rise of such intense reaction inflamed hopes on the radical fringe. The most formidable challenge was led by Huey Long, senator from Louisiana and virtual dictator of that state. Brilliantly attuned to the discontent of those who felt cheated out of their fair share as the Depression dragged them down, Long attacked the greed of the few with millions in the midst of deprivation and launched a Share Our Wealth movement that claimed in 1935 to have 27,000 clubs and a mailing list of 7,500,000. Long publicized his aims in a brash fantasy called *My First Days in the White House* (1935), which talked of a vast coalition of leaders from left to right and a time when President Long would restore the Common Man to his traditional place at the center. Observing Long's skillful hoopla, nervous Democrats pondered a poll that showed a Long candidacy could take away as many as three to four million votes, most of them Democratic. That broad support indicated the complexity of Long's appeal. Certainly he had a demagogic, authoritarian side that conjured up comparisons with the fascist dictators multiplying abroad and led some to call him the "Redneck Messiah," thus stigmatizing Long's followers as well. Yet Long was also progressive by southern standards on race issues and thus popular among the state's long dispossessed and disenfranchised blacks. His activist administration, which broke the stranglehold of an old planter and big oil oligarchy, delivered on its promises to build roads and schools with free books and so earned him the love of the state's poor. If Long could redistribute opportunity in such a regressive state, what, some wondered, might he be able to do for—or to—the rest of the nation?

Another threat to the New Deal with comparable magnetism was Father Charles Coughlin, pastor of the Shrine of the Little Flower in the Royal Oak suburb of Detroit. Coughlin, who had been giving radio sermons since 1926, greeted the New Deal victory in 1932 as a kind of redemption for suffering humanity. But because Roosevelt had turned away from the populist campaign for free silver—the "gentile metal," as distinct from the gold that Jews were said to covet—the "Radio Priest" became a foe. No longer bringing "Christ's Deal" but rather the "Pagan Deal," Roosevelt's administration was decried as a captive of the international conspiracy of Jewish financiers to squeeze the masses by keeping gold the only basis for money. A marvelously expressive baritone, Coughlin was reckoned by 1934 to command the largest radio audience ever and to receive the most mail of any public figure. His defection from the New Deal posed a serious problem in the eyes of Democratic strategists.

Hanging on as a third menace was the dogged Dr. Francis Townsend. His humiliation at the hands of Congress and eclipse by Social Security left him embittered, ripe for recruitment in a radical challenge to the New Deal. Support for the Townsend movement had not evaporated with the passage of the Social Security Act, partly because from that time to the 1936 elections the new program was collecting worker and employer contributions but not yet paying dividends.

Despite some affinities on economic issues, radicals on the left tended to view populist agitators like Long, Coughlin, and Townsend with alarm. Unlettered lower-class belligerence toward much of the modern world and particularly the notable undercurrent of anti-Semitism made the populist challenge seem an American version of fascism. Fear of fascism also guided the approach taken toward the New Deal in 1936 by Norman Thomas, the thoughtful leader of the Socialist Party. While conceding that the New Deal was not itself fascist, as more radical leftists had frequently charged, Thomas warned that the administration could not adequately resist the tide of fascism because of its ties to southern Democrats and big business. The fascist menace also moved the Communist Party to a major change of direction. After many years of bitter hostility toward the Socialists for their willingness to reform the system rather than overthrow it, Kremlin spokesman Georgi Dimitrov announced at the Seventh World Congress of the Communist International in the summer of 1935 that henceforth, Communists should join in a "Popular Front" with Socialists, New Dealers, and all others who opposed fascism. American Communists thus took to parading their fealty to the democratic values of the Founding Fathers. "Communism," their new slogan proclaimed, "is twentieth century Americanism."

As the Second Hundred Days ended and the swirls of discontent from the left and right intensified, Roosevelt agreed with his friend, publisher Roy Howard, that a "breathing spell" was needed. So he set out to tour the nation and gather wisdom about the state of affairs. His speeches to friendly crowds glowed with assurances about sustaining American ideals and reviving enterprise. He dedicated the giant Boulder Dam as testimony to fruitful government service to recovery and progress and then embarked on his favorite recreation—a fishing trip that would carry him through the Panama Canal and back to Washington by November.

The breathing spell stretched into 1936, with little in the way of government initiative but some satisfaction over signs of returning prosperity. Unemployment was drifting downward from a high of close to 30 percent in 1933 to about 20 percent by 1935, heading toward a low of 14 percent in 1937. Corporate profits had risen correspondingly from a dismal $2 billion in 1933 to nearly $5 billion in 1936, and the Dow Jones industrial average of stock prices was up 80 percent over 1933. Company earnings soared; by the end of 1936 they would be 50 percent higher than in 1935. So strong was the business rebound that worriers turned their attention from depression, so long endemic, to a fear of inflation. In all this was impressive evidence that the New Deal had wrought well—even, perhaps, that its innovative work was done.

But there were dark overtones. Roosevelt's standing in the polls remained low. His advisers were divided over the wisdom of planning versus regulation, and in January the administration's nemesis, the Supreme Court, struck again, this time invalidating the AAA. Although a substitute had been devised for such an emergency, the government was still stuck with the loss of about $1 billion in revenue from the outlawed processing tax at just the time a $2 billion veteran's bonus was passed over Roosevelt's veto. In response, the administration jammed through Congress a tax on undistributed corporation profits in order to meet the new expenses, but only after a hard fight that revealed growing pockets of resistance to the New Deal.

In planning the election campaign, Roosevelt realized that he had become the major issue. That conclusion dismayed Moley and Tugwell, who disliked the politics of personality and wanted to devise a new planned design. But there was sense in Roosevelt's judgment. No major new legislative program was in the works, and none seemed urgent in view of rising prosperity. The original Brains Trust vision had dissipated, leaving in its wake a number of reforms and agencies but no concerted movement to debate. What remained for the electorate was the question of whether to endorse the leader and give him a chance to devise new initiatives, repudiate the New Deal in favor of Republican restoration, or take a radical leap in a new direction.

Roosevelt chose to take to the offensive in two ways. He would depart from the original New Deal strategy of unifying all elements in society and instead draw a sharp distinction between idealistic friends of recovery and their enemies. Rather than stress the organic unity sought by the Brains Trust planners, Roosevelt set out to build a coalition of believers in himself and his administration's policies—and isolate those who would not join.

For his enemies in the business community, who by 1936 had become legion, Roosevelt reserved his greatest fury. His campaign tapped a deep contempt for the corporate arrogance and greed that had long offended Roosevelt's cooperative commonwealth ethic. As early as November 1933, Roosevelt had written to Wilson's old adviser, Colonel Edward House, that "the real truth of the matter is, as you and I know, that a financial element in the larger centers has owned the government ever since the days of Andrew Jackson. . . . The country is going through a repetition of Jackson's fight with the Bank of the United States—only on a far bigger and broader basis." By 1936, after trying to mollify the business sector and fashion a new, mutually beneficial relationship between it and the public welfare, Roosevelt was stung by big business attacks on him. The ingratitude and foolishness of it all moved him to stress traditional Democratic Party ties with small businesses and family farms. Roosevelt used his renomination speech in Philadelphia on June 27 to make it clear that the divisive view he had declared to Colonel House would dominate his campaign pitch. He thundered that after the Revolution of 1776 had been won, "economic royalists" entered the temple, led by Roosevelt's old nemesis, Alexander Hamilton, to corrupt the Founding Father's ideals: "It was natural and perhaps human that the privileged princes of those new economic dynasties, thirsting for power, reached out for control over government itself. They created a new despotism and wrapped it in the robes of legal sanction."

Roosevelt then connected his presidency with a patriotic attempt to revivify the original dream. Fully engaged in the occasion, he was willing to cast aside his usual caution and reveal the egalitarian fervor that linked him to the classic ideal of a cooperative commonwealth, from Jefferson's advocacy of a yeoman democracy through its utopian expression by Edward Bellamy and the workingman's republicanism of the Knights of Labor to the progressive causes that made up the common man core of the New Deal. Counting on the reformist moment to seize the crowd of 105,000 which jammed Franklin Field for the moonlit drama, he declared:

> The election of 1932 was the people's mandate to end [the despotism]. Under that mandate, it is being ended. . . . The royalists of the economic order have conceded that political freedom was the business of government, but they have maintained that economic slavery was nobody's business. . . . In the place of the palace of privilege we seek to build a temple out of faith and hope and charity. It is a sobering thing to be a servant of this great cause.
>
> To some generations much is given. Of others much is expected. This generation of Americans has a rendezvous with destiny.

To join him at the "rendezvous with destiny," Roosevelt sought allies far and wide among those with a similar sense of partisan cause against big money and anti-democratic forces. He courted Progressive Republicans like Nebraska Senator George Norris and Farm-Laborites in Minnesota and Wisconsin, even though it meant abandoning duly nominated Democrats. To blacks he stressed the sympathies New Dealers felt for their lot and the way the "royalist" Republicans, with their indifference to "economic slavery," had taken the black vote for granted ever since the Civil War. In an expansive twist, he radiated similar compassion to the poor southern and ethnic minority whites who were the closest competitors of the blacks for jobs and housing. To gain the labor vote, Roosevelt displayed the Wagner Act as a talisman; to farmers he boasted of the AAA. Intellectuals, impressed by New Deal reforms and the use of specialized brain power, flocked to the banner. So, too, did the champions of women's rights, drawn both by Eleanor Roosevelt's active promotion of good causes and the New Deal's compassionate openness to outsiders. The Women's Division, led by Eleanor Roosevelt, did its part by mobilizing Democratic women at the local level, as they had done in 1932, to blanket the grass roots with "rainbow fliers" extolling the ways the New Deal had alleviated hardship for ordinary citizens. In a tribute to the growing inclusiveness of the New Deal, these women produced and distributed about 80 percent of the campaign literature. In these ways the campaign developed into the ultimate forging and testing of the New Deal coalition.

The effort paid off handsomely. John L. Lewis and organized labor's new Non-Partisan League lined up behind Roosevelt's candidacy early in the campaign. Endorsement by the NAACP and the leading black journal, *Crisis,* made the shift of black allegiance to the Democratic Party all but official. And in September the Progressive National Committee swept a broad array of reformers into the fold by naming Roosevelt their candidate.

The force of Roosevelt's reelection juggernaut caught opponents by surprise. Populist dissidents were in an especially vulnerable position. In September 1935, Huey Long had been assassinated in a corridor of the statehouse in Baton Rouge, and his place was taken by a fundamentalist preacher, Gerald L. K. Smith, who lacked Long's political stature and organizational ability and made his mark instead with his talent for rousing the rabble by denouncing the Jews, blacks, fat cats, and foreigners supposedly blocking the common man's path to shared wealth. In June of that year, Father Coughlin, beguiled by his own rhetoric and a dip in the president's popularity, launched the National Union for Social Justice and managed to persuade veteran Populist congressman William Lemke of North Dakota to be its presidential candidate on the Union Party ticket. They were soon joined out on that shaky limb by Townsend and Smith, even though their differences on political programs had not been reconciled.

The alliance was primarily powered by hate and resentment. Coughlin had been inspired to form the party by anger over the defeat of a silver monetization bill in Congress sponsored by the hard-bitten Lemke. Smith's trademark was bigoted scapegoating for those wanting revenge for their troubles. And Townsend fumed over his slight at the hands of a hardhearted congressional investigation into his movement and its finances. Altogether, the Unionists were a perfect foil for Roosevelt. Their strident call for a strongman leader and repression of dissidents served as an example of the fascist alternative that might follow repudiation of the New Deal.

The left also played into Roosevelt's hands. Norman Thomas's warning against fascism further solidified belief that the real challenge to Roosevelt—and to American democracy—was on the right and that Roosevelt was a necessary bulwark against totalitarianism. And the Popular Front strategy of the Communists led to a campaign that, for all its efforts to gain votes for folksy Kansan Earl Browder, also left voters thinking of Roosevelt as a candidate who would lead the common cause against fascism.

Roosevelt's main rival, Republican candidate Alf Landon, faced an impossible task. The progressive record on reform and civil rights he had forged as Governor of Kansas was upstaged, and his mildly conservative counters to the New Deal only caused him to be confused with the extremism of the Liberty League. In a last, desperate fling, Landon tried to scare the public about the way Social Security would confiscate money from their payrolls and reduce people to mere numbers. But the campaign boomeranged against Landon's stature as the kindly midwesterner able to arouse nostalgia for the good old days of Republican dominance. He started to seem a stingy alarmist rather than the genial fossil everyone wanted to like while they voted for Roosevelt.

An acquaintance of Roosevelt captured the amused disdain Landon's campaign aroused. Fixing on the use of the Kansas sunflower as the Republican symbol, he reminded Roosevelt that the sunflower is yellow, has a black heart, is only good for parrot food, and dies before November. Roosevelt laughed at that, but he so resented the attack on Social Security that he ended his campaign in Madison Square Garden on October 31 with some fighting remarks about black hearts. To an excited crush of followers, Roosevelt decried his "old enemies" of "monopoly, speculation, reckless banking, class antagonism. . . . Never before in all our history have these forces been so united against one candidate as they stand today. They are unanimous in their hate for me—and I welcome their hatred." Against the surging roar of the crowd's sympathetic anger Roosevelt concluded for posterity: "I should like to have it said of my first Administration that in it the forces of selfishness and of lust for power met their match. I should like to have it said of my second Administration that in it these forces met their master."

On election day the Roosevelt coalition captured every state but Maine and Vermont. His vote total of 27 million was 5 million over his 1932 result and swamped Landon by 11 million votes. Right and left suffered even worse disasters. With a scant million votes, the Union Party fell 90 percent short of Coughlin's prediction, and the share of the Communist and Socialist Parties dropped below their 1932 count. In a crushing demonstration that the New Deal coalition had taken the urban masses away from its radical challengers, Roosevelt carried all but two of the 106 cities with a population over 100,000. Clearly, the center of gravity of Roosevelt's coalition had moved ever more decisively away from its traditional support in the rural South to the urban centers whose working-class and white-collar residents benefited most from New Deal labor and regulatory policies.

The *New Republic,* which had supported Norman Thomas, editorialized that Roosevelt had been given a "blank check" and should now press ahead with the national planning inherent in the idea of New Deal. Yet with no specific new programs as part of the campaign, New Dealers had reason to speculate whether the landslide was, indeed, a blank check for future undertakings or rather an endorsement of what was deemed to be a successful—and completed—experiment. Amid the victorious euphoria there was much talk of an unbeatable new Democratic coalition but very little about yet another Hundred Days of reform.

CHAPTER TEN

The Judicial Revolution

When the sound and fury of Roosevelt's campaign died down, a decision to reflect on mandates and prospects was indicated by an atmosphere more like a resumption of the "breathing spell" than of a crusade in motion. Roosevelt, who had a sometimes destructive weakness for being a man of mystery, took to his favorite retreat, the sea, for a month's cruise off of South America. There he could contemplate ideas for the new term while the nation waited in suspense. When he returned for his inauguration on January 20, 1937, Roosevelt restated some of the old campaign militancy in deploring the disgrace of "one-third of a nation ill-housed, ill-clad, ill-nourished" but unveiled no new proposals for eliminating the problem. Nor was there a powerful clamor by the public and the critics for more innovation. In doubt also was the actual range of opportunity for new political initiatives. Roosevelt had dramatically burned his bridges to conservatives and business forces on the right, and the lack of any significant voter appeal for populist and radical candidates dampened whatever inclination there might have been to reach out for cooperation with the left. The strategy of necessity was to find room to maneuver in the center.

Roosevelt, the shrewd exploiter of appearance, could not, however, let the opportunity pass to hail congressional majorities of 331 Democrats to 89 Republicans in the House and 76 Democrats to 16 Republicans in the Senate as a grand mandate for progress and an endorsement of his leadership. Some, like Raymond Moley, who thought of themselves as voices of modesty and caution, deplored the way Roosevelt cast the election in personal terms as a dangerous overreaching toward power. But Roosevelt realized that he had little choice but to emphasize his central role. Only he, the wielder of symbols and the voice of reassurance, could be the focal point for the vast but fragile coalition that gave the Democrats victory. A charismatic appeal to compassion and shared values had to be made if there were to be any hope of getting past regional differences and short-term interests. His great challenge was to find a way of bringing southern segregationists, long-rooted rural and small-town midwesterners, and urban ethnic northerners together to create the coordinated will necessary to eliminate the causes and consequences of the Depression. Put another way, Roosevelt had presided over the creation of a coalition able to defeat the Republican Party and its vested economic interests; now the task was to find some way of mobilizing the coalition to advance worthy causes.

The high priority Roosevelt gave to judicial reform surprised many observers but fitted these realities. It aimed at the reactionary strongholds in the judiciary that had long obstructed the humane and centralizing reforms that appealed to the traditional, middle-class progressives who occupied the middle ground Roosevelt sought to cultivate. Early in his 1932 campaign for the presidency, Roosevelt spoke bluntly about the threat to the New Deal posed by the Supreme Court: "After March 4, 1929, the Republican party was in complete control of all branches of the government—the Legislature, with the Senate and Congress; and the executive departments; and I may add, for full measure, to make it complete, the United States Supreme Court as well."

Roosevelt had grounds for seeing the Supreme Court as the linchpin of the Republican era he sought to end. The appointment of William Howard Taft as chief justice of the Supreme Court in 1921 made plain the determination of the new Harding administration to end the era of progressive reform. As head of the highest court, Taft could give substance to the bitter words in his book *Popular Government* (1913) against the progressive tide that had swept him from the presidency in 1912: "The change advocated by the social reformers is really that the object of law should be social interests and not individual interests. . . . The proposals made for progress have been so radical, so entirely a departure from all the lessons of the past and so dangerous to what we regard as essential in preserving the inestimable social advances we have made . . . that we have been forced to protest."

His subsequent effort to "mass" the Court to protect vested property interests was aided by a phalanx of fellow Justices who presided throughout most of the 1920s and 1930s in a way that earned them the nickname "the Four Horsemen of Reaction." Until their accession, the Court in all its history had extended its power of judicial review to only nine federal laws. Between 1922 and 1924 alone, the Court faulted thirteen federal statutes; by the time Taft stepped down in 1930, the Court under him had ruled unconstitutional more legislation than it had during the previous fifty years.

The main opponent of conservative reaction on the Court was Louis Brandeis, whom Wilson had appointed in 1916. Brandeis, described by Taft as "a muckraker, an emotionalist for his own purposes, a Socialist . . . a man of much power for evil," had gained fame as a progressive lawyer by relying on massive data of hardship and inequity rather than technical legal analysis. His most famous sociological brief, argued in 1908 on behalf of the right of the state of Oregon to regulate working conditions for women, was so detailed and cogent that it was reprinted as a book. Before the Court it won grudging majority acceptance for demonstrating a "reasonable" case for state interference with worker "freedom" to negotiate a contract no matter how bad the terms or how helpless the "free" worker actually was to change them. At the time of his appointment, against bitter opposition to his "judicial temperament" and scarcely veiled references to his Jewishness, Brandeis spoke out in an article called "The Living Law" against the failure of lawyers and judges to "keep pace with the rapid development of . . . political, economic and social ideals." Thus, as Brandeis concluded on a later occasion, "the process of trial and error, so fruitful in the physical sciences, is appropriate also in the judicial function." The crux of the matter was contained in a favorite aphorism of his: "If we would guide by the light of reason, we must let our minds be bold."

Other important voices appealed to experience somewhat differently. Brandeis's most famous fellow dissenter against the law as a set of fixed precepts, Oliver Wendell Holmes, was less inclined toward reform and reliance on sociological data than were the progressives. He came to the bench in 1902 with a rather melancholy view of mankind, partly because his harrowing military service in the Civil War, during which he was severely wounded, convinced him that a high degree of rationality was beyond any social system. As early as 1881, in *The Common Law*, Holmes urged his readers to keep in mind that "the life of the law has not been logic; it has been experience." Attempts to discover permanent canons of Moral or Constitutional Truth or to impose objectively rational standards were futile. The most a judge could arrogate to himself, Holmes concluded, was the power to determine whether an action under review was based upon a reasonable interpretation (not necessarily the judge's interpretation) of what the Constitution did not clearly forbid. It followed that Holmes's "latitudinarianism," as Taft disapprovingly labeled it, involved him in a string of dissents, famous for their lucidity, against the righteously restrictive logic of the conservative defense of property and self-reliance.

The third and most far-reaching protest against judicial dogmatism in favor of experience was made by the so-called legal Realists. The emergence of that viewpoint in the troubled period just before the New Deal marked both the climax of frustration over the way judicial decisions during the 1920s tried to make defenses of the status quo appear literal applications of the Constitution and the growing use of psychological analysis. Drawing upon Freud's insistence that subconscious motivations often governed what purported to be rational thought, the Realists, most of whom identified with thwarted progressive reform, argued that legal doctrine evolved in accord with social changes and at any particular moment reflected a judge's own experience and his subjective understanding of the issues confronting him in his courtroom. Indeed, the role of judges, arrayed in priestly robes and governing society's taboos, struck the Realists as especially attuned to Freud's understanding of human experience in terms of mythology and patriarchal authority.

Jerome Frank, a Harvard-trained lawyer destined to become an important New Dealer, provided the most influential summary of the Realist position in his book *Law and the Modern Mind* (1930). After undergoing psychoanalysis, Frank concluded that the urge to judge stemmed from a childhood desire for security and certainty. Anxious personal needs taking root in the subconscious determined that judging would be primarily intuitive and idiosyncratic. With their basic needs at the fore, judges quite naturally tend to begin with conclusions and then work backward through technical detail to find justification. Frank recognized the ominous implications of such a theory for the cause of objective justice and sought to reassure his readers that there was a path to true "realism." If members of the legal profession would give up their pretensions to certainty, fixed in place by abstract principles and a literal reading of the law, they could come to grips with their own psyches and overcome "robeism," the delusion that one can employ perfect and unalterable legal truths. The wise jurist would then be in a position to appreciate the finding of legal scholar Edward Corwin that, with a boundless array of cross-grained legal precedents to choose from, the Supreme Court could decide cases almost any way it wished on the basis of some constitutionally certified premise. In the unfolding New Deal Frank discovered the political implications of his position. Brought into the administration as legal counsel, Frank referred to his fellow Realists as "experimental" jurisprudes and concluded that they were meant to be "humble servants to that master experimentalist, Franklin Roosevelt."

Frank's *Law and the Modern Mind* appeared just as Taft died, a month after he retired. The uproar attending the choices Hoover made to succeed the chief justice and his colleague Edward Sanford, who died on the same day as Taft, befitted the old reactionary's anxious fear of reform. For chief justice, Hoover turned to Charles Evans Hughes, a man of impressive dignity who had served on the Supreme Court before World War I until he resigned for a narrowly lost run at the presidency against Woodrow Wilson in 1916 and then became secretary of state under Harding and Coolidge. A middle-of-the-roader whose mildly progressive record as associate justice from 1910 to 1916 had gained general approval, Hughes seemed, as the *New York Times* put it, a "case of the office seeking the fit man." But reformers instead used Hughes as a lightning rod for their frustrations. Reflecting on the big money contacts Hughes had made as a corporate lawyer, George Norris, chairman of the Senate Judiciary Committee, decided to oppose the nomination out of concern that "we have reached a time in our history when the power and influence of monopoly and organized wealth are reaching into every governmental activity." Unfortunately, he added, "no man in public life so exemplifies the influence of powerful combinations in the political and financial world as does Mr. Hughes." With reform Democrats and his fellow progressive Republicans joining Norris, a spirited debate on the influence of wealth in American life preceded Hughes's confirmation. The episode was revealing. With the nation sliding into the pit of depression, the Supreme Court was joining big business as a symbol of a discredited era. Senator Clarence Dill of Washington conveyed that conviction to the Senate floor in bitter terms: "The last resort of organized capital that plunders the common people of America," he cried, "has turned out to be the Supreme Court of the United States."

The clamor over Hughes was muted, however, by the candidate's eminence and moderation, which carried the day for the nomination. But when Hoover, insensitive to populist feelings as always, nominated Judge John J. Parker of North Carolina to fill the seat vacated by Sanford, a decisive number of senators took deadly aim at Parker's remark that the participation of blacks in politics was "a source of evil." Hoover turned then to competent, inoffensive Philadelphia lawyer Owen J. Roberts, but the overtones of the Hughes and Parker fights lingered on as a storm signal for future relations between the Court and its reformers.

Hughes was aware of the delicate situation. He had always, in fact, been sensitive to the need to protect the Court's reputation and was adept at drawing opposing views into fine-sounding compromise. This time, faced with the difficulty of reconciling a conservative Court with a rising demand for reform, Hughes decided to play down federal issues and emphasize state authority. The tactic was a shrewd one for getting the Court out of its increasingly notorious role as chief obstacle to reform efforts, some of which Hughes favored. It squared with

Hoover's approach to the troubles of Depression; it fit Brandeis's decentralist views; it suited Holmes's insistence that local authorities be left alone to reform as they saw fit; and it could not very well be opposed by free-enterprise conservatives who had conceded in their invocation of the Tenth Amendment against federal regulation that important powers were reserved to the states.

With so much to offer reformers and moderates, Hughes was able to fashion a majority without abandoning the Court's longstanding defense of private enterprise against federal intervention. Swiftly, the new majority upheld the police powers of the states in disputes over how best to serve the general welfare. This dictum covered many issues—from regulating insurance companies and protecting labor from company unions to allowing free textbooks in public schools and licensing cotton gins. Impressed by the scope of Court activity, commentators even began speaking of a "Hughes rebellion."

Hughes's attempt at reconciling the conservative and liberal poles was only marginally successful, however. There was grumbling from the left that the new majority was granting the private sector too much immunity from federal regulation and thus slighting the need to recognize how the Constitution must evolve to meet new circumstances. From the dissenting right the reaction was sharper. Justice George Sutherland, the most articulate of the Four Horsemen, insisted on the permanent, literal truth of the Constitution, written "in such plain English words that it would seem that the ingenuity of man could not evade them." No emergency could justify abridging the self-evident Constitutional requirement that contracts be upheld. Thus the divided nature of the Court became clear: increasingly antagonized liberals and conservatives on the wings and a "swing" vote of the meliorative Hughes and Roberts in between. Only direct testing of the New Deal statutes before such a volatile body could determine the sort of legitimacy they would eventually have. The test would also go far in determining what changes the Court would be willing to make in accommodating the Constitution to the New Deal influence in shifting federal activism toward collective planning and a national system of welfare.

The New Deal began its long ordeal before the Court in 1934 when it faced a challenge to a NIRA order forbidding the shipment of oil in excess of the code quota—"hot oil"—across state lines. The New Deal image suffered when it was revealed that the Justice Department had jailed the Panama Oil Company official who had defied the order, even though there was no provision in the law to do so. With ominous reproof for such high-handed carelessness, the Court invalidated the "hot oil" proviso. But the rest of the NIRA was untouched, leaving the relationship of New Deal planning to the Constitution an anxiously open issue.

The second skirmish heightened the tension. It concerned holders of government bonds who wanted to exercise their contractual right to turn them in for gold. The New Deal opposed funding, however, because its re-evaluation of gold upward to $35 an ounce meant that redeeming the bonds would be expensive for the government to the point of bankruptcy. Desperately, the New Deal inner council resolved that, should the government lose the case, the president would defy the Court, citing the example of Lincoln's refusal to obey the Court in wartime, and then take to the air to explain to the public how payment would impoverish local and state governments. But, luckily, after a dramatic pause of several days, the Court headed off the crisis by allowing the government to pay the debt in dollars equivalent to the original gold figure. For a brief moment the administration could enjoy its reprieve.

Then came the deluge, which swept away a dozen New Deal laws. Most discouraging to New Dealers was the tilt of Roberts to the right in striking down the Railroad Retirement Act of 1934. Reaching back to a conservative view of the commerce clause that New Dealers believed had long since been discredited by progressive reform trends, Roberts declared that pensions were not part of the flow of commerce across state lines and thus could not be required by federal law. The ruling against compelling employers to provide pensions as a violation of due process raised fears that the Social Security Act, then a-borning, might be killed in its cradle. Despair mounted to a climax on Black Monday, when both the NIRA and the Frazier-Lemke Act for relief of farm mortgages were leveled and the President was denied the authority to fire Federal Trade Commissioner William E. Humphrey. All three cases were unanimous, and the president was left to wonder aloud: "Well, where was [liberal Justice] Ben Cardozo? And what about old Isaiah?"—as he liked to call Brandeis. Then, with widely felt effect, he lashed out in a press conference at the way the Court was pushing the country back into "horse and buggy" days.

But Roosevelt need not have been so surprised. Hughes's favoring of state reform and the decentralist progressive sympathies of "old Isaiah" caused the liberals to join the conservatives against federal powers that seemed to reach too far. These cases provided the strongest indication that New Deal reform, rather than being a mere extension of the progressivism of Roosevelt's youth, had significantly different leanings in a collectivist federal direction that went against the grain of both older progressives and conservatives by seeming to undermine self-reliance and state prerogative and intrude on property and contract rights.

Although the Court in February 1936 supported the administration in *Ashwander v. TVA*, allowing the government to sell the power it generated at Wilson

Dam, the drift against collectivism continued. The conservative Justices, while upholding the TVA, pointed out that stockholders could sue company officials for carrying out laws they considered unconstitutional. In response, lower courts issued hundreds of injunctions against New Deal laws that seemed about to be embroiled in litigation and apt to be struck down by the Supreme Court.

It was in the gathering shadow of that trend that the AAA and NRA were invalidated as federal trespasses into state and private affairs. Then, with Sutherland again insisting that the commerce clause was being violated, the Court ruled against the Bituminous Coal Conservation Act of 1935. What made the situation especially vivid was the fact that the act, drawn up by Joseph Guffey, Democratic reform governor of Pennsylvania and then senator, related to an industry and a region in such dire straits that everyone conceded the need for rescue. A ruling against the act would appear tantamount to denying the classic progressive position that conditions must have a crucial bearing on the validity of a law. George Sutherland was up to that task. In reiterating the notion that the commerce clause only referred to transporting goods across state lines—not to manufacture or mining in any locale within a state—Sutherland declared that the "logical" distinction between direct and indirect effects was "essential to the maintenance of our constitutional system." The disastrous effects of denying federal intervention made no difference: "The extent of the effect bears no logical relation to its character. . . . An increase in the greatness of the effect adds to its importance. It does not alter its character."

The dismay of Court critics over the coal case was topped by the reaction to a ruling soon afterward against a New York minimum wage law. Invoking the right of contract, the Court virtually closed the door against any governmental action to keep jobholders from falling below a decent subsistence level. New Deal reformers were galled as usual by the judicial argument that the sacred right of freely contracting one's labor overrode the community's right to protect the welfare of citizens.

But moderates and some conservatives were also angered because the decision reversed the efforts of Hughes to restore the police powers of the states as a bulwark against both excessive federal powers and the pains of Depression. As many as seventeen state welfare plans for meeting the crisis were in jeopardy. Accordingly, although the press was heavily Republican and hostile to Roosevelt, about 80 percent of its commentary decried the decision. Herbert Hoover, himself, was so aroused that he even proposed an amendment to bestow on the states "the power they thought they already had." And from the bench Harlan Stone wrote to Felix Frankfurter that the Court had committed a kind of "indecent exposure," showing through its twists and turns that it was primarily concerned with stopping certain social action rather than with defending the letter of the unambiguous Constitution. At the end of the 1936 session, Stone unburdened himself to his sister: "We finished the term of the Court yesterday, I think in many ways one of the most disastrous in its history. . . . Since the Court last week said that [regulating minimum wages] could not be done by the national government, as the matter was local, and now it is said that it cannot be done by local governments even though it is local, we seem to have tied Uncle Sam up in a hard knot."

Although he remarked on how the Court's reaction had left the New Deal "fairly completely undermined," Roosevelt resisted the temptation to belabor the Court with any more "horse and buggy" quips. He recognized the sacrosanct aura around the Court and may have seen a Gallup poll in the fall of 1935 showing that only 31 percent of the sample interviewed favored limitations on the Court's authority to declare acts of Congress unconstitutional. But when he gained reelection, Roosevelt returned to the charge. A volatile mixture of frustration, personal ambition, and civic responsibility shone through his resolve to fend off reactionary judges: "When I retire to private life on January 20, 1941, I do not want to leave the country in the condition Buchanan left it to Lincoln. If I cannot, in the brief time given me to attack its deep and disturbing problems, solve those problems, I hope at least to have moved them well on the way to solution by my successor. It is absolutely essential that the solving process begin at once."

On the docket for 1937 were cases involving Social Security, the Wagner Act, the Railway Labor Act, the Commodity Exchange Act, and the powers of the PWA, SEC, and FTC. Should the Court rule against these measures, the New Deal would be devastated.

In contemplating their options, the president and his advisers saw that resort to constitutional amendment to curb the Court's power had one great advantage over legislation: Public opinion generally would be more receptive to a formal change in the Constitution to affect what it believed to be a constitutionally sanctioned power of judicial review. A congressional attempt at tempering the Court would smack of a violation of the sacred immunity the checks and balances system seemed to confer on each branch of government from interference by another branch. There were grave disadvantages to the Amendment route, however. One was slowness. Roosevelt, sensitized to the problems of poor children by his wife's years of work for settlement houses and welfare legislation, ruefully observed that the Amendment to forbid child labor had already burned up thirteen years of its earnest advocates' lives without success. That futile lapse of time reflected on another disadvantage: the difficulties in getting advocates of an amendment to agree on its shape. Certainly, from the welter of proposals for action against the Court, gaining a consensus on a judicial change would be a touchy matter. Finally, there was the arduous requirement of consent from three fourths of the state legislatures. Although Roosevelt still looked to the states as laboratories for reform, he had experienced enough disappointment in past efforts to fuse them into a cooperative commonwealth to have become quite cynical. Pointedly, he joshed an old New York friend: "If you were not as scrupulous and ethical as you happen to be, you could make five million dollars as easy as rolling off a log by undertaking a campaign to prevent the ratification by one house of the Legislature, or even the summoning of a constitutional convention in thirteen states for the next four years. Easy money." Harold Ickes remembered that Roosevelt confided in him, half-seriously, that he could name at least thirteen states where money could arrange to defeat an amendment.

After mulling all these variables in the heady aftermath of his reelection, Roosevelt informed Homer Cummings, the attorney general, just before leaving for South America that he had decided on getting some congressional device to defeat the Court conservatives. Just how that was to be fashioned he left to Cummings's ingenuity; the president would spend the time on board with a battery of papers, planning a wide array of initiatives for the new term.

Soon after Roosevelt's return in December, Cummings settled on a strategy. From Edward Corwin, the leading scholarly commentator on judicial trends, he took the suggestion for a bill to increase the size of the Court in order to provide help for Justices over 70. The plan had the additional advantage of being able to cite the precedent of numerous past instances when Congress had changed the size of the Court. By coincidence, Cummings also found, while editing the draft of a book he was preparing on federal justice, that in 1913 none other than Justice James McReynolds, the most intractable of the Four Horsemen, had proposed that the federal judiciary be enlarged for the same purpose of compensating for the diminished effectiveness of judges over 70. This emphasis on age went beautifully with the complaints from many citizens in letters to the administration that antiquated judges were a serious problem and with a sensationally popular attack on the superannuated Court by the muckraking journalists Drew Pearson and Robert S. Allen called *The Nine Old Men*.

With the President's chuckling approval—for the humorous irony of ancient Justice McReynolds's falling victim to his own idea for an age proviso was not lost on him—Cummings moved vigorously to draft a complete judicial reform bill. It contained four main features: (1) power for the president to name a judge to preside alongside any judge of a federal court who declined to resign six months after turning 70; (2) a limit on the addition of new judges to six for the Supreme Court and two for any lower court, the entirety to number no more than fifty; (3) allowance for lower-court judges to be assigned to unusually busy courts; and (4) supervision of lower courts by proctors of the Supreme Court.

The provisions to enlarge and modernize the lower courts met general approval, but the power given the president to enlarge the Supreme Court proved highly provocative. Roosevelt sought to finesse criticism that the proposal was self-serving. In a "fireside chat" to the nation on the radio he unconvincingly claimed his intent was not, as critics charged, to "pack" the Court but to bring in "new blood," younger judges who would be more alert to their surroundings than the judges over 70.

Roosevelt's way of dealing with Congress was even more maladroit. Partly to gain the greatest shock value and thus to get the public's attention, partly because of his love for surprises—and perhaps because Moley had a point about the triumphant president's arrogance—Roosevelt announced his court reform plan on February 5 without consulting his congressional allies. He thus faced the disgruntlement of an institution filled with men over 70 in numbers unusual anywhere outside a retirement home. Under the circumstances, the president's message could hardly be too delicate and, unfortunately, did not come close. "In exceptional cases, of course," he began, "judges, like other men, retain to an advanced age full mental and physical vigor." But apparently most were not so blessed: "A lower mental or physical vigor leads men to avoid an examination of complicated and changed conditions. Little by little, new facts become blurred through old glasses fitted, as it were, for the needs of another generation." Stumbling on in this way, the argument said what everyone knew but what those called on to recognize were least willing to acknowledge. Looking on from the concerned bystander's vantage, Hughes recalled an earlier time when Justice John Marshall Harlan had approached flagging old Stephen Field to urge him to face the need to retire. Gently reminding Field that he had once asked the same of an elderly associate, Harlan watched the old man come alive: "Yes!" Field growled. "And a dirtier day's work I never did in my life!"

Roosevelt sought to defuse the situation by sending his aide Thomas Corcoran to see Justice Brandeis, then 81, to explain that the geriatric argument was not aimed at him. Brandeis was gracious but made it plain that he considered it a primary duty to defend the Court against political incursion.

Soon after the Senate Judiciary Committee hearings on the bill began in March, administration witnesses gave up the detached posture of caring most about efficiency and age and acknowledged that the main thrust of the bill went to breaking the logjam on the Court so that the New Deal work of recovery from Depression could go forward. "Yes," said Assistant Attorney General Robert Jackson, later himself to be appointed to the Supreme Court by Roosevelt, "I think it is fair to say that it is absolutely true that [whether Roosevelt's plan works] will depend on the men appointed."

The touch of arrogance revealed by such a direct statement of intent to manage the Court was matched by the administration's approach to Congress. Riding high from the November election, the New Dealers showed that they expected the vast Democratic majority to act at the administration's behest. Democratic Party Chairman Jim Farley spelled it out bluntly at a press conference: "Before I close, I just want to call something to your attention regarding the Supreme Court issue. We have let the Senate talk all they want to. Then the House will take up the matter, and there they will talk until they are tired. After they are all talked out we will call the roll. You will find we have plenty of votes to put over the President's program."

Congress, however, decided to debate a great deal longer than Farley had anticipated. The high volume of mail and public protest against the proposal, the blitz publicity campaign decrying Court packing, and, in some cases, their own opposition made many otherwise loyal New Dealers seek ways of evading the administration steamroller, none more deftly than the man in charge of the Senate hearings, Judiciary Committee chairman Henry Fountain Ashurst from Arizona. A wit who had the imperturbability of one who believes he can talk himself out of anything, Ashurst decided to bamboozle the administration by making a virtue of lengthy committee hearings that were actually designed to smother the bill by calling hostile witnesses. After a brief administration statement to the committee based on the expectation of quick action and belief in the chairman's loyalty, Ashurst opened the gates to all who could conjure up some objection. In March, after three weeks of hearings had already elapsed, Ashurst told amused reporters: "I could win easily in June, more easily in July, quite easily in August, and by September it would be no fight at all." When asked if he would be unduly influenced by so much negative input, the chairman wryly reminded the questioner that he was a Fountain, not a cistern.

To spur on the faltering campaign, Roosevelt turned to his natural allies, farm and labor leaders. They, however, were hesitantly of two minds. In the midwest, insurgents revived the Non-Partisan League as a vehicle to bring a team of farm and labor reformers to bear on social issues; Ed O'Neal, president of the American Farm Bureau, cautioned that "those who believe the American farmer will stand idly by and watch his program for economic justice fall without a fight are badly mistaken. The fight is on—and this time it will be with the gloves off." But the opposition of James Taber of the Grange to the scheme echoed a strong farm belt streak of reverence for the Supreme Court that inhibited farmers from offering much active support to the administration.

Organized labor, in contrast, stepped in vigorously to support the president. Editorials in the labor press hammered on the need for a national economic policy and the foolishness of judicial distinctions between interstate and intrastate commerce. The plan to stop reactionaries from using the commerce clause, the power to tax, and due process against the right of labor to organize was not, labor spokesmen insisted, a plan for packing the court but for unpacking it. The ideal was for a court that would refrain from much judicial review and, as the great dissenter, Oliver Wendell Holmes, and unionism's patriarch, Samuel Gompers, had urged, would let the people's elected representatives decide what laws were appropriate.

Finally, the Supreme Court broke the deadlock. At the end of March, Hughes, in one of the moves that has left his reputation a clouded blend of statesman and Machiavellian, composed a letter rebutting the administration argument that a larger Court was needed to handle the expanding number of cases. Hughes obtained the signature of Justice Brandeis, loyal to the Court as he had assured Corcoran he would be, and sent the letter to the Senate Committee where the most prominent Democratic defector, Burton Wheeler of Montana, dramatically revealed its documented assurance that the Court had kept pace with its docket. Privately, members of the Court who had not been shown the letter seethed at Hughes's stratagem for the way it involved the Court as lobbyist; Roosevelt noted accurately that a major reason the Court was able to keep up with its business was that it took excessive advantage of the 1925 Judiciary Act allowing it to refuse to hear appeals more easily. But Hughes's perfect timing enabled him to make the greatest impact on Congress.

Then the scene moved to the courtroom. On March 29, 1937—"White Monday" as it came to be known, in contrast to "Black Monday," when the New Deal suffered its greatest reversal—the Supreme Court handed down decisions stunningly favorable to the administration. The central case, *West Coast Hotel Co. v. Parrish,* reversed by a five to four vote the Taft Court's refusal to allow state welfare laws to interfere with freedom of contract by upholding a statute in the state of Washington regulating minimum wages for women and minors. The case was not a landmark for that reason only. It was pivotal because it marked the shift of Hughes and Roberts from the conservative to the liberal side of the Court, although both Justices stoutly denied any change of position. They had not endorsed such state welfare power in the case disallowing a similar New York law a few months earlier, they explained, because the Taft Doctrine's lack of firm precedent had not been explicitly addressed. In the West Coast Hotel case, however, the weak precedent was challenged, and so they felt entitled to reverse it. Though legal scholars have argued over whether that explanation saved Hughes and Roberts from gross inconsistency, court-watchers at the time, taking the Realist position, concluded that the Justices had sensed political danger, if not from Court packing then by some other means to curb their power, and simply decided that "a switch in time saves nine." The cynical saw signs of personal political ambition. After having voted conservatively early in the year to position himself as the next Republican presidential candidate, so the argument ran, Roberts decided that Roosevelt's sweeping victory left him no chance in a future election and so changed his stripes to accommodate the winning side. Whatever the reason, the change was fraught with great political implications.

Alongside the West Coast Hotel case that fateful day were a number of other cases in which the new majority extended the commerce and general welfare powers of the states and federal government to include regulation of mortgage contracts, restriction of trade in dangerous firearms, and protection of collective bargaining. Astutely, Roosevelt noted at a press conference the day after "White Monday" that the New Deal had arrived at the perilous shores of "Roberts Land." In the hands of that changeable justice rested the balance of power between the laissez-faire world and the New Deal welfare state. There was, indeed, something to the contention by one expert observer that for a crucial moment Owen Roberts was the single most powerful man in the United States.

Attention next settled on a challenge to the Wagner Act made by the Jones & Laughlin company, one of the most atavistically defiant of the Pittsburgh steel enterprises, in defense of its policy of firing workers who claimed their right to unionize. Should the unpopular steel barons prevail, the New Dealers might gain enough indignant sympathy in Congress to push the Court reform bill through. Could any degree of conviction and the precedent of the Schechter and Carter cases be strong enough for a majority of Justices to take such a risk? On the other hand, could the Court afford to reverse its judgment against the NRA and perhaps set off a stampede toward acceptance of the entire New Deal case that legislative discretion should determine how the commerce clause would be used to advance the general welfare?

The answer came at a packed session on April 12, 1937. New Dealers took heart when they learned that the chief justice would read the decision himself, for Hughes, always careful about his image and posterity, preferred to write the popular liberal decisions and shied away from conservative opinions that drew the barbs of legal critics, the most celebrated of whom disdained the old pieties. As anticipated, Hughes spoke for a five to four majority, including Roberts, in favor of the National Labor Relations Board position. Still trying to preserve a sense of the Court's continuity, Hughes sought to swallow up the Schechter and Carter cases within the all-encompassing concept of experience. "These cases are not controlling here," Hughes stated in broad endorsement of the Progressive and legal Realist positions, because the nature of each instance of governmental intervention "must be appraised by a judgment that does not ignore actual experience." The affronts to workers' rights and needs, unlike the issues of meddling with poultry businesses and coal fields, were of crisis proportions. It was pointless to debate whether the labor wars the Jones & Laughlin position incited would have an effect on interstate commerce that "would be indirect or remote. It is obvious that it would be immediate and might be catastrophic."

Hughes's expansive appeal to experience and consequences enabled him to draw upon precedents of widely differing character and implications, and to do so with a sonorous ring of fealty to the Larger Truths of the Law. But the stance aroused suspicions of opportunism and alienated fellow Justices—conservative and moderate alike—who wanted more literal consistency and an avowal that the Jones & Laughlin decision was a reversal, not an extension, of the previous majority position. Justice Harlan Stone, a champion of the Holmesian view that courts should allow legislatures and persons to do what they chose unless the law expressly forbade it, tartly summed up the aversion to Hughes's zigzag style in writing to prominent Realist critic Karl Llewellyn: "I can hardly see the use of writing judicial opinions unless they are to embody methods of analysis and of exposition which will serve the profession as a guide to the decision of future cases. If they are not better than an excursion ticket, good for this day and trip only, they do not serve even as protective coloration for the writer of the opinion and would much better be left unsaid." Roosevelt, with his usual shrewd skepticism, did not doubt that a fundamental shift had taken place. "It would be a little naive," he concluded, "to refuse to recognize some connection between these 1937 decisions and the Supreme Court fight."

Victory in the courtroom took most of the steam out of Roosevelt's congressional campaign to expand the Court, and the retirement soon afterward of the New Deal's most adamant foes on the bench sealed the fate of the effort altogether as irrelevant. As the Senate voted to recommit the Court reform bill to the Judiciary Committee, where it was stripped of the packing proviso, excitement shifted to the revelation that Senator Hugo Black of Alabama, chosen to replace conservative Justice Willis Van Devanter, had once been a member of the Ku Klux Klan. With that sudden turn of fate Roosevelt was able to make new appointments that set the stage for completing what has aptly been termed "the Constitutional Revolution of 1937."

Powerful confirmation of the new trend came soon afterward in a series of decisions that upheld Social Security by proclaiming the right of the federal government to decide on the ends to which it chose to use its taxing and spending powers. The conservative insistence that taxing bills had to be limited to raising revenue and to funding initiatives the Court deemed duly respectful of property, free trade, and states rights gave way to legislative discretion about what was in the public interest. In one of his last pronouncements, Justice Cardozo hailed the trend with an appeal to experience that fit the New Deal cooperative commonwealth credo: "The purge of nation-wide calamity that began in 1929 has taught us many lessons. Not the least is the solidarity of interests that may once have seemed to be divided." Now we must see, he concluded, that "unemployment is an ill not particular but general, which may be checked, if Congress so determines, by the resources of the Nation. . . . The problem is plainly national in area and dimensions. Moreover, laws of the separate states cannot deal with it effectively. . . . Only a power that is national can serve the interests of all."

The last major inhibition set by the old Court against the Constitutional authority of the New Deal to implement its conception of a welfare state lost its hold in 1940 when Justice Stone stated bluntly, and without contradiction, that the Tenth Amendment was a mere truism, tacked onto the Bill of Rights to soothe the raw feelings of the anti-Federalists who wanted some specific word that the states would retain powers of their own under the new Constitution. By no means was the declaration of powers reserved for the states intended to curb the federal government's ultimate authority to decide for itself how federal legislation would apply to the nation at large. Roosevelt Supreme Court appointee Frank Murphy drew the ultimate economic inference in 1946 when he declared flatly that the national government's power to regulate under the commerce clause "was as broad as the economic needs of the nation." Left essentially unchallenged, the statement signaled the end of the Court's power, or disposition, to inhibit the passage of legislation placing national concerns ahead of local, state, or private interests. The Constitutional defilers haunting the imagination of Taft and Sutherland had won the day. But economic woes and the resurgence of conservative political opposition would keep the New Dealers from taking immediate advantage of their hard-won opportunity.

CHAPTER ELEVEN

The Rendezvous with Destiny

As the judicial revolution cleared away constitutional obstacles to the New Deal welfare state, other impediments gathered to take their place. The court-packing plan heightened policy differences between Roosevelt and Congress and lowered the president's esteem within a public that reverenced judicial independence. Comprehensive planning was set back by the National Recovery Administration fiasco. And the business community, after the stinging campaign attacks on "economic royalists," became increasingly estranged. Thus the president was forced to walk a tightrope between the continued need of bold action for recovery and the growing chorus of critics crying "farewell to reform"—all the while trying to juggle the planner and decentralist rivals within his administration. Confined to a narrow field of possibility, the administration ran the gauntlet of congressional resistance, economic recession, business counterattack, and retrenchment of social programs under the cloak of defense against subversive menace. The "rendezvous with destiny" Roosevelt had triumphantly proclaimed for his second term turned out to be a far less glorious outcome than the optimists in his camp expected would crown his smashing reelection.

In an effort to maintain New Deal momentum, Roosevelt sought immediately to reward his working class electoral base. He pressured Congress to provide another $1.5 billion for the emergency relief effort and endorsed the Black-Connery Fair Labor Standards bill, which, following the West Coast Hotel decision, set out federal guidelines for working conditions and minimum wages. Alongside these measures, reformers who operated with White House approval but little explicit endorsement because of fear of antagonizing conservative allies introduced the

Wagner Fair Housing Bill and a measure to end the nefarious practice of lynching, then on the rise as blacks turned to the New Deal in search of a better, freer life while hard times pitted them against whites in the struggle for scarce economic opportunities.

Faced with congressional reluctance to accept even that limited agenda, the administration explored new ways to achieve a cooperative commonwealth through planning. Since the fall of 1933 a committee of the National Planning Board had been studying ways of reorganizing the executive branch so that it would gain the authority that seemed necessary to run a complex modern state. Urged on by eager members of that committee—all veterans of progressive reform and commissions to manage cities and natural resources—Roosevelt in the spring of 1936 set up the Committee on Administrative Management to study reorganization. From its deliberations an executive reorganization bill made its way to Congress calling for an expansion of presidential staff, greater executive authority over civil service, and a transfer of the Bureau of the Budget to the White House.

These recommendations reflected longstanding institutional thought by social scientists concerned about efficient management. Yet in the wake of the Court fight and alarming news of dictatorial tyranny abroad, an uproar ensued. In Congress, voices rose, some of them Democrats, to accuse the president of once again trying to infringe on the authority of other branches of government. Newspaper editorials accused the president of a power grab, and there were even outdoor rallies to rouse public sentiment against reorganization. A quieter, yet still intense, protest came from veteran reformers who from early progressive days had preached the virtue of regulatory agencies free from either legislative or executive control. Because of a provision in the new bill to give the president appointment power over the agencies, even members of Roosevelt's administration like James Landis, head of the SEC, registered their opposition. Unnerved, the House defeated the measure despite a large Democratic majority, and the administration was left with no better recourse than to accept a weak substitute bill, supplemented by an executive order in September 1939 that did move the Bureau of the Budget to the White House and also provided means for the president to issue planning reports and carry out reviews of governmental policies. The shift by the New Deal to greater reliance on executive authority, after the Courts and Congress slighted the cause of planning and made the president's ability to control the Democratic party uncertain, prompted one critical observer in 1937 to speak of a Third New Deal—one bent on victory by creating an administrative state that would eclipse the legislative branch. Roosevelt's lack of enthusiasm for the meager results of executive reorganization, however, and the increasingly effective inclination of Congress to stymie what was left of the New Deal made the concept of a Third New Deal a dubious way to explain the events of Roosevelt's second term.

The waning of New Deal crisis-time magic was ironically tied to the fact that the very success of New Deal liberalism had enabled some conservative anti–New Deal Democrats to ride into office on Roosevelt's coattails. As well, many Congressmen with progressive records were tiring of reform, especially the new-fangled welfare state kind. Those who came out of the Wilsonian tradition distrusted centralization, and old-time Democrats could be heard muttering louder than usual against the horde of fancy new bureaucrats who "murdered the broad 'a'" and tried to change everything. Because these old stalwarts were often from rural areas, especially in the South, their complaints included the urban emphasis of Roosevelt's new coalition, with its clamoring mass of blacks and ethnics. This growing hostility from the hinterland cast a disturbing shadow over the New Deal's pursuit of cooperative unity. Though the Common Man ideal retained much symbolic influence, it could not wish away traditional antagonisms between farmers and workers or the resistance to change built into local customs and views about race, class, and other characteristics that emphasized fixed individual differences rather than the possibilities of finding common ground.

The Republican ranks, though small, gained significant spirit and unity from the divisiveness that climaxed in the Court fight. Even progressives like George Norris and William Borah who had sided with the New Deal on many reforms returned to the Republican fold. Their suspicion of Rooseveltian high-handedness carried over to increased doubts about any further initiatives he might take, especially those apt to produce regional and racial friction or entangle the nation in risky foreign adventures.

As the New Deal momentum waned, its modest legislative proposals of 1937 all squeaked through the Senate except for the Court bill and were ready for House consideration during the next year. Less fortunate were the anti-lynching bills and the Wagner housing proposal in 1938. In stark terms southerners noted that the housing measure had been proposed by a New York champion of labor and would tend to shore up decayed northern industrial centers against southern economic competition. Senator Harry F. Byrd of Virginia, a wealthy apple grower who owned vast stretches of the state but liked to preach abstemiousness to others, managed to attach a proviso to the housing act that limited the amount of money available for a family home to $4,000—only marginally useful for any low-level housing. The anti-lynching bill was throttled altogether by filibuster, the windy anticlimax to an effort that had engaged the fullest efforts by the NAACP and other civil rights groups since the advent of the New Deal.

In the course of their resistance, southern diehards heightened white supremacy agitation to a point that gave some credence to claims that fascism and racism were twin alternatives to progressive reform. Senator Theodore Bilbo of Mississippi brought those fears to a chilling head in 1938 with the concept he flung out to his Senate colleagues: "Race consciousness is developing in all parts of the world. Consider Italy, consider Germany. It is beginning to be recognized by the thoughtful minds of our age that the conservation of racial values is the only hope for future civilization. It will be recalled that Hitler . . . gave as the basis of his program to unite Germany and Austria 'German blood ties.' The Germans appreciate the importance of race values." The logical conclusion, Bilbo hammered home, is to make more living space for American whites by shipping blacks to Africa—the counterpart of Nazi policy toward Jews of "resettling them in the east" so that there would be space in the Fatherland for Aryans.

As reform stalled amid rancor in Congress, Roosevelt came to fateful conclusions about stabilizing the economy. The rise in business indicators suggested to him and his secretary of the Treasury, Henry Morgenthau, that the time had come for return to the strict budget-balancing frugality government had traditionally favored. Accordingly, the Federal Reserve raised its lending rates in 1937, and Roosevelt, who had always fretted about the danger of inflation, cut appropriations for the WPA and PWA.

But the policy backfired. With federal spending stimuli reduced, along with some $2 billion more of purchasing power siphoned off for the Social Security reserve fund, the still fragile economy went into a dive just as the Senate session ended in August. Construction slowed and factories shut down in the course of a sharper decline during the ten months beginning in the fall of 1937 than had been suffered in 1929. Industrial production dropped 33 percent and national income by 12 percent, while unemployment soared by 50 percent to about 11.5 million persons midway through 1938. Almost all the gains registered in the *New York Times* Business Index since 1933 vanished.

An alarmed Roosevelt called a special session of Congress in November, while New Dealers divided into nervous factions that further elaborated the classic distinctions between liberal planning and progressive decentralization. Henry Morgenthau and Jesse Jones of the Reconstruction Finance Corporation spoke for the monetarist view that recovery would come through restoring liquidity and increasing the credit supply to private business. To them the key was restoration of business confidence, which meant easing the campaign to clean up business practices and redistribute wealth. On the other side, Ickes, Henderson, and Jackson insisted that businessmen had not been handled roughly enough and were still pushing for "a strike against capital" to force the New Deal to ease taxes and regulation. The solution, these progressives maintained, was to break up the reactionary giants into small enterprises willing to compete without special favors or inflated expectations. Against this cure through competition former NRA official Donald Richberg argued the planning case that only a newly perfected, Court-proof NRA could bring business into efficient association that would end "destructive competition." An even more fully collectivist group, led by Jerome Frank and Mordecai Ezekiel, contended that central planning to circumvent all of the ills of private competition was the answer.

The view destined to have the greatest influence, however, made a late entrance into the debate through an unorthodox side door. When Lauchlin Currie, Harvard economist and adviser to Marriner Eccles at the Federal Reserve, argued for a return to deficit spending, he unknowingly echoed a strategy offered by the great English economist John Maynard Keynes in his book *The General Theory of Employment, Interest, and Money*, which was published in 1936.

Though most New Dealers were unfamiliar with *The General Theory* when the recession hit, Keynes did have some presence in the New Deal scene, especially through his admiring acquaintance Felix Frankfurter. Keynes had also been directly in touch with Roosevelt. On December 31, 1933, the economist suggested in a letter to the *New York Times* but meant for the eye of the president that the NRA strategy was fundamentally misconceived. Planned limits on production were exactly the wrong cure for falling national wealth and production; artificially fixing high prices merely weakened already anemic consumption. Instead of these self-defeating measures, Keynes proposed that governments worldwide make a New Year's resolution to "lay overwhelming emphasis on the increase of national purchasing power resulting from government expenditure which is financed by loans." The following spring Keynes came to the United States to receive an honorary degree from Columbia and used the occasion to visit Roosevelt, armed with a letter of introduction from Frankfurter that described him, plausibly, as "perhaps the single most powerful supporter of the New Deal in England."

Keynes commanded attention on several grounds. He was the widely admired critic—and satirist—of the discredited Versailles Treaty, which had set the terms for reordering the world after the Great War; a wizard at making profitable investments; and the eminent author of technical treatises on money and public policy. Keynes also distinguished himself among the English Bloomsbury group of artists and literary lions by his elegant wit and debating skill. Bertrand Russell, the most eminent social thinker of the time in England, summed up the feeling of many who had encountered Keynes's rapier mind with his declaration that "Keynes's intellect was the sharpest and clearest that I have ever known. When I argued with him, I felt that I took my life in my hands, and I seldom emerged without feeling something of a fool."

On New Year's Day of 1935, Keynes was on the verge of his greatest triumph and wrote the playwright and social reformer, George Bernard Shaw, of a very special excitement: "To understand my state of mind, you have to know that I believe myself to be writing a book on economic theory which will largely revolutionize—not, I suppose, at once but in the course of the next ten years—the way the world thinks about economic problems." The next year Keynes's *General Theory* appeared, and by the end of the subsequent decade his prophecy was essentially fulfilled.

The *General Theory* was one of those rare revelations of how long-cherished truisms are the opposite of the truth. In this case the glare was cast on a prevalent belief that harked back to the eighteenth-century French economist Jean-Baptiste Say and the faith in progress and scientific law that characterized his Enlightenment world. Say's Law described the marketplace as a kind of perpetual motion machine. Since man's desire for possessions is infinite, Say argued, and the manufacture of goods generates wages that will be used to buy them, it follows that all things produced will find a buyer. Further, labor will always be employable because in an insatiable market there is ample incentive for new productive enterprises to absorb available workers. To all of which the great economist David Ricardo, who guided the Industrial Revolution in England, added a word about the tendency of some to withdraw purchasing power from the market in the form of savings. "To save is to spend," Ricardo aphorized, meaning that the purpose for saving is to have capital available for new investment. The result was a neat assurance that the marketplace, *if left free*, would follow natural laws toward full capital formation, full employment, and the consumption of all goods produced.

But with the wreckage of the Depression all around him, Keynes insisted to the contrary that a society might reach economic equilibrium at far less than full employment and productive capacity. The reason was to be found in limitations on the urge to invest. At a certain point in the onward march of prosperity, inducement for investment is bound to falter. Say and the classical economists who followed failed to comprehend that fact because they did not fully consider the difference between *desire* and *demand*. True, desire is infinite—but business-men need to produce according to effective *demand,* or purchasing power. For example, merely because there are always people who would like to take a cruise does not mean that they are prepared to buy an ocean liner—or even reserve a cabin on one. Throughout the economy the supply of particular goods tends to reach a point where consumer demand is satiated far short of desire. To drive home the point of how vulnerable the modern economy is to market saturation, Keynes made one of his characteristically sardonic comparisons: "Ancient Egypt was doubly fortunate and doubtless owed to this its fabled wealth, in that it pos-sessed two activities, namely pyramid-building and the search for precious met-als, the fruits of which, since they could not serve the needs of man by being con-sumed, did not stale with abundance. The Middle Ages built two cathedrals and sang dirges. Two pyramids, two masses for the dead are twice as good as one; but not so two railways from London to York."

The hesitation of investors in the face of tightening demand has an ominous chain-reaction effect, Keynes explained. Contracting investment means lowered pro-duction, fewer jobs, and, thus, less purchasing power. That cluster of events in turn lowers demand still further, setting off a new round of decline in investment, production, employment, and consumption. The downward spiral at some point will find a new equilibrium, but at far less than full production and employment. Conceivably, fresh initiative can start the spiral upward again, thus beginning a new cycle. But it might also turn out that the debased equilibrium stays frozen.

Keynes even ruled out the hope for salvation from savings clung to by Her-bert Hoover and the orthodox diehards around him. Confronted with a slump in opportunity, conventional wisdom argued, investors characteristically with-hold their money in line with the virtue of saving for a rainy day. Eventually the savings accumulated find new opportunity and the economy rebounds. Not so, Keynes argued. Saving for investment was a luxury that only applied to sunny days. When it rains people spend their savings to keep dry—or avoid drowning. Thus, the $4 billion Americans put in savings during the prosperity of 1929 swiftly dissipated in hard times. By 1933 the citizenry was not saving at all; cor-porations, which in flush times sought to bypass banks and keep their own in-vestment funds tucked away, had gone from $2.45 billion in savings in 1929 to deficits of nearly $6 billion by the end of 1932. The moral was that the more des-perately savings are needed to finance a climb out of the pit, the more they are apt to be missing. No more conclusive evidence of this could be found than the fact that the United States economy, which at the peak of prosperity in 1929 had generated $15 billion for wages, salaries, and profits, could only provide $886 million in 1932. The dropoff of 94 percent was something Say and Ricardo could not explain.

Keynes was not given to unrelieved gloom, however. He offered a way out with the jaunty wit he used to pierce the armor of respectability layered around classical concepts. The thing to do, he insisted, was to use the government in times of free market paralysis as the only agency capable of providing investment funds. While useful projects were to be preferred, any sort of paying proposition would do: "If the Treasury were to fill old bottles with banknotes, bury them at suitable depths in disused coal-mines which are then filled up to the surface with town rubbish, and leave it to private enterprise on well-tried principles of *laissez-faire* to dig the notes up again . . . there need be no more unemployment. . . . It would indeed be more sensible to build houses and the like; but if there are political and practical difficulties in the way of this, the above would be better than nothing."

Keynes's prescription was, of course, directly in line with the "pump-priming" relief projects that the New Deal—and even Hoover—had mounted. What he added was a densely reasoned rationale that carried such measures out of the realm of sheer crisis management and onto the plane of august professional and theoretical reputability. His comprehensive formulation also added immensely to the ability of governments to gear their pump-priming to actual need. Beyond that, Keynes looked to a theory of counter-cyclical intervention that would control the entire business cycle. To balance pump-priming for starting a sluggish economy, the theory also included consideration of how to take money out of circulation when the pump overheated. In the United States that balanced strategy entailed unemployment relief and public works combined with redistribution of wealth through tax policy and regulating the money supply through manipulation of interest rates by the Federal Reserve. It was a formula that called for state intervention but not socialism, for macroeconomic tuning that would leave microeconomic decisions about prices and production to the marketplace. Ideally, the Keynesian approach would thus protect capitalist economies from boom and bust cycles and reduce the cruel gap between rich and poor while preserving free enterprise. It was thus a formulation remarkably well suited to advancing the cooperative commonwealth goals at the heart of New Deal reform.

For all the logical affinities between the two men, Roosevelt found reasons to resist Keynes's brilliant case. The President was dubious both about the "moral" value of speculative business and Keynes's occasional air of cynical superiority. Thus Keynes failed to get a very positive response when he chided Roosevelt about his righteous rejection of businessmen as "economic royalists": "You could do anything you liked with them, if you would treat them (even the big ones) not as wolves and tigers, but as domestic animals by nature, even though they have been badly brought up and not trained as you would wish. It is a mistake to think that they are more immoral than politicians. If you work them into the surly, obstinate, terrified mood, of which domestic animals, wrongly handled, are so capable, the nation's burdens will not get carried to markets, and in the end public opinion will veer their way." Also annoying was the way Keynes in *The Economic Consequences of the Peace* derided Wilson as a hypocritical Presbyterian prig who was disastrously blind to the worldly ways of Europe—the bitch gone rotten in the teeth, as Keynes's poetic counterpart, Ezra Pound, put it. Roosevelt could not take kindly to such disrespect for his early political hero and the administration he served, especially when the slur came from an economist, whose profession Roosevelt tended to disparage in a bemused way. To the economist booster of the private entrepreneurial spirit, Joseph Schumpeter, Roosevelt wrote in 1936, just before Keynes's *General Theory* appeared, that after many years of "a more or less intensive study of economics and economists [I am] compelled to admit—or boast—which ever way you care to put it, that I know nothing of economics and that nobody else does either!" The rising exasperation of the indifferent Harvard economics student with the way the profession failed to come to his rescue bristled through Roosevelt's complaint at a press conference: "I brought down several books by English economists and leading American economists. . . . I suppose I must have read different articles by fifteen different experts. Two things stand out: The first is that no two of them agree, and the other thing is that they are so foggy in what they say that it is almost impossible to figure out what they mean. It is jargon; absolute jargon."

Nor was Roosevelt merely a querulous outsider in a tight spot. Throughout the decade the major journals, the *American Economic Review* and the *Quarterly Journal of Economics,* showed scant recognition that the Crash and ensuing Depression called for radically new analyses. Indeed, the American economic profession became increasingly impersonal and detached from social issues during the 1930s, as the vogue of value-free social science carried it further into the realm of abstract classical theorizing. In a rare moment of interest in unorthodox ideas among the professional economists, John M. Clark in his 1936 address as outgoing president of the American Economic Association decried the inertia and pressed his colleagues to devise urgently needed new ideas for recovery. But the advice died away after faint applause.

Under the circumstances, it was not surprising that Keynes's talk with Roosevelt has left a murky record of men with different talents and dispositions trying to find some common ground in a time of uncertainty. Frances Perkins remembered Roosevelt grumbling about Keynes's way of reeling out "a whole rigama-role of figures" that made him seem more a mathematician than an economist. Keynes seemed equally disappointed, remarking that he had "supposed the President more literate, economically speaking." On the other hand, Rexford Tugwell, who was present for some of the talk, recalled that "Keynes' attitude was more that of an admiring observer than that of an instructor." Afterward, when each wrote to Frankfurter, Keynes spoke of a "tête-à-tête" with the president which was fascinating and illuminating; Roosevelt exclaimed that he had "had a grand talk with Keynes and liked him immensely."

Whatever the effect of Keynes's visit, his concepts moved steadily to fill the void of effective economic strategies. A young government economist named John Kenneth Galbraith set out a program in *Toward Full Employment* (1938) that pointed the way toward subsequent efforts to apply compensatory fiscal policy and to resort to deficits where necessary in order to raise employment levels. Keynesian doctrine was also securing a strong beachhead in the academic world. An enthusiastic coterie at Harvard and Tufts led by Alvin Hansen, an economist who after reading *The General Theory* renounced classical laissez-faire to become an ardent disciple of Keynes, most effectively answered Clark's call for new ideas. Their manifesto, *An Economic Program for American Democracy* (1938), declared that "the New Deal has not failed. Rather its great weakness has been a wavering adherence to its own principles." Regaining a firm grasp on fundamentals called for a crisis mentality: "Here in America we can save our free democratic institutions only by using them to expand our national income." That must be done in recognition that business was even more the problem than Roosevelt had indicated in his anti-royalist campaign for reelection: "For private enterprise, left to its own devices, is no longer capable of achieving anything. . . . The need for immediate action to achieve this end cannot be over-emphasized. For the danger exists that businessmen, obsessed with a devil theory of government, will attempt to use their economic power to suppress democracy and place in its stead a dictatorship supposedly dedicated to the fulfillment of their desires."

The impact of the new economic thought was dangerously delayed, however. Despite the deepening recession, the president hesitated to call off his decision to reduce federal spending in an attempt to balance the budget. Only when a group spearheaded by Hopkins and Leon Henderson managed in the spring of 1938 to get Roosevelt alone at Warm Springs, away from the distractions of Washington, could they drive the Keynesian message home. The decisive argument was an appeal to history by Beardsley Ruml, chairman of the New York Federal Reserve, who possessed broad business and academic experience.

Ruml persuaded Roosevelt that governmental stimulation of business was an old story. By disbursing the public lands, making grants to railroads, coining the gold discovered in California, granting franchises, setting tariffs, and other such devices, the federal government had always primed the pump. "It follows," Ruml concluded in his memorandum, "that the competitive capitalist system has been sustained from the beginning by federal intervention to create purchasing power." Ruml's comparison between earlier subsidies to powerful enterprises and Keynesian policies to help the disadvantaged and redistribute income downward was strained. Subsidies in the past to productive enterprises like canals and railroads, designed to speed the nation's economic development, had little directly to do with New Deal social spending aimed at circulating wealth and fostering high levels of consumption. Nonetheless, the appeal was effective. Moved by his keen appreciation of historical experience, rather than by any newfound admiration for economic theory, Roosevelt consented to a massive reversal of the balanced austerity budget that Morgenthau had pressed on him in 1937.

The most prominent result was a $3.75 billion omnibus relief bill passed by Congress in June 1938, which bolstered the faltering WPA and brought the PWA out of mothballs. More in line with Ruml's analogy was the funding distributed to the RFC to pump loans into faltering banks and railroads. That revival of the RFC as a key agency for capital formation indicated the administration's willingness to improve relationships with business without having to abandon efforts to restrict monopoly and redistribute income.

But all the new pump-priming was not enough to reverse the downward slide. The recession trouble unleashed by the 1937 policies struck most heavily in 1938. Unemployment rose sharply by 3 million to 19 percent of the workforce and did not descend to the 1937 level for two years. All the other prime indices took the same dip: the Gross National Product went from $90.8 billion to $85.2 billion; corporate profits fell from $6.2 billion to $4.3 billion; savings were especially devastated—the sure sign, as Keynes had explained, of economic trouble—off 75 percent in the personal sector and pushing undistributed corporate profits below the break-even point, just a year after the first profit in the decade had been registered in 1937. Accordingly, the business failure rate was grim—up almost 50 percent. Recovery to the 1937 level would not occur until after World War II had vastly increased federal spending and demonstrated Keynes's case. The old entrenched concepts would make it virtually impossible, as he put it, "for a capitalistic democracy to organize expenditure on the scale necessary to make the grand experiment to prove my case—except in war conditions."

Against that dark backdrop, the 1938 congressional session proceeded contentiously. The spending measure went through on the wings of sheer necessity; beyond that the only major success of the administration was passage of a watered-down version of the Fair Labor Standards Act first proposed in 1937. Conservatives, gaining momentum and confidence, succeeded in exempting many agricultural workers from minimum wage standards and forced postponements in certain other categories. Southern hardliners thus prevailed for a time in their 50¢/day concept against the caustic outrage of Roosevelt and his northern allies. Less predictable was the hesitation of the AFL to endorse the minimum wage concept. Still unable to trust that government was more likely to be supportive than restrictive of labor interests, Green and his inner council warned against any interference in the collective bargaining process. As an official of the United Textile Workers put it—speaking from within the industry that had had the least overall success in trying to organize its workers and should have been most eager for outside help—"Any attempt by statute law to interfere with labor unions' rights to carry out the contract with the employer is an interference with organization in the field."

Roosevelt responded to the turmoil by resuming his attacks on the "economic royalists" and giving his blessing to the desire of progressive decentralists in the administration, Corcoran and Ickes prime among them, to declare war on monopoly. On April 29 Roosevelt accused the "concentration of private power without equal in history" of arranging for the "disappearance of price competition." In June Congress responded to the president's call for an investigation of concentrated wealth by creating the Temporary National Economic Committee (TNEC) with Senator Joseph O'Mahoney of Wyoming as chairman. O'Mahoney was a moderate progressive who wished to find ways of supporting scaled-down business enterprise, not punish any "malefactors of great wealth." Others on the committee, however, prevailed on the Justice Department to launch the most extensive antitrust drive ever undertaken.

In the choice of Yale Law School professor Thurman Arnold to head the Antitrust Division, the New Deal gained one of its most vivid characters. Arnold was an outspoken member of the legal realists and in his writings on practical politics and business had captured the experimental spirit of the New Deal well enough to have earned a reputation as the administration's unofficial philosopher. His widely read books *The Symbols of Government* (1935) and *The Folklore of Capitalism* (1937) with irreverent wit championed the idea that bigness was sometimes a blessing and that good management called for a subtle meshing of reality with myth and symbols at the hands of a master manipulator like Franklin

Roosevelt. Such a collectivist approach was well suited to the first New Deal, and Arnold was conspicuously in sympathy with the NRA's desire to suspend aspects of the antitrust laws while the work of coordinating the nation's industry was going on. The Sherman Antitrust Act, Arnold contended offhandedly at that time, was a mere ceremonial affair of "economic meaninglessness" that should not be allowed to stand in the way of recovery.

Could this, onlookers wondered in 1938, be the right person to lead an antitrust investigation, at a time when the "symbols" of the New Deal were losing the force Arnold sought to gain for them? Arnold's answer showed that he had been attentive to the failure of NRA and had now decided that a dangerous proportion of American business had grown too big and arrogant to be brought together under a blue eagle or any other symbol of government authority. His cynicism about the man in the street since tempered by the failure of the powerful men in Washington and corporate boardrooms to make a go of NRA, Arnold turned more respectfully to the general citizenry. In "The War on Monopoly" (1939), he contended that "the idea of antitrust laws is to create a situation in which competition compels passing on to the consumers the savings of mass distribution and production." Arnold argued that this turnaround on antitrust was more apparent than real. His complaints had always been about failures of administration, not the Sherman Act itself. The fundamental motive of practical enforcement made for its own kind of consistency; within that framework the Sherman Act could change from being "futile" to symbolizing "our traditional ideals." The fervent terms in which he expressed his views, drawing on his cowboy individualist upbringing in Wyoming and Thorstein Veblen's skewerings of business, could make Arnold seem exaggerated and inconsistent, but his steady concern to enlarge the area of personal freedom, combined with his shrewdness in exposing balderdash put forward by captains of industry to advance their interests at the expense of the general welfare, made him a key spokesman for the evolving New Deal.

Arnold expressed his view of the changed times by presiding over the initiation of 44 percent of all the antitrust suits filed since the passage of the Sherman Act in 1890. Much of that activity, which saw the personnel of the Antitrust Division increase from 111 to 496 and its budget swell from $473,000 to $1.8 million, stemmed from his charisma and shrewdness in getting businesses under the gun to sign "consent decrees." Both his public relations appeal to cherished symbols and the Machiavellian sureness of his tactics illustrated Arnold's mastery of New Deal maneuver. Yet the resourceful resistance of business and another change in circumstances ultimately thwarted the antitrust drive. By 1942, when the wartime need for expanded and unified productivity brought Arnold's crusade for smaller-scale competition to an end, only the Pullman Company and Paramount Pictures had been significantly changed by antitrust action. Eventually, persuasive doubts were cast on whether monopolies had taken much advantage of the public. One study presented in 1954 indicated that preventing the development of monopolies during the 1920s would only have given consumers about a tenth of a percent more for their money. At best, the Sherman Act and Arnold's labors served as a holding action against a pattern of business combination that has since grown well beyond the point that so concerned trustbusters during the 1930s.

As the economic shadows of 1938 lengthened, Roosevelt decided to launch an offensive on the political front to match Arnold's economic campaign. He had become increasingly annoyed at Democratic congressmen who were defecting from the New Deal and decided to come out against several offenders in their attempts to win reelection that year. But the "purge" effort backfired, proving conclusively that the mandate Roosevelt thought he had won in 1936 had dwindled in the face of new fears and an old distrust of activist government. Despite enlisting the shrewd Jim Farley as coordinator of the effort and barnstorming himself in the key congressional districts, Roosevelt succeeded in ousting only one Democratic defector: Representative John O'Connor of New York City who as chairman of the House Rules Committee had been a bottleneck for numerous New Deal measures that he considered radical attempts to redistribute wealth and give the federal government too much control over individual and state actions. Elsewhere, efforts against Senators Guy Gillette of Iowa, Frederick Van Nuys of California, Walter George of Georgia, "Cotton Ed" Smith of South Carolina, and Millard Tydings of Maryland were bitterly thwarted. The purge campaign not only inflamed party loyalists but also revealed the strong attachment of voters to their local representatives, even those who did not support the popular will on national issues. Roper Public Opinion Research Center polls showed that even Democrats generally opposed the "purge" tactic as an encroachment on state and local affairs.

In Congress Roosevelt had little voting support to lose in opposing the incumbents, who would have resisted many of his policies in any case—but the cost in prestige was high and no doubt emboldened some of his enemies. They were swift to level an ugly charge that Hopkins and other WPA officials had conspired with local relief administrators to deliver the votes of their clients against those on the purge list. Hopkins and his administrators emerged free from any taint of illegal use of WPA funds, but the Senate investigation of the Kentucky election came up with enough evidence of arm-twisting to convince Congress to pass the Hatch Act in 1939, forbidding federal employees from engaging in political activity.

Rising domestic antagonisms darkened when alarm over totalitarian oppression abroad triggered an old reflex to find foreign causes for domestic troubles. That scapegoating could be seen in the action of the Justice Department in 1939 to curb entry of Jewish refugees from Hitler and other "undesirable" aliens on the grounds that they were apt to introduce dangerous ideas and would prolong hard times by taking jobs away from real Americans. Congress provided a forum for anti-foreign fears when it created the House Un-American Activities Committee (HUAC) in 1938. Ostensibly designed to reveal fascist subversion, the committee became tainted by a vehement campaign against attempts to pass anti-lynching legislation. A filibuster filled with inflammatory rhetoric about red radicals and enemies of states' rights stirring up racial discontent defeated the anti-lynching bill. Out of that ugly scene one of the more outspokenly racist congressmen, Representative Martin Dies of Texas, emerged to become chairman of HUAC. Dies proved to be a zealot of shifty ethics and oratorical power who used the committee to aid the conservative attack on the New Deal. Within public opinion fearful of war and socialist subversion, Dies's technique of badgering witnesses whose right to respond was consistently cut short was very successful. The fate of Representative Kent Keller of Illinois marked the futility of trying to contest Dies's authority within Congress. Keller sought to have the funds for HUAC cut off, charging that the only "ism" the committee's members were against was the "progressivism of the New Deal." The House rebuffed the effort, however, and Keller then returned to Illinois to be defeated in the election of 1940 as the subversives' friend whose plan for a power plant dam on Crab Orchard Creek was attacked as a totalitarian attempt to create "Lenin Lake." Other progressives, feeling the hot breath, subsided from earlier activism and, especially in Keller's midwest, were pressured to avoid entanglements with anything "foreign," whether imported or domestic.

The Federal Arts Projects were also prime targets for HUAC. During the heyday of support for relief spending, when critics of experimentation and federal involvement in traditionally private sectors were subdued by crisis, artists on the projects could extend their freedom to the point of defying the established order. Discredited capitalists and the misery left behind by the Crash were prime targets for artists in their new stance as workers in charge of inspiring the "People" to "make America over." The setback of Roosevelt's plans for his second term now gave the other side a chance to retaliate. Poignantly indicative was the fate of painters Anton Refregier and Philip Guston. At the start of the Arts Program Refregier rejoiced that federal support for group effort made it possible to revive the large mural form. "The work is going full swing," explained the artist.

"The workshop is the closest to the Renaissance of anything, I am sure, that has ever happened before in the States." But in 1940 the prize-winning results Refregier and Guston derived from the workshop were destroyed as a frill. At the time of that debacle a crowd of government officials gathered before some other WPA murals at the Brooklyn and Newark airports and debated such questions as whether the red star on a fighter plane was supposed to be an American Air Force insignia or a Soviet icon. Solemnly, the officials decided to take no chances and the murals disappeared.

The strain between artist workers and government managers became acute in 1937 when sharp budget cuts in the relief program were announced in line with Roosevelt's decision that recovery had alleviated the need for more federal pump-priming. Desperately, those cut adrift from the Arts Project, most of them in New York City, converged on the WPA office. The Workers Alliance of writers led a one-day stoppage and takeover of the office of newly designated administrative chief Harold Stein. When six hundred shouting, fist-brandishing demonstrators moved in on him, Stein decided not to call the police for fear that rescuers running up the stairs might be too much for the old floors to bear. Instead Stein agreed to send a plea to Washington for a stay of execution.

The situation was little better at the offices of the Arts Project. There director Audrey McMahon, whose fiery temper had cowed many a worker, debated passionately with invading strikers over how the funding cuts might be restored. Finally, the group composed a telegram with the right mixture of fire and pleading to persuade Washington to restore the funds.

But the projects had only reached the eye of the storm. In 1938 Hopkins left the WPA to become the secretary of commerce, a move designed to make him more accessible to Roosevelt, who had become increasingly reliant on Hopkins since the death of his first mentor, Louis Howe, in 1936. Hopkins's replacement was a strict Army colonel who announced that he had no eye for art and a tin ear. He was merely fulfilling his duty and in a stolid mood, light years removed from the idealist fervor that had created the projects, let it be known that he was perfectly well reconciled to presiding over their demise. Roosevelt added a stern word of his own by making it plain he would not become a party to brawling. He insisted that the artist-workers must not organize militantly, an insistence that was partly a reflection of his sense of the fitness of things when it came to art and government patronage and partly a sign of the need he felt to repair damaged relations with Congress.

The Arts Project had an even more tenuous relationship with Congress than with Roosevelt. The concentration of its workers in New York City alienated many congressmen, whose resentment came to the fore when Representative William Sirovich of New York proposed in 1938 that WPA support for the arts be made permanent by creation of an independent Bureau of Fine Arts. In a response that shocked Sirovich in its vehemence, Congress buried the idea with ridicule. Reverend Dewey Short, congressman from Missouri, started the farce when he declared he couldn't see how anybody could "feel comfortable or enjoy listening to the strains of Mendelssohn with the seat of his pants out." That made the main point: relief money should go for practical needs. Having set the tone, Short pranced down the aisle to exhibit his claims for taking over the division of dance and allied arts himself. In a storm of yahoo hilarity, his colleagues voted accordingly to kill Sirovich's suggestion.

The final blows came more from the patriotic and frugal side than from the philistine. In 1938 HUAC member J. Parnell Thomas of Connecticut announced that the Arts Project was a hotbed of Communism and needed to be investigated. Surprised, WPA officials decided to take a low profile and wait until the wild talk had passed. But Thomas and Dies pressed the attack, and the WPA, faced with Dies's skill at drawing headlines and a Gallup poll showing that 75 percent of those queried favored the committee's investigations, finally agreed to appear. The testimony of their star witness, Hallie Flanagan, director of the Theatre Project, which was especially strongly vilified, should have been a triumph in its skillful and spirited rebuttal of charges. Instead it revealed how a congressional committee determined to scourge a program could turn almost anything to its advantage. When it became clear that Flanagan was not to be bested, Dies simply reneged on his promise to put her statements in the record; the newspapers, more alert to scandal than defense, obliged HUAC by headlining the charges and playing down Flanagan's rebuttal. The committee's work was done so thoroughly that for the arts, as someone put it, the New Deal turned into the Dies Deal. The Relief Bill of 1940 exacted full revenge on Flanagan's uppityness by eliminating the Theatre Project altogether and further placated the Dies Committee by imposing a loyalty oath on the other severely reduced projects. In 1943 the Arts Project was abruptly ended altogether. With that departure went much of the New Deal's ability to wrap its work in symbolism. The cultural programs had always carried a great deal of the weight of defining the New Deal's core values: democracy, community, and the moral primacy of the common man. Only common cause in war could offer a plausible substitute, albeit a temporary one.

The demoralizing end of the Arts Project belied their impressive contribution. The great volume of completed works, though many were lost through hasty disposal at the end, left a sizable legacy. There were moments of high quality, especially in the plastic arts. The subsequent careers of WPA artists further in-dicated the project's significance. Such notables as Ivan Albright, Jack Levine, Marsden Hartley, Mark Tobey, and Jackson Pollock spent time on the project; indeed, by 1941, at the end of the project, fully half the Guggenheim awards to support artists went to project alumni.

The general encouragement to the arts afforded by the WPA and its network of community centers helps explain why more Americans visited art museums in 1940 than in 1930. Along with the rise in museum attendance went an in-crease in the number of art professionals—practitioners and teachers alike—up to 66,000 by 1940, a 12 percent rise in a period when the population only ex-panded by 7 percent.

The Federal Theatre experience also indicated that there were audiences in the hinterlands waiting to be tapped. The documentary drama favored by Fla-nagan because it was both relevant and relatively easy to mount spurred on a new realism in the commercial theater. Most significant was the band of hard-pressed young actors who formed the Group Theater in New York. Their innova-tive leaders, such as Harold Clurman, Lee Strasberg, Elia Kazan, John Garfield, and Clifford Odets, all bound for permanent fame, showed the influence of the Federal Theatre Project in their stress on social reform themes and stark realism.

The Federal Music Project joined in the highly influential emphasis on Amer-ican roots. At last taking up the plea Antonín Dvořák had made forty years ear-lier when he visited the United States, the Project sponsored a rediscovery of folk music, mated with the often folk-rooted works of new composers, black and white. Aaron Copland added to that a reworking of the Gallic forms learned in Paris to develop themes of the Wild West and Appalachia. From other points on the compass Roy Harris expressed his origins on the Great Plains, and European refugee musicians brought the most recent developments from the continent to mesh in unprecedented direct contact with American sources.

The documentary ventures of the New Deal managed to survive the conser-vative assault longer than the arts did. Curving in conformity with the national mood, the photographic section steadfastly promoted New Deal reform by cham-pioning basic folk values. By 1938 Stryker had shifted the focus of FSA photo-graphic concern away from social evils toward signs of progress, alert to the grumbling of critics that, if conditions are still as bad as the FSA pictures show, then what are we getting for all our relief money? Stryker countered both that question and the fascist claims of American degeneracy with instructions to get pictures showing the bountiful American heritage. From the desolate Dust Bowl the FSA turned to the northern countryside where Thanksgiving and Christmas scenes restored old images of well-being harking back to Currier and Ives. On the eve of war Stryker endorsed the view of documentary's poetic ally, Archibald MacLeish, that "the real test may come in the towns." Then, as fighting began in Europe, Stryker instructed his staff to get "pictures of men, women and children who appear as if they really believed in the U.S. Get people with a little spirit. Too many in our file now paint the U.S. as an old person's home and that just about everybody is too old to work and too malnourished to care much what happens. . . . We particularly need young men and women who work in our factories. . . . Housewives in their kitchen or in their yard picking flowers. More contented old couples."

That charge ironically doomed the mystique that had first borne the FSA along. By turning from the dispossessed to the traditionally stable small town, Stryker's camera fodder abandoned those best served by the communal values of the FSA in order to show strongholds of conservative individualism. During the crisis of war the self-defeating aspect of the new focus was masked by the patriotic common purpose of rural America in feeding the troops and sending its sturdy sons to the front. After the war, as Stryker noted regretfully, purpose ebbed out of the towns. Some people eased back into set ways. Others moved to city centers of postwar affluence, far from the mystique of the 1930s documentaries. Stryker himself spoke an elegy for the 1930s spirit on the occasion of publishing a selection of FSA photos in 1972: "Sure the kids looked grim sometimes. So did their parents. Nobody had a dime. But they had a whole lot more. They had each other, as corny as that sounds today. A family stuck together. It's all there was. They did such simple things. A man would sit on a street corner for hours, talking to his friends. What would they talk about? I don't know. It didn't matter so long as somebody listened. Who listens now?"

Though it faded swiftly, the New Deal documentary effort left a bedrock legacy. The usable past gained more substantial shape as the photographic record complemented the recovery of folk roots and the encouragement to the creative spirit carried on by the WPA Arts Project. But Walt Whitman's idea that what the country needed most was a class of poets was decidedly not what most congressmen considered the main civic concern. So the immediate, official presence of this spiritual side of the New Deal was snuffed out on the grounds that all resources were needed for material recovery and mobilization for war.

Another important contributing factor to the dissipation of the New Deal progressive and artistic impulse in the documentary was subtly inherent in the movement itself. In order to gain help for the dispossessed, the rescuers sought to arouse respect for the common life. Thus, it followed that change of that common life would eventually be seen as a violation of its integrity. The most poignant instance of this paradox was provided by the collaboration during the mid-1930s between photographer Walker Evans and writer James Agee, which was finally published as a book, *Let Us Now Praise Famous Men* (1941). With evocative pathos, the Evans and Agee study of southern sharecropper families brought out the plain beauty and nobility of their hard lives. Evans's photographs preserved every detail in severe, crystalline images—the placement of household objects, a pair of boots sculpted by many rounds of toil, the angular postures and weathered faces of exhausted cotton pickers. Agee's prose, often cadenced like the Bible, established an aura around Evans's pictures that strained toward reverence. *Let Us Now Praise Famous Men,* appearing on the threshold of war, was the most beautiful and powerful statement of the widespread documentary intention to fix an uplifted characterization of America's most victimized folk in place. But behind the fixity, as behind Stryker's later scenes of bounty, remained the basic woes and structural flaws of the Depression. With haunting permanence, the documentary venture of the 1930s fixed an ambivalent image in place. The dignity of the poor, closest to nature and simple virtue, graces the FSA photographs—but so does indignation that such poverty should exist in a land of rich resources. The decade ended with the vital question posed by the effort to rediscover roots and purposes: was the mission of the New Deal to honor the common man, in all his commonness, or was it to raise him out of that commonness into the affluent middle class? Left with that unresolved question, the search for a usable past and a distinct image of America remained unfulfilled. The rendezvous with destiny, so beset by forces opposed to New Deal aims, was thus itself obscured by uncertainty about how to define what recovery from Depression meant and what the shape of a reformed society and the rightful lot of its citizens within it would really be.

CHAPTER TWELVE

The Common Man at the End of the Decade

The stymie after 1936 of New Deal aspirations to expand its reforms meant that the central thrust of that period moved from change to consolidation. Within an uncompleted design for a cooperative commonwealth remained a New Deal voting coalition, welfare programs for unemployment and social security, farm and labor legislation, a Supreme Court reconstituted to favor economic regulation and civil rights, oversight of banking and finance, and a series of planned conservation and resource initiatives. All of these achievements through which the New Deal sought to enlist public support were centered in the celebration of the Common Man. The status, then, of the working class in the city and on the farms gave the best measure of where the New Deal stood as Roosevelt's conflicted second term reached its end.

The New Deal struggle to cure the ills of agriculture arrived at a crucial divide by mid-decade. A purge of the more insistent reformers in the Department of Agriculture gave the established forces and their Farm Bureau allies a strong central position. And yet, the effort made by New Dealers to advance tenant farmer rights and racial justice also brought the plight of the dispossessed to the fore. Significantly, within that effort, the aid given to destitute farm workers by Federal Emergency Relief Administration (FERA) marked the first time that federal relief had been extended directly to the countryside, where it underscored the problem of rural unemployment.

The sharply divergent claims on the New Deal by large landowners, seeking expert advice and subsidies, and by the agrarian poor in need of rescue reflected farmers' long unresolved struggle to find common cultural and economic ground. Despite the friction between them, established and marginal farmers shared a common agrarian tradition whose folkways the New Deal sought to express in its relief programs for artists and workers. Observers of the massive Tennessee Valley project tended to dwell on how, with help from the New Deal, the folk life of the region had been preserved, even while they marveled at the vast transformation. On the other hand, science and technology, spurred on by the progressive policies of the Department of Agriculture Extension Service, transformed farming into a modern big business. Farm price supports were most effective in helping large landowners, who were in the best position to weather the Depression, regain their momentum toward full-scale modernization. Shaping policy so that it would bring the "forgotten man" into balance with inducements to modernize was thus a matter of great subtlety and posed a strong challenge to New Deal aspirations.

These countervailing initiatives helped shape the substitute for the first AAA after it was downed by the Supreme Court in 1936. In addition to the conservation aspect so central to the strategy of avoiding another Supreme Court veto, the new bill offered other possibilities for bringing the administration into the sort of association with the land and the yeoman farmer that reformers had long favored. Henry Wallace entered the lists with a book called *Whose Constitution? An Inquiry into the General Welfare* (1936), where he argued that individual property rights should be subordinated to the larger interests of society. Following Tugwell, he called for a "Council of the General Welfare" to include economists who would plan a balanced prosperity and have the right to call for national referenda on Supreme Court decisions. Reaching further back into the reform tradition in which Roosevelt's hopes also resided, Wallace concluded that creation of a "cooperative commonwealth" remained central to the New Deal.

In that spirit Wallace presided over the transformation of the stopgap 1936 farm bill into the permanent Agricultural Adjustment Act of 1938. The bill encouraged a social welfare incomes approach by providing that payments on land withdrawn from cash crops would be apportioned to landlords and tenants according to the normal distribution of crop sale proceeds. Furthermore, persons other than the established growers gained an opening by the bill's proviso that land recently switched to crops eligible for support payment could be included in the program.

The heart of the act, though, retained the original focus on eliminating the surplus. Three means were designated: the shift of land to soil-conserving crops; the designation of marketing quotas; and, should the first two means fail to curb production enough, loans that essentially constituted payments for the removal of excess crops from the market. An important safety valve for crops stockpiled by the government was the Federal Surplus Commodities Corporation, whose campaign to dispose of the surplus led to the formation of export agreements, the 1946 National School Lunch Act, and a plan to issue food stamps for those who could not afford to buy what they needed.

Into this intricate web came farmers seeking the share of national prosperity they felt had long been denied them. This mood of restitution tended to make them feel narrowly righteous about their interests and fitted the position taken by M. L. Wilson and others from the farm establishment that the Department of Agriculture should confine itself to raising farm prosperity and leave other national concerns to other agencies. Wallace's address to the 1937 national convention of the Farm Bureau roused little warmth with its plea that farmers realize their mutually dependent relationship with industry, labor, and the consumer. After many years trying to get out from under competing special interest groups, farmers resisted such entangling alliances, especially with the government, and approached the New Deal shelter warily.

At first, sheer duress had drawn even the most reluctant individualists into association. Nobody, for example, has ever been more averse to "regimentation" than cattle ranchers and their lonesome cowboys. Yet when drought joined depression at the outset of the New Deal, cattlemen flocked to the Drought Relief Service oasis created by AAA. Millions of head of cattle were sold to the government for distribution to the needy, with producers receiving about $110 million. From that emergency both the cattlemen and the AAA drew the lesson that production controls were necessary. Cattlemen resisted long-term planning, however, and even balked at joining the AAA—complaining of controls they felt to be coercive and the extraction of processing taxes. Rising cattle prices by mid-decade completed the cycle as the cattlemen bowed out of any involvement with production controls and made it clear that the keystone of their participation in governmental programs had been their need for relief, not any deep-seated desire for production planning or social cooperation. Indeed, cattlemen stood out as the group receiving crucial assistance that gave back the least in terms of loyalty to New Deal aims and the Democratic Party.

In other cases, the lure of high profits, rather than mere survival, fastened farm interests tightly on the New Deal. Subsidies for the cotton industry, for example, were funneled through Oscar Johnston, a Mississippi politician who also happened to be owner of the Delta and Pure Land Company, the largest cotton plantation in the capitalist world. Through his positions as finance director of the AAA, vice president of the Commodity Credit Corporation, and manager of the

Federal Cotton Producers' Pool, Johnston arranged for his company to receive over $750,000 in subsidies. Only at the end of the decade did reform, led by Republican Senator Arthur Vandenberg of Michigan far from the New Deal and far from cotton country, succeed in making every subsidy payment public and in limiting soil-conservation payments to $10,000.

By then, as the action by a business-minded Republican like Vandenberg indicated, the issue for the established farms was coming to be not recovery but rather how much to curb their government-supplied profits. Farm prices rose to 93 percent of parity before the recession of 1938 and income to more than double the low point of 1932. It followed that, as the New Deal farm program turned a profit, ardor for reaching out beyond the boundaries of the status quo to further the ideal of a cooperative commonwealth would decline.

The businesslike détente between agriculture and government that developed early in the New Deal left marginal and small family farms in a quandary. Sympathy for these victims of the Depression had done much to move Congress and the administration toward reform and to shape dominant New Deal conceptions of how to balance progress and preservation. But as the new policies went forward, questions arose about survival. To what extent should new relief programs seek to maintain traditional ways that failed to meet modern technologically sophisticated competition? At what point would New Deal assistance best serve marginal farmers by urging them to abandon their hopelessly downtrodden existence for the city? To help resolve the issue, Calvin Hoover, a sociologist from Duke, was engaged in 1934 to investigate the conditions of southern agriculture where the most hard-pressed farmers were concentrated. Soon afterward the Land Planning Committee of the Department of Agriculture endorsed his conclusion that a "comprehensive policy for the economic rehabilitation of Southern agriculture" was "plainly required." For Hoover the correct policy was the one long pressed by advocates of the "New South"—the growth of an industrial base that would raise the South economically while giving the poorest rural element someplace to go. New Deal reformers found it hard to disagree with that formula, especially considering the hope of escape from abject dependency it offered to sharecroppers and tenant farmers—yet their vision of transforming agricultural life was never entirely at ease with the idea of urging people to leave the land and their own past.

Overwhelming evidence of poverty no yeoman ethic could be expected to overcome finally drove the New Deal to act. By executive order in April 1935, the Resettlement Administration was formed to help break the cycle of chronic farm poverty by moving victims to new ways of life. Rexford Tugwell as head of the program carried the planning zeal of the time to the task. In Los Angeles in 1936 he went so far in his enthusiasm for systematic overhaul as to call for a new progressive party to embody the frustrated dream of a coalition between farmers and workers against their moneyed oppressors. Tugwell, who came from a farm and small-town background in upstate New York, had ambivalent memories and sentiments. He was proudly nostalgic about his roots, but he also admired critiques of rural harshness and prejudice that were characteristic of writers during the 1920s who had also fled to New York City from the hinterland. With special attention to Thorstein Veblen's bitter wisdom about small-town bankers and absentee landowners, Tugwell spoke bluntly about the chronic misery he wished to help farmers escape: "A farm is an area of vicious, ill-tempered toil with a not very good house, inadequate barns, make-shift machinery, happenstance stock, tired, over-worked men and women—and all the pests and bucolic plagues that nature has evolved . . . a place where ugly, brooding monotony, that haunts by day and night, unseats the mind."

This biting characterization may have seemed familiar to resettlement clients, but it did not sit well with the booster pride of farm organization leaders. Tugwell's affront—and his city address—became especially problematic when mixed with the race problem of the South and the Resettlement Administration's tampering with landholding patterns. The longtime head of the Farm Bureau, Ed O'Neal, held views significantly different from Tugwell's about the nature of race and poverty. Proprietor of a large Alabama plantation, O'Neal was affably pleased with life as he had always seen it. He included both races in his idyll: "When you talk to one of these niggers [on my plantation], you say, 'Robert, are you happy out here?' 'Why, Mr. Ed, this is your land, your home. I don't pay you any rent for the house. I've got plenty of water, plenty of wood, a nice garden, some pigs, a couple of Jersey cows. I got a nice little pasture. When I make something, you get it, and when I don't make anything, you don't get anything. It's heaven here.'"

Tugwell knew that any efforts to aid the downtrodden would run up against powerful forces, but he was fired by the possibilities the Department of Agriculture offered for creating constructive solutions to the problems of poverty that had always moved him in his powerless role as a professor of economics. The first annual report of the Resettlement Administration, accompanied by a barrage of news releases describing the scarred face of rural America, stressed the urgency of reform. To drive the need home, Tugwell took Henry Wallace on a two-thousand-mile tour of destitute farm country just before the 1936 elections. Wallace, despite his own farm background, was shocked and arranged to incorporate the RA within the Department of Agriculture and, from that stronghold, to press for drastic legislation. Diverse support from groups that had been persuaded by the RA informational campaign, such as the Catholic Rural Life Bureau headed by the reform priest John Ryan and the Federal Council of Churches of Christ in America, expressed determination to give relief to desperate tenant farmers.

But the RA effort had a hard road to travel. Tugwell's Los Angeles speech helped galvanize support for the forgotten rural poor, but its call for a new progressive party, which was in accord with what Roosevelt had privately told him was his own aim, so inflamed traditional Democrats that Jim Farley barred Tugwell from the campaign trail. Tugwell was encountering other discouragement as well. His aim of using the RA to advance cooperative planning was hampered by the persistent appeals of private land ownership. Tugwell's assistant, Will Alexander, liked to recall one poignant interview with an RA client. After the earnest fellow recited how everything was going along just fine—the best house and best land he ever had to use, plenty to eat, the children enjoying good schooling—he concluded with his plan to abandon it all: "A few more years on this project and we can buy us a piece of land."

As the RA's communal vision faltered, a congressional act of 1937 empowered Wallace to create the Farm Security Administration for the purpose of rehabilitating poor farms through low-cost loans. The FSA thus endorsed the ideal of private ownership, and yet the conservative turn in Congress away from social programs prevented it from becoming a triumph for free enterprise or from rescuing the traditional small farmers it was mainly designed to help. Steadily, the assistance the FSA was able to give fell behind the increase in tenant farming. Although the law allowed fewer than 10,000 loans per year, the number of additional tenant farmers per year had increased to 40,000 by 1940. The year before that drastic figure was reached, 146,000 applications for loans had reached the FSA, which could only muster funds to answer slightly over 6,000 of the appeals.

The shortfall of the loan program was partially a reflection of the inadequacy of the small farmer/entrepreneur concept in an age of mechanized agribusiness. Trying to set up numerous small landholders would tend to drive land prices up beyond any capacity of government or clients to afford them. Furthermore, the newly created small farms would be in a poor position to compete with the larger farms that, ironically, were the chief beneficiaries of New Deal policies. To encompass both the economies of scale and the ideal of yeoman ownership, the FSA sought to establish cooperative farm communities of small landholders. But these undertakings were plowed under by Congress as socialistic, even though the FSA reasonably insisted that they reflected the frontier spirit of sharing and were the only way small farmers could compete with corporate farms.

For all these difficulties, the RA and the FSA did achieve some notable results. By June 1937, some 17.5 million acres of marginal land, mostly in the semi-
arid eastern plains, had been shifted from unstable crop production to other
uses, especially grazing. To gain options on the land, the government had spent
$52,283,950 and assisted in the resettlement of the people displaced. More ex-
tensive than resettlement was the rehabilitation program favored by Alexander.
By the time the FSA was phased out in 1943, loans and technical assistance had
been granted to 354,000 farm families.

The clash over reform policy toward the underprivileged took place against a
background of depressed prices and extended drought, climaxing in the winter
and spring of 1932–33. A disastrous combination of cold that killed the crops, flash
rains that eroded the bare ground, and high winds that lifted the soil beset the area
from Kansas to Texas. In March and April of 1933, great "rollers" of dust began to
sweep over fields and towns, leaving farms in drifts of sand, like the Sahara. The
spectacular disaster excited public alarm and vaulted residents of the Dust Bowl
into prominence as Depression victims in extremis. When the winds of November carried the black cloud far eastward, observers could speculate on the grim
symbolism of the dust settling, literally, on the government in Washington.

Out of that melodramatic setting a half million folk set out for the "promised land" of California in numbers rivaling those of the great pioneer epic of
the nineteenth century. But unlike earlier pioneers who sought to improve on
established, if meager, successes or simply sought adventure, depression migrants were for the most part bedraggled refugees from disaster. Their affinity
was more to the uprooted immigrants who had flooded across the Atlantic until the "Golden Door" was shut in the 1920s. Like those earlier newcomers, the
migrants heading west in the 1930s were poor enough to feel that they had little
to lose by leaving yet also resolute enough to risk survival in a new place, unlike
those at the very bottom of socioeconomic degradation who stayed put. Like their
immigrant counterparts, as well, the daring and ingenuity of the new migrants
were not much appreciated. Instead, they entered the public imagination as the
antithesis of the pioneers—as victims of lost opportunity, not creators of new
ones; examples of the ravaged environment, not the improving of it. Reproachfully, these "Okies," a name that stuck because so many came from Oklahoma,
were held out as embodiments of the failure of the American Dream that the
pioneers had done so much to define.

The material and mythic importance of the Okie migration benefited from
a remarkably expressive group of observers. In 1934 Paul Taylor, an economist
at the University of California at Berkeley who worked with the California Rural

Rehabilitation Division of FERA, took the lead after he observed ragged migrants camped in tents outside the vast agribusiness farms, looking for work. Taylor managed to get $20,000 for emergency shelter—the first peacetime public housing in the United States, he could rightly claim. More important in terms of public consciousness was Taylor's wife, photographer Dorothea Lange, whose pictures of migrant families surpassed those of the FSA in translating the abstract term *Depression* into very concrete images.

In 1939 the chronicling of the migration epic reached its height. Carey McWilliams, a skillful and compassionate journalist who had been made chief of the California Division of Immigration and Housing by reform governor Culbert L. Olson, summed up his official findings in *Factories in the Fields,* a devastating exposé demonstrating how migrant laborers on large California farms lived in just the sort of assembly line degradation the New Deal was seeking to eliminate from the industrial workplace. Taylor and Lange buttressed those findings in *An American Exodus: A Record of Human Erosion,* a written and pictorial record of the automobile journey they had taken to retrace the flight of migrants from Oklahoma to California. As its title indicates, the book in very graphic terms linked natural disaster in the Southwest with the wrath of God and the subsequent Okie migration with the Old Testament flight from Egypt.

That dramatic interpretation crystallized standard New Deal policy and moralizing with regard to farm relief and the conservation of natural resources. The acclaimed film documentaries made by Pare Lorentz under the auspices of the FSA brought an awareness of the link between misuse of the land and poverty into movie theaters all over the country. Alongside that New Deal campaign California novelist John Steinbeck transformed the tragic tie between poor land and poor people into literary myth. A survivor of lower-class poverty himself, Steinbeck waded militantly into Depression woes as soon as they began gathering around him. His proletarian novel *In Dubious Battle* (1934) exalted the losing struggle of farm laborers to unionize. Stunned by the ferocious power of farm owners to subdue any revolt from below, Steinbeck turned his attention to the irony of the Dustbowl migration leading not to the promised land but to something closer to a Babylonian captivity. His novel *The Grapes of Wrath* (1939) evoked the biblical and nationalist fervor that "The Battle Hymn of the Republic"—from which the book derived its title—had mobilized for another downtrodden group before the Civil War. It told of a poor and ignorant, yet devoted, Okie family that endured the westward trek and the oppression of ruthless farm owners. Steinbeck's morality tale, coupled with a highly praised film version the following year, provided the most effective dramatization of the common people as the true American heroes.

There was much weight to the Dust Bowl epic. Americans had reason to be awed and frightened by the great dust storms that blotted out the sun and made farm fields look like Saharan dunes. The displacement of farmers by dust and drought certainly was a denial of Jefferson's and Lincoln's ideal of a nation of prosperous, intelligent, independent yeomen. Per capita income in the afflicted areas was less than $300 per year; only somewhat over half of southwesterners could bring more than a grammar school education to bear on the effort of finding new opportunity.

Not everyone reacted sympathetically. Alarmed at the influx of these hapless folk, California authorities sought ways to bar their entry. On Highway 66, just outside Tulsa, Oklahoma, a billboard warned that there were no jobs in California. Those who pressed on anyway were met at the border by the California Indigent Act of 1933, which sought to deny recruitment of Okies as farm labor by making it a misdemeanor to bring an "indigent person" into the state. Local officials, interpreting the law with the looseness its framers intended, put up roadblocks against the desperate refugees.

Those who made it across the line had then to endure alienation and scorn. A Kern County doctor who attended to many Okies in his public health duties described them as "a strange people" who were unable to read and knew nothing of the world around them. They disturbed him as a foreign "breed"—"like a different race." A neighboring schoolteacher added detail about their abject behavior: "I can spot a migrant on the street every time by watching him walk. He shuffles. He doesn't hold up his shoulders and face the world. His glance is often timid and wandering." In short, the Okies were perceived as having traits long considered the inheritance of deviates and degenerates. This stereotype extended to the Southwest the earlier portrait of brutalized poor whites with which Georgia author Erskine Caldwell shocked the nation in his bestseller and later long-running Broadway play, *Tobacco Road* (1932). As one journalist taken in by the stereotype put it, Californians thought *Tobacco Road* was just a stage caricature—"until the same kind of folks landed here on us."

That stereotype of ignorant, depraved subhumanity made it easier for overseers on the giant California farms, which included more than a third of the nation's richest agricultural land, to hire the Okies on terms much like those dictated earlier to the Chinese coolies and Mexican underclass whom the Okies displaced. Living in tents or makeshift shacks, the migrants could get by all right during the growing season when the weather was mild. But cold winter coincided with the end of work opportunities, and many of the helpless, stranded Okies, denied relief for a year under California residency rules, suffered and even died from exposure, malnutrition, and poorly treated disease. Something like 400,000 of their number who could muster the will and resources acknowledged defeat by turning back eastward and vanishing into the cities and back country of the Southwest and Midwest.

Certainly, there was much truth to the vividly expressed Dust Bowl saga. Nearly half of those who left the Southwest for California had no high school education, and their average annual income for the rest of the decade stayed at $850, well below the California norm. They were indeed disadvantaged and set apart. Yet they were also part of a larger story. Rather than establishing a new pattern of migration, the Okie refugees exemplified long-standing trends. Between 1910 and 1930 farm workers had already declined in the Southwest by 300,000. In part, that movement, which hard times in the 1930s accelerated, was an internal one of people seeking opportunity with practical skills that could be useful in the city as well as in the countryside. When these "tumbleweeds" eventually left the region, over half departed from cities. The majority of whites and virtually all the blacks went north rather than west, where the treatment of Asians had made racism and subjugation notorious. Ultimately, in the booming economy of World War II sharecropping and tenant farming largely disappeared. In place of Okie poverty a new balance in the Southwest of burgeoning cities and farms that had survived with New Deal support left the Dust Bowl episode to recede into a romanticized, vanished past.

New Deal programs were crucially involved in the Dust Bowl epic. The disasters of wind and weather made it difficult to tell how much of the general decline in farm production could be attributed to AAA and how much to nature. Since increased productivity per farm worker and per acre during the decade more than made up for the planned removal of land from production, drought and dust had a large role to play in reducing the surplus. The relation between scientific agriculture and nature came into question, also, when one harked back to the warning of the great nineteenth-century surveyor of western lands, John Wesley Powell, that the dry plains would not support conventional agriculture. In *The Plow That Broke the Plain*, the FSA popularized the notion that plowing away the grasslands binding the plains together left the topsoil vulnerable to blowing in dry seasons. Accordingly, the New Deal decided to follow the land-use plan outlined by Lewis C. Gray of the Bureau of Agricultural Economics in the *Yearbook of Agriculture* for 1923. In Gray's scheme, the nation would be divided into regions classified as supermarginal, marginal, and submarginal and their farmers either supported or removed to subsistence homesteads or industrial centers. Much of this conception was incorporated into the RA and then applied to the

Dust Bowl. The decision to remove stricken Plains farmers from their submarginal land accounted for much of the $52 million spent on government land acquisition; the rehabilitation loans and community formation related heavily to the displaced Dust Bowlers.

A final assessment is hard to make. Dust storms plagued the area long before any plows broke the plains. And during the Depression, despite the drought, the economy of the Dust Bowl remained on a par with the nation generally, while the greatest area of farm distress was in the humid regions of the Southeast. For those forced off the land by New Deal policy, life was undoubtedly hard; yet the ultimate fate of the migrants shaded off into unrecorded mystery after they left the New Deal rolls—in some cases to enter the "factories in the fields," in others to try their luck at a new life in the burgeoning cities. Perhaps there never was a need for New Deal planners to drive people out of the parched Southwest; perhaps the imposition of land-use plans from afar failed to appreciate the inevitable cycles of nature and local ingenuity in moderating them. One bitter historian from the Plains goes so far as to argue that the "attitude on the part of all land-utilization policy makers toward residents of the dust bowl was remarkably similar to the thinking of Thomas Jefferson concerning the Indians." Both groups were forced from their homes by "men inflicted with a missionary spirit and little understanding of the problems or their solutions."

The imponderables of the New Deal agricultural program characterized an uncertain decade. Only the coming of war would be able to tip the balance toward a definite resolution. Bumper crops in the early 1940s enjoyed a prosperous wartime market, and many of the migrants to the north and the west found well-paid work in the defense industry rather than on the margins of agriculture. As the image of the farmer changed from charity recipient to national asset, an increasingly conservative Congress drew the old lesson that self-help, not the humiliation of relief, had prevailed. The time had come, it seemed, to end government support for the unproductive. Let those who would grow do so and those who could not manage to support themselves on the land find some other work for which they might have a talent, perhaps in the war effort. The ragged victims of depression who were once invested with heroic stature had become something of an embarrassment.

The FSA was a prime target of budget-cutters and believers in free enterprise almost from the outset, with the House Appropriations Committee under John Taber of New York at the forefront. In 1940 Will Alexander stepped down, lamenting twin pressures from northern reactionaries and southerners who were afraid that the New Deal would undercut white supremacy. Alexander's doughty successor, C. B. "Beanie" Baldwin, showed statistically in 1942 that large and medium-sized farms were producing close to capacity but that small farmers could move 10 percent closer to meeting the national need if they were granted FSA loans. This dual appeal to evidence and patriotism moved Congress—not to increase loan grants but to decrease appropriations for the FSA. The majority was in no mood to prop up marginal farmers when there was other patriotic work for them to do in the armed forces or in mobilizing resources for the war effort. The following year Baldwin resigned and the FSA petered out. While reeling from that setback, the Bureau of Agricultural Economics was also attacked by southern congressmen who had uncovered a report discussing race relations by Will Alexander. For stating the existence of segregation on the basis of white supremacy, Alexander was vilified as a disturber of the peace. Representative Dan McGehee of Mississippi insisted that the Negro in the South enjoyed full opportunity to realize his potential and that, referring to Alexander, "the bird that concocted all this rot . . . should be kicked into Kingdom Come, and it should be in the lower region of purgatory." After that blacks might continue to claim, as did the author of a poem written about the FSA, that "Uncle Sam Is My Shepherd," but the reality was a retreat by the last of the New Deal reformers from attempts at improving the lot of rural blacks which had been vague and tentative even at their fullest realization.

Thus the farm policy at the end of the decade moved ambivalently into the wartime period of reviving prices and flagging social reform. The legacy of the New Deal was a farm policy that emphasized large-scale production promoted and insured by crop subsidies and parity price supports. The century-long campaign to link the mainstream of farm prosperity explicitly with the national interest had been won, but those in the countryside who persisted on the fringe of that prosperity, often as landless tenants and migrants, existed far from the traditional agrarian ideal, updated by the New Deal, of self-sufficient independence.

The final phase of organized labor's transformation during the last years of the New Deal was a different sort of ordeal. Although the Jones & Laughlin decision established the validity of the Wagner Act, it did not reconcile labor's opponents. The tenet of the open shop was so staunchly held that as late as 1957 United Steel's president, Benjamin Fairless, condemned the requirement of a worker to join a union as tantamount to compelling him to join a particular church. Action to back up that conviction was still possible after the Wagner Act because the law did not mandate collective bargaining but merely conferred on workers the right to be represented. Further, labor had not by 1937 overcome the traditional preference of the general public and its law enforcement officials for management's concept of private property rights, which asserted full control over the use of its productive machinery. Finally, the recession of 1937 made strikes seem dubious, for any work stoppage both deepened the general decline and weakened the workers' position.

And yet, despite the handicaps, labor recognized that, should it back off from its hard-won militancy, it would risk losing momentum—a momentum that the CIO sought to maintain by making inflated claims of having four million members, more than the AFL. By nature a gambler, John L. Lewis realized at that recession crossroads that the CIO must keep pressing. Ahead lay the twin fortresses of American heavy manufacturing: automobiles and steel.

Although Lewis intended to start with steel, whose "captive" coal mines had long bedeviled the UMW with their open shop ways, circumstances favored an initial campaign against the auto industry. To a great extent that resulted from the desperate state of affairs in the Detroit area. As early as 1930 the Depression laid Detroit low. The drop in employee income in auto manufacture was almost three times as large as for others in manufacturing—by 32.5 percent as compared to 14 percent. And those figures counted only the lucky ones with jobs. Fully 43 percent of the automobile workforce, about 725,000 persons, were out of work by the fall of 1932. They provided an angry contingent in Detroit to stun Herbert Hoover with jeers when he campaigned in the city he had carried handily in 1928.

The city's welfare department was ill equipped to meet the crisis. Revenue fell $19 million short of the strict budget in 1931; under pressure from the committee of bankers given custody of city finances, food allotments to the destitute were limited to bread and flour. Because there was no money left for rent subsidies, evictions rose to 4,500 families per month. Tent cities sprang up and gave parts of the city the look of a Bedouin slum.

Throughout the debacle Detroit's financial and industrial oligarchy continued to maintain its affluence, or at least keep up appearances. Only on the eve of Roosevelt's inaugural was it revealed that the solvency bankers had been reporting was illusory. In the automobile industry, despite dropping sales, which forced out most of the small firms, the large companies managed to reward their executives well and pay substantial dividends to stockholders. In a famous boast after three years of Depression, Alfred Sloan, head of General Motors, declared that "in no year did the corporation fail to earn a profit." Once the New Deal recovery program got underway, corporate fortunes rose sharply higher. The index of industrial productivity showed a 50 percent increase in 1935 over 1932, with the number of passenger cars tripling from 1.1 million to 3.7 million and met by a rise in consumer spending of $7.1 billion.

Unfortunately, the prosperity did not trickle down accordingly to the working-class base. Nationwide between 1932 and 1935 employment in manufacturing rose by only 2.1 million—30 percent as against the 50 percent rise in industrial productivity. Even worse, payrolls increased by only 20 percent. And, as usual, Detroit fared worse than the average. Automation meant that fewer men working shorter hours turned out more vehicles in 1936 than in 1928, and 17 percent of the labor force in Detroit was still out of work in 1936, as against only 13 percent in the first Depression year of the decade.

Violent tremors of worker discontent preceded a climactic campaign for unionization. On March 6, 1930, a large turnout of workers in Detroit answered a Communist Party call for International Unemployment Day demonstrations. When throngs converged on Cadillac Square and Grand Circus Park, the Detroit police played the part the Communists had always assigned to them by attacking the demonstrators with clubs and tear gas. Almost exactly two years later, after an ominous lull, another momentous crowd gathered for a hunger march on the Ford plant in Dearborn, the citadel from which many of them had been discharged in an austerity move that helped keep corporate profits up. Although leftist organizers were once again prominently involved, the demands of the marchers featured such un-revolutionary basics as elimination of kickbacks in hiring, a six-hour day to spread the work, free medical care, and the right to organize collective bargaining unions. This time the police were joined by Ford secret service men. Gunfire followed the usual exchange of rocks and billy clubs, and scores of strikers were carried off the field dead or wounded.

On the other side, the major casualty was Henry Ford's reputation. As the naive hopes of the marchers were cut down, so too were all reasons to believe that the industrialist who was lionized as the man who first gave workers the five-dollar day was dedicated to the general welfare. His policy in hard times of abandoning many of his workers and squeezing the rest by an assembly line speed-up indicated how the auto industry was dead set against attaining the "concert of interests" the New Deal sought through its NRA or calm union bargaining.

The rise of industrial unionism made an effective response in the auto industry viable. By joining the CIO in August of 1936, the United Auto Workers escaped the AFL insistence on keeping its 25,000 workers divided into separate "craft" unions along an automated production line that made such fine distinctions mostly irrelevant. The reelection of Roosevelt and the election as governor of Michigan of staunch New Deal liberal Frank Murphy gave further encouragement. Behind the slogan, "You voted New Deal at the polls. . . . Now get a New Deal in the shop," the UAW gathered 15,500 new members into the fold in December, raising its total to some 60,000. The reform wave sweeping Roosevelt to reelection also produced important pro-labor legislation, including unemployment insurance, guarantees of maximum hours and minimum wages, and a law forbidding the importation of strikebreakers across state lines.

The pressures of this union growth and the success of its political allies were felt most acutely in the General Motors stronghold of Flint. In that city of 160,000, more than two thirds of the wage earners—about 47,000 in all—worked for General Motors. The company's assets were $1.5 billion by the end of 1936, comprising 37 percent of the world's sales of motor vehicles. Such magnificence acted as a goad to the workers whose share of New Deal recovery was so small as to place them on the lower rungs of the wage-earner ladder.

As 1936 came to an end, the pressures finally erupted, before the time planned by Lewis. Influenced by similar tactics used successfully by the rubber workers of Akron, employees in General Motor's Fisher Body Plant #2 simply sat down on the job on December 30 and refused to move. Later the same day workers in the larger Plant #1 followed suit. Like a row of dominos other General Motors plants underwent sit-downs in the ensuing weeks, until the entire 136,000 man workforce was idled.

Few Americans could have been more outraged and astounded over the sin of trespass than auto executives, who had become used to virtual sovereignty in a domain where even public officials were disposed to do their bidding. For similar reasons, the strikers drew psychological strength from the situation. For years they had been among the most downtrodden of workers, subject to the peculiarly tight discipline of the production line. Now they could raise their self-esteem by a coup d'état that reversed the roles of owners and peons. A festive air began to well up through the long-repressed surface. Sympathetic entertainers who appeared at the barricaded plants were raucously applauded; there were songs and pro-union skits, and across the street from Fisher Body Plant #1 the chef of the elegant Detroit Athletic Club set himself up in a rented restaurant to prepare food fit for heroes. All the while, a large public, given to rooting for the underdog and increasingly antagonistic to high-binding business, cheered from the sidelines.

On the other side of the barricade, consternation mounted. General Motors, headed by icy, ascetic Alfred Sloan, had long been opposed to unionization. Sloan was also averse to violence and other crude tactics of the sort that had tarnished Ford's image. Instead, he preferred the subtleties of spying and had built up the most formidable undercover apparatus in business history. At the time of the sit-down strike, the National Labor Relations Board (NLRB) was fighting an injunction against its investigation into Sloan's million-dollar spy network, and the Civil Liberties Committee, chaired by Wisconsin Senator Robert La Follette Jr., was conducting an investigation that flushed many timeworn means of intimidation out of the industrial world. What finally stymied General Motors, however, was the low value that espionage had in the bold open warfare of a sit-down strike. Frustrated, the corporation decided to try appealing to the law.

While General Motors fought to get an injunction against trespass, the workers in Fisher Plant #2 fended off police with a barrage of pop bottles, car parts, and whatever came to hand in what they jubilantly called the "Battle of the Running Bulls." A standoff ensued at the factory and in the courts. Governor Murphy then became the center of attention. Bitterly opposed by the industrial old guard for his pro-labor views, he was also an enigmatic figure among fellow progressives— either admired for his eloquent attachment to civil liberties or deplored for a streak of vanity and his slipshod administration. Fortunately, Roosevelt was one of Murphy's admirers. They were also of one mind in disapproving of the sit-down, while convinced that calling in the militia to drive the strikers out was not worth the probable bloodshed. The strikers added staunch determination to the do-or-die situation. A message to Murphy on February 2 declared, "We have decided to stay in the plant. . . . We fully expect that if a violent effort is made to oust us, many of us will be killed, and we take this means of making it known to our wives, to our children, to the people of the state of Michigan and of the country that if this result follows from the attempt to eject us you are the one who must be held responsible for our deaths." Lewis added his promise that, if the soldiers were called out, "I shall leave this conference and I shall enter one of those plants with my own people."

Roosevelt and Murphy adroitly devised a mediation panel that held off demands to evict the strikers while pressuring the evasive Sloan ("a scoundrel and a skunk," Perkins called him to his face for one of his maneuvers to avoid settlement) into negotiation. On February 11 General Motors decided to sign a contract. Only one page long, the contract distilled the essence of the union struggle to gain an independent share of authority in the workplace by giving the UAW status as the sole representative of GM workers. To buttress its authority, the union gained the right to have shop stewards in GM plants to monitor conditions and handle worker grievances. With its brief bill of rights in hand, the victorious strikers ended their sit-down within the aura of having revolutionized unionism in America. Chrysler added to the aura by signing a similar contract after a brief sit-down in April. And that left only the Ford Motor Company among the major producers outside the fold.

Ford was the most formidable foe for the UAW, and so was wisely left for last. The irascible eccentricity of Henry Ford was apt to confound any strategy used against him. Trying to make old Henry "see reason" was a bit like trying to teach the proverbial shrimp to whistle. "I don't want to know the facts!" shouted Ford to an aide who sought to change his mind. He was given instead to private reveries, laced with paranoia against those who seemed to differ—which included belief that a conspiracy of Jews, DuPonts, New Dealers, and many others was out to get him. From acclaim as a friend of the workers and prophet of affluence through technology, Ford had retreated into tyranny. Whatever degree of benevolence had been in Ford's original vision by the mid-1930s had given way to his passion for perfect efficiency. He took advantage of the assembly line process to speed up tasks to the limit of workers' endurance, and his five-dollar day stayed in force until rising prices made it far from generous. To maintain order, Ford hired a private army, replete with spies to infiltrate the line and spot deviants. The leader of the army was Harry Bennett, an ex-prizefighter who used the situation to work out a Napoleonic complex. Often called "the little guy," the five-foot-seven Bennett imitated the toughness of a screen gangster and surrounded himself with the largest plug-uglies he could find, many of them with prison records. Ford considered him a godsend because he not only kept a resentful work force in line but was fanatically loyal to the chief.

The union contest opened brutally. On May 26, 1937, several UAW organizers, including the man who was to become the union's leading strategist, Walter Reuther, set out to distribute handbills at the River Rouge plant. They were met there by several of Bennett's more impressive specimens and savagely beaten—while news cameramen snapped away. The indifference of Ford to the violence his thugs were wreaking in broad daylight indicated that capitulation would come hard. A combination of intimidation and grim times kept the firm on a nonunion basis for the next four years.

Yet the changes of the era rolled on inexorably, however much Ford chose to barricade himself against them. The NLRB developed comprehensive measures for ensuring the right of workers to unionize against traditional lockout and intimidation tactics. The access to violence declined correspondingly. So, too, did labor's resort to its most melodramatic device, the sit-down. In 1939 the Supreme Court ruled that the workers of the Fansteel Metallurgical Corporation had trespassed when they used the sit-down. To no avail the NLRB pointed out that the company had repeatedly violated the Wagner Act and thus did not come to the Court with "clean hands" but had provoked the sit-down. Property rights prevailed and the sit-down faded from the scene—not to be revived until the turbulence of the 1960s, when peace protesters called it the sit-in.

In the twilight of permissible violence, with his company threatened with bankruptcy, Ford tried to stand fast. He was shocked when black workers, so long patronized by Ford and little involved in the early sit-downs for fear of rejection by industry and union alike, heeded the urging of the NAACP to show solidarity with the union. Yet, still not comprehending the logic of events, Ford was tearfully devastated when an election ordered by the NLRB showed that workers favored the UAW rather than perpetuating the cherished myth of their loyalty to his person. In June, his empire tottering, Ford finally agreed to sign a contract with the union when his wife threatened to leave him if he were to refuse and thus trigger more violence. To the astonishment of many observers and even of UAW organizers, Ford's concessions went far beyond those of GM and Chrysler to set lasting benchmarks. Ford workers gained the highest pay in the industry and were freed from the autocratic system that had long oppressed them. In its stead, the UAW became the exclusive agent for workers. New standards, written by the union, were to govern seniority and grievances and provide pay for workers when plants were closed for overhaul. At last, it seemed that the Ford mass production revolution might actually lead to the good life for workers it had originally promised.

The campaign against the steel companies was a drama of similar intensity but unfolded differently. Philip Murray, Lewis's mild lieutenant, directed a strategy from his simple frame house in the Pittsburgh coal country that opened steel mills to union organizers for the first time. Crucial help came from the New Deal. On September 21, 1933, the captive mines owned by steel companies had at last been forced from their anti-union open shop stance by Roosevelt's personal intervention on behalf of Section 7(a) of the NIRA so that a code for the mines allowing collective bargaining might be written and a strike damaging to recovery be averted. Within that breach the organizing drive managed by Murray swelled the union ranks so that the Steel Workers Organizing Committee (SWOC), at 500,000 members, had the largest membership within the CIO by the time of the crucial push in 1937. The capitulation of General Motors in February 1937 was an electrifying development whose significance both Lewis and the president of United States Steel, Myron Taylor, were quick to recognize. After a series of conferences, both men decided to avoid confrontation and signed a collective bargaining agreement on March 2.

While the amazing acquiescence of one of the most stubborn foes of organized labor greatly boosted the status of the CIO, a cluster of "Little Steel" companies, especially Bethlehem, Republic, Inland, and Youngstown Sheet and Tube, dug in their heels. In May 1937 the surging SWOC called a strike against Republic Steel, whose president, Thomas Girdler, was the leader of Little Steel's militant resistance to sharing any of its autocratic authority. Girdler liked to refer to his reign as "a benevolent dictatorship"; a congressional investigating committee, noting the segregation of workers by ethnic group and the use of company police to curb expressions of discontent, chose to call the situation one of "systematic terror." In Lewis's grandiloquent judgment Girdler was "a heavily armed monomaniac, with murderous tendencies, who has gone berserk." True to his view that collective bargaining was "a bad thing for our companies, for our employees; indeed for the United States of America," Girdler declared that, rather than traffic with unions, he would go off to "raise apples and potatoes." Soon afterward Little Steel cohorts gained control of the Iron and Steel Institute from U.S. Steel and named Girdler president.

That was the morning after the SWOC had declared a strike in answer to Girdler's closing of his steel plants on May 20. The clash of rampant wills soon came to a head. On Memorial Day, strikers and their supporters marched toward the Republic plant in Chicago under cover of recent court decisions upholding the Fourteenth Amendment right for such demonstrations. The Chicago police, adhering to an older view of union agitation as disturbance of the peace, sought to break up the march. When a tree branch was thrown toward the police ranks, they opened fire and charged the crowd. Ten marchers died in the onslaught, mostly shot in the back as they tried to flee; scores more were injured.

Public opinion bestowed sympathy on the victims of the "Memorial Day Massacre," but the union lost the war. Republic resisted the SWOC, and others in Little Steel, thus fortified, held off union incursions with only minor concessions. Roosevelt himself contributed one of his few diplomatic gaffes when he became annoyed that his appeals to Girdler as a fellow "gentleman" were rebuffed and that labor continued to act militantly outside the paternal harmony the president sought to bestow. As tension increased, he told a press conference that the public was looking on at the fracas between labor and management and saying "a plague on both your houses." John L. Lewis took mortal offense and thereafter pitted his influence relentlessly against the president and much of his New Deal.

The feud between Lewis and Roosevelt, which became increasingly bitter, anchored a labor stalemate. Lewis was convinced that Roosevelt and his allies in the labor movement, chief among them Sidney Hillman, wished merely to restore the old economic system. Lewis argued instead for a shift of power to a farmer-labor alliance that would take unjustified wealth and influence away from the industrial and financial barons and armor a newly secure workforce against the appeals of "isms" on the left and the right. As Lewis argued that position against the New Deal with increasing heat, other setbacks further stilled the momentum that had been slowed by the Little Steel defeat. Rising unemployment during the recession of 1937–38 depleted the number of union members at work. That weakness in numbers, along with uncoordinated leadership, left the CIO vulnerable to AFL competition for membership and employer resistance to collective bargaining. An important source of internal conflict that also brought hostile public attention was the presence of Communists within union ranks. Warnings by union members against the threat to democracy posed by leftists, most powerfully within the UAW and Harry Bridges's longshoremen's organizing effort, resonated with newspaper scare stories and alarmist outcries on the right about Communist domination over an un-American labor movement. John L. Lewis, always aggressively confident of his ability to face down rivals, Communist or otherwise, resisted pressure to expel the Communists in favor of continuing to use them as shock troops in the labor wars. Once Lewis stepped down in 1940, however, the issue came to a head in a purge of the Communists that by the end of the decade left the CIO a less militant part of the mainstream.

Racial, regional, and gender divisions also played a role in the troubles of the union movement. AFL craft unions routinely excluded blacks from their ranks, whereas the workforce the CIO sought to mobilize included many mass production industries, most prominently steel and auto manufacture, where blacks and whites had long worked side by side. The difficulty in finding integrated common ground proved a painful factor in keeping the two major unions from merging until the 1950s. Race helped shape sharply contrasting regional patterns as well. In the textile mills of the South, where unions had made valiant efforts to organize, segregation and local custom thwarted collective bargaining. Unlike the North, where unions were attractive to a working class composed heavily of cohesive ethnic communities bound by their own cultural solidarity, community in the South was more tied to locale, which meant that workers more readily deferred to traditional hierarchies and caste distinctions. The suspicion of outsiders that accompanied those rooted loyalties and discrimination further splintered the southern work force and stymied union organizing. Ironically, the NLRB in the South sometimes also became part of labor's problem. Mill owners used the board's guidelines, under which collective bargaining could only begin after the establishment of a well-organized local unit, to forestall union drives. Inhibited by customary class roles and economic insecurity, southern workers balked at meeting NLRB standards. Management was similarly put off by the lack of fit between New Deal policy for business recovery and southern tradition. For all its talk of cooperative commonwealth, the New Deal stress on modern corporate organization and planning strained, rather than strengthened, south-ern commitment to community as defined in egalitarian New Deal terms. The way New Deal agencies differentiated between management and labor and then broke each side down into distinct professional and vocational categories in or-der to distribute benefits and regulate practices went against the preference of paternal southern mores to regard the workplace as an extension of tight-knit family and local paternalism.

This institutional trend also had consequences for gender relations within the labor movement. Even though the union workforce was increasingly composed of females, and local activists and their community support networks during the early 1930s had often been heavily female, the labor bureaucrats who ran the unions established under the auspices of the Wagner Act were, like the NLRB, almost invariably men. No doubt the rough and ready militancy of the era con-tributed to the rise of men with a touch or more of machismo; the solidifying of a union establishment also tended toward favoring the socially conservative, clubby sort of men who usually dominated bureaucracies.

A shortage of jobs reinforced traditional attitudes. In order to spread scarce work across as many families as possible, the Economy Act of 1932 specified that women could not hold federal jobs if their husbands were also employed by the government. Reluctant to stretch its thin resources beyond conventional indus-trial workplaces, the NRA declined to bring under its code umbrella farm labor and those occupations mainly left to women—clerical jobs, domestic service, nursing, and social work. The general public agreed with the principle of support first for the male breadwinner, 82 percent of those polled in 1936 expressing a view that wives with working husbands should not also seek jobs. In much the same restrictive way, unions made little effort to organize female- and minority-centered clerical and social service workers and domestic servants.

The situation was further complicated by the AFL's ingrained distrust of gov-ernment. AFL leaders feared that, however benevolently the NLRB and the courts acted under New Deal guidance, they could always turn on unions at any time in the future. That realization was far less inhibiting to the insurgent CIO union, partly because many of their members held socialist ideals and partly because their very ability to come into being and survive early challenges had depended on NLRB certification.

In this turmoil of differing views, New Deal labor policies and efforts to re-inforce its political coalition through labor alliances and regulation of industry and commerce generally prevailed. A volatile mix of hardship and opportunity shifted worker activism away from the sort of autonomous grassroots activity that had first produced unions and had sparked the great labor uprisings of 1934 toward dependence on the benevolence of the NLRB and the courts. In the favorable climate of the New Deal era for large-scale union growth, AFL worries about the negative possibilities of government oversight retained little influence, and the union movement surged toward the peak of its numbers and influence. Indeed, in ways that lacked the conspicuous drama of sit-downs and pitched battles, the AFL became the chief beneficiary of New Deal efforts to regulate economic behavior in the interest of a fairly distributed recovery. Banking reform and agencies to facilitate home buying, for example, proved a boon to the increasingly unionized building trades. In efforts to salvage the dream of efficient cooperation between management and labor from the wreckage of the NRA, the New Deal often sought advice from both sides in devising new regulatory laws. So it was that the Motor Carriers Act of 1935 gave companies protection from cutthroat competition and workers latitude to organize. The security and rising fortunes of transport companies that resulted made them less determined to resist unionization, and the Teamsters union, in turn, could offer workers a solid opportunity to benefit from collective bargaining. With the creation of the NLRB, a mechanism for holding peaceful elections and settling disputes further stimulated union growth. Not surprisingly, membership in the Teamsters between 1935 and 1940 increased threefold to 450,000.

Much the same beneficial change held true in other sectors, where, for example, the Railroad Labor Act of 1934 set conditions that led to forty-five union elections, more than thirty of which were won by AFL unions. So, too, legislation helped AFL electrical and utility unions add 210,000 members and the Airline Pilots Association become firmly established. Through elections, then, set by federal law rather than the grassroots strikes and agitation typical of CIO growth, the way was prepared for the revival of the AFL and an atmosphere of comity between workers and their bosses. The Common Man ideal moved toward greater respectability as unions became part of the establishment, and workers were able to glimpse a future as part of the great American middle class. In the form of unionized worker, then, the Common Man standard attained its fullest success. As for Roosevelt's prized independent family farmer, plains elegist David Danbom has spoken truly that the journey was in the opposite direction, from majority to minority to curiosity.

CHAPTER THIRTEEN

The International Climax

During the 1932 campaign for the presidency, Roosevelt made no major foreign policy addresses and steadfastly deflected questions on the subject. Partly that was because he realized the great issue of the campaign was economic hardship and agreed with the voters that he should focus on improving their lot. Yet, with frustrated resignation Roosevelt also realized that public approval of America's refusal to join the League of Nations or World Court made it prudent for him to underplay his true internationalist outlook.

In his inaugural address the one specific mention of foreign policy Roosevelt allowed to intrude on the theme of domestic recovery was his statement that he wished the United States to be a "good neighbor." That cheery but vague pronouncement indicated that the internationalism Roosevelt had expressed in Wilsonian times still flickered. Behind his early enthusiasm lay tours abroad, of the sort that young people of Roosevelt's class and generation characteristically made and, of course, the impressions derived from having as a cousin that most exuberant and influential of world-beaters, Theodore Roosevelt. After the defeat of the League, however, Franklin Roosevelt moved with the current of doubt about internationalism far enough so that by 1928, in an article for *Foreign Affairs,* he denied that it would be to the advantage of the United States to join the League. Roosevelt offered a hopeful view that cooperation with the League might be rewarding. But mostly he remained silent on foreign policy during the 1920s and concentrated on establishing himself in New York politics.

It was in responding to events in the Western Hemisphere that Republican foreign policy left Roosevelt the best opening for reinvigorating his dormant

commitment to international cooperation. After many years of Yankee intervention into Latin American affairs in order to protect American economic interests,
which created a chronic air of resentment toward the "Colossus of the North," a
shift of direction was stimulated by Coolidge's appointment of Dwight Morrow,
an intellectually alert businessman and former governor of New Jersey, as ambassador to Mexico in 1927. Morrow's rapport with the Mexicans and his ability
to communicate the results fit well with a rising interest north of the border in
Latin American culture as an antidote to excess materialism.

Hoover, more warmly than his predecessor, endorsed this unaccustomed embrace of Hemisphere neighbors by an American ambassador by declaring that
he was out of sympathy with the use of intervention as a diplomatic weapon. At a
conference in Havana, Secretary of State Charles Evans Hughes echoed the new
deferral to Latin American sovereignty by condemning the way the Monroe Doctrine had served as a "cover for extravagant utterances and pretension."

Roosevelt expressed full sympathy with the idea of democratic self-determina-
tion in Latin America; yet his first encounter with that region as president was a
response to dictatorial maneuvers. Just as he was assuming office, Cuba erupted
in a revolution displacing the harsh rule of General Gerardo Machado in favor of
Grau San Martin, perceived by Roosevelt's ambassador to Cuba, Sumner Welles,
as an indecisive intellectual who would not be able to keep order. Not wanting to
tie itself to Grau's unpromising government, Roosevelt decided instead to with-
hold recognition, thus inviting a more stable insurgent element to take over. Unfortunately, the successful agent of overthrow was Fulgencio Batista, who would
prove a notorious and long-lived dictator. Aside from that misadventure, the administration disavowed any further efforts to determine other nations' fates and
announced its intent to become a benevolently neutral "good neighbor" to Latin
America.

Soon after the setback to democracy in Cuba, the Roosevelt administration
went on record against intervention. At the seventh International Conference
of American States, held in Montevideo in December 1933, Cordell Hull was
enthusiastically received as the first American secretary of state since 1889 to
attend an American States conference and announced full American support of
the nonintervention proposal placed before the body as a main order of business.
This Good Neighbor concept, repeatedly endorsed by the United States, passed
its most severe test after Mexico announced in 1938 that it was taking over the
oil holdings of foreign investors. Despite the anguished appeals of American oil
companies to past precedent and national manhood, the New Deal held to its
hands-off policy.

Nonintervention was the self-effacing aspect of the Good Neighbor policy. At the Montevideo Conference, Hull also unveiled his dearly cherished activist component, a reciprocal trade design for circumventing the world's tariff barriers in the interests of free trade and peace, which to his old-fashioned southern agrarian mind were the blood brothers of sound foreign policy. Hull's belief that tariff walls were too entrenched to pull down in their entirety inclined him toward the reciprocal trade concept. It would allow the United States and foreign states to lower tariff schedules by up to 50 percent and then extend a welcome to other nations, who would abide by the same terms. Called the "most favored nation" concept—a label Hull never cared for because it belied his free trade ethic of including *all* nations—the device seemed a satisfactory way to most critics of keeping the advantages of tariff barriers while adding a flexibility that would both allay the tendency of other nations to retaliate against tariffs and encourage new trading relations. With overwhelming support in Congress and abroad, the Reciprocal Trade Agreements Act was signed into law in 1934, and by the end of the decade twenty-two countries, eleven of them in Latin America, joined in a network of reciprocal trade agreements.

An accompaniment to reciprocal trade that rounded out the importance of Latin America to the formation of New Deal economic foreign policy was the development of the Export-Import Bank in 1934. Created to finance trade with the Soviet Union after Roosevelt's recognition ended a sixteen-year diplomatic exclusion of that revolutionary nation, the device actually became effective when a second Export-Import Bank instituted trade with the Batista dictatorship in Cuba. Although the bank did not do a large volume of business in Latin America before World War II, it brought a measure of order into a free enterprise jungle where almost all the bonds floated in the United States by Latin governments between 1921 and 1934 had fallen into default. The perplexity from the Latin American side was, of course, that the stabilizing agency was a creature of the United States government and always apt to insinuate Yankee power into the economic life of its neighbors. But it was the only reasonably effective device at hand. Through a tentative series of small loans and the underwriting of shaky financial institutions, the Export-Import Bank established its role as mediator between what one pungent Latin American critic called "the shark and the sardines."

Elsewhere in the world, most impasses admitted of no such technical alleviation. Disarmament talks dragged, and the near universal default of debt payment in the face of Depression (only Finland maintained its schedule) was not reversed by the angry Debt Default Act of 1934 forbidding the exchange of loans and bonds with nations in default, which Senator Hiram Johnson of California, an avowed isolationist, rammed through Congress. When Roosevelt sought to expand his Good Neighbor policy to include membership in the World Court, an isolationist coalition of unlikely bedfellows—including Father Coughlin, anti–New Deal newspaper tycoon William Randolph Hearst, and comic folk hero Will Rogers—drummed up enough Senate opposition to cause the enabling bill to fall seven votes short of the two-thirds majority required. By cutting itself off from participation in both the League of Nations and the World Court, the United States relinquished its chance to wield the influence its power warranted. For all its promise as a way to draw nations toward cooperative peace and prosperity, the Reciprocal Trade Act was not an innovation that could have much effect on the main march of events throughout the world.

By force of circumstances, American foreign relations increasingly centered on two nations. In the Far East, Japan, though willing to have trade with the United States, interfered with the Open Door policy America had imposed on it by imposing a self-sufficient, closed "Asian Co-Prosperity Sphere" on its neighbors. In Europe Germany showed similar tendencies. Rather than entering into most-favored-nation agreements with the United States, which could be shared by other willing traders, the Germans sought exclusive barter arrangements. Hull's opposition persuaded Roosevelt not to accept such unorthodox ways, and Germany in its search for markets was left to drift toward the sort of hegemony over neighbors in the West that Japan sought in the East. With such developments on both sides of the globe, made more ominous by German and Japanese militarization to enforce their aims, hopes for a broadly successful New Deal transformation of international economic life steadily dwindled.

The situation aroused in Roosevelt a longstanding streak of distrust for Germany and Japan. He stated in exasperation on one occasion that the merely 8 percent of the world's population concentrated in those two nations was denying the other 92 percent the right to move toward disarmament and cooperative free trade. The militarist style of the two he linked by describing Japan as the "Prussia of the East." Yet despite that facile comparison Roosevelt approached the two spheres quite differently. The Far East did not attract him very strongly, and he was willing to fall back on the offhanded impressionism he often used to slide by secondary interests. He claimed special insight into the Far East because his grandfather on the Delano side had been a China trader. To emphasize his distaste for the aggressive Japanese policy, he was even willing to credit the rumor told him by a Japanese student at Harvard in 1902 that the Japanese high command had since the 1880s been developing a secret plan to conquer the southwest Pacific. Most other issues affecting the Orient Roosevelt tended to duck by referring to the mysterious mind of the East. Moreover, he declared, since occidentals had long exploited orientals and so were resented as intruders, it was futile to seek solutions to Asiatic problems through an enlightened American economic policy. In that spirit the president dismissed complaints by a governor of the Federal Reserve that the Silver Purchase Act of 1934 was wreaking havoc by draining silver from China's silver standard backing of its currency to the artificially high-priced silver market in the United States. Such a view was far too mundane, Roosevelt answered: "Silver is not the problem of the Chinese past, nor the Chinese present, nor the Chinese future. There are forces there which neither you nor I understand, but at least I know that they are almost incomprehensible to us Westerners. Do not let so-called figures or facts lead you to believe that any of Western Civilization's actions can ever affect the people of China very deeply." Roosevelt added to his stereotyped view of the inscrutable East that he would not recommend any action on the matter because the "forces" in China could in their "incomprehensible" way stop the outflow of silver if they really chose to do so.

At first Roosevelt was almost as cavalier toward Europe. But the rise of Hitler and to a lesser extent Mussolini soon made him take more careful notice. Public opinion accompanied him, turning decisively against Hitler after the dictator's murderous 1934 purge of dissident military elements. From then until the advent of World War II the New Deal trained its foreign policy attention on containing the Nazi menace.

Fortunately, Roosevelt picked an ambassador to Germany who perceived the German situation with uncompromised moral clarity. William Dodd, an eminent historian who embodied a courtly southern sense of honor, was offended by the brutal and boorish nature of the Nazis. Conscientiously, he refused Hitler's blandishments. He would not lend Hitler respectability by attending Nazi rallies and would not countenance the treatment of the Jews. By 1936 Dodd had compiled a full enough "book" on Hitler to write a 173-page report to Washington whose main point was the simple truth that Hitler 's viciously anti-Semitic tract *Mein Kampf* gave a true description of the man and his aims.

In Washington, however, the State Department, used to the old-fashioned politesse of international relationships, could not readily bring itself to believe the stern word from Berlin. Hull, who was pained by unpleasantness, tried to smooth things over. When 20,000 aroused spectators packed Madison Square Garden for a rally sponsored by the AFL and the American Jewish Congress to present "the Case of Civilization against Hitlerism," Hull commiserated with the German Ambassador, Hans Luther, about not being able to find legal means to stop the affair. With hope against hope of averting a blowup, the administration and most of the nation held tight and watched the drama unfold across the Atlantic.

The violent implications of fascism were first aimed toward outlying areas that would serve as tests of will. In response to the loud posturing of Mussolini about restoring the Roman Empire (for which the American newspaperman George Seldes dubbed him the "Sawdust Caesar") on August 31, 1935, Roosevelt signed a Neutrality Act forbidding shipment of war materials to belligerent nations. Two days later the League of Nations announced similar sanctions as part of its policy of collective security.

Roosevelt's acceptance of the Neutrality Act as a way of joining the international community in punishing an aggressor opened up a confused and troubled chapter in foreign relations. At odds with the president's support for international sanctions against aggressor nations, pacifists and isolationists backed neutrality legislation as a way to shield the United States from violent engagement in the world's troubles. Out of the well of disillusionment with America's failed idealism in World War I came suspicions that an influential number of those who opposed the neutrality law, like many who had supported America's entry into World War I, were part of an industrial-financial conspiracy that stood to profit from producing war materiel. The Women's International League for Peace and Freedom, a pacifist group begun in 1915 by Jane Addams to oppose American participation in the Great War, lobbied for a congressional investigation of the munitions industry. Senator Gerald Nye of North Dakota, a stalwart of midwestern populism's aversion to foreign adventures, was appointed chairman of a special committee that spoke of the "merchants of death" with a vehemence that set public opinion solidly against American intervention in foreign wars.

America's neutral stance was swiftly challenged. Openly disdainful of those not given to manly aggression, Mussolini on October 3 launched an attack on Ethiopia to bring it back within the colonial framework that had come to an end after World War I. At this crucial juncture the international community's commitment to collective security crumbled and American noninvolvement held, even though a main tenet of the neutrality concept had been violated. Fecklessly, the quarantine declared against Italy failed to include an embargo against oil—the one critical item Mussolini's war machine had to import; the administration's plea that United States shippers enact a "moral embargo" by voluntarily refusing to send oil failed to stem the free enterprise urge. The Neutrality Act's purpose was further perverted by preventing shipment of armaments that the Ethiopian victims needed and the Italian aggressors did not. To complete the fiasco, British Foreign Minister Sir Samuel Hoare and French Premier Pierre Laval abjectly acquiesced in the Italian annexation of Ethiopia through an agreement reached with Italy in December 1935.

No sooner had deposed Ethiopian Emperor Haile Selassie's plea for help died away from the League's Assembly Chamber than an even more poignant and serious upheaval began in Spain. In the summer of 1936, General Francisco Franco and a band of rebel followers crossed the Mediterranean from their outpost in Morocco to launch an assault on the Republican government, which had recently replaced a decrepit monarchy. Franco argued that he was striving to rescue Spain—and the Catholic Church—from Communism and anarchism. His campaign attracted considerable support from Mussolini, who welcomed the chance to pose alongside his fellow fascists as a defender of the faith. The Nazis were lured into the fray by the prospect of a kindred authoritarian regime that might help outflank France in case of war. Other nations and partisan groups also found cause for concern, and Spain soon became an arena for testing the relative strength and wisdom of leading social beliefs and contenders for power. Russia sped arms and organizers to the war in order to promote a Marxist-Leninist front against fascism. Anarchists also headed for the front to aid their comrades in a struggle against fascist enemies on one side and Communist rivals on the other. Drawn by the sense that Spain was a great test for free institutions, people along a broad spectrum of democratic and autocratic fervor converged on the war to bear witness.

In the United States, where partisans of all the embroiled factions existed, the crisis in Spain became an emotional and symbolic test of support for the common man against the forces of feudal and fascist oppression. For the New Deal it also posed a challenge to the policy of nonintervention. Franklin Roosevelt chose Chautauqua, New York, the center of nineteenth-century moralistic popular lecturing, to speak fervently against American involvement in a foreign war. Recalling in bloody detail his experience with World War I, Roosevelt called instead for a moral embargo: "If war should break out again in another country we would find in this country thousands of Americans who, seeking immediate riches— fool's gold—would attempt to break down or evade our neutrality. They would tell you—and, unfortunately, their views would get wide publicity—that if they could produce and ship this and that and the other article to belligerent Nations, the unemployed of America would all find work. . . . It would be hard to resist." Nonetheless, Roosevelt contended, "We can keep out of war if those who watch and decide . . . possess the courage to say 'no' to those who selfishly or unwisely would let us go to war."

When the moral embargo was breached by a company that insisted on its legal right to a license to ship airplane parts and engines to the Spanish government, Roosevelt went the next step in sponsoring special legislation in January 1937 embargoing strategic shipments to either side in the Spanish conflict.

Roosevelt's blanket opposition to war as the cat's-paw of profiteers enabled him to fend off partisans of both sides. Neither the Catholic spokesmen who favored Franco's defense of order and faith nor the leftist defenders of democratic institutions who supported the Loyalists could sway Roosevelt, though he was sympathetic to the latter. Instead Roosevelt retreated into the gray area of neutrality, buffered by the 25 percent of the population shown by the polls to have no opinion on the civil war.

Closer to the scene of war, twenty-seven nations, led by France and England, and including Germany and Italy, formed the International Non-intervention Committee and pledged not to ship war materials to the combatants on the pious grounds that this aloofness would "contain" the war to a local stage and keep the conflict brief. Once again the post-Versailles strategy of peace through aversion was being tried; once again its effect was to give an advantage to those nations who would use violence to advance their expansionist ends. Italy and Germany, in brazen contempt of the fact that they were co-founders of the Non-Intervention Committee, sent masses of men and weapons to Franco's aid. They were so intent on joining the battle in Spain that foreign observers moved toward the conclusion that those bellicose powers, looking forward to another Great War, were engaging in a "Rehearsal in Spain." The Nazis, in their blood-chilling way, were not even shy about the terrible symbolism of calling their expeditionary force the "Condor Legion."

As the devastating way Germany and Italy preyed upon Spain became more difficult to ignore, Roosevelt pondered accepting the resolution of Senator Gerald Nye to lift the embargo on the grounds that its effect was almost wholly to cripple the Loyalist efforts. But Hull, deferring to the British and French reluctance to antagonize the Fascists, persuaded Roosevelt to maintain the embargo. Not even the outcry after the infamous Nazi dive-bombing of Guernica on April 26, 1937, could shake that strategic resolve.

But in the hush that followed the collapse of Loyalist Spain in 1939 a significant change of heart occurred. Popular remorse took to the novel Ernest Hemingway wrote out of his experience in the war zone. The poignant account of American volunteers futilely trying to help the outgunned Loyalist troops Hemingway called For Whom the Bell Tolls (1939). Abashed, Roosevelt admitted that it tolled for him, that he and Congress had made a tragic error in blocking aid to the Loyalists. Neutrality legislation left the United States an island unto itself, unable to help the League of Nations apply collective security force against an aggressor.

Roosevelt was not willing to be completely silent throughout the period of Spain's trial, however. Outraged by the Japanese use of a minor incident at the Marco Polo Bridge outside Beijing as a pretext for launching an offensive to conquer the whole of China, Roosevelt delivered a speech in Chicago on October 5, 1937, urging the imposition of a "quarantine" against aggressor nations. Immediately afterward Undersecretary of State Welles proposed a conference of many nations to give international principles of law binding force. Public response, however, vehemently opposed what looked like the tricky maneuvering of an adventurer president who wanted to get around the isolationist will of the people expressed shortly before in the Neutrality Act. Roosevelt swiftly retreated, and Welles's plan was quashed with equal speed by Secretary of State Hull.

Roosevelt revived his plea for collective security at the start of the next year when he asked in his annual message to Congress for stronger efforts to secure international peace. Loyal New Dealers in the House Foreign Relations Committee were then struggling to defeat the amendment offered by Louis Ludlow of Indiana that would force approval in a national referendum before the government could declare war. Under White House and State Department pressure, however, Congress on January 10 acceded to Roosevelt's insistence that the conduct of foreign policy would be crippled by such a war referendum. Simultaneously, Sumner Welles managed to persuade the ever-cautious Hull to drop his objection to a world conference on international law and then, with Roosevelt's encouragement, issued an invitation to Great Britain to help plan the conference.

The brief New Deal initiative for a stronger foreign policy soon stalled, however, when Welles met with brusque refusal in England. Prime Minister Neville Chamberlain derided the idea as "woolly," a hapless notion that would be scorned by the very totalitarian powers it was meant to impress. Chamberlain had devised another plan for dealing with the fascist menace. His neat, businesslike mind, combined with an old world disdain of Americans—not least the bumptious Roosevelt—led to Chamberlain's resolve that it would be best to forego American moral lectures and get right on, by himself, to direct parley with Hitler. Did the Germans wish living space for their cramped population? Very well, their desires should be considered with detailed reference to the land available. Were the Germans sensitive about the slights they had received from the Versailles treaty? Then it would be the better part of valor discretely to examine what changes in the treaty and Germany's reparations debt might mollify them. Most sensitive was the last question: were the Germans keen on reunion with the Germanic elements situated across the borders of other nations? Then one needed to confer with Herr Hitler to learn just how a rearrangement of allegiances might be achieved with a minimum of discomfort to those nations that had to cede territory. Chamberlain adopted for his policy of acquiescence to Nazi demands the term *appeasement* and prided himself on how tactfully he was able to alter established policies and obligations to serve the larger requirements of "peace in our time."

Chamberlain's youthful assistant, Anthony Eden, later to become prime minister himself, resigned in despair when his superior refused Welles's invitation. Forever afterward Eden argued that the best chance to avert war had been thrown away—as a supporter put it, like a life buoy refused by a drowning man. It could, Eden insisted, have provided the means for the British and Americans to buck up each other's courage and form a military alliance strong enough to face down Hitler's threatening gestures. Given Hitler's belligerence and the timidity of his opponents, however, the chances that the conference Welles proposed would have found a way to head off the threat of war were slight. Certainly, there was no indication in Welles's proposal that the United States was ready to engage in the sort of military action needed if mere talk failed and Hitler resumed his aggression.

Thus free of effective opposition, Nazi ambitions to bring all Germans under Hitler's control took hold. At the start of 1938 Hitler called Austria forward for a reckoning. Chancellor Kurt von Schuschnigg was summoned to Hitler's mountain retreat at Berchtesgaden and told that he must appoint as minister of the interior the Austrian Nazi Arthur Seyss-Inquart. This demand, which Austria did not have the strength to deny, was the prelude to imposing Seyss-Inquart as chancellor and the incorporation of Austria into the German state soon afterward. That shotgun marriage of March 12—the "*Anschluss*" (meaning "junction")—had, for all its crude bullying, an electrifying effect on Germans, who for about two centuries had been slowly moving along a tortuous path of war and negotiation from a collection of minor principalities toward unification as a great power. Suddenly, Austrian autonomy—the last barrier left to complete unification of the German-speaking states, which not even Chancellor von Bismarck, the architect of German unity, had been able to overcome—was ended. Borne along by a surge of the messianic excitement that ignited his countrymen after the *Anschluss,* Hitler could now contemplate spreading his version of the old "pan-German" ideal of empire across the continent.

The immediate target was Czechoslovakia. In the Sudetenland section of Czechoslovakia a large, ethnically German element, stirred by what had occurred in Austria, accepted the counsel of Hitler to make demands on the Czech government for autonomy, which amounted to the dissolution of the Czech state. As outside nations watched tensions mount and tried desperately to think of means either to preserve the Czech state or to meet German demands without general war or humiliation, Hitler drove straight toward what he told his generals in private was his "unalterable" intent to "smash" Czechoslovakia and end its existence as an independent state. It was left to Neville Chamberlain, after inducing the reluctant French to hold back from their treaty obligation to aid the Czechs in event of war, to fly to Berchtesgaden for one of those calm, businesslike meetings he so favored. American Ambassadors William Bullitt in Paris and Joseph Kennedy in London endorsed the appeasement, advising against regarding anything that happened in Czechoslovakia as justification for war—Bullitt by warning that Russia would step in after the slaughter of western youth to establish an "asiatic despotism" and Kennedy by offering to tour Germany and talk with Hitler to ease tension and help Roosevelt understand that Hitler, who had "done wonders" for his people, was being maligned.

On September 30, the Czech government announced that it would cede the Sudeten region to Germany. Understanding that the remnant of the Czech state had no means to resist and would get no outside help, Hitler occupied the rest of Czechoslovakia on March 30, 1939, without even a show of justification. Then he turned his inflamed attention on Poland.

The scenario with Poland was the by then familiar one of theatrical outrage over the alleged sufferings of the German minority in that country, unreasonable demands for restitution, which were then "unreasonably" refused, mobilization, and, finally, on September 1, 1939, armed invasion. This time, even though Bullitt and Kennedy were still counseling appeasement, the British and French did not back down. With their declaration of war against Germany, World War II began.

The American response to war was sharply divided. The Keep America Out of the War Congress, founded in 1938 to oppose New Deal leanings toward international involvement, and its successor in 1940 after World War II had begun, the America First Committee, attracted diverse followings of anti-interventionists. There were socialists, including the head of the Socialist Party, Norman Thomas, who had always been averse to war as the device of capitalist rulers to sacrifice working-class soldiers to suit their profit-making ends; believers in religious and humane principles who considered war an insupportable threat to civilized decency; isolationists who would let foreigners fight their own battles; and even America's most famous aviator hero, Charles Lindbergh, who spoke for those who feared that opposing the Nazi juggernaut would not be worth the cost. On the other side those who would have the United States enter the fight against totalitarian aggression made the practical argument that modern advances in naval and air warfare meant Americans were no longer safe behind their ocean barriers as well as the moral argument that it was America's duty to stand beside the Allies in defense of civilized values.

Most Americans existed—confused and apprehensive—between the two poles. The most broadly representative citizen group, headed by the patriarch of Republican journalists, William Allen White, called itself the Committee to Defend America by Aiding the Allies—to which was usually added the term "by all means short of war." The group's ambivalence showed acutely when the German blitzkrieg broke through the supposedly impregnable Maginot Line and forced France to surrender in June 1940. White met the heightened threat by urging that the motto of the CDAAA should be "The Yanks are not coming," thereby offending those who wanted to stress active support of the Allies. At the same time he declared that everything "short of war" must be done to defeat the Axis, which antagonized those who emphasized the need to keep America uninvolved. Yet the CDAAA ambivalence was close to the heart of American sentiment. Polls taken during the three years before Pearl Harbor showed rising hostility toward the Axis but steady refusal to recommend American entry into a war. By the spring of 1940, when France fell, emotions became acutely mixed. As often happens with apprehensive subjects, the Gallup poll was contradictory: a majority was convinced that defeating Hitler was more important than staying out of war, yet a comparable majority stated that they opposed America's participation in the war.

Under the circumstances the American government had to be shrewd in devising ways to help save Britain, the last ally left against Germany. Advised in December 1940 that Britain had only $2 billion available to pay for $5 billion worth of arms that had been ordered from American manufacturers, Roosevelt came up with one of his inspired improvisations. Remembering Ickes's disgruntled remark earlier in the summer that American neutrality legislation left the nation like the householder who refused to lend or sell his fire extinguisher to a neighbor whose house was on fire, Roosevelt suggested a device that came to be called Lend-Lease. At a news conference he urged that Britain be granted the right to acquire arms in the United States on the promise that their worth would be paid back in kind after the war. Thus, aid could be sent to an ally without technically violating the neutrality acts' prohibition against selling or shipping arms. In a fireside chat a few days later, Roosevelt convinced most listeners that this measure would enable the people of Europe to fight for their liberty, and so provide security, without drawing America into the war. The overwhelmingly favorable response in letters to the White House was followed by the Lend-Lease Act of

March 11, 1941, which authorized $7 billion to underwrite the British acquisition of the materials they desperately needed. Winston Churchill captured the mood of common-sense compromise when he declared with dubious bravado: "You give us the tools and we'll finish the job."

And yet, however cleverly Lend-Lease stopped short of outright intervention, such participation in the British war effort contributed to a momentum that moved toward full partnership. Underlying the drift was Roosevelt's declaration in his annual message to Congress on January 6, 1941, that the United States supported victory over the dictatorships in order to protect "four essential human freedoms"—freedom of speech, freedom of religion, freedom from want, and freedom from fear. Lend-Lease translated that advocacy into partisan action; thus mobilized, the partisan spirit quickly deployed American naval vessels to help British patrols track marauders in the north Atlantic and thus ensured that the distance to outright war would dwindle steadily.

America was first drawn into war in the Pacific, however. Japan, after feeling the effects of gradual American economic pressures against its expansionist campaign, concluded a pact with Italy and Germany in Berlin on September 27, 1940. Emboldened by Germany's swift defeat of France, which forced Britain's isolated forces to flee across the Channel for a last-ditch defense of the home island, Japan then invoked its alliance with Germany as a justification to overrun French Indochina in July 1941. Roosevelt, faced with the choice of taking drastic measures or allowing Japan to incorporate all the vast southwest Pacific area beyond Australia into her Greater East Asia Co-Prosperity Sphere, chose to tighten the economic noose a crucial twist further by halting the sale of gasoline to Japan and freezing that nation's assets in the United States. From the Japanese side, the drive for self-sufficiency had been a great success, and the thought of halting it was unbearable. Thus the American boycott of vital raw materials prompted further Japanese expansion to secure replacements. To head off American military opposition, Japan set in motion plans for a preemptive strike against American naval forces. While Japan's negotiators in Washington diverted attention by talking of peace, the Japanese government unleashed its aircraft carrier fleet. On the morning of December 7, 1941, waves of Japanese planes devastated the American ships at anchor in Pearl Harbor, Hawaii, and destroyed most of the American warplanes there and at distant bases in the Philippines and Wake Island before they could even get off the ground. Germany, also taken by surprise, swiftly followed the Japanese lead and declared war. The tightrope walk of American neutrality had ended with a fiery fall into the pit of war.

Another Cycle?

The onslaught of World War II had the paradoxical result of both achieving recovery from the Depression through massive spending and job creation and displacing the aim of a cooperative commonwealth with a centralized command structure devoted to military victory. Accordingly, Roosevelt declared that he had ceased being "Dr. New Deal" and had become "Dr. Win-the-War." This, he made plain, was to be a total war leading to unconditional surrender, and all domestic policies were to follow in the wake. Quite aside from Roosevelt's position, New Deal reform was bound to slip out of favor in a crisis that stressed national unity on the basis of loyalty to traditional values and institutions.

The congressional elections of 1942 indicated the turn of politics away from reform. Though the Democrats retained their majority, Republican newcomers announced the return of midwestern districts to their pre–New Deal conservatism and urged that the country be streamlined for war by ridding it of further New Deal experiments and kindred socialistic and foreign influences. By the end of 1943, agencies that exemplified the New Deal were feeling the heat. Roosevelt gave the Works Progress Administration an "honorable discharge," and Congress dispatched the Civilian Conservation Corps and the National Resources Planning Board while reducing the Farm Security Administration and the Rural Electrification Administration to mere paper status.

Those still committed to the New Deal creed worried about the reentry of the "Economic Royalists" into the administrative temple. When Roosevelt mobilized the nation's resources for war, he followed the precedent set in World War I of calling to the colors the big businessmen who alone had the experience to run giant productive combines. With the business influx came the free enterprise notion of incentive. Secretary of War Henry L. Stimson, the stern and able Republican whom Roosevelt had chosen according to his principle of putting the war effort ahead of ideology, stated the position succinctly: "If you are going to . . . go to war . . . in a capitalist country, you have to let business make money out of the process or business won't work." And on that principle the money rolled in. Conversion of industry to war purposes was cushioned by lower excess profits taxes, long-term government loans, and that most notorious of arrangements, the cost-plus proviso enabling defense contractors to be paid for work that was more expensive than promised.

So encouraged, business enterprise moved toward ever greater concentration. The way was eased when Stimson scuttled Thurman Arnold's vigorous trust-busting campaign in 1942, calling Arnold "a self-seeking fanatic" who was inhibiting the war effort. By 1945 the majority of the nation's manufacturing concerns had more than 500 workers, where before the war most businesses were well below that number. The trend toward bigness was speeded by a policy that awarded the dwindling third of small companies with only slightly over 10 percent of the Army's contracts.

The increasing sway of big corporations in the war effort was balanced by efforts to bring labor in as a partner. The attack on Pearl Harbor came at the end of a year of great labor upheaval, marked especially by the capitulation of the Ford Motor Company and "Little Steel" to the CIO juggernaut. In all, some 2.3 million workers had gone out on strike in 1941—a higher number than for any years except 1919 and 1937. It seemed imperative, then, for the war economy to bring order to the workplace by insisting on labor's cooperation. In January 1942, Roosevelt created the National War Labor Board, composed of representatives from business, labor, and the general public, and gave it the power to impose arbitration and call on the president to take over plants where disputes were hindering the war effort. As their great contribution, the unions agreed to a general application of terms reached with "Little Steel" in which workers would gain a 15 percent pay raise and not resort to strikes. Within those guidelines the NWLB adjudicated over seventeen thousand disputes involving twelve million workers, and production rose dramatically.

The way war imperatives swiftly ended the economic stagnation that had so defied peacetime measures has naturally led to the conclusion that it was war, not the New Deal, that solved the Depression and brought unemployment virtually to an end by the close of 1942. It would seem more accurate to say that war accelerated measures that were already in place before the war, that it made use of deficit spending ideas from Eccles to Keynes which had entrenched themselves as the preferred means to rapid economic expansion during the recession of 1938. Wartime expenditures also demonstrated the monetarist claims for the stimulus to be gained from expanding the money supply. Rising prosperity and the imposition of income tax withholding overcame the chronic shortage of revenues needed to operate government welfare, regulatory, and managerial functions, thus fueling hopes that, once the war and its voracious appetite for resources ended, there would be the means to revive New Deal programs.

As the surging economy revived the workplace, the CIO scored a dual triumph. In 1941 its UAW affiliate successfully completed its campaign to organize the auto industry. Soon afterward the steelworkers' union gained a measure of vindication for the Memorial Day Massacre by using an urgent need for armaments to force a contract out of diehard Little Steel. Most of all the trend helped the AFL, however. Building on its successful use of the right to organize through federally supervised elections, the AFL brought two million newcomers into its ranks between 1940 and 1945. With high demand from the military buildup for skilled workers, the AFL grew so vigorously that by the outbreak of war it had become the majority union movement once again. The rebound of the AFL depended on the submergence of the old leadership to an extent that left the AFL and CIO overlapping and steadily less antagonistic. In 1954 the rivals were finally reconciled in a merger that brought the labor revolution to a unified resolution.

But the new system ran into a measure of trouble as well. Workers were rebuffed in their attempt to get an increase in the minimum wage scale through Congress. Where was the money to come from, Roosevelt asked, ignoring the fact that high managerial costs were part of the reason that half of the war effort had to be financed by deficit loans. Also brushed aside were the low wages—one fourth of the workers in manufacturing, about ten million in all, were still making less than 60¢ an hour at the peak of the war boom. Most provocative was the plain fact that inflation, which benefited business and finance, pushed the cost of living well beyond the maximum 15 percent salary rise accorded to labor.

The mutually supportive tie between labor and the New Deal, which had made so many of labor's gains possible, withstood the strain. For one thing, despite the acrimony, Roosevelt now had the sort of cooperative system that he had always favored over the adversarial model that prevailed after the failure of the NRA. Further strengthening the new arrangement's hold on Roosevelt was the way this revived cooperation reflected his formative experience in World War I with its ardent Wilsonian commitment to a common cause. Organized labor also recognized, for the most part, that its participation was virtually a command performance.

Still, labor was pinched. Economic advance was stayed, and the ideal of heroic working stiffs battling industrialists for economic justice took on the taint of undermining the war effort. Most degrading as a sign of an ebbing reform spirit was the sharp rise in the employment of children to take the place of those who had gone to war, while officials looked the other way. Conditions among the common men in the fields were also troubled. With the FSA reduced to a nullity, many poor farmers had little to hold them. A great migration to the towns, often to take advantage of war plant work, drained three million persons off the land between 1940 and 1945, a decline in farm population of 17 percent. Progressives like Tugwell, who had favored planned resettlement rather than flight to the cities, looked upon those figures as a defeat. Obscuring their disappointment was the fact that agriculture prospered in the way favored by the Farm Bureau Federation. Increasing numbers of large, "modern" farms garnered a cash income that rose from $2.3 billion in 1940 to $9.5 billion in 1945, and Farm Bureau Federation membership expanded accordingly, from 400,000 to well over a million at war's end. Farming moved decisively into an era of agribusiness, and the yeoman ideal, kept alive during the lean years of the Depression by the New Deal, faded into nostalgia.

There was, then, much to dismay New Deal liberals as the war period wrought its changes. Archibald MacLeish, a highly visible champion of the New Deal and head of the wartime government information service, expressed that dismay when he told a gathering of liberal peers in 1944 that "it is no longer feared, it is assumed, that the country is headed back to normalcy, that Harding is just around the corner, that the twenties will repeat themselves." Other New Dealers were even more alarmed. Felix Frankfurter's protégé Max Lerner, always attuned to trends, warned that "America is today more reactionary in its prevailing mood than any other country where the fascists are not openly in power. The counter-revolution is gathering its forces in America." Then, as the presidential election of 1944 approached, Roosevelt dampened liberal ardor for his decision to run for a fourth term by replacing the favorite of reformers, Vice President Henry Wallace, with the safely obscure product of urban machine politics, Missouri Senator Harry S. Truman. Roosevelt's victorious campaign was essentially an uninspiring effort to discredit his opponent, Governor Thomas E. Dewey of New York, as another Hoover, while Dewey, in even less helpful style, warned against the Red Menace lurking behind the New Deal.

The liberal doldrums were deepened by widespread expectation that the Depression would resume once the artificial wartime prosperity ended. There had always been slumps after war; in this case Americans had the recession of 1937 to keep in mind as evidence that the deep-seated flaws in the economy had not been dispelled by the New Deal. The "normalcy" to which the nation expected to return was that of the Depression, not the prosperous sort that followed victory in World War I. That was the central message in the studies sponsored by the Twentieth Century Fund, "Guide Lines to America's Future." Issued between 1942 and 1946, the studies warned of the need to resume overhaul of the system that had characterized the cutting edge of the New Deal. The first priority was to secure full employment, with ample pay so that there would be enough money in circulation to absorb the goods the nation was capable of producing. In close agreement, pollster Elmo Roper, writing for the social documentary journal *Survey Graphic*, in 1943 warned that "if full employment is denied . . . opposition to more radical proposals is likely to wither rapidly." More anxious voices pressed the ominous implications further. *Fortune* contended that "the American soldier is depression-conscious and . . . worried sick about postwar joblessness. . . . The soldier himself is most deeply interested in the quest for personal security."

That fearfulness about personal economic well-being sapping the idealism of the New Deal touched off some alarmed condemnations of American society. Novelist and social critic Philip Wylie in a hotly debated slash at social mores concluded that an obsession with material security to the exclusion of higher aims had made Americans "a generation of vipers." To which Henry Miller, recoiling from a cross-country survey made after years in exile from American aversion to his "dirty" books, added that the crass regimentation of American life amounted to an "air-conditioned nightmare." Wylie and Miller and others of like mind who were appearing in increasing numbers to challenge the New Deal affirmation of the common man saw in the war effort portents of a fascist society in which those controlling money and opinion would turn America into a nation of sheep. John Dewey, still America's most eminent social philosopher, did not share that loss of faith in the Common Man, but on the eve of Pearl Harbor he warned in his *New Republic* article, "No Matter What Happens, Stay Out," that war would move the nation's leaders to impose authoritarian controls in order to eliminate dissent. War would thus play into the hands of reactionary business leaders who had been waiting on the sidelines for the chance to regain what they had lost to New Deal reform. Once the nation had taken the leap into the dark of war, such fears gained in power to haunt the dreams of all those contemplating the shape of the world to come after the bloodshed and brutalization.

The anti-liberal aspects of fear and crisis did not prove fatal, however. Because the New Deal had gained powerful stature, the tides of war and conservative reaction were never able to drown it. They did slow the momentum of the New Deal and left many of its programs awash. But they also stimulated new resolve by making the need to carry on reform, and to seize wartime opportunities, especially vivid. Rexford Tugwell, remembering the way World War I had given planners their chance, hailed the occasion for "disciplined cooperation." For "the fact is that only war has up to now proved to be such a transcending objective that doctrine is willingly sacrificed for efficiency in its service." Roosevelt added an appeal to idealism when he told Congress on January 6, 1941, that Lend-Lease to Britain would help establish a "moral order" guaranteeing "the supremacy of human rights." Such rhetoric, echoed many times, indicated that Roosevelt remained true to the Wilsonian intention to "make the world safe for democracy." For all his bending to conservative pressures for the sake of wartime unity and productivity, Roosevelt, unlike some disheartened liberal allies, stayed with his conviction that the struggle to defeat the Axis would lead to a securer and more progressive world. He was in that sense, as his biographer, James MacGregor Burns has written, a "soldier of freedom," intent on translating the sentiments of the Four Freedoms into the Atlantic Charter, which Britain and the United States signed in middle of the ocean in 1941, and then using the Charter as the basis for a postwar United Nations.

Domestically, Roosevelt showed his intention to make wartime prosperity permanent by maneuvering through Congress a G.I. Bill of Rights that expanded unemployment insurance, social security, and educational benefits for a group not even conservatives could deny. Other citizens, Roosevelt believed, could view the G.I. Bill as a prototype of what they should gain after the war when the progressive spirit again took charge. A nation fighting for its rights, Roosevelt contended, should realize that a decent standard of living was one of those rights and be prepared "to move forward . . . to new goals of happiness and well-being" after victory was gained. In his State of the Union message on January 11, 1944, Roosevelt summed up his agenda as a Second Bill of Rights, guaranteeing certain conditions as a matter of right: well-paid employment, livable housing, fair business competition, medical benefits to be added to social insurance, protection from economic fears of old age and disability, and an education offering citizens full opportunity to develop their talents.

Roosevelt did not live to test his postwar vision. Late in the afternoon of April 12, 1945, word arrived from Warm Springs, Georgia, that the president had died of a massive stroke. Those who had been recently shocked by Roosevelt's haggard appearance were not surprised. But most people who heard the news when it was first flashed over the radio recalled being stunned, unable for a time to imagine how the nation would be run by anyone other than the man they had become so used to thinking of as the president. With so much left to do to insure world stability and the issue of domestic prosperity hanging in the balance, it was well that the minister presiding at the White House funeral repeated Roosevelt's famous reassurance: "The only thing we have to fear is fear itself." But how long the old New Deal optimism could be sustained was impossible to predict.

The imperatives of the war effort helped matters move forward without the commander-in-chief. The vast outlays needed for the armed forces, coupled with the successful effort by conservatives to curb rising taxes, had forced the government to borrow heavily. That massive departure from the shibboleth of a balanced budget gave impetus to the Keynesian view of an activist government resorting to deficit spending when its plans required it. In turn, businessmen involved in the war effort naturally came to see the government as a partner. Free enterprise and public purpose converged, though not for New Deal reform aims, and corporations thus became more socialized, even as the New Deal was coming to terms with "economic royalists."

The most revealing episode of this period of convergence was the movement to enact a full employment bill. Spokesmen from both sides of the business-government partnership praised the enlightened aim of full employment, but in the end conservative reluctance to tamper with free enterprise pared the bill down from mandating full employment to mere advocacy of the "maximum" that could be done and to establishing the presidential Council of Economic Advisers.

Postwar resistance to the New Deal cooperative commonwealth ideal stressed the shortcomings of human nature that made such high hopes seem dangerously utopian. In the era's most influential biography of Roosevelt, James MacGregor Burns's *The Lion and the Fox*, the president emerges as master Machiavellian power broker and the New Deal as piecemeal maneuvering to get as much as possible for its constituency by any means available. Historian Richard Hofstadter brought class into the picture by closing his widely admired book on *The American Political Tradition* with a sketch of Roosevelt that labels him "the Patrician as Opportunist." In these scenarios the presidential hero does not let innocent idealism stand in the way of opportunity, nor inflict unintended bad consequences by trying for more than the partial solutions that are practical and popular. The Roosevelt who spoke of comprehensive planning, of subduing big business and redistributing income, and of realigning American politics so that a dominant progressive party might emerge appears only occasionally, and then in an overwrought moment or as a master manipulator of public emotion exaggerating for effect. To such praise of unillusioned shrewdness another admirer of the New Deal, theologian Reinhold Niebuhr, added the darker Calvinist insight that human beings are innately depraved and that history is therefore essentially a tragic record of flawed action. During the 1930s, Niebuhr as a passionate Christian Socialist had contended that New Deal measures were not sweeping enough. After the war, no longer romantic or irresponsible, as he saw it, Niebuhr urged Americans to realize that in such a sinful world they must adjust their expectations for success lower than the New Deal had sought.

The concept of limits found its most important application to the New Deal in the magisterial series of books on *The Age of Roosevelt,* written by Niebuhr's protégé, Arthur Schlesinger Jr. Like his mentor, Schlesinger saw history as a tragic record of unfulfilled hopes against which great men like Lincoln or Roosevelt struggled valiantly. In the midst of telling his story Schlesinger paused long enough to write *The Vital Center* (1949), in which he urged heirs of the New Deal to pursue their goals within established mainstream institutions, far from the ideological extremes of right and left. Thus, Niebuhr and Schlesinger, who were founders of the Americans for Democratic Action dedicated to carrying on the New Deal reform spirit, accepted the sort of limitations that John Chamberlain had taken as grounds for bidding farewell to reform. Adopting that view meant tempering the use of state power to complete the creation of the cooperative commonwealth to which Roosevelt had pledged the New Deal. Democrats came instead to rely on the economic boom, guided by regulation and Keynesian fiscal and monetary controls, to lift society toward the point where Roosevelt's goals would be affordable for all Americans, either with or without government support.

New Dealers who saw this reliance on affluence as a departure from the cooperative commonwealth ideal of the sharing of modest means, tended to agree with Chamberlain that what remained was a rather degraded "limited racket" politics of a state brokering deals with special interests. These critics of the broker state either drifted away from politics or found themselves in self-defeating dissent to the way New Deal aims were being compromised after the war. Rexford Tugwell in a bitter critique, *Off Course* (1971), decried the Truman administration for its abandonment of social and economic planning and for belligerent Cold War confrontation with the Soviet Union. In a kind of last gasp effort to rally support for policies that aimed to get the cooperative commonwealth ideal back on course, Tugwell had joined other disaffected reformers in 1948 to create the Progressive Party and back his former boss, Henry Wallace, in a run against Truman for the presidency. The Progressives hoped to foster a working relationship with Russia, advance black civil rights, and remedy the welfare system so that it would include all in need. Instead, attacks on Wallace's campaign by liberals as well as conservatives for not barring Communist support made his cause notorious and intensified doubts about the state as an agent of change. In his upset victory over Governor Dewey, Truman gained the support of anti-communist liberals as well as of many progressives who might otherwise have supported Wallace were it not for their fear that such a conscience vote would hand the election over to conservative Republicans.

Studies of American life at the time indicated that the sense of limitation governing appraisals of the New Deal and the policies of its successors extended far beyond politics. Sociologist David Riesman picked up the theme in terms of the alienation and loss of confidence suffered by his countrymen whom the pressures of modern life had turned into a "lonely crowd" of "other-directed" persons. Much the same message resided at the heart of David Potter's description of Americans as "people of plenty," more closely attached to material abundance than to the democratic creed that the New Deal had sought to develop into a cooperative commonwealth. Predictably, in an atmosphere that stressed safe limits, what the New Deal had managed to accomplish was mostly left in place as part of the undergirding of prosperity, but the spirit was lacking for any strong new liberal reform ventures. When a commission was appointed by Truman's Republican successor Dwight Eisenhower to determine how a sense of national purpose might be created, it drew the uninspiring conclusion that a nation as large and diverse as the United States could hardly do more than provide a setting for citizens to develop their own separate purposes.

Yet, despite the chastened mood of the 1950s—more like a subdued middle road than a "vital center"—the chances for recovering the New Deal momentum seemed to be growing at the end of the decade. The anti-communist hysteria that had cast suspicion on collectivist reform subsided as events discredited Wisconsin Senator Joseph McCarthy and other red-hunters. To the clamor for fair play, the courts added an important measure of relief by invalidating laws that restricted political association and reversing court convictions that had violated civil rights. Climaxing the series of judicial victories against racial discrimination that began in 1938, the Supreme Court in the *Brown v. Board of Education* case of 1954 outlawed segregation as inherently destructive of the Fourteenth Amendment's guarantee of equal protection under the law.

Veteran New Dealers, including Arthur Schlesinger, made the most of the new reform spirit in guiding the only presidential aspirant since Roosevelt with charisma toward a revival of the New Deal crusade. Young, dashing, a devotee of physical fitness, John F. Kennedy borrowed extensively from a speech Roosevelt gave in 1935 to lay out his "New Frontier" concept in 1960 and then propelled his winning campaign with a Rooseveltian insistence that it was time to "get America moving again." Once in office Kennedy further evoked the New Deal spirit when he created the Peace Corps and exhorted the comfortable to help the "invisible poor" tucked away in remote regions and mostly forgotten since the reformers of the 1930s had thrust their suffering peoples into the public consciousness.

Certain aspects of the situation, however, cast doubt that a full revival of the New Deal spirit would take place. Eleanor Roosevelt, still the standard-bearer for the fight against poverty and injustice, regarded Kennedy as a dubious choice because he had not compiled a strong Senate record of support for minority civil rights and programs to expand welfare. Widespread affluence also ruled out a sense of shared economic crisis such as had dominated the 1930s. Instead, the Cold War seemed most urgent, and analogies to Munich appeasement abounded as reasons for taking care of national security over social ills. In any event, Kennedy's sense of the ideal was different from Roosevelt's. Narrowly escaping death in World War II, he displayed a well-developed fatalism about life as unfair and fragile, even tragic. Kennedy was inspired more by a spirit of individual adventure than common man security, and did not lament the necessity of abandoning New Deal economic planning in the face of widespread opposition to collectivism.

Before events could determine whether the Kennedy administration could simultaneously project toughness abroad and New Deal compassion at home, assassination cut down the charismatic president. Kennedy's successor, Lyndon Johnson, a Texan forever loyal to the New Deal for its help in lifting him out of his bleak rural beginnings, pressed the case for New Deal revival more fervently than Kennedy. To create a "Great Society," Johnson pressured Congress into granting voting rights to blacks and allocating large sums to his "war on poverty," which intended to complete New Deal housing programs and provide the education, training, and job creation needed to reach the goal of full employment and protection of the helpless that had eluded Roosevelt's New Deal and Truman's Fair Deal.

But Johnson's good intentions came to unanticipated grief. His insistence on pursuing a strategically and morally disastrous war in Vietnam splintered the coalition of old New Dealers and idealistic young followers of Kennedy that had produced Democratic reform majorities. When protesters eventually forced Johnson out of office and halted the escalation of the conflict, they also derailed the Great Society effort.

After Johnson's departure, political power flowed from a Democratic reform majority toward realignment of an ambiguous sort. The recoil of middle-class Americans from radicalism and the shift of conservative southerners away from their traditional home in the Democratic Party, now committed to civil rights, led to a more dominant and conservative Republican Party. Prospects for regaining momentum for Great Society transformation dimmed accordingly. Yet the changing balance also moved national politics toward the clear demarcation between a progressive Democratic Party and a conservative Republican Party that Roosevelt had optimistically believed would aid the New Deal cause. The possibility that a progressive majority would develop someday seemed remote, however, as a conservative coalition of economic and religious conservatives solidified in the 1990s.

At the close of its Great Society revival, the New Deal legacy could certainly show a record of prosperous advance. By 1970 about half of the New Deal aim of bringing all Americans out of poverty had been achieved. During the 1950s and 1960s the gross domestic product rose annually by over 4 percent, with 70 percent of whites achieving comfortable middle-class status. Driving these pathbreaking changes was a steady increase in workplace productivity by about one-third in each decade, which suggested that the case New Dealers had made for industrial efficiency was being borne out in economic well-being. The New Deal goal of inclusiveness seemed on track as well. Though separate figures on Asians and Hispanics were not kept prior to 1970, the rise in the earnings of black men from 55 percent those of white men in 1950 to 64 percent in 1970 indicated that barriers against minorities entering the economic mainstream had weakened.

Then new circumstances tilted the balance away from progressive reform. In addition to a conservative reaction against the Great Society's war on poverty, worldwide economic conditions spelled trouble. Of signal importance was the decision by OPEC (Organization of the Petroleum Exporting Countries) in 1973 to decrease the export of oil to the United States in order to profit from higher prices and protect their resources. Faced with doubled or tripled energy and transportation costs, manufacturers had to raise prices and, even so, showed declining profits. Against the conventional wisdom that prices and prosperity rose and fell together, Americans found themselves caught in what came to be called "stagflation"—a simultaneous slump in economic activity and rise in prices and interest rates. Adding to the misery was the invasion of foreign manufactures, especially from Japan, and the lure of cheap labor drawing jobs from American factories to the third world. As American manufacturing declined, enterprise focused more on service industries, whose workers had never been well-organized or reliable supporters of the New Deal. Consumption mirrored that shift. In 1960, 60 percent of America's income was spent on manufactured goods and 40 percent on services; thirty years later the situation was reversed—60 percent of disposable income going to services, 40 percent to manufactured goods.

A worrisome aspect of growth in the service sector for the New Deal legacy was the rapid escalation of health costs. Between 1960 and 1990 per capita
spending on health care went up more than 300 percent, increasing the percentage of national wealth absorbed from 5.3 to 14.9. In part this phenomenon
resulted from the greater availability of health coverage that the Great Society's
Medicare and Medicaid programs granted. It also reflected the longer lifespans
that improved medical science and affluence bestowed. As these trends developed, Social Security old age assistance and its Great Society health care counterparts became both increasingly essential to social well-being and at greater risk
because of their rising costs.

The response of business and its conservative allies to these troubling changes
was the traditional one of containing expenses and increasing profit by reducing
the size and cost of the workforce through mergers, lowered pay, and longer hours.
As a result American workers, in the words of economists Bennett Harrison and
Barry Bluestone, executed a "great U-turn" from rising wages between 1940 and
1973 to falling wages afterward, even as time on the job lengthened. The downward slide of wages also reflected the decline of labor unions. By 2005 less than 14
percent of the workforce was unionized, little more than a third of the high-water
mark of 35.5 percent in 1945. Making the picture bleaker was the fact that in private
industry even unionized workers suffered a wage decline from 1977 on.

A loss of militancy within a fragmented workforce accounted for some of the
decline of unions. The rest derived from strategies developed in a society less
sympathetic to the Common Man than in the 1930s. The change in direction
of the National Labor Relations Board was a key case in point. In its first twenty
years, the NLRB granted certification to almost 75 percent of those petitioning
for union status; from the mid-1980s to the present, as a result of more conservative appointments to the board, fewer than half of union petitions were looked
upon favorably. So, too, judges chosen by conservative presidents and governors
showed increased willingness to endorse managerial challenges to union formation and petition. Feeling little risk, officers of companies found guilty of blocking
union organizers from the workplace or firing employees who sought to unionize
were apt to shrug off fines as an affordable cost of keeping unions at bay.

The weakening of union solidarity as the bedrock of Common Man integrity
left the working classes without a secure base of support, let alone a share in
a cooperative commonwealth. Long-term employment grew rarer as companies
moved to save costs by relying on independent contracting and even piecework
in the home, reminiscent of the sweatshop system of a century before. All of this
made it harder for unions to organize the workforce. In addition to the loss of pay,

employees in such a situation of disconnect and temporary assignments faced mounting difficulties in trying to hold on to the New Deal ideal of community.

Instead, the fading of the corporation and the union as places of long-term loyalty made it easier for opponents of the New Deal legacy to oppose welfare and economic planning with the old doctrine of rugged individualism. At the behest of just such conservative lobbyists and lawmakers, state and federal law increasingly forced welfare recipients off the rolls and into whatever jobs they might find. Funds for public housing of the sort New Deal legislation provided for people only a step away from public assistance dried up. And in ways mostly irrelevant to the low-income Common Man, calls escalated for the privatization of Social Security so that beneficiaries could choose their own investment strategies for retirement.

Predictably, these trends encouraged the very social conditions against which the New Deal had pitted itself: a wide disparity of wealth that left many in poverty and ill health, unaccountable corporate power, restricted opportunity, and an alienated loss of morale—all anchored in a widespread conviction that government cannot or should not act to ensure decent living standards. A report by the United for a Fair Economy Foundation in 1999 on "Shifting Fortunes: The Perils of the Growing American Wealth Gap" reported stark contrasts. For the richest one percent, the years between 1993 and 1995 saw a rise in net worth of 17 percent, leaving them with 40 percent of the nation's household wealth. During the next few years their share would rise beyond the previous high-water mark in the doomed year of 1929. In that surge, the gains of the richest 1 percent rose from 100 to 560 times that of the national average.

Thus the twentieth century ended with the top fifth of the American public earning eleven times as much as the bottom fifth, a gap significantly wider than in any other industrialized country. The disparity in part reflected a reduction by the 500 largest corporations of five million jobs, many of them transferred to low-wage foreign countries. With the paring down of the workforce, which helped corporations achieve record profits, unemployment rose to an official level of five percent by 2005. According to some experts, however, the true figure was anywhere from 13 to 35 percent in places where jobs had become so scarce that many cast-off workers were too discouraged to look for positions and so were not included in official unemployment figures. As for those still working, wages fell below the level of western European nations, while hours lengthened. During the 1950s and 1960s Americans generally worked shorter days than citizens in other industrial nations. By 2002 the situation had reversed to the point where the average American spent 350 more hours on the job per year than the typical European—the equivalent of nearly nine extra work weeks.

Not surprisingly, the situation of longer hours and dwindling purchasing power within a workplace setting of mergers, layoffs, and outsourcing produced stress. As the twenty-first century got underway, the American Institute of Stress, its very existence a clear symptom of anxious times, estimated that workplace stress was costing the nation more than $300 billion a year in health care, missed work, and the expense of stress reduction programs. Polling and other measurements of the happiness Americans were supposed to pursue were consistent, albeit necessarily subjective, in showing a decline in contentment and confidence.

This turn of events made a mockery of Henry Wallace's claim that the twentieth century was the Century of the Common Man and bolstered charges that the New Deal was a flawed or futile attempt to overcome the limitations of the American system of government and of the public it was meant to serve. The more apocalyptic critics have seen the future in terms of end points: *The End of Liberalism, The End of Reform, The End of Affluence, The Jobless Future, The Rise and Fall of the New Deal Order, Class War in America, The Coming Class War and How to Avoid It, The Great Betrayal,* and *Dark Age Ahead,* to name a few examples of what one critic has called "terminal visions."

The situation appears brighter when one considers the New Deal goal of equal opportunity, spearheaded by Eleanor Roosevelt's tireless efforts on behalf of civil rights and the advancement of women. Drawing on the massive civil rights changes that the New Deal launched, women have been most successful among disadvantaged groups in improving their status. While the earnings of men overall have fallen since 1970, women at all levels of education have risen in pay and opportunity, and their entry into both blue- and white-collar positions formerly closed to them has steadily escalated.

African Americans, who have suffered most from discrimination, gained ground as well. In the aftermath of the Voting Rights Act of 1965, black representation in Congress rose from three in 1964 to forty in 1995. Income increased alongside influence, creating a significantly expanded black middle class. In the mid-1960s a scant 5 percent of black households had incomes over $50,000; by 1993 the number had risen to 15 percent. Across the entire spectrum, earnings of black men rose from only 43 percent of whites in 1940 to 73 percent by 1980. African Americans also showed improvement in education, included in Roosevelt's "second bill of rights" as the traditional hallmark of American social mobility. Though only 45 percent of African Americans in the 1920s and 1930s graduated from high school, their children's graduation rate rose to 75 percent by 1991, not very far below the 83 percent achieved by whites.

Other than the relatively small portion who moved up into the middle class, however, blacks and Hispanics have been slow to escape the old racist and socioeconomic traps. Because they have served disproportionately in blue-collar ranks, the ups and downs of industrial manufacturing have most severely affected their fortunes. From the end of World War II to the early 1970s, a period in which the working class saw palpable gains, black and Hispanic income rose and their numbers beneath the poverty line shrank accordingly. Since then, however, the U-turn to falling wages, as high-wage manufacturing jobs for workers disappeared, has blighted that advance. Between 1999 and 2001 both Hispanics and blacks lost nearly 27 percent of their net worth. Although both groups regained some of their wealth in the subsequent recovery, the Pew Hispanic Center reported in 2004 that at the end of 2002 median white household worth was 11 times greater than that of Hispanics and more than 14 times that of blacks.

The division between most Americans and an upper-income elite that burgeoned after 1980 signaled a reversal of the New Deal ethos. Rather than viewing economic regulation, taxes, and welfare policy as ways of bringing Americans closer together on a plane of modest security, appeals to traditional self-reliance and distrust of collectivism led to the easement of controls on industry and the insistence that the dependency of welfare recipients on Great Society handouts meant that the poor were, in the words of Charles Murray's vehement attack on welfare, *Losing Ground* (1984). A decisive middle-class voting bloc, fearful that they also might be losing ground, heeded voices of regression. In 1981 their newly inaugurated choice for president, Ronald Reagan, could announce to an admiring public that both Franklin Roosevelt and Calvin Coolidge were his presidential models. Reagan's economic adviser Murray Weidenbaum explained the appeal of the long discredited and mocked Coolidge by declaring that America had enjoyed a great economic boom in the 1920s under Coolidge and that it was time for America to cut loose from welfare state inhibitions for another such fling.

Following Reagan's lead, subsequent Republican administrations shrewdly sought to include the legacy of the New Deal as a way of stabilizing a system that would funnel benefits upward to Coolidge admirers. In this reverse version of the welfare state, regulation was bent to favor large corporate mergers; compassion for the poor was redefined as a matter of releasing them from relief rolls into the beneficial "magic of the marketplace"; lower taxes, which most directly benefited the rich, were advertised as the best means to raise additional revenue that the government could use to aid the needy; and Keynesian fiscal policy was taken to mean adjusting interest rates so as to strike the optimal balance between economic growth and the maintenance of a 5-6 percent unemployment rate cal-

culated to minimize labor costs and thus increase corporate profits and investment returns with low inflation.

The reverse spin on the New Deal of "Reaganomics" coincided with the emergence of historian critics who, in their disenchantment with centralized power
and the perceived imperfections of the New Deal approach, advanced the case
that the social and economic views prevailing in the 1920s and the 1950s (what
a wag called "Eisenhooverism") were the norm for modern America and that
the New Deal, rather than effecting a permanent revolution, is best understood
as an aberration. The comparison only dealt with formulas for success, but the
nervous citizen might reasonably wonder whether, if Coolidge was the hero of
a booming economy and Hoover was truly the forgotten progressive and his approach reflective of the national norm, it wasn't evident that another economic
calamity was expected as part of the ongoing natural cycle.

Shadowed by such questions of what constituted sound policy and a logical progression of events, Americans entered the new millennium uncertain
whether the New Deal agenda would, or should, ever be completed. A third of
the nation remained below the poverty line "ill-housed, ill clothed, and ill-fed,"
and in the void left by the failure to reach the New Deal goal of universal health
coverage about 44 million persons—a seventh of the population—were without
medical insurance. At the bottom of the record gulf between rich and poor, those
falling fastest into poverty were children under the age of five. Among those a
little older, child labor with all its old miseries was again on the rise.

As the wealthy pulled away, the Common Man ideal flagged. Education as the
favored means of self-improvement was in decline, according to federal research
reports that showed almost half the public lacking in the literacy needed to meet
the social and vocational challenges confronting them. Independent farmers
and labor unions, the basic working-class components of the New Deal coalition, were unable to make much collective difference. Agribusiness continued
to drive family farms into bankruptcy; unions, facing legal challenges and the
transfer of jobs to cheap labor in the third world, suffered a decline in membership and influence. In fundamental violation of the New Deal prescription for
progress, American workers, even as they became the most productive in the
world, suffered a steady decline in their standard of living.

And yet, despite the crumbling of the New Deal coalition, the foundations of
the welfare state were still standing at the end of the century. Confidence that
there were apt means for building a cooperative commonwealth upon them was
lacking, however. As E. J. Dionne summed it up in his study of *Why Americans
Hate Politics* (1991), the public in large measure had come to look on the federal

government as an island of special privilege in a sea of disorder and economic troubles. Regulatory agencies, the fruit of progressive reform energy, wore the aspect of training grounds to supply private companies with experts who had learned to evade or control agency policy. Electoral politics increasingly were dominated by money, class privilege, and special interests. Half or more of eligible voters, especially those at the lowest socioeconomic level, found no good reason for going to the polls.

The grip of the new elite seemed strong, but as the twenty-first century got underway, cracks appeared in the facade. Doubts about the true worth of the technology sector, promoted as the key to America's economic boom, led to a shocking decline in the value of computer, internet, and biotech stocks. Between March 2000 and the following April, the NASDAQ exchange, centered on technology, lost two-thirds of its value. Shaken by that decline, the New York Stock Exchange also suffered a sharp decline. Then the suicide attack on the World Trade Center on September 11, 2001, signaled that the United States was a target of foreign enemies and sent the stock market downward in the steepest single-week loss since 1933. Overall, the economic slump from early 2000 to the end of 2001 resulted in vanished equity equal to a greater amount of Gross Domestic Product than was lost after the 1929 crash. Other similarities emerged. Investigators sifting through the wreckage of bankrupt companies discovered fraudulent practices akin to those used in the Roaring Twenties to present a false picture of assets and earnings. Buffeted by the threat of further terrorist attacks and a corporate financial system of dubious integrity, the public lost confidence in those who promised rising prosperity. They could still cling to the remaining New Deal safeguards, yet who could blame them for doubting Roosevelt's words that all they had to fear was fear itself?

In the wake of the close reelection of George W. Bush in 2004, the question intensified as to how much better the plutocratic blend of skewed wealth and a government run by businessmen and those who owed their election to rich contributors would fare than its counterpart in the 1920s. While conducting a war in Iraq and presiding over the largest federal expenditures in history, the Bush administration pursued objectives that mirrored the tax and welfare policies of the 1920s. Just as Coolidge's treasury secretary, Andrew Mellon, argued that tax cuts for the rich would spur investment that would trickle down to the poor in the form of jobs, so, with the same promise of job creation, did the din of anti-tax rhetoric within Republican circles result in a proposal to reduce capital gains and corporate taxes, repeal the estate tax (disingenuously mislabeled the "death tax"), and slash income tax rates across the board. Analysts pointed out that the bill would result in everyone earning over $75,000 paying lower taxes, while the 49 percent of taxpayers making between $10,000 and $20,000 would receive no cut at all. One could appreciate the vastness of the disparity by realizing that there would be forty times as many taxpayers getting no benefit from the tax bill (including 2.5 million single parents with children at home) as millionaires, who in all would gain 44 percent of the tax cut total in 2005.

Alongside its tax policy, the Bush administration also offered a plan for returning to pre–New Deal self-reliance in the form of diverting a share of Social Security payroll taxes to individual investment accounts, contending, in an echo of the 1920s, that the stock market would bring higher rewards than a guaranteed government benefit. Partly in order to fund private accounts, the Bush administration proposed cuts in assured Social Security payments, arguing that current Social Security funding levels could not sustain the program, while also refusing to consider higher taxes to make up the shortfall. Given the facts that the average worker could only at present expect to receive $900 a month from Social Security upon retirement and that the average family headed by a worker between 55 and 64 years of age in 2002 had retirement savings with a monthly worth upon retirement of $408 a month, cuts in Social Security foreshadowed a future in which older Americans would slip back toward the end-of-life poverty that prevailed before Social Security was enacted.

Dire uncertainty had preceded the rise of Franklin Roosevelt in 1933 as the unexpected hero of a New Deal. How much further the Common Man had to sink in the new century before rallying to another reform champion was an open question. Yet all the elements of distress were in place that had in the past led to uniquely American moments of reform in order to reinvigorate hope in the nation's original promise of a free and equal commonwealth and the abundant pursuit of happiness.

Essay on Sources

PREFACE

Historians have generally seen the late nineteenth century as a period of consolidation. See, for example, Alan Trachtenberg, *The Incorporation of American Life*, and Robert Wiebe, *The Search for Order, 1877–1920* (1967) and *Self-Rule: A Cultural History of American Democracy* (1995), where Wiebe describes the creation of a professional and administrative class that favored expertise over democracy.

John Garraty in *The New Commonwealth, 1877–1890* (1968) argues instead that modern complexity required cooperation. Yet, as James L. Huston shows in *Securing the Fruits of Labor, 1765–1900* (1998), self-interested striving resulted in a widening division of wealth and privilege. To the dissenters from that inequality described by John L. Thomas in *Alternative America* (1983), cooperation was so central that Christopher Lasch could contend in *The New Radicalism in America, 1889–1963* (1965) that turning America into a cooperative commonwealth had become "the vision common to all" radicals.

Daniel Aaron, *Men of Good Hope* (1951) and David B. Danbom, *The World of Hope* (1987) sympathetically describe cooperative commonwealth thought. Revival of interest in the main thinkers is indicated by Toby Widdicombe and Herman S. Preiser, eds., *Revisiting the Legacy of Edward Bellamy* (2002); Rick Tilman, *Veblen's Century* (2002); Michael Spindler, *Veblen and Modern America* (2002); and Richard Digby-Junger, *The Journalist as Reformer: Henry Demarest Lloyd and Wealth Against Commonwealth* (1996). The populist movement, which gave the fullest political expression to the cooperative commonwealth ideal, once decried by Richard Hofstadter in *The Age of Reform* (1955) for its paranoid intolerance, has more recently been lamented for the loss of its democratic spirit by Lawrence Goodwyn, *Democratic Promise: The Populist Moment in America* (1976) and Michael Kazin, *The Populist Persuasion* (1995). A work of great importance in setting American democratic reform within a transatlantic context is Daniel T. Rodgers, *Atlantic Crossings* (1998).

INTRODUCTION

Arthur M. Schlesinger Jr. led the way for generally favorable accounts of the New Deal in *The Age of Roosevelt*, 3 vols. (1956–60). Carl Degler, in *Out of Our Past* (1959) and Mario Einaudi, *The Roosevelt Revolution* (1959) credit the New Deal with revolutionary change, while Eric Goldman, *Rendezvous with Destiny* (1952) and Richard Hofstadter, *The American Political Tradition* (1973) judge the New Deal as a flawed attempt to patch the prevailing system. The unsurpassed single volume summation, William E. Leuchtenburg, *Franklin D. Roosevelt and the New Deal, 1932–1940* (1963), offers a judicious appraisal by a committed liberal activist, while Paul Conkin in his brief *The New Deal* (1968) expresses disapproval of ethical looseness and muddled thinking.

The turn in the 1960s toward criticism of the New Deal for failing to take advantage of opportunities for radical change was best expressed in Barton J. Bernstein, "The New Deal: The Conservative Achievements of Liberal Reform," in his edited volume *Toward a New Past: Dissenting Essays in American History* (1967), pp. 263–88, and Ronald Radosh, "The Myth of the New Deal," in *A New History of Leviathan: Essays on the Rise of the American Corporate State* (1972), pp. 146–87. Jerold S. Auerbach defended the New Deal against radical revision in "New Deal, Old Deal, or Raw Deal: Some Thoughts on New Left Historiography," *Journal of Southern History* 35 (1960), pp. 18–30.

Among recent surveys, Anthony Badger, *The New Deal: The Depression Years, 1933–1940* (1989) is important both for its sensible coverage and for its thorough bibliographical essay. Notable briefer works include Roger Biles, *A New Deal for the American People* (1991); Ronald Edsforth, *The New Deal* (2000); and two collections of essays: Robert Eden, ed., *The New Deal and its Legacy* (1989) and Harvard Sitkoff, ed., *Fifty Years Later* (1985). The essays in Steve Fraser and Gary Gerstle, eds., *The Rise and Fall of the New Deal Order, 1930–1980* (1989) demonstrate the persistence of the leftist critique. Overshadowing all in massive comprehensiveness is David M. Kennedy, *Freedom from Fear* (1999).

William Leuchtenburg's argument for the continued centrality of the New Deal in his *In the Shadow of FDR* (2001) is countered by Alan Brinkley's lament for the decline of New Deal reform in his *Liberalism and Its Discontents* (1998). Hopeful social scientists, including Sidney M. Milkis in *Political Parties and Constitutional Government; Remaking American Democracy* (1999) and, with Jerome M. Mileur as coeditor, *The New Deal and the Triumph of Liberalism* (2002); Stephen Skowronek and Karen Orren in *The Search for American Political Development* (2004); and David Plotke in *Building a Democratic Political Order* (1996) focus on the New Deal as a model for modern political practice.

CHAPTER 1. PRELUDE

Ellis Hawley in *The Great War and the Search for a Modern Order* (1979) describes the 1920s from the standpoint of efforts to develop efficient means of coordinating government and private institutions. Most other texts stress disorder: William Leuchtenburg, *The Perils of Prosperity*; Stanley Coben, *Reform, War, and Reaction, 1912–1932* (1973); David J. Goldberg, *Discontented America* (1999); and Michael Parrish, *Anxious Decades* (1992).

John Kenneth Galbraith, *The Great Crash* (1960) and Gordon Thomas, *The Day the Bubble Burst: A Social History of the Wall Street Crash of 1929* (1979) are especially readable.

To explain the Crash, Milton Friedman and Anna Schwartz in *The Great Contraction, 1929–33* (1963) argue that the economic woes of that time resulted from a drastic lack of currency because of a shortage of gold backing and restrictive Federal Reserve policies. Peter Temin in *Did Monetary Forces Cause the Great Depression?* (1979) contends that the real problem was maldistribution of wealth leading to the inability of the general public to consume enough to sustain the economy. Starting with Charles Kindleberger, *The World in Depression, 1929–1939* (1973), economists have compared America with other countries. Barry Eichengreen in *Golden Fetters: The Gold Standard and the Great Depression, 1919–1939* (1992) concludes that international forces other than sound money were key. On the other hand, Ben S. Bernanke in "Macroeconomics of the Great Depression," in his edited volume *Essays on the Great Depression* (2000), endorses a consensus view that money had a key role to play, whether from scarcity or lack of consumer purchasing power. Michael Bernstein in *The Great Depression: Delayed Recovery and Economic Change in America, 1929–1939* (1987) offers yet another view, that recovery was slow because the Depression retarded the development of key new industries. Whatever strategy might have been called for, James Prothro's analysis of the pronouncements of the National Association of Manufacturers and the Chamber of Commerce during the 1920s in *The Dollar Decade* (1954) indicates that the business establishment's rigid concepts ill equipped it to adapt successfully to any radical change.

Valuable overall accounts of the Depression include John Garraty, *The Great Depression* (1987); Lester V. Chandler, *America's Greatest Depression* (1970); and two accounts by Peter Fearon, *The Origins and Nature of the Great Slump, 1929–1932* (1979) and *War, Prosperity, and Depression: U.S. Economy, 1917–1945* (1987). James R. McGovern's *And a Time for Hope* (2000) insists that low expectations and communal cooperation enabled Americans to weather Depression hardships.

Radical critic Edmund Wilson's reports from his travels around the country, collected in *American Earthquake* (1952), did not include much in the way of self-help optimism. The recovery of oral testimony from the times by Tom Terrill and Jerrold Hirsch, *Such as Us: Southern Voices of the Thirties* (1978); Ann Banks, *First-Person America* (1980); and John F. Bauman and Thomas H. Coode, *In the Eye of the Great Depression* (1988) resemble Wilson in revealing mostly bitterness and despair. Bernard Sternsher, *Hitting Home* (1970) shows growing anger over Hoover's inaction, which the New Deal changed to *Hope Restored* (1999). Charles Alexander in *Nationalism in American Thought, 1930–1945* (1969) adds that recovery efforts stimulated a resurgence of national pride. The letters to Roosevelt collected by Robert S. McElvaine in *Down and Out in the Great Depression* (1983) and Lawrence W. Levine and Cornelia P. Levine in *The People and the President* (2002) display gratitude and hopefulness. Accordingly, McElvaine's survey, *The Great Depression in America* (1984), shows a feeling for the common life. T. H. Watkins also conveys basic realities and personal stories in *The Great Depression in the 1930s* (1993) and *The Hungry Years* (1999).

Herbert Hoover in his *Memoirs: The Great Depression, 1929–1941* (1951) attributes the crisis to foreign economic instability. Joan Hoff Wilson, *Herbert Hoover: Forgotten Progressive* (1975) presents Hoover as a progressive activist. In contrast, John Gerring, *Party Ideologies in America, 1828–1996* (1998) holds that Hoover moved the Republican Party from activism to favoring governmental restraint. Biographers who see Hoover as a reluctant progressive include David Burner, *Herbert Hoover: a Public Life* (1979) and Herbert Fausold, *The Presidency of Herbert Hoover* (1985). George Nash presents Hoover as a man of the right in *The Life of Herbert Hoover*, 3 vols. (1983). Ellis Hawley in J. Joseph Hutmacher and Warren Susman, eds., *Herbert Hoover and the Crisis of American Capitalism* (1973) and in his own edited volume *Herbert Hoover as Secretary of Commerce* (1981) offers the most insightful appreciation of Hoover's concept of voluntary association between government and business. William H. Mullins in *The Depression and the Urban West Coast, 1929–1933* (1991) finds that "cooperative individualism" to have been ineffective in meeting urban problems. The best study of Hoover's farm policy, David E. Hamilton, *From New Day to New Deal* (1991), sees Hoover's version of cooperative agriculture leaving farmers with little to share but misery.

CHAPTER 2. THE SHAPING OF FRANKLIN ROOSEVELT

Frank Freidel's four-volume biography, *Franklin D. Roosevelt* (1952–73), ends just after Roosevelt begins his presidency. Freidel's far briefer overview, *Franklin D. Roosevelt: A Rendezvous with Destiny* (1990), covers his entire life. James MacGregor Burns in *Roosevelt: The Lion and the Fox* (1956) contends that more forthright lion and less devious fox would have enabled Roosevelt to advance the cause of progressive democracy further.

Kenneth S. Davis, in his five-part biography, *F.D.R.* (1971–2000) regrets that the earnest but unreflective young Roosevelt never did develop an ability to inquire deeply enough to develop a viable plan for the postwar world. So, too, Rexford Tugwell, in *The Democratic Roosevelt* (1957) and *In Search of Roosevelt* (1972) conveys appreciation of Roosevelt's tactical genius along with ruefulness that Roosevelt did not plan more systematically. Journalist Joseph Alsop, Roosevelt's cousin and a member of his social circle, gives a plausible firsthand interpretation of Roosevelt's outlook and career in *FDR, 1882–1945: A Centenary Remembrance* (1982). Geoffrey C. Ward combines a full account of Roosevelt's public career with a probing appraisal of Roosevelt's family history in *Before the Trumpet* (1985) and *A First Class Temperament* (1989). Other worthy biographies include Ted Morgan, *FDR: A Biography* (1985); Conrad Black, *Franklin Delano Roosevelt: Champion of Freedom* (2003); and Patrick Maney, *The Roosevelt Presence* (1992). Two works that make clear the lifelong mental and physical toll of Roosevelt's polio affliction are Richard T. Goldberg, *The Making of Franklin D. Roosevelt: Triumph over Disability* (1981) and Hugh Gregory Gallagher, *FDR's Splendid Deception* (1985).

Eleanor Roosevelt's frank autobiographies *This is My Story* (1937) and *This I Remember* (1949) are a good starting point for understanding her role. Joseph P. Lash provides the most affecting account of Eleanor Roosevelt's troubled childhood and difficult marriage in *Eleanor and Franklin* (1971). The central biography is Blanche Wiesen Cook's two-volume study, *Eleanor Roosevelt* (1992, 1999). Susan Ware provides valuable information about the political milieu in *Beyond Suffrage: Women in the New Deal* (1981), *Holding Their Own: American Women in the 1930s* (1982), and *Partner and*

I: *Molly Dewson, Feminism, and New Deal Politics* (1987). Robyn Muncy, *Creating a Female Dominion in American Reform; 1890–1935* (1991); Kristi Andersen, *After Suffrage: Women in Partisan and Electoral Politics before the New Deal* (1996); and Suzanne Mettler, *Dividing Citizens: Gender and Federalism in New Deal Public Policy* (1998) add important dimensions.

Helpful works relating to aspects of Franklin Roosevelt's early development are Frank D. Ashburn, *Fifty Years of Groton School* (1934); Alfred Rollins, *Roosevelt and Howe* (1962, 2002); and Robert Wesser in *A Response to Progressivism: The Democratic Party and New York Politics, 1902–1918* (1986). David Burner, *The Politics of Provincialism: The Democratic Party In Transition, 1918–1932* (1968) effectively portrays a party whose urban outreach was obstructed by an older rural base. The importance of Al Smith in overcoming that provincialism is clarified in Oscar Handlin, *Al Smith and His America* (1987); Paula Eldot, *Governor Alfred E. Smith: The Politician as Reformer* (1983); Donn C. Neal, *The World beyond the Hudson: Alfred E. Smith and National Politics, 1918–1928* (1983); and Robert A. Slayton, *Empire Statesman: The Rise and Redemption of Al Smith* (2001). David Sarasohn, *The Party of Reform: Democrats in the Progressive Era* (1989) argues that the Democrats, rather than Republicans, were the main agents of Progressive change.

CHAPTER 3. LANDSLIDE

Steve Neal, *Happy Days Are Here Again* (2004) shows how narrowly Roosevelt managed to gain the nomination. Kristi Andersen in *The Creation of a Democratic Majority, 1928–1936* (1979) explains that Democratic victory was mainly due to new voters, many of them recent immigrants. John M. Allswang astutely analyzes the politics of the new coalition in *The New Deal and American Politics* (1978).

The Bonus Army incident is well covered in two contrasting accounts: Roger Daniels, *The Bonus March* (1971), which excoriates Hoover's handling of the event, and Donald J. Lisio, *The President and Protest* (1994), which shifts the blame from Hoover to MacArthur for going against the president's orders.

Rexford Tugwell loyally describes the formation and function of Roosevelt's closest advisers in *The Brains Trust* (1968), while Raymond Moley looks back with disillusionment in *After Seven Years* (1939) and *The First New Deal* (1966). Bernard Sternsher, *Rexford Tugwell and the New Deal* (1964), and Michael Namorato, *Rexford Tugwell: a Biography* (1988) supplemented by Namorato's edition of *The Diary of Rexford G. Tugwell* (1992), defend Tugwell's role. Jordan A. Schwarz has contributed three valuable works: *The Interregnum of Despair* (1970); *Liberal: Adolf A. Berle and the Vision of an American Era* (1987); and *The New Dealers* (1993). Elliot A. Rosen in *Hoover, Roosevelt, and the Brains Trust* (1977) agrees that the change of administrations was beneficial. Clyde P. Weed, *The Nemesis of Reform: The Republican Party during the New Deal* (1994) emphasizes the weak disorganization of the Republicans in 1932 and their gradual shaping of an effective opposition. Albert U. Romasco in *The Politics of Recovery* (1983) reveals the business establishment's opposition to state capitalism and economic planning that doomed New Deal attempts to cooperate with business, while

Theodore Rosenof in *Dogma, Depression, and the New Deal* (1975) explains how New Dealers' own inhibitions balked democratic planning.

Marion Clawson, *New Deal Planning: The National Resources Planning Board* (1981) credits the NRPB with being an "idea stimulator." Planning precedents are explained in Patrick D. Reagan, *Designing a New America* (2000), and Otis Graham, *Toward a Planned Society* (1976) adds discussion of planning after the New Deal.

The cross-purposes that stymied Congress and state governments are explained in James T. Patterson, *Congressional Conservatism and the New Deal* (1967) and *The New Deal and the States* (1969); John Braeman, Robert H. Bremner, and David Brody, eds., *The State and Local Levels* (1975); and Anthony J. Badger, "The New Deal and the Localities" in Rhodri Jeffreys-Jones and Bruce Collins, eds., *The Growth of Federal Power in American History* (1983). Ronald L. Feinman, *Twilight of Progressivism* (1981) and Ronald Mulder, *The Insurgent Progressives in the United States Senate and the New Deal, 1933–1939* (1979) point out that New Deal state capitalism and planning also alienated many progressives.

The claim in George McJimsey, *The Presidency of Franklin Delano Roosevelt* (2000) that Roosevelt had a "vision of a cooperative pluralism" is buttressed in Sean J. Savage, *Roosevelt: The Party Leader, 1932–1945* (1991); Philip Abbott, *The Exemplary Presidency* (1990); and Robert Eden, ed., *The New Deal and its Legacy* (1989). Betty Houchin Winfield in *FDR and the New Media* (1990) gives a favorable account of Roosevelt's tactical success in projecting an inspiring image, while Richard W. Steele in *Propaganda in an Open Society* (1985) decries that success for its slanted presentations and intimidation of newsmen.

CHAPTER 4. THE STRUGGLE FOR FINANCIAL STABILITY

Herbert Stein's central work on *The Fiscal Revolution in America* (1969, 1996) argues that the New Deal deliberately engaged in "fiscal drift," and E. Cary Brown, "Fiscal Policy in the Thirties: A Reappraisal," *American Economic Review* 46 (1956) agrees that drift kept New Deal fiscal policy too weak to effect full recovery. Perry G. Mehrling in *The Money Interest and the Public Interest* (1997) sees greater purposiveness in the institutionalist economists who guided monetary thought toward fiscal policy. Michael D. Bordo, Claudia Goldin, and Eugene N. White, eds. *The Defining Moment: The Great Depression and the American Economy in the Twentieth Century* (1998) describe how the shock of Depression changed economic behavior. Alonzo L. Hamby in *For the Survival of Democracy: Franklin Roosevelt and the World Crisis of the 1930s* (2004) goes further in arguing that the Depression was the defining event of the twentieth century, to which Great Britain and Germany responded more effectively than the United States.

The key works on emergency banking reforms are Susan Estabrook Kennedy, *The Banking Crisis of 1933* (1973) and Helen M. Burns, *The American Banking Community and New Deal Banking Reforms, 1933–1935* (1974). Michael Parrish, *Securities Regulation and the New Deal* (1970) astutely covers reform of the stock market. Regarding the World Economic Conference, Robert Dallek, *Franklin D. Roosevelt and American*

Foreign Policy, 1932–1945 (1979) and Arthur Schlesinger, *The Coming of the New Deal* (1958) credit Roosevelt with a wish to find international accord that was thwarted by lack of European cooperation. Moley, Hamby, and Kindleberger agree that Roosevelt missed an opportunity to foster recovery through stabilizing the international monetary system. Patricia Clavin, *The Failure of Economic Diplomacy: Britain, Germany, France, and the United States, 1931–1936* (1996) sees that botched diplomacy as an object lesson that led to a viable international system after World War II.

CHAPTER 5. THE RECOVERY OF INDUSTRY

Senator George Norris of Nebraska explains in his autobiography *Fighting Liberal* (1945) that the TVA was the core of his public life, and Richard Lowitt, *George W. Norris*, 3 vols. (1963–78) shows the accuracy of Norris's claim. Divergent views, however, plagued the project. TVA co-director Arthur Morgan in *The Making of the TVA* (1974) and Roy Talbert in *FDR's Utopian: Arthur Morgan of the TVA* (1987) indicate how Edward Bellamy's utopian thought inspired Morgan's vision of remaking the Tennessee Valley. In *TVA: Democracy on the March* (1944, 1977), David Lilienthal stresses the significance of the TVA as an experiment in grassroots democracy. Lilienthal's career as an evangelist for public power is well told in Steven M. Neuse, *David E. Lilienthal: The Journey of an American Liberal* (1996). Philip Selznick, *TVA and the Grass Roots* (1949, 1966) and Erwin C. Hargrove, *Prisoners of Myth: The Leadership of the Tennessee Valley Authority, 1933–1990* (1994) describe how the TVA evolved from a grassroots ideal into a hierarchical federal agency. Thomas K. McCraw, *TVA and the Power Fight, 1933–1939* (1971); North Callahan, *TVA: Bridge over Troubled Waters* (1980); and Walter L. Creese, *TVA's Public Planning: The Vision, the Reality* (1990) agree that the TVA has been beneficial despite the displacement of traditional culture deplored by Michael J. McDonald and John Muldowny in *TVA and the Dispossessed* (1982) and Jane S. Becker in *Selling Tradition: Appalachia and the Construction of an American Folk, 1930–1940* (1998). Philip Fungiello, *Toward a National Power Policy* (1973) charts TVA's vast technological effect. For a spirited defense of New Deal energy and conservation policy, see Henry L. Henderson and David B. Woolner, eds., *FDR and the Environment* (2005).

Gerard Swope's idea for government-business cooperation is well recounted in David Loth, *Swope of GE* (1958). Ellis Hawley, *The New Deal and the Problem of Monopoly* (1966) is the primary account of the troubled NRA that followed. Bernard Bellush, *The Failure of the NRA* (1975) and Robert Himmelberg, *The Origins of the National Recovery Administration* (1976) echo Hawley's contention that business used NRA ineptness to advance selfish interests, while Donald R. Brand in *Corporatism and the Rule of Law* (1988) provides a meticulous refinement of ousted NRA chief Hugh Johnson's contention in *The Blue Eagle from Egg to Earth* (1935, 1968) that NRA troubles stemmed from the unwillingness of business leaders to sacrifice for the common good. John K. Ohl, *Hugh S. Johnson and the New Deal* (1985) credits Johnson's claim but cannot help revealing his hero's erratic flaws.

The aspect of the NRA devoted to relief projects is best approached through Harold Ickes. *The Secret Diaries of Harold Ickes* (1953) must be used with skeptical awareness of Ickes's penchant for special pleading. Graham White, *Harold Ickes of the New Deal: His Private Life and Public Career* (1985) dwells more on Ickes's psychological quirks than on his public career. Most thorough is T. H. Watkins, *Righteous Pilgrim: The Life and Times of Harold L. Ickes, 1874–1952* (1990).

On the militant reform spirit of labor and its allies, see the empathetic accounts by Irving Bernstein, *The Turbulent Years* (1970) and *A Caring Society* (1985). Melvyn Dubofsky's collection of essays, *Hard Work: The Making of Labor History* (2000), shows a wide variety of labor responses to the Depression that were not always caring or turbulent. Three works on linked business and political attempts to co-opt labor law and contain union activity are Christopher L. Tomlins, *The State and the Unions* (1985); Colin Gordon, *New Deal: Business, Labor, and Politics in America, 1920–1935* (1994); and Ruth O'Brien, *Workers' Paradox: The Republican Origins of New Deal Labor Policy, 1886–1935* (1998).

Staughton Lynd, ed., *"We Are All Leaders"* (1996) touts democratic union militancy. In contrast, Elizabeth Faue, *Community of Suffering and Struggle: Women, Men, and the Labor Movement in Minneapolis, 1915–1945* (1991) laments that the all-out labor wars of 1934 broke down older community patterns in favor of desperate union struggle. Lizabeth Cohen in *Making a New Deal: Industrial Workers in Chicago, 1919–1939* (1990) tells a similar story of labor strife undermining ethnic community life. Labor insurgency and community on the West Coast in 1934 are vividly described in Kevin Starr, *Endangered Dreams* (1996).

The effects of mill owner paternalism and the New Deal reluctance to challenge it are well covered in James A. Hodges, *New Deal Labor Policy and the Southern Cotton Textile Industry, 1933–1941* (1986); Janet Irons, *Testing the New Deal: The General Textile Strike of 1934 in the American South* (2000); and G. C. Waldrep, *Southern Workers and the Search for Community* (2000). John A. Salmond in *The General Textile Strike of 1934* (2002) takes consolation from the way strikers recognized that the New Deal was not the enemy and in *Southern Struggles: The Southern Labor Movement and the Civil Rights Struggle* (2004) tells of the partial victory workers gained in the 1960s. For the effect of radical "outside agitators" on black hopes, see Robin D. G. Kelley, *Hammer and Hoe: Alabama Communists during the Great Depression* (1990).

J. Joseph Hutmacher, *Senator Robert F. Wagner and the Rise of Urban Liberalism* (1968) and Daniel Nelson, "The Other New Deal and Labor: The Regulatory State and the Unions, 1933–1940," *Journal of Policy History* (2001) describe the balance that was struck during the rise of labor in the 1930s between bottom-up union activism and top-down government regulation. The transition from the NRA attempt to secure union rights to the Wagner Act is closely examined in James A. Gross, *The Making of the National Labor Relations Board* (1974).

CHAPTER 6. SAVING THE FARMS

Theodore Saloutos, *The American Farmer and the New Deal* (1972) traces New Deal farm policy from its roots in the 1920s. The growth and success of the farm lobby are well told in John Mark Hansen, *Gaining Access: Congress and the Farm Lobby, 1919–*

1981 (1991) and Christiana McFadyen Campbell, *The Farm Bureau* (1962). Elegies for the family farm are given by Dennis S. Nordin and Roy V. Scott, *From Prairie Farmer to Entrepreneur: The Transformation of Midwestern Agriculture* (2005) and Jack Temple Kirby, *Rural Worlds Lost* (1987). Partial success for New Deal conservation policy is recounted in Tim Lehman, *Public Values, Private Lands, 1933–1985* (1995) and Richard Lowitt, *The New Deal and the West* (1984). New Deal efforts to prop up the agricultural economy are described in William D. Rowley, *M. L. Wilson and the Campaign for the Domestic Allotment* (1971); Van L. Perkins, *Crisis in Agriculture: The Agricultural Adjustment Administration and the New Deal, 1933* (1969); and Richard S. Kirkendall, *Social Scientists and Farm Politics in the Age of Roosevelt* (1967). The cornerstone biography by Edward L. Schapsmeier, *Henry A. Wallace of Iowa: The Agrarian Years, 1910–1940* (1968), is usefully supplemented by John C. Culver and John Hyde, *American Dreamer: The Life and Times of Henry A. Wallace* (2000); Graham White and John Maze, *Henry A. Wallace: His Search for a New World Order* (1995); and Mark L. Kleinman, *A World of Hope, a World of Fear* (2000). Insurgencies wanting more drastic action than the New Deal offered are described in John L. Shover, *Cornbelt Rebellion: The Farmers' Holiday Association* (1965) and Lowell K. Dyson, *Red Harvest: The Communist Party and American Farmers* (1982).

Persistent hardship beyond the reach of New Deal policies is explored in Paul E. Mertz, *New Deal Policy and Southern Rural Poverty* (1978) and David E. Conrad, *The Forgotten Farmers: The Story of the Share-Croppers in the New Deal* (1965). A failed attempt of sharecroppers to organize an escape from misery is poignantly told in Donald H. Grubbs, *Cry from the Cotton: The Southern Farm Tenants' Union and the New Deal* (1971) and by one of their own in H. L. Mitchell, *Mean Things Happening in This Land* (1979). Paul Conkin's *Tomorrow a New World* (1959) is an enlightening study of the effort by the Farm Security Administration to build model communities for displaced farmers.

CHAPTER 7. LAUNCHING THE WELFARE STATE

The persistence of hardship is revealed in James T. Patterson, *America's Struggle against Poverty, 1900–1980* (1981) and Walter Trattner, *From Poor Law to Welfare State: A History of Social Welfare* (1999). Donald S. Howard describes a breakthrough in *The WPA and Federal Relief Policy* (1943; 1973), and Harry Hopkins explains his view of work relief as an investment in people in *Spending to Save* (1936). Sympathetic portraits of Hopkins are provided in Searle F. Charles, *Minister of Relief* (1963); Paul A. Kurzman, *Harry Hopkins and the New Deal* (1974); and George T. McJimsey, *Harry Hopkins: Ally of the Poor and Defender of Democracy* (1987). Hopkins's granddaughter June Hopkins in *Harry Hopkins: Sudden Hero, Brash Reformer* (1999) dwells on Hopkins's early years. Jeff Singleton in *The American Dole* (2000) intelligently amplifies the finding in Daniel Nelson, *Unemployment Insurance; The American Experience, 1915–1935* (1969) and Udo Sautter, *Three Cheers for the Unemployed* (1991) that relief programs derived from progressive efforts, as against the social control thesis advanced by Frances Fox Piven and Richard Cloward in *Regulating the Poor* (1971). The two most popular relief programs receive favorable coverage in Bonnie Fox Schwartz, *The Civil Works Administration, 1933–1934* (1984); John Salmond, *The Civilian Conservation Corps, 1933–1942* (1967); and Edwin G. Hill, *In the Shadow of the Mountain: The Spirit of the CCC* (1990).

Daniel Rodgers, *Atlantic Crossings* (1998) illuminatingly compares the patchwork inadequacy of America's welfare approach to comprehensive European systems. Theda Scocpol in *Protecting Soldiers and Mothers: The Political Origins of Social Policy in the United States* (1992) argues that American welfare evolved from pensions given to Civil War veterans. In contrast, Roy Lubove in *The Struggle for Social Security, 1900–1935* (1968) and *The Professional Altruist* (1983); James Leiby, *A History of Social Welfare and Social Work in the United States* (1978); and David A. Moss, *Socializing Security: Progressive-Era Economists and the Origins of American Social Policy* (1996) attribute the genesis of welfare policy to a loose reform coalition. Linda Gordon in *Pitied But Not Entitled: Single Mothers and the History of Welfare, 1890–1935* (1994) and Alice Kessler-Harris, *In Pursuit of Equity* (2001) provide crucial understanding of how gender and racial discrimination affected welfare law and practice. William Graebner, *A History of Retirement* (1980) adds a stark picture of what the life of the retired was before 1935. Edward Berkowitz and Kim McQuaid in *Creating the Welfare State* (1980) assert that business and government bureaucrats used commercial life insurance as the model for Social Security. Jennifer Klein, *For All These Rights: Business, Labor, and the Shaping of America's Public Private Welfare State* (2004) extends that view to explain how the insurance industry and the American Hospital Association devised private health plans that derailed New Deal hopes for public health insurance. William R. Brock, *Welfare, Democracy, and the New Deal* (1988) adds an incisive discussion of the many ways the states forced the New Deal to settle for meager welfare measures.

CHAPTER 8. REVIVAL OF THE SPIRIT

Recollections by two important social critics, Matthew Josephson, *Infidel in the Temple: A Memoir of the Nineteen-Thirties* (1967) and Malcolm Cowley, *The Dream of the Golden Mountains* (1980), explain the excitement intellectuals and artists felt about new opportunities in the Depression. Within the general public novelist Sherwood Anderson in *Puzzled America* (1935) finds anxious uncertainty. The search for cultural revival by artists and ordinary citizens alike is explored in Richard H. Pells, *Radical Visions and American Dreams* (1973); Charles Alexander, *Here the Country Lies* (1980); David Peeler, *Hope Among Us Yet* (1987); Michael Denning, *The Cultural Front* (1996); Laura Browder, *Rousing the Nation: Radical Culture in Depression America* (1998); and Michael Szalay, *New Deal Modernism* (2000). Roosevelt's use of cultural symbolism to foster commitment to the New Deal is explained in Alfred Haworth Jones, *Roosevelt's Image Brokers: Poets, Playwrights, and the Use of the Lincoln Symbol* (1974).

Use of U.S. Treasury funds to commission artworks is recounted in Marlene Park and Gerald Markowitz, *Democratic Vistas: Post Offices and Public Art in the New Deal*

(1984); Karal Ann Marling, *Wall to Wall Art* (1982); and Belasario R. Contreras, *Tradition and Innovation in New Deal Art* (1983). William F. McDonald in *Federal Relief Administration and the Arts* (1969) exhaustively summarizes the WPA Arts Project. Milton Meltzer, *Violins and Shovels: The WPA Arts Projects* (1976) gives an intelligently condensed overview, to which Jonathan Harris adds cogent interpretation in *Federal Art and National Culture* (1995). Histories of each subset include, for painters and sculptors, Richard McKinzie, *The New Deal for Artists* (1973) and Francis O'Connor, *Art for the Millions* (1973); for writers, Jerre Mangione, *The Dream and the Deal* (1972) and Monty N. Penkower, *The Federal Writer's Project* (1977); for music, Kenneth J. Bindas, *All of This Music Belongs to the Nation* (1969); and for the theatre project, Jane DeHart Matthews, *The Federal Theater, 1935–1939* (1967); E. Quita Craig, *Black Drama of the Federal Theater Era* (1980); and a spirited memoir by the project director, Hallie Flanagan, *Arena* (1940).

The New Deal use of film is favorably described in Robert L. Snyder, *Pare Lorentz and the Documentary Film* (1968); Richard Dyer McCann, *The People's Films: A Political History of U.S. Government Motion Pictures* (1973); and Garth Jowett, *Film: The Democratic Art* (1976). William L. Stott, *Documentary Expression and Thirties America* (1973) is the fundamental account of that genre. Roy Stryker, with Nancy Wood, offers a well-chosen collection of Farm Security Administration photographs in *In This Proud Land* (1973), and the significance of FSA photography is discussed in James Curtis, *Mind's Eye, Mind's Truth: FSA Photography Reconsidered* (1989) and Maren Stange, *Symbols of Ideal Life* (1989).

CHAPTER 9. RENEWING THE NEW DEAL LEASE

The meager gains for African Americans are described with varying degrees of criticism for the New Deal in Harvard Sitkoff, *A New Deal for Blacks* (1978); Nancy Weiss, *Farewell to the Party of Lincoln: Black Politics in the Age of FDR* (1983); and Patricia Sullivan, *Days of Hope: Race and Democracy in the New Deal Era* (1996). New Deal revision of Indian policy is well set out in Graham D. Taylor, *The New Deal and American Indian Tribalism* (1980). Christine Bolt in *American Indian Policy and American Reform* (1987) situates Native American issues within a larger progressive framework. And Donald L. Fixico, in *The Invasion of Indian Country in the Twentieth Century* (1998) critically analyzes the effects of capitalism on Indian autonomy.

Stephen W. Baskerville, *Of Laws and Limitations: An Intellectual Portrait of Louis Dembitz Brandeis* (1994); Nelson Lloyd Dawson, *Louis D. Brandeis, Felix Frankfurter, and the New Deal* (1980); and Michael E. Parrish, *Felix Frankfurter and His Times* (1982) describe Frankfurter's role in promoting Brandeis's views and staffing the New Deal. The troubled career of Frankfurter's protégé, James Landis, director of the SEC, is sensitively related in Thomas McCraw, *Prophets of Regulation* (1984). Two other key Frankfurter protégés have recently received their biographical due in William Lasser, *Benjamin V. Cohen: Architect of the New Deal* (2002) and David McKean, *Tommy the Cork* (2004). Joseph P. Lash in *Dealers and Dreamers* (1988) adds insider detail from interviews and friendship with Cohen and Corcoran.

W. Elliot Brownlee, *Federal Taxation in America: A Short History* (2004) offers a useful overview, and Mark Leff in *The Limits of Symbolic Reform* (1984) criticizes inequities in the Wealth Tax and the payroll tax system for funding Social Security. David Beito takes a similarly negative position in *Taxpayers in Revolt* (1989), while Brian R. Sala in *Partisan Politics in the New Deal Era: Essays on Income Taxation* (1994) explains how contention within political circles minimized the degree to which taxes of any sort could be imposed.

Samuel Lubell, *The Future of American Politics* (1952) broke new ground by arguing that the election of 1936 signaled a shift from Republican to Democratic national dominance. Lyle W. Dorsett, *Franklin D. Roosevelt and the City Bosses* (1977) finds that Roosevelt was successful but sometimes at the cost of using dubious tactics. Martin Shefter in *Political Parties and the State* (1994) explains how fitting alliances with the left into the Democratic Party framework created a coalition that gave the poor and marginalized power for the first time to defeat old-guard wealth and status.

Organized labor's role in fundraising and voter turnout is explained in J. David Greenstone, *Labor in American Politics* (1977) and Ruth Horowitz, *Political Ideologies of Organized Labor* (1978). New Deal ties with urban ethnic political machines are analyzed in Bruce H. Stave, *The New Deal and the Last Hurrah: Pittsburgh Machine Politics* (1970); Gerald H. Gamm, *The Making of New Deal Democrats: Voting Behavior and Realignment in Boston, 1920–1940* (1989); Charles Garrett, *The LaGuardia Years: Machine and Reform Politics in New York City* (1961); and Thomas Kressner, *Fiorello H. LaGuardia and the Making of Modern New York* (1989).

The role of religious minority groups is described in George Q. Flynn, *American Catholics and the Roosevelt Presidency, 1932–1936* (1968); Howard M. Sachar, *A History of the Jews in America* (1992); and Beth S. Wenger, *New York Jews and the Great Depression* (1996). Sociologist Michael J. Webber in *New Deal for Fat Cats: Business, Labor, and Campaign Finance in the 1936 Election* (2000) makes the important point that, with little money from the wealthy classes, the New Deal had to place its electoral fate in the hands of its new ethnically and racially mixed coalition. .

Alfred Landon's futile campaign is presented with some sympathy in Donald McCoy, *Landon of Kansas* (1967). On losers further to the right, see Leo P. Ribuffo, *The Old Christian Right* (1983) and George Wolfskill, *The Revolt of the Conservatives: A History of the American Liberty League, 1934–1940* (1962). The electoral failure of the communist left is explained in Harvey Klehr, *The Heyday of American Communism* (1984) and Fraser Ottanelli, *The Communist Party of the United States* (1991). Alan Brinkley sensibly analyzes the challenge from the Union of Social Justice coalition in *Voices of Protest: Huey Long, Father Coughlin, and the Great Depression* (1983). T. Harry Williams in *Huey Long* (1969) contends that Long's rough tactics were the only way any reform effort could stand a chance in corrupt Louisiana. Two well-crafted biographies, William Ivy Hair, *The Kingfish and His Realm* (1991) and Glen Jeansonne, *Messiah of the Masses: Huey P. Long and the Great Depression* (1993), dispute Williams's claim and conclude that Long brought little constructive change.

CHAPTER 10. THE JUDICIAL REVOLUTION

For the prevailing reaction to court-packing of praise for ends and condemnation of tactics, see journalists Joseph Alsop and Turner Catledge, *The 168 Days* (1938); legal scholar Edwin Corwin, *Court Over Constitution* (1938); and Supreme Court Justice Robert H. Jackson, *The Struggle for Judicial Supremacy* (1941). Later studies of the judicial scene from that standpoint include Richard Cortner, *The Wagner Act Cases* (1964); Alpheus T. Mason, *Harlan Fiske Stone: Pillar of the Law* (1956); Robert McCloskey, *The American Supreme Court* (1960); and Walter F. Murphy, *Congress and the Court* (1962). Louis Brandeis's legal reasoning is admiringly explained in Melvin Urofsky, *Louis D. Brandeis and the Progressive Tradition* (1981); Philippa Strum, *Brandeis: Beyond Progressivism* (1993); and Edward Purcell, *Brandeis and the Progressive Constitution* (2000). Jerome Frank, *Law and the Modern Mind* (1937); Robert Jerome Glennon, *The Iconoclast as Reformer: Jerome Frank's Impact on American Law* (1985); Laura Kalman, *The Strange Career of Legal Realism (1996)*; and Peter H. Irons, *The New Deal Lawyers* (1982) supportively explain legal realism and show that Frank's frame of reference was widely shared by lawyers who came to work for New Deal agencies.

William E. Leuchtenburg in *The Supreme Court Reborn* (1995) argues that Roosevelt's court reform was based on sound precedent and driven by the need to save the New Deal from judicial defeat. G. Edward White in *The Constitution and the New Deal* (2000) contends that the modernizing of court doctrine, not immediate political pressure, caused the change in court rulings. . Barry Cushman in *Rethinking the New Deal Court* (1998), adds that the legal reasoning of Supreme and lower court justices had prepared the way for change prior to New Deal action. Richard A. Maidment, *The Judicial Response to the New Deal* (1992), defends the Hughes Court case against New Deal use of the Commerce Clause; and George I. Lovell, *Legislative Deferrals* (2003), blames Congress for hindering court protection of individual rights. Hadley Arkes, *The Return of George Sutherland: Restoring a Jurisprudence of Natural Rights* (1994) defends in rigorous analysis the strict constructionist challenge to New Deal pragmatism.

CHAPTER 11. THE RENDEZVOUS WITH DESTINY

Roosevelt's executive reorganization is covered well in Barry D. Karl, *Executive Reorganization and Reform in the New Deal* (1963); Richard Polenberg, *Reorganizing Roosevelt's Government, 1936–1939* (1966); Peri Arnold, *Making the Managerial Presidency* (1998); and Robert Harrison, *State and Society in Twentieth-Century America* (1997). The latter concludes that the current state seems no better suited to meet the demands of the new century than the pre–New Deal version was.

Mark Gelfand, *A Nation of Cities: The Federal Government and Urban America, 1933–1965* (1975) is a thorough overview, while C. Lowell Harriss, *History and Policies of the Home Owners' Loan Corporation* (1951) provides a dry but uniquely informative account of the key housing agency. Kenneth T. Jackson, *Crabgrass Frontier* (1985) traces revolutionary changes in residential patterns, and Ronald C. Tobey in *Technol-*

ogy as Freedom (1996) astutely links New Deal electric power policy with a technologically improved standard of living.

The recession of 1937–38 as a catalyst to new thinking is well conveyed in Dean L. May, *From New Deal to New Economics* (1981). Marriner Eccles, head of the Federal Reserve, explains in his memoir *Beckoning Frontiers: Public and Personal Recollections* (1951) how he drew from banking the lesson that experience, not theory, was the key to recovery and foreshadowed Keynesian fiscal policy. Robert Skidelsky's preeminent biography, *John Maynard Keynes* (1983), is informative on Keynes's support for the New Deal and his ambivalent relationship with Roosevelt. Encompassing all the major economic thinking associated with the New Deal is Theodore Rosenof's astute analysis *Economics in the Long Run* (1997). An ironic tale of how those concepts were later wrenched into an alleged basis for Reagan's anti-government supply-side economics is told by Nicolas Spulber in *Managing the American Economy, from Roosevelt to Reagan* (1989).

The valuable role of the Reconstruction Finance Corporation is examined in Bascom Timmons, *Jesse H. Jones: The Man and the Statesman* (1956) and Jones's forthright autobiography, *Fifty Billion Dollars: My Thirteen Years with the R.F.C.* (1951). David Lynch ardently recounts the work of the Temporary National Economic Committee in *The Concentration of Economic Power* (1946), and Thurman Arnold, head of the Anti-Trust Division, defends the campaign that followed in *The Bottlenecks of Business* (1940).

The effort to purge unsupportive Democratic senators is best told in James Patterson, *Congressional Conservatism and the New Deal*. David L. Porter, *Congress and the Waning of the New Deal* (1980) further clarifies why those whom Roosevelt would purge were able to resist. Walter Goodman, *The Committee* (1968) describes the wily takeover of the House Un-American Activities Committee for use as a weapon against New Deal liberalism, to which John Houchin in *Censorship of the American Theatre in the Twentieth Century* (2003) adds mention of the gallantly futile attempt to save the Federal Theatre Program from red-baiters.

The last major New Deal initiatives are described perceptively in George E. Paulsen, *A Living Wage for the Forgotten Man: The Quest for Fair Labor Standards, 1933–1941* (1996) and Robert L. Zangrando, *The NAACP Crusade against Lynching, 1909–1950* (1980).

CHAPTER 12. THE COMMON MAN AT THE END OF THE DECADE

Theodore Saloutos, *The American Farmer and the New Deal* (1982) and Bruce L. Gardiner, *American Agriculture in the Twentieth Century* (2002) present agriculture as mainly a success story. More somberly, Theodore Saloutos and John D. Hicks, *Twentieth Century Populism: Agricultural Discontent in the Middle West, 1900–1939* (1964), describes how the waning of populist hopes cost farmers their self-confident image of themselves as the backbone of the nation; Gilbert C. Fite, *George N. Peek and the Fight for Farm Parity* (1954) regrets the lost fight for the McNary-Haugen; Jean Choate, *Disputed Ground: Farm Groups That Opposed the New Deal Agricultural Program* (2002) relates how dissidents went from high hopes to defeat; and Sidney Baldwin, *Poverty and Politics: The Rise and Decline of the Farm Security Administration* (1968) laments the doomed effort to help the helpless. Looking with sadness on the loss of farm community after 1945 are John L. Shover, *First Majority–Last Minority: The Transforming of Rural Life in America* (1976); Gilbert C. Fite, *American Farmers: The New Minority* (1981); and David Danbom, *Born in the Country: A History of Rural America* (1995).

Drought and dust storms have produced two schools of thought. Donald Worster, *Dust Bowl: The Southern Plains in the 1930s* (1979) and R. Douglas Hurt, *The Dust Bowl: An Agricultural and Social History* (1981) describe a situation of prostrate farmers in the Southwest with little choice but to leave their ruined lands. In rebuttal, Paul Bonniefield, *The Dust Bowl: Men, Dirt, and Depression* (1979) insists that the real heroes were those dust bowl victims who stayed and reclaimed the land. In *The Worst of Times* (2006) Timothy Egan describes how hard it was to stay. Paul Taylor and Dorothea Lange, *An American Exodus* (1939) and James N. Gregory, *American Exodus: The Dust Bowl Migration and Okie Culture in California* (1989) tell of the flight from the Southwest as a reversal of earlier hopeful pioneer migrations. The sufferings of refugees once they reached California are conveyed in Cletus E. Daniel, *Bitter Harvest: A History of California Farmworkers, 1870–1941* (1981) and Devra Weber, *Dark Sweat, White Gold: California Farm Workers, Cotton, and the New Deal* (1994). Brad D. Lookingbill, *Dust Bowl, USA: Depression America and the Ecological Imagination, 1929–1941* (2001) insightfully reflects on dust bowl imagery.

The history of national unions, with the formation of the CIO at its center, is well told in Walter Galenson, *The CIO Challenge to the AFL: A History of the American Labor Movement, 1935–1941* (1960); Robert H. Zieger, *The CIO, 1935–1955* (1995); and Zieger with Gilbert J. Gall, *American Workers, American Unions: The Twentieth Century* (2002). Veteran union activist David Milton in *The Politics of United States Labor* (1980) lauds the ability of workers in the 1930s to devise strong-minded theoretical positions. Zieger's *John L. Lewis, Labor Leader* (1988) and Melvyn Dubofsky and Warren Van Tine, *John L. Lewis* (1977) provide vivid portraits of the complex and combative labor leader. Climactic events are covered by Sidney Fine, *Sit-Down: The General Motors Strike of 1936–37* (1969) and *Frank Murphy: The Detroit Years* (1975); August Meier and Elliott Rudwick, *Black Detroit and the Rise of the UAW* (1979); Nelson Lichtenstein, *The Most Dangerous Man in Detroit: Walter Reuther and the Fate of American Labor* (1996); and Steve Fraser, *Labor Will Rule: Sidney Hillman and the Rise of American Labor* (1991). Bert Cochran in *Labor and Communism* (1977) and Roger Keeran in *The Communist Party and the Auto Workers Union* (1980) credit Communist organizers with genuine dedication, while Harvey Klehr in *The Heyday of American Communism* (1984) sees them as essentially troublesome.

A wide range of labor and New Deal relations are thoroughly covered in James A. Gross, *The Reshaping of the National Labor Relations Board: National Labor Policy in Transition, 1937–1947* (1981); Jerold S. Auerbach, *Labor and Liberty: The LaFollette Committee and the New Deal* (1966); and Colin Gordon, *New Deals: Business, Labor and Politics in America* (1994).

CHAPTER 13. THE INTERNATIONAL CLIMAX

The most comprehensive overview, Robert Dallek, *Franklin D. Roosevelt and American Foreign Policy* (1979), takes a generally favorable view of its subject. In contrast, Frederick W. Marks, *Wind over Sand: The Diplomacy of Franklin Roosevelt* (1988) charges that New Deal policy was misconceived. Lloyd C. Gardner, *Economic Aspects of New Deal Diplomacy* (1964) emphasizes the influence of business interests. Far different is the indication of old-fashioned rectitude in the memoirs of Cordell Hull and biographies by Julius W. Pratt, *Cordell Hull*, 2 vols. (1964) and Michael A. Butler, *Cautious Visionary: Cordell Hull and Trade Reform, 1933–1937* (1998).

Key works on reciprocal trade and Good Neighbor policy include Bryce Wood, *The Making of a Good Neighbor Policy* (1961); Dick Steward, *Trade and Hemisphere* (1975); and Erwin F. Gellman, *Good Neighbor Diplomacy: United States Policies in Latin America, 1933–1945* (1979), the last of which credits the New Deal with taking a very incomplete Good Neighbor effort by Hoover on to a hemispheric consensus. In *Roosevelt and Batista: Good Neighbor Diplomacy in Cuba, 1933–1945* (1973), Gellman acknowledges that outreach could also involve the New Deal in unsavory ties to dictators. David F. Schmitz in *Thank God They're on Our Side: The United States and Right-Wing Dictators, 1921–1965* (1999) makes the balancing point that the New Deal drew back from Latin dictators after 1935.

The decision to normalize relations with the Soviet Union is described as a controversial attempt to promote good will and trade in Edward M. Bennett, *Recognition of Russia* (1970) and Mary E. Glantz, *FDR and the Soviet Union* (2005). The hesitation of the New Deal to act on its disapproval of the dictatorships in Germany, Italy, and Japan is described in David F. Schmitz, *The United States and Fascist Italy* (1988) and Dorothy Borg, *The United States and the Far Eastern Crisis of 1933–1938* (1964). Steven Casey in *Cautious Crusade: FDR, American Public Opinion, and the War against Nazi Germany* (2001) dwells on the difficulties in gaining public support for involvement in European conflicts. That caution in the face of evil is criticized in Arnold Offner, *American Appeasement: United States Foreign Policy and Germany, 1933–1938* (1969) and C. A. MacDonald, *The United States, Britain, and Appeasement, 1936–1939* (1981). The essays in David F. Schmitz and Richard D. Challener, eds., *Appeasement in Europe: A Reassessment of U.S. Policies* (1990) tend toward the view that United States inaction was more a matter of uncertainty than appeasement. John E. Wiltz, *In Search of Peace: The Senate Munitions Inquiry of the 1930s* (1963) and Matthew Ware Coulter, *The Senate Munitions Inquiry of the 1930s* (1997) explain how the belief that profit-making was behind the call for military preparedness influenced Congress to mandate neutrality. The power of suspicion wielded by the inquiry's chairman is made clear in Wayne S. Cole, *Senator Gerald P. Nye and American Foreign Relations* (1980). The nature of noninterventionist activity is ably described in Wayne S. Cole, *America First: the Battle Against Intervention, 1940–1941* (1953) and *Roosevelt and the Isolationists, 1932–1945* (1983); Geoffrey S. Smith, *To Save a Nation* (1992); and Justus D. Doenecke, *Storm on the Horizon* (2000). Douglas Little in *Malevolent Neutrality* (1985) makes the case that United States inaction indirectly aided aggression. The policy of neutrality is put in specific context in Brice Harris Jr., *The United States and the Italo-Ethiopian Crisis* (1964), and the tragic consequences are set out in George W. Baer, *Test Case: Italy, Ethiopia, and the League of Nations* (1976), and Alberto Sbacchi, *Ethiopia and Fascist Italy, 1935–1941* (1997). Key sources on the political response to the even more demoralizing civil war in Spain include F. Jay Taylor, *The United States and the Spanish Civil War* (1956) and Richard P. Traina, *American Diplomacy and the Spanish Civil War* (1968). The impact of the democratic defeat in Spain is expressively conveyed in Allen Guttmann, *The Wound in the Heart* (1962). Robert Rosenstone adds an empathetic account of Communist-recruited volunteers in *Crusade of the Left: The Lincoln Brigade in the Spanish Civil War* (1969) that is buttressed by highly personalized accounts of gallant futility in Stanley Weintraub, *The Last Great Cause* (1968) and Arthur Landis, *Death in the Olive Groves* (1989)

Richard Ketchum, *The Borrowed Years* (1989) and Kenneth S. Davis, *FDR: Into the Storm, 1937–1940* (1993) chart the unfocused response to the approach of war. The unfolding of events is thoroughly described in William L. Langer and S. Everett Gleason, *The Challenge to Isolation, 1937–1940* (1952) and *The Undeclared War* (1953); Herbert Feis, *The Road to Pearl Harbor* (1964); and John E. Wiltz, *From Isolation to War* (1968). The struggle to meet the Axis challenge is analyzed in Dorothy Borg, *The United States and the Far Eastern Crisis of 1933–1938* (1964); Jonathan Utley, *Going to War with Japan, 1937–1942* (1985); David F. Schmitz, *The United States and Fascist Italy* (1988); and Waldo Heinrichs, *Threshold of War: Franklin D. Roosevelt and American Entry into Word War II* (1988).

Robert B. Stinnett, *Day of Deceit: The Truth about FDR and Pearl Harbor* (2000) perpetuates the belief that Roosevelt deliberately lured the Japanese into attack. Most scholarly accounts see no such deceit and include notably Roberta Wohlstetter, *Pearl Harbor: Warning and Decision* (1962) and Gordon W. Prange, *At Dawn We Slept* (1981). Akira Irye, *Pearl Harbor and the Coming of the Pacific War* (1999) presents valuable discussion of Japanese strategy and motivation.

EPILOGUE

The unanimity of commitment to World War II and anxiety about many other things are captured in Richard Polenberg, *War and Society* (1972); John Morton Blum, *V Was for Victory* (1977); and William L. O'Neill, *A Democracy at War* (1993). Organized labor's difficult situation is analyzed in Nelson Lichtenstein, *Labor's War at Home* (1983). Philip W. Warken in *A History of the National Resources Planning Board, 1933–1944* (1979) and Marion Clawson in *New Deal Planning: the National Resources Planning Board* (1981) explain the central role of the NRPB in Roosevelt's hopes for a postwar revival based on shared prosperity through planned resources management. Elizabeth Borgwardt in *A New Deal for the World* (2005) argues cogently that Roosevelt's international policies from the Atlantic Charter on sought to apply New Deal principles. Stephen Kemp Bailey, *Congress Makes a Law: The Story behind the Employment Act of 1946* (1950) thoroughly recounts how the original bill for *full* employment was scaled back. Philip J. Fungiello in *The Challenge to Urban Liberalism: Federal-City Relations during World War II* (1978) tells how most plans by New Dealers for postwar renovation of cities were thwarted by newly ascendant conservatives in state and federal government.

John P. Diggins in *The Proud Decades* (1988) applauds the postwar commitment to prosperity through consumption. William L. O'Neill, *American High: The Years of Confidence, 1945–1950* (1986) and James T. Patterson, *Grand Expectations: The United States, 1945–1950* (1996) show less enthusiasm for complacent materialism, while Daniel Horowitz, *The Anxieties of Affluence* (2004) focuses on fears and doubts. The baleful effects of the Cold War in stigmatizing radicals and liberals are emphasized in Randall B. Woods and Howard Jones, *Dawning of the Cold War: The United States Quest for Order* (1994) and Ellen Schrecker, *The Age of McCarthyism* (1994). Richard Gid Powers in *Not Without Honor: The History of American Anticommunism* (1995) condemns unjust repression as well but also notes that the work of moderate anticommunists in helping to bring down communism has only been appreciated in former Iron Curtain countries.

The minority view that Henry Wallace was the true inheritor of New Deal leadership is expressed in Rexford Tugwell, *Off Course* (1971) and Norman D. Markowitz, *The Rise and Fall of the People's Century* (1973). John F. Kennedy's claims for succession are found wanting by his recent biographers: Thomas C. Reeves, *A Question of Character: A Life of John F. Kennedy* (1991); Richard Reeves, *President Kennedy: Profile of Power* (1993); Geoffrey Perrett, *Jack: A Life Like No Other* (2001); and Robert Dallek, *An Unfinished Life: John F. Kennedy, 1917–1963* (2003). The factors that undermined Lyndon Johnson's ambitious attempt to build on New Deal foundations are shrewdly assessed in Henry J. Aaron, *Politics and the Professors: The Great Society in Perspective* (1978) and Irwin Unger, *The Best of Intentions: The Triumph and Failure of the Great Society* (1996). Jill Quadagno in *The Color of Welfare* (1994) shows how Johnson's campaign against segregation prompted a backlash. The self-immolating radical dissent that followed is most bitingly described by participants Todd Gitlin, *The Sixties: Years of Hope, Days of Rage* (1987) and Maurice Isserman and Michael Kazin, *America Divided: The Civil War of the 1960s* (2000).

Informative discussions of a sea change toward conservatism include Thomas Ferguson and Joel Rogers, *Right Turn: The Decline of the Democrats and the Future of American Politics* (1986); Matthew Dallek, *The Right Moment* (2000); and William C. Berman, *America's Right Turn* (1998). Kevin Phillips details the growing income gap in *The Politics of Rich and Poor* (1990) and follows up in *Wealth and Democracy* (2002) with a brilliant analysis of how the skewed American economy threatens democracy and risks collapse. In *Two Nations* (1992), Andrew Hacker demonstrates statistically how race is implicated in the income gap. David K. Shipler, *The Working Poor: Invisible in America* (2004) explains how racial minorities, once the main concern of the New Deal, are now ignored. Issues of deindustrialization and the decline of unions are treated in Barry Bluestone and Bennett Harrison, *The Great U-Turn* (1988); Thomas Geoghegan, *Which Side Are You On?* (1991); and Stanley Aronowitz, *From the Ashes of the Old: American Labor and America's Future* (1998).

The conservative case that welfare corrupts its recipients is made abstractly in Charles Murray, *Losing Ground* (1984). Among the majority of analysts who deplore the reaction against welfare, Michael Katz in *The Undeserving Poor* (1989) offers copious facts to show that Murray is wrong, and Michael K. Brown in *Race, Money, and the American Welfare State* (1999) draws upon his experience as a poverty policy analyst focused on poverty to advocate revival of New Deal cooperative federalism. Robert E. Goodin et al., *The Real Worlds of Welfare Capitalism* (2000) unfavorably compare the American welfare system with those in the Netherlands and Germany. Representative voices in the debate on Social Security include Max J. Skidmore, *Social Security and its Enemies* (1999), arguing on behalf of the current system; Alicia Munnell, *Coming Up Short* (2004), warning that Americans are not saving enough; and Sylvester J. Schieber and John B. Shoven, *The Real Deal: The History and Future of Social Security* (1999), offering an investment banker's case for partial privatization. With echoes of failed New Deal proposals for government-funded health care, Colin Gordon in *Dead on Arrival: The Politics of Health Care in Twentieth-Century America* (2003) and Jennifer Klein in *For All These Rights* (2004) explain why "socialized medicine" has never come about in America.

Index